MINORITIES
IN A
CHANGING WORLD

MINORITIES
IN A
CHANGING
WORLD

EDITED BY

MILTON L. BARRON

The City College of
The City University of New York

New York ALFRED·A·KNOPF

1967

THIS IS A BORZOI BOOK,
PUBLISHED BY ALFRED A. KNOPF, INC.

FIRST PRINTING

Library of Congress Catalog Card Number: 67–10716

Manufactured in the United States of America.

IN MEMORY OF

HARRY AND ANNA BARRON

*who, like countless other European emigrants,
gave their American children far more than
they themselves had received.*

Preface

THE ORIGINAL plans for this book called for a major revision of *American Minorities*, published in 1957. It seemed appropriate to both the publisher and to me that, after a decade of unabated dynamism in the struggle for equality by minorities in American society, the first volume should be brought up to date. As the project took shape, however, the quantity and quality of fresh source material pointed unequivocally to a redefinition of our goal, namely, to a new set of readings and therefore a new book. We have now brought together thirty-three articles and essays, all but one of which—an essay on "ethnic anomie," written expressly for this volume—have been published elsewhere in a total of fourteen journals, magazines and reports. The earliest articles are two that first appeared in 1959.

The "mixed-bag" character of *American Minorities* has been retained in *Minorities in a Changing World* because I still feel it is presumptuous to call only on "card-carrying" sociologists for contributions to our understanding of such complex social problems. Thus we have articles by such diversified practitioners as philosophers, geographers, historians, lawyers and journalists, with sociologists comprising the statistical majority.

The major difference between this volume and its predecessor is implicit in their respective titles. Whereas *American Minorities* was concerned almost entirely with the problems of minorities in American society, *Minorities in a Changing World* views the problems of minority groups in the broader context of a world-wide struggle. After a short introductory section on the meaning of minority and dominant groups, and on the nature and ambiguity of ethnic differentiation, the new volume deals extensively in Section II with a sampling of minority problems in various societies outside the mainland of the United States. Section III takes up general aspects of ethnic differentiation and inequality in American society. In Section IV, there are articles and essays on four American racial, nationality and religious minorities of immigrant extraction—the Chinese, Puerto Ricans, Mexicans and Roman Catholics. Section V deals exclusively with the dynamics of the status and role of the American Negro—the most conspicuous minority in our society and the most publicized in the entire world. This, in turn, is followed by two concluding sections, one on assimilation and intermarriage and the other on new programs and techniques that seek to induce harmony and equality in American race relations.

Like its predecessor, *Minorities in a Changing World* is designed primarily for use in courses on minority problems either as the textbook or as a supplementary book of readings in conjunction with the more conventional textbook assignments.

MILTON L. BARRON

Dobbs Ferry, N.Y.

Acknowledgments

FOR THE permission they so graciously extended to reprint the copyrighted materials in this volume, I wish to thank the following publications, organizations and publishers:

American Jewish Committee, American Sociological Association, *The Annals of the American Academy of Political and Social Science*, Anti-Defamation League of B'nai B'rith, Antioch Press, *Daedalus*, Harper & Row, McGraw-Hill Book Company, The Nation Associates, Inc., National Association of Intergroup Relations Officials, *The New York Times Magazine*, *Phylon*, Prentice-Hall, Inc., *Race: The Journal of the Institute of Race Relations*, *Sociology and Social Research*, the University of Chicago Press, and the University of North Carolina Press.

To the authors of the articles and essays in this volume, I offer my deep appreciation and gratitude. Whatever merit the reader finds in the book is due overwhelmingly to their efforts. As editor, I assume full responsibility for any and all deficiencies.

Contents

I INTRODUCTION TO MINORITY GROUPS

The INTERACTIONS among races, religious groups and nationalities in multigroup societies have become one of the most serious complexes of social problems in modern times. This is true not only in American society and the Western World, but, with few exceptions, wherever these "ethnic" groups have converged, either voluntarily or involuntarily. Those who are subordinated in these intergroup relations are typically referred to as minorities, whereas their superordinates in status are called both majority and dominant groups. The concepts of dominant and minority groups are traditionally applied only to ethnic units—primarily races, religious groups and nationalities—and to three other ethnic bases of social differentiation of secondary importance, namely, nation-state (country of origin), nativity and linguistic affiliation.

Numerical size undoubtedly has played an important role in the struggle for power between interacting ethnic groups. It is not surprising, therefore, to find that in most societies of the world, statistically smaller groups are in fact sociological minorities and the larger ones are usually dominant. But social power is not dependent solely upon the variable of size or numbers; other variables such as weapons, organizational skill, leadership, resources and literacy can offset numerical strength so that statistical majorities can become sociological minorities and some statistical minorities become sociological majorities.

Memberships in minority and dominant groups are not mutually exclusive, for it is possible to occupy dominant and minority statuses simultaneously. This possibility is based upon the multifaceted ethnicity underlying the dominant-minority typology. For instance, while American Negroes are a minority racially, they are at the same time overwhelmingly

Gentile, Protestant, native-born and English-speaking. As such they share significantly in dominant-group attitudes and behavior directed against the Jews, Roman Catholics, foreign-born and non-English-speaking people in American society.

As a leading world power professing an official creed of equality, justice and fair play, the United States has found that hostility and tension among its own ethnic groups are exploited more effectively than anything else as propaganda weapons by our political and economic rivals in the struggle for retaining or attaining power among the uncommitted blocs.

In the article that follows, Professor Richard A. Schermer-horn compares European and American minorities, noting, among other things, that "the minority situation in America, in contrast with that of Europe, is not a function of simple conquest."

1 ► MINORITIES: EUROPEAN AND AMERICAN

R. A. SCHERMERHORN

► THE POWER relations between people in Europe have been largely those of military conquest. The continuous shifting of boundary lines as one people after another became dominant has occurred for centuries; the uncertain vicissitudes of war have led at times to the engulfing of whole peoples in the territory of another, and at other times to the incorporation of mere fragments. Changes in the power structure have been legitimated by treaties, and the plethora of these treaties can be aptly illustrated by the numerous partitions of Poland in 1772, 1793 and 1795, and the later subdivision established by the Congress of Vienna (1814–15).

The rise of nationalism in the period between 1800 and the Treaty of Versailles suffused both dominant and subordinate peoples with a value system of a highly volatile and dynamic character. Social boundaries came to have more validity than political ones as each subordinate people acclaimed the necessity of a common language, common customs, common historical experience, putative biological relatedness, and especially common aspirations for a separate autonomous existence. The amalgam of all these was the national whole, potential or actual. The right of self-determination for such national wholes reached its climax in 1918 when Lithuanians, Latvians, Esthonians, Poles, Ukranians, Ruthenians, Czechs, Slovaks, Rumanians and many others found their cause championed by Woodrow Wilson at the close of World

From *Phylon* (Summer, 1959), 178–85. Reprinted by permission of the author and publisher.

Based on a lecture delivered before the Salzburg Seminar in American Studies during the summer of 1958.

War I. At this moment the popular nineteenth century slogan came as near realization as it has ever done: *"Jede Nation soll einen Staat bilden; Jeder Staat soll nur eine Nation umfassen."* [1]

However, boundaries could never be drawn with the exactitude demanded by this ideal, with those of one language and culture neatly on one side and those of a different ethnic composition on the other. Each new treaty created a new crop of minorities; and the Versailles Treaty, which probably came closest to the realization of the nationalistic norm, perhaps originated the largest number of minorities—or at least some sort of a case could probably be built to show this.

At any rate, Professors E. C. and Helen Hughes of the University of Chicago are probably correct in their description of the situation in Europe. They comment, "For the term 'minority' was historically applied in Europe to a group of people living on soil which they have occupied from time immemorial, but who, through change of boundaries, have become politically subordinate. They are strangers, though at home. These we may call, 'charter-member' minorities." [2]

However, it is not sufficient to localize the position of European minorities as a function of historical conditions and to conclude that this will serve to determine their characteristics. So far, we have been considering mainly one side of the power relationship, the side of the dominant group. To make the picture more complete it is necessary to focus attention on the subordinates and their responses to minority status. At this point the most useful set of conceptualizations has been furnished by the late Louis Wirth who presents four ideal-types of minorities in terms of their aims: (1) pluralistic, (2) assimilationist, (3) secessionist, and (4) militant. While he recognizes that no minority is unanimous and that each one may have its crosscurrents or internal factions, he nevertheless suggests that any specific minority will, in all likelihood, have one of these four aims as a "characteristic orientation and directing social movement."

The minority with pluralistic aims "seeks toleration for its differences on the part of the dominant group." The one with assimilationist objectives "craves the fullest opportunity for participation in the life of the larger society." Secessionists wish "to achieve political as well as cultural independence from the dominant group," while the militant minority, as Wirth defines it in a very special sense, "has set domination over others as its goal." [3]

Wirth's typology has definite implications for the analysis of European minorities. It means, in the first place, that previous to the end of the eighteenth century when nationalism became an overriding issue, most minorities in Europe were pluralistic and aimed chiefly at cultural autonomy; however, with the coming of the nineteenth century and the stimulus of nationalism minorities became secessionist with the possible exception of the Jews, who did not catch the fever until Zionism made its inroads at the end of the century. In fact, the Jews of Germany in pre-Hitler days were predominantly assimilationist, in Wirth's opinion, though they remained cultural pluralists in other lands. It seems difficult to find any other minority in Europe that was truly assimilationist in character during this period; for, no matter how small the ethnic group,[4] if it had a distinctive language, culture, and historical tradition, it tried to establish claims for independent national status.

The assimilationist ideal was, for the most part, adopted by majorities and by dominant nations—actually a one-way assimilation. Usually the term assimilation in the sociological literature has denoted the merging of two cultures so that those who share the merger become indistinguishable from each other. One-way assimilation, however, is primarily a power process in which the dominant group, believing in its cultural superiority, imposes its way of life upon a less powerful group of subjects. As Claude defines it in the European context, "Assimilation demands that minorities consent to abandon the ethnic, cultural, and linguistic characteristics which distinguish them from the national majorities with whom they live, and to become merged into nationally uniform communities with the majorities." [5]

The attempt of the League of Nations to extend some protection to national minorities was really premised on the ideal that these minorities would be culturally pluralistic in character—i.e., that they would be satisfied with their own language, institutions, schools and associations. On the other hand, the phenomenon of the kin-state gave the dominant nations many doubts about the validity of this assumption. Claude reminds us that "a state which regards itself as standing in a special relationship to a national minority in another state, by reason of ethnic affinity, is designated as a 'kin-state.'" [6] Thus for Czechoslovakia of the 1920's and 30's, Hungary was a kin-state of the Hungarian minority in Slovakia, and Germany was the kin-state of the Sudeten Germans in Bohemia and Moravia. As these kin-states regarded their fellow-nationals in Czechoslovakia as having a claim on their protection, and as they began to encourage the display of nationalistic sentiment among their fellow-ethnics, nation states like Czechoslovakia were not always convinced that the demands of minorities would remain culturally pluralistic, but regarded the outgrowth of secessionism or even militancy as quite likely.

At all events, the relations between majorities and minorities among European nations in the nineteenth and twentieth centuries have been those of chronic conflict. The value clash of different cultures and traditions was, for the most part, transmuted into a political clash in which the attempt to impose assimilation by force became an accepted weapon of minority treatment.

Applying a power analysis in broad terms we can hypothesize that: in periods of rapid social change, the loosening of the social structure permits either superordinate or subordinate groups to find access to new power resources that enable them to alter the balance of power. Such were the conditions of World Wars I and II. If we wished to be epigrammatic, we might almost say that after the first war, many minorities became nations, while after the second, many nations became minorities. In the latter case one thinks of the satellite nations of the Soviet orbit which may be called minorities in one respect, or colonies in another—the choice is in many ways a semantic one. To sum up the European situation in a word, however, it seems fair to say that her minority problem has been a nationality problem.[7]

The minority situation in America, in contrast with that of Europe, is not a function of simple conquest. The American experience has been more like that of Australia and New Zealand with European colonists gradually penetrating areas of sparse aboriginal populations. The newcomers at first were minorities themselves, but due to their technological and military superiority they extended what at first was an economic penetration to a large scale invasion that displaced the older inhabitants; as immigration enlarged the numbers of the incoming population, it changed likewise the whole nature of the minority situation. This broad difference distinguishes the European from the American minority occasions in a significant way; in Europe, the incessant changes in political boundaries, while recurrent and repetitive, did not alter the essential nature of the minority problem which remained one of nationality conflict. The French aphorism, *plus ça change, plus c'est la même chose* fits the European experience.

In America, on the other hand, historical development continually brought about the emergence of new situations, qualitative differences in the power relationships that might be characterized better by the phrase *plus ça change, plus c'est l'autre chose*. What are some of these changes? First, in the nature of immigration. The first American census was taken in 1790, and it is now estimated that ninety percent of the population at that time was from Northern and Western Europe, with sixty-four percent being from the British Isles. This process continued in the years 1800 to 1882, which era is generally known as the period of the "old immigration," when the vast majority of immigrants continued to come from Northern and Western Europe, which includes Germany. This group, though mixed from the European point of view, regarded themselves as more or less homogeneous in America and established themselves as the majority, giving a characteristic stamp to American culture and institutions.[8] Since the English came first, they took precedence as cultural leaders; English became the accepted tongue, English common law became the basis of the legal code, and the philosophy of Locke and Burke was embodied in the American Constitution. Likewise, the vast majority of this first group were Protestants, giving to American culture its peculiar Protestant slant.[9] In recent years this dominant group has been facetiously referred to as the WASPS—the capital letters standing for White Anglo-Saxon Protestants. Of course not all members were Anglo-Saxon, but the popular fiction more or less regarded them as such.[10] However, with the rise of industrialism, the stream of immigration changed in the general period of 1882 to 1920 when the newcomers from Europe for the first time came in greater numbers from Southern and Eastern Europe in what is known as the "new immigration." These new immigrants, because of cultural and religious differences, were regarded more as outsiders by the dominant group and were assigned a definite minority status.

In the meantime, the march of settlers toward frontier areas in the American West resulted in two major changes in the power configuration. The steady infiltration of Indian territory, punctuated by intermittent warfare, resulted in the forcible removal of the Indian population to segregated areas known as reservations, finally isolating the Indians in separate areas where they have been excluded from the main currents of American life. Concurrently the frontiersmen pushing westward came into conflict with Mexico and, after a conflict with that country, imposed the cession of territory to the United States of California, Nevada, Utah, New Mexico, Arizona, plus parts of other states (the recognition of Texas as a United States possession came at the same time). This shift of boundaries, exceptional in American history, resembled the more typical conditions in Europe, and resulted in the shift of large Spanish-American populations to the status of United States subjects—the majority of them being in New Mexico.

Finally, in the Southern states, the development of cash crops such as tobacco, indigo, rice, but especially cotton, coincided with the growth of similar systems in the West Indies which had satisfied the demands for cheap labor by the importation of slaves from Africa. This solution, in the early period, was congenial to Americans both of the South and of New England; it suited the former because it provided the growing demands of plantation owners for a controllable labor supply; and it suited the Yankee traders of New England because it was a major contribution to their enrichment in the most lucrative form of ocean commerce then known, the slave traffic. However, the slave system, as a peculiar set of power relationships, became characteristic only of the Southern regions.

Thus the pluralistic pattern of American minorities may be traced not only in the emergent relations of dominant and subordinate with historical changes traced chronologically but also tends to differentiate sectionally in terms of geographical areas.

It now becomes evident that American minorities, unlike the European of the same era, are not exclusively of the nationality type. To understand them on the basis of a power analysis it will be convenient to arrange them in terms of power pressures. If we construct a scale with the most severe power pressures at one end of the scale and the most mild ones at the other, a provisional outline could then be constructed as follows:

Scale of
increasing
power
pressure

↑	Subordination by slavery followed by social segregation	Negroes
	Subordination by displacement followed by geographical segregation	Indians
	Subordination by boundary absorption	Spanish Americans
	Subordination by assignment to inferior status: occupationally and socially	Later immigrants—especially those from Southern and Eastern Europe

(This outline is an illustrative sample and does not attempt to include all American minorities.)

Useful as this general scheme may be—and we trust it will prove its utility—it omits something important. The power typology may have certain validity from the viewpoint of the social scientist, but we must remember that it is an abstraction from the situation, one which presents the underlying realities in an explanatory way. Nevertheless, this is not the way most Americans perceive the members of minority groups; and before we can understand the American scene, we must know what the popular perceptions are. Long ago, W. I. Thomas, a pioneer in American sociology, made the pregnant observation that "if men define situations as real, they are real in their consequences." Even social fictions believed to be real will be made the basis for social action on the part of those who believe them, for they become a part of the value system. How then does the dominant majority in America, the WASPS, if you will, define those outside their charmed circle? First of all, they categorize them as either colored or noncolored as compared with their own white status. The largest colored element, the most dispersed, and on the whole, the most easily distinguishable from the dominant group are the Negroes. But in certain limited geographical areas there are numerous colored aggregations like Indians, Japanese, Chinese, Mexican, and Puerto Rican. For all such groups, the dominant majority displays a definite aversion and sets up social distance systems occupationally and residentially to separate them from themselves.

A second category employed popularly to distinguish the ins from the outs is that of foreigner. Sometimes this overlaps with the colored category, but most of the time it does not since the predominant foreign population stems from Europe. The height of anti-foreign feeling probably arose prior to and during World War I when the assimilationist philosophy had its major influence with the dominant group in America. It even penetrated into high places politically as well; for example, Woodrow Wilson, who urged upon European nations the importance of cultural pluralism where boundary lines could not be adjusted in accordance with the uniformity principle, had quite different words to say of the American scene. At that time he declared, "America does not consist of groups. A man who thinks of himself as belonging to a particular national group in America has not yet become an American." [11] It is this philosophy which had much to do with the growing restrictions on immigration to America which occurred in the 1920's; along with this view went the emphasis on speaking English as a sign of assimilation, while a noticeable accent became an indication of alien character.

Religious labels are also used to differentiate the dominant group from others; at times they are applied to non-Protestants, at others to non-Christians. The flash fire of anti-Catholic feeling in the 1830's and 40's when the Know-Nothing Party began to stir up nativist sentiment left some charred embers behind and veiled forms of this hostility are still endemic in a minor sort of way. On the other hand, opposition to the Jews has developed at a much later period, and while nominally stated in the form of non-Christian labels, has been either a reaction to mobility or the perception of Jews as somehow of an alien racial stock.

The popular labels and conceptions are often illogical and contradictory. For example the Mexicans, defined popularly as a colored population, are nevertheless listed in the United States census as whites rather than non-whites. This makes no difference to the social perceptions of an Anglo-Saxon Texan who continues to see them as before. On the basis of color distinctions a stranger to America might hypothesize that when color discrimination is added to that against foreigners, colored aliens might be subject to the most severe power pressures of all. Such is not the case, as can be shown by the case of the Chinese and Japanese, who are not subject to many of the severe restrictions imposed upon Negroes who are native-born Americans. As for the Indians, another colored element in the population, distance lends enchantment to the view. The whites who live farthest from the Indian reservations are most likely to have a semi-romantic conception of the "noble red man," but the whites living in the same states with the Indian are the most harsh in their judgments of Indian behavior and in everyday treatment of the Indians in general. Many other contradictory views might be cited in support of this thesis.

It may be worthwhile to present the popular view by imposing on it somewhat more order than it actually has. Such an attempt would result in the following typology:

1. Non-Caucasian non-immigrants
   A. Descendants of the slave population—Negroes
   B. Subjugated and segregated indigenous population—Indians
2. Non-Caucasian immigrants
   Japanese, Chinese, Mexican, Puerto Rican, etc.
3. Caucasian immigrants of the nationality or cultural type
   A. Nationality groups: Italians, Poles, Yugoslavs, etc.
   B. Cultural group: Jews

More to the point is the observation that the popular typology depends on the racial factor as its most distinctive defining characteristic. It is racism cross-fertilized with power subordination that has characterized the American ethos in the treatment of minorities.

Notes ▶

1. Mentioned by Otto Bauer, *Die Nationalitätsfrage und die Sozialdemokratie*, p. 171, quoted in Inis L. Claude, *National Minorities, An International Problem* (Cambridge, Mass., 1955), p. 92.
2. E. C. Hughes and H. M. Hughes, *Where Peoples Meet, Racial and Ethnic Frontiers* (Glencoe, Ill., 1952).
3. Louis Wirth, "The Problem of Minority Groups," in Ralph Linton, ed., *The Science of Man in the World Crisis* (New York, 1954), pp. 354, 357–58, 360, 361, 362–63.
4. "Ethnic group" is here defined as a group having common traditions and culture with putative continuity of biological heredity.
5. Claude, *op. cit.*, p. 79.
6. *Ibid.*, p. 5.
7. So typical is this trend that twentieth century refugees and

immigrants have hardly been categorized as minorities at first. Only gradually have European countries come to regard them in this light. See Sydney Collins, *Coloured Minorities in Britain: Studies in British Race Relations Based on African, West Indian and Asiatic Immigrants* (London, 1957).

8. Arnold Green, *Sociology* (2nd ed., New York, 1956), p. 240.

9. R. A. Schermerhorn, *These Our People, Minorities in American Culture* (Boston, 1949), p. 6.

10. Sinclair Lewis' description of one of his characters is worth quoting at this point: "Martin was, like most inhabitants of Elk Mills before the Slavo-Italian immigration, a Typical Purebred Anglo-Saxon American, which means that he was a union of German, French, Scotch, Irish, perhaps a little Spanish, conceivably a little of the strains lumped together as 'Jewish,' and a great deal of English, which is itself a combination of Primitive Britain, Celt, Phoenician, Roman, German, Dane and Swede."

11. Quoted in *New York Times Magazine*, May 16, 1948, p. 26. Taken from Claude, *op. cit.*, p. 227.

2 ▸ ETHNIC ANOMIE

MILTON L. BARRON

The following essay, on ambiguous ethnic identification and problems of ethnic closure, evolved out of an extensive study begun in 1962–63 when its author was a Fulbright lecturer in Israel. The study was provoked by the perennial questions "Who is a Jew?" and "What is a Jew?" both of which have been enhanced in recent years as new cases in Jewish identification and closure developed—in Israel as well as in the Diaspora—and were widely publicized. It must be stressed, however, that the implications of this study extend far beyond the relations between Jews and Gentiles to those among ethnic groups in general in contemporary multigroup societies.

▸ STUDENTS OF ethnic relations cannot avoid the observation that the lines presumably delineating and differentiating one group from another are in fact porous and enigmatic. Racial, religious and nationality groups in mass, Western societies are singularly unsuccessful in their efforts to formulate and implement the centripetal requisites of identification and membership closure, the social psychological and sociological criteria to which people are expected to adhere in order to obtain mutually exclusive ethnicity. Among the major centrifugal social forces and processes leading to "ethnic anomie," especially on the peripheries between two or more groups, are secularization, emancipation, alienation and individuation; apostasy, proselytism and conversion; intermarriage, miscegenation and ethnically mixed parentage; cultural deviation and sectarianism by ethnic subgroups; and multiple and incongruous criteria of ethnic membership.

Ethnic Anomie

In the Weberian sense of the term, "ideal" properly describes ethnic differentiation if two or more ethnic groups in a society are each sufficiently integrated within themselves and sufficiently differentiated from each other to be recognized and identified as such. Despite the claims that some groups do indeed approximate this ideal centripetal form even in Western societies,[1] it is proposed here that some ethnic anomie is inevitable under urban and industrial conditions. Gordon maintains [2] that ideal ethnic differentiation and its social psychological consequence of uncomplicated and consistent self-identification are realities only in the steadily dwindling nonliterate societies of the world; elsewhere "population increases, stimulation to social class formation, wars, migrations, creations of cities, proliferation of religious variation, and grouping in progressively larger political units have, in accelerating tempo, shattered and fragmented . . . this ethnicity—detaching one by one each of the elements which composed the once unified whole, and isolating each element from the other. . . ."

What, then, is ethnic anomie? It has been noted, first of all, that Durkheim, who established the general concept of anomie in sociological vocabulary and related it to urban, industrial and mobile conditions, derived it from its Greek root where it meant "broken limits," later adding the connotations of deregulation and normlessness.[3] *By ethnic anomie, therefore, we mean "broken group limits" and their disposition toward social anarchy in modern, ethnic intergroup relations, typically in the form of dilemmas of ethnic identification.* Relevant to our discussion is Ruitenbeek's exploration of the impact of anomie on identity in general, as follows:

The human environment is reduced to a series of fleeting contacts with strangers or near strangers. . . . In this situation, identity is endangered, for it is bound to reflect the discontinuity of the social environment. A man living in so mobile a world will be less sure of himself and of others than a person in more stable surroundings. . . . In so mobile a society, group membership is often short-lived. *Group as well as individual relationships tend to become more shallow, less differentiated, more interchangeable, as it were.*[4] [Italics ours]

The purpose of this essay is to review the conceptualizations and typologies formulated by sociologists and social psychologists seeking to clarify the enigmatic consequences of ethnic anomie and to propose a new, consolidated typology of centripetal and centrifugal ethnicity which may serve modestly as a fresh starting point for further empirical and theoretical study.

Inadequacies of Classical Concepts

Fundamental to any analysis of ethnic anomie is recognition of the gross inadequacies of classical concepts such as Giddings' "consciousness of like and unlike kind," and Sumner's "in-group," "out-group" and "ethnocentrism"—which fail to deal with the complexities and subtleties of group peripherality, porousness and ambivalent identification in contemporary Western societies.[5] For instance, in the following statement that serves as the basis for his much-admired typology allegedly distinguishing the in-group from the out-group, Sumner made no adequate allowance for any of the enigmatic social situations involving two or more groups except in his casual and unsophisticated reference to exogamous wives and "other foreigners":

A group of groups may have some relation to each other (kin, neighborhood, alliance, connubium and commercium) which draws them together and differentiates them from others. Thus a differentiation arises between ourselves, the we-group, or in-group, and everybody else, or the others-groups, out-groups. The insiders in a we-group are in a relation of peace, order, law, government, and industry, to each other. Their relation to all outsiders or others-groups is one of war and plunder, except so far as agreements have modified it. If a group is exogamic, the women in it were born abroad somewhere. Other foreigners who might be found in it are adopted persons, guest friends and slaves.[6]

It is regrettable that recent generations of sociologists and other social scientists have been generally complacent concerning these important but, in retrospect, oversimplified and naive concepts and typologies formulated by the founding fathers—employing them uncritically for the most part. The outstanding exceptions in this respect have been the social psychologists Daniel J. Levinson and Kurt Lewin, and the sociologists Everett V. Stonequist and Joseph H. Fichter; each has recognized at least one phase of the problem to which we are addressing ourselves and each has tried to cope with it conceptually or typologically.[7]

Levinson's Motivated Upward and Downward Mobility

Levinson observed, first of all, that ethnocentrism in Sumner's mode of thought meant a rigid identification by people with those with whom they share a culture (the in-group), and their equally rigid contra-identification with the culturally dissimilar (the out-group). This was a consistent and unyielding way of perceiving the fellow members of one's own group as distinguished from aliens. For Sumner, in the absence of a sense of basic conflict, antithesis and mutual exclusiveness with regard to the in-group, there was no contra-identification, and therefore no out-group.

Initially, Levinson's contribution was to see the in-group and the out-group as social psychological rather than purely sociological concepts, for they refer not to formal memberships in groups but rather to frames of mind. People may feel identified with groups in which they actually have no membership, as happens in cases of "motivated upward and downward mobility"—wherein they identify with groups of higher or lower status than those to which they now belong. Levinson further refined our understanding of ethnocentric ideology by discerning that the out-group shifts in accordance with different levels of social organization. Whereas ethnocentrism takes the form of patriotism in international relations, this superior notion of "we" disintegrates when the social context encompasses only intranational relations. Most ethnocentrists see the social world as a series of concentric circles revolving around a bull's-eye, with each circle representing a distinction between the in-group and the out-group. The line of each circle functions as a barrier excluding all outside groups from the insiders, and each group in turn finds itself excluded by a slightly narrower circle.

Lewin's Central and Peripheral Layers

Levinson's emphasis upon the vertical pull of identification with groups higher or lower in status than the group with which one is formally affiliated is similar to Kurt Lewin's concepts of the "central" and "peripheral" layers of the ethnic group. The members of any group, according to Lewin, are subject to diametrically opposed forces. Some attract members inward and tend to enclose them, as contrasted with other forces that repel people from the group either because of its unattractive features or the greater attractiveness of a competing, alternative group. Assuming that a person's own inclinations, needs and goals are allowed socially uninhibited expression, he would be lost to another group if the balance of attraction and repulsion favored the latter. On the other hand, the group would retain the person as a member if its positive features outweighed the negative. Lewin pointed out, however, that the forces pulling to the center and to the periphery of groups are not pure expressions of individual idiosyncrasies, but are often imposed upon persons by external social powers. Consequently, some of us are compelled reluctantly to remain in groups we prefer to leave, or are excluded from groups we would choose to join.

What are the external powers that intrude upon the individual's free choice? They have to do with the uneven distribution of status and privilege among groups in modern society. Privileged groups obviously offer higher status, attracting their membership more and repelling them less than do underprivileged groups. The former, therefore, may be said to have a stronger positive balance and the latter a more negative one. But the privileged groups—or influential segments within them—tend to develop exclusiveness, inhibiting and resisting infiltration across their boundaries from the underprivileged out-groups. Consequently, members of the underprivileged are hampered in their group belonging; they are retained in groups not by personal preference but by outside restraints.

The effects on the structure of such "minority" groups and on the social psychology of its membership are far-reaching. Unlike the privileged groups' membership, whose orientation is centripetally toward their central stratum, the underprivileged produce members oriented by negative chauvinism centrifugally toward their peripheral layers. They are as distant from the crux of minority-group life as is socially tolerable and they are in a chronic state of frustration and self-hatred. Here, according to Lewin, one even finds the paradox of "the leader from the periphery." In summary, the structure of an underprivileged group is fundamentally turned against itself.

Stonequist's Marginal Man and Organized Dualism

In much the same manner that Levinson's work meshes with that of Lewin, the latter's concept of the peripheral layer in the underprivileged group closely resembles "the marginal man," first conceptualized by Robert E. Park and later given more elaboration, precision and application by Everett V. Stonequist and others.[8] Essentially, however, these sociologists viewed the marginal man as an occupant of the peripheries of two or more groups simultaneously, and not just one, as seen by Lewin.

The marginal man, claimed Stonequist, is the person who typically inhabits, or has kinship ties with, at least two interacting but incompatible groups; thus he is not wholly acceptable or accepting in either. Marginality comes about as a social consequence of the cultural and ethnic disparity between the individual's dual or multiple affiliations, his inadequate acculturation to any, his rejection at least partially by all, and the persistence of inhibitions and loyalties in multigroup societies. It characterizes not only individuals, but even entire groups in whose cases minority status and limitations in identification have crystallized into patterns of organized dualism.

Fichter's Nuclear, Modal, Marginal and Dormant Membership

Unlike Lewin and Stonequist, who applied their concepts with special reference to problems of enigmatic Jewish identification and membership, Joseph H. Fichter's central concern was the white Roman Catholic in the urban parishes of the South. Yet he was obviously mindful of the relevance of the contributions by other social scientists to his own analysis of the push and pull of competing institutions and social forces as they affect the Catholic layman in the urban community.

According to Fichter, in its attempt to pattern the behavior of its members, the Roman Catholic Church's ideal is personalized in its so-called nuclear parishioners. These are people who are cooperative with other laymen and with priests in parochial activities, exemplify Christian norms in their personal affairs, esteem Catholic religious values and fulfill the formal sacramental expectations of the Church. But nuclear Catholics in the United States represent only a statistical minority because, like other Americans, Catholics are subject to institutional conflict and the patterned evasions so commonplace in the urban community. For them, the values and role demands of secular institutions tend to mitigate the centripetal pull of their religious institution toward their own nuclei. Four of the centrifugal forces—contrasting assumptions, relative morality, anti-authoritarianism and the dysfunctional parish—influence all urban Catholics, but in varying degrees. Thus most Catholics partially accept their religious value system and partially reject it when it conflicts with other institutionalized values. Their religious status therefore becomes ambiguous, for in the clearly defined and formal institutionalism of the Roman Catholic Church those who are "neither hot nor cold" Catholics lack social position.

Utilizing several subjective and objective criteria of socioreligious distance to classify and stratify Catholics who are not nuclear, Fichter conceptualized these people as modal, marginal or dormant in their membership. Dormant Catholics fall within the outer limit of the circumference of Catholic affiliation—the polar opposite of nuclear members. They retain a foothold in the Catholic circle because they meet such criteria as baptism in infancy, reception of the sacrament of matrimony, occasional attendance at services of the Roman Catholic Church, infant christening for their own children and reluctance to join another church.

Between the dormant or minimal, and nuclear or maximal extremes are the modal and marginal Catholics. Both of these types are generally negligent of three Catholic religious obligations: attendance at mass, paschal reception of the Eucharist and of sacramental penance, and religious education of their children. The key difference between the two types is that the modal, unlike the marginal Catholic, is unaware of his inconsistency and is not psychologically frustrated in the tug of war between Catholic religious and non-Catholic secular forces.

Alienation and Correlative Concepts

This brief review of sociological and social psychological concepts and typologies that deal with the enigmas in ethnic identification and membership closure created by centripetal and centrifugal forces would be incomplete without reference to alienation and its conditional and correlative processes. Alienation is obviously socially centrifugal and conducive to upward and downward mobility, the production of peripheral layers, the marginal man and dormant membership as seen in the works of Levinson, Lewin, Stonequist and Fichter.

The idea seemingly central to the concept—and one in use since ancient times to refer to a variety of psychological as well as social disorders—is man's loss of identity and selfhood.[9] If, in the first place, one achieves these social psychological states through social interaction within clearly defined groups, then to be deprived of such interaction and meaningful relationships produces people who are unable to answer without hesitation the questions: "What am I?" and "Who am I?" [10] Concepts frequently associated with—and even confused with—alienation are anomie, social isolation and social disorganization. If they are not actually etiological factors of alienation, at least they are important conditions or correlates of it.[11]

The Jews as the Prototype of Ethnic Anomie

This essay offers an existential typology of ethnic anomie that advances beyond the valiant contributions just reviewed. The rudiments of this typology appeared more than a generation ago when the anthropologist Herskovits joined in the apparently endless task of defining the Jews, the classic case of an enigmatic ethnic group.[12] But before we examine Herskovits' work and the new typology based upon it, we need to explore historically in outline form the problems of ambiguous Jewish identification and group closure that scholars like Herskovits have had to confront. Peter L. Berger recently asserted that "the problem of 'Jewish identity' arose only among modern Western Jews when assimilation into the surrounding Gentile society had begun to weaken the power of the Jewish community itself to bestow alternate identities on its members as against the identities assigned to them by anti-Semitism." [13] The evidence, however, suggests a much earlier beginning for Jewish enigmatism, perhaps as early as the first historical records of the group itself.

Jews have introspectively but unsuccessfully posed the questions "What is a Jew?" and "Who is a Jew?" to an extent unparalleled by any other ethnic group.[14] One of the most perplexing anomalies in this regard is that although no other group seems to have had as much difficulty in clarifying and reconciling its identification and membership requirements, the Jews surpass all others in sociological illustrations of in-group versus out-group differentiation, consciousness of like and unlike kind and ethnocentrism.[15] According to some scholars, exaggerated group-consciousness is actually the most characteristic Jewish trait, as follows: [16]

The ultimate and residual distinguishing trait of a Jewish group anywhere in the world is the consciousness of being heirs to an old tradition. . . . This tradition manifests itself mainly in mental orientation, in a knowledge and awareness of an historical past different from that of the non-Jewish environment. All the tangible expressions of Jewish cultural life are derived from this single source of group-consciousness; it is this awareness of tradition which is the motive power behind such cultural phenomena as the community organization, the synagogue and its services, and is the driving force towards self-perpetuation achievable only by establishing and maintaining the proper mechanisms of cultural transmission in the form of educational institutions and of other, less formal processes of socialization.

Yet from the time of their historically recorded emergence, although a number of dynamic social, cultural and religious forces have operated centripetally to forge and consolidate the group out of what were originally only loosely federated tribes, others worked centrifugally to diffuse the several foundations of Jewish social structure. By standard historical accounts the earliest Jews on the banks of the Euphrates River mixed with the Canaanites of the lowlands, the Amorites of the highlands, and with the Hivites, Amalekites, Kenites, Egyptians and Hittites. About 2000 B.C., the patriarch Abraham and his pastoral family departed from their home community, Ur of the Chaldees near the Persian Gulf, toward Mesopotamia in the north. Later they migrated slowly southwest toward Canaan (Palestine), the strip of land along the eastern Mediterranean between the two key Biblical terminals, Dan and Beersheba, and an area exposed by turn to the powerful influences of the two great river-valley powers of Mesopotamia and Egypt—the cultural and political centers of the ancient Middle East. Generations later some went south into Egypt and settled in the fertile land of Goshen east of the Nile Delta. About 1200 B.C. they rebelled against the Egyptians and set out again for Canaan, and after years of migration and warfare, they finally broke into Canaan north of the Dead Sea.

It is very much to the point to examine the name of these early Jews, the "Hebrews." Ausubel [17] brings to our attention the prevailing scholarly opinion that links the Hebrews with the mass migration of the "Habiru," a Semitic word referring loosely to all nomads from beyond the Jordan or Euphrates rather than to any specific group. Of diverse ethnic origins, the Habiru were linked together by a language having a common Semitic character and by similar cultural patterns. In two relatively recent issues of a Biblical research journal,[18] the problem of the identity of the Biblical Hebrews of 1500 B.C. was pursued along this vein after noting that a century ago, the French Egyptologist, M. Chabs, argued that the "Apiru," the name of foreigners working for the Pharaohs, was actually that of the ancient Hebrews. When the Tel-el-Amarna letters were discovered, the argument widened to include the "Habiru" who were harassing Egyptian colonial officers stationed in Canaan and whose name was also found in a variety of inscriptions in Asia Minor, Mesopotamia, Syria and Egypt, covering a period of approximately 1000 years. Scholars have concluded that the names "Apiru" and "Habiru" denoted an ancient foreign element living on the fringe of society. That these names are identical with the name for the Hebrews (Ivri) is supported by the fact that the latter name appears in the Bible thirty times, typically in stories in which the Jews confronted or interacted with other ethnic groups. Otherwise they were referred to as the Israelites.[19] This ancient intergroup denotation of "Ivri" is comparable to the early usage of "Welsh"—the term for "foreigner" applied by the invading and conquering Saxons to refer to the indigenous Bretons. Eventually this term too, as in the case of the Hebrews, came to denote the proper name of an ethnic group.

Although they were initially nomadic tribes, the ancient Jews adjusted to the requirements of agricultural and peasant cultures in the promised land of Israel. The later books of the Old Testament, describing this sedentary period of Jewish history, are replete with indications that the group's norms were repeatedly violated—the prophets in particular having great difficulty securing the people from social and cultural deviations. Throughout their early and middle years as a nation, the Jews were far from having achieved centripetal unity, manifesting instead many peripheral shades and layers of intragroup differences and intergroup liaisons. For example, the first kingdom, established under David and Solomon a thousand years before the Christian era, was ostensibly a union of twelve tribes. It disintegrated after Solomon's death, however, and gave way to Israel, comprising ten of the tribes, and Judah, made up of the remaining two. When Assyria destroyed the state of Israel in 722 B.C., Jewish history began, the word "Jew" being an abbreviation of Judaean.[20]

It is a well-established historical fact that Christianity—as a new religious movement almost two thousand years ago—attracted both Jews and non-Jews, and that Jewish Christians remained marginally distinguishable from Gentile Christians for the several centuries they were in the process of coalescence. The Roman conquest of Israel in 70 A.D. finally destroyed all semblance of the national independence of Jews, dispersed them after 137 A.D., and transformed them into one of the first and most sustained of urban-dwelling peoples in the Western world.[21] Throughout this long period of dispersion, better known as the Diaspora,[22] the processes of genocide, acculturation, apostasy, assimilation and horizontal mobility created divergence, ambiguity and disruption in Jewish identification, especially on the group's peripheries. Strongly conscious of like and unlike kind, the Jews nevertheless witnessed a blurring of their social edges. This social attrition by social interaction was most profound in Western Europe, where, under the banner of modern rationalism following the French Revolution and the onset of the industrial revolution, the multi-group societies were subjected to emancipation and secularism. The reform religious branch of Judaism took shape there, seeking to retain within a Jewish framework those who, in any case, were rejecting large portions of Jewish tradition, and to enable them to reconcile their old Jewish affiliation with their new social and intellectual premises. In the nineteenth century there were also significant emancipatory trends among eastern European Jews, such as the Haskalah movement in Hungary. But that region remained the last bastion of traditionalism and hard-core identification among the so-called Ashkenazi (Western European) Jews until their dispersal and destruction by the Nazis in the twentieth century. Sephardic Jews—the descendants of medieval Spanish Jews who were expelled in 1492 and thereafter scattered in small communities elsewhere in Europe, North Africa and the Middle East—lived in comparative seclusion and were touched less by the new trends, thus preserving their special identity. The third major branch of the Jewish people—the Oriental or Middle Eastern Jews —retained more of their Jewish identity and culture than did most of their Western counterparts. This was especially true of the remote communities such as the Yemenites and the Kurds, but it was also characteristic of the more sophisticated Oriental Jews as represented by the Iraqis and the Jews in the coastal areas of North Africa. All three branches—the Ashkenazi, the Sephardic and the Oriental Jews—had diverged from each other sufficiently by the present century to become markedly different in physical appearance, culture and social organization.

Jews were not excepted from the disruptive influence on group identification and membership that came with migration to the new Transatlantic frontier of American society. As one prominent Jewish social historian has observed:

American history began with the Puritan conception of Commonwealth of the seventeenth century, the ideal of which was the completely uniform society of the town meeting—one state, one community, one church. But the conditions of colonization exerted a steadily disruptive effect, broke up closely-knit, homogeneous communities. The constant influx of outsiders and the unsettling frontier left this country with a society in which no form of association was completely coterminous with every other. Every man was a stranger to some extent and "belonging" was a relative term. The result was the persistent sprouting of all sorts of religious, cultural, and social groups among which the prospective member had the capacity freely to choose. Out of enormous diversity grew an exhilarating sense of spontaneity, a taste for experimentation and improvisation, and the urge toward liberty. . . .[23]

It is not surprising that in a recent study [24] of Jewish-American consciousness as it emerged over the last two decades in the works of seven prominent writers—Karl Shapiro, Delmore Schwartz, Isaac Rosenfeld, Leslie Fiedler, Saul Bellow, Bernard Malamud and Philip Roth—the author Irving Malin found all concerned with the ambiguities of Jewish-American identity. These writers defined "Jewishness" in various ways, but each was conscious of alienation not only as a Jew (the eternal exile), but from Jewish life itself, both traditional and modern. Each asserted that the Jew starts with tension and never finds complete relief.

In the meantime, during the late nineteenth and the first half of the twentieth centuries, the reconvergent movements of Zionism and Jewish nationalism—culminating in the European holocaust under the Nazis and the subsequent establishment of the new state of Israel in 1948—effected the return of approximately two million Jews to the ancient homeland. The immigrants, an influx coming from more than a hundred countries of origin, all claimed Jewish identification despite deep cleavages in physiognomy, religion, nationality and cultural traits. Beginning in 1958, a decade after the founding of the new state, Israeli Jews began to provide the world with an almost continuous series of cases—reinforcing those endemically spawned in the Diaspora—that served to dramatize a group's inability to reach consensus on its identification and membership requirements. The historical background, as we have seen, offered no firm bases for distinguishing Jew from non-Jew.[25] The search for the essential criteria of differentiation had ranged from the rabbinical position that Jewish identification is either ascriptive matrilineally (i.e., a person is Jewish if his or her mother was Jewish), or achieved by religious conversion to Judaism—to the purely ascriptive anti-Semitic decrees and definitions of European ultranationalists (e.g., the Nuremberg Racial Law of 1935 defined anyone as a Jew, baptized or not, who had at least one Jewish grandparent). Now the Israelis were compelled to probe beyond the examination of each other's faces, mannerisms and background in the introspective manner so typical of the Diaspora, to puzzle over the essential common core of their renewed composite structure.

The Israeli legislature, the Knesset, was understandably reluctant from the very beginning to attempt to formulate explicit answers to the questions "Who is a Jew?" and "What is a Jew?" Are Jewish nationality and religious identification one and the same, or can they be separated? Is an individual able to be Jewish without being a member of the Jewish faith? It was not only too complex to answer these questions but politically dangerous to try. Yet the daily operating needs of the new society have created seemingly inexorable problems—in connection with immigration policy, religious conversion, marriage eligibility and the affiliation of the offspring of mixed marriages—that call for policy decisions on Jewish ethnic identification and definition. The most controversial of these has been the application of the Israeli immigration policy known as the "Law of the Return," passed by the Knesset in 1950, and recognizing the right of every Jew to return to the ancestral homeland and to assume Israeli citizenship voluntarily, unless he poses a threat to public health or security, or has been guilty of offenses against the Jewish people.

In summary, the Jews form an ethnic group whose origins were classically marginal and whose history typically found them splintered and centripetally dispersed. Under the conditions of anomie in the contemporary world, they continue to generate problems of peripheral identification and group closure. This has come to be the case even for the Jews of Israel after having achieved dominant status, and has marked the lives of minority Jews in non-Jewish societies.

Multiple, Inarticulated and Ambivalent Criteria

An important feature of the dilemma in the new state of Israel —and one that has long plagued Jews and non-Jews elsewhere—is the use of such multiple, imperfectly articulated and ambivalent criteria of identification and membership as race, religion, and nationality. No one or combination of these offers the precision and consistency of intragroup inclusiveness and extragroup exclusiveness that would satisfy all. For example, the small but significant group of "Hebrew Christians" both in the Diaspora and in Israel, illustrate voluntary religious conversion to Christianity by Jews who at the same time have retained Jewish self-identification and have resisted complete assimilation into non-Jewish groups. For our purpose, they illustrate that Jewish religiosity and other aspects of Jewish ethnicity are imperfectly meshed.[26] The anthropologist Herskovits [27] skillfully defined the issue as follows:

Of all human groupings, there is none wherein the problem of definition has proved to be more difficult than for the Jews. Even when all possibilities seem to have been exhausted—race, people, nation, religion, cultural entity, historic group, linguistic unit—we find students casting about for other, more precise, more comprehensive designations. . . . It must be clear from . . . the many attempts that have been made to define the term "Jew" and to arrive at some formula to describe those who are to be placed in the category of Jews that there is certainly no agreement. The failure to obtain a consensus of opinion would seem to derive, in part at least, from the difficulty of drawing a definition when the very terms that must apparently be employed so lack preciseness.

What, for example, is an "ethnic group"? It is obviously not a race, yet it is stated to have subracial status, with certain distinguishing physical characteristics and certain way of life. And how does an "ethnic group" differ from a "people" or a "socio-religious group"? What does it mean to say they are a "population," or that they are those who belong to "a Jewish community" or that they are a "religio-national group"? What, even, does it mean to state that Jews are "a religion," when the views of the nature and functioning of the universe held by those included in a Jewish "ethnic group," "population," or "community" are so heterogeneous that, as one Jewish wit has said, "Where there are two Jews, there are three opinions!". . .

They (definitions of Jews) almost invariably attempt to encompass both dimensions of man, physical and cultural. That is, Jews are held to have delimitable physical traits . . . and they are also held to be marked by certain beliefs or habits, or traditions, or points of view, or values that mark them off from other peoples. Hence any attempt to draw a logically valid definition, it is felt, since it must describe as well as delimit, has to include two terms which, because they vary independently, rarely, if ever, exhibit a one-to-one correspondence. . . . No such order of correspondence holds for the Jews.

The matter of definition is especially baffling because there is enough similarity in physical type between enough Jews to permit the development of a stereotype that in the minds of the laity receives daily reinforcement and even justifies certain scientific classifications for certain Jewish subgroups. There is, also, enough of a least common denominator of belief, a certain minimum of traditionally accepted values, a certain sense of historic continuity held by enough Jews to make these aspects of Jewish life loom large in the minds of those concerned with definition. Yet whether on the level of physical type or of culture, the exceptions remain, exceeding any limits that can seemingly be drawn. This is undoubtedly the reason why it is far easier to say what Jews are not than to describe what they are.

Even so tentative a discussion as that of Bram (Joseph Bram, "The Social Identity of the Jews," *Trans. N.Y. Acad. of Sciences,* Ser. II, Vol. VI, No. 6, 1944, pp. 194–99) does not elude the common dilemma. Admitting the "picture of the Jewish people" to be "one of heterogeneity . . . of a changing people interacting with diverse national societies and whose social identity is constantly subjected by both sides to fluctuating interpretations," he still frames his concept of his task as an understanding of "the problems of social and 'ethnic identity' of the Jews." "The two extreme groups," he says, with insight, "those who want to be Jewish and those who cannot escape being Jewish, have, for a common denominator, only common ancestry and the recurrent hostility of the surrounding world."

Silcox and Fisher [28] made the same critical observation with special reference to Canadian and American Jews. There are Jewish racial (more so in the psychological and sociological meanings of the term than by physical and genetic measures), religious and nationality characteristics, but none is absolutely determinative. It can be argued that Jews are, and at the same time are not, a race; similarly it can be demonstrated that Jews and non-Jews are not mutually exclusive in religion and in nationality.

Classification of Controversies of Jewish Ethnic Anomie

At first glance, the many controversial and publicized cases of Jewish ethnic anomie in contemporary Israel [29] and the Diaspora, especially the United States, appear to be too diversified to submit to any meaningful classification. Careful examination, however, suggests that despite some overlap they fall into the following fourfold scheme: (1) Population registry and census; (2) Quasi-Jewish subgroups; (3) Apostates; (4) Children of mixed ethnic parentage.

Israeli Cases

(1) *Population registry and census.* The first classification of cases has to do with Israel's attempt, like those of other modern states, to keep an account of its demographic resources. In 1958, ten years after the establishment of the state, an agnostic Minister of Interior, Bar Yehuda, issued administrative directives to his staff concerning the people who could be registered as Jewish in the government's population directory. The directives were in defiance of rabbinic law that Jewish religious and nationality identification were identical and therefore indivisible. Bar Yehuda insisted instead that the two forms of identification were independent of each other and therefore a Jew could be anyone declaring in good faith that he or she is Jewish by nationality even if that person were nonreligious. Defending his Minister against the protesting rabbis, Premier Ben Gurion said:

The government does not consider itself qualified to decide who is a religious Jew. The question we had to decide is: Who is a Jew by nationality? I know there is an opinion that there is no such thing as a Jew without religion, but unfortunately there are many Jews who are not religious.[30]

This liberal position concerning Jewish identification was modified when the religious ministers in Ben Gurion's government took the issue to the cabinet. The latter amended Bar Yehuda's directives with a provision that adults belonging to a religion other than Judaism may not be registered as Jews in nationality, thereby going far toward recognizing the position that Jewish religion and nationality are indeed identical. In the case of children, however, the cabinet refused to meet the objections raised by the religious members, for it provided that in cases of intermarriage and miscegenation, if the parents concur that a child is Jewish, he or she shall be so registered. This was in contradiction of rabbinic law which recognizes the children of mixed parentage as Jewish only when the mother is Jewish and which insists that when the mother is Gentile the children be required to undergo the rituals of conversion in order to become Jewish. Confronted by an obstinate cabinet, the religious ministers resigned from the government in protest. At this point, Premier Ben Gurion relented and announced he would head a committee of three ministers to reexamine the whole question of Jewish identification and then formulate new registration rules.

In 1960, new government directives on the question "What is a Jew?" were issued by a new, religiously orthodox Minister of Interior, Moshe Shapiro. The directives now defined a Jew in Israel as a person born of Jewish mother and who does not belong to another religion, or one who was converted to Judaism in accordance with Jewish religious law. Like the amended directives of 1958, the new directives contradicted rabbinic law which states that apostates remain Jews, but unlike their predecessors they supported rabbinic law in maintaining that children follow the religion of their mother with the requirement that those whose mother is not Jewish undergo rabbinic conversion in order to become Jewish.[31]

A census in Israel in 1961 once again raised the vexing question: "What is a Jew?" In framing the census queries an attempt was made to circumvent the heart of the issue, but to no avail. For example, a key question was: "Are you a Jew, Moslem, Christian, Druse or other?" The alleged purpose in posing the question in this manner was to offer people a chance to register as Jews without stating whether they thought that their Jewishness was based upon religious or nationality criteria. But an association known as "The League to Prevent Religious Coercion" organized a movement to persuade Jews to register as "other" on the ground that the state failed to make the distinction between "Jew by religion" and "Jew by nationality." The League insisted that, under the existing directives, if a Jew informed the government officially that he was leaving the Jewish religion, the word "Jew" would be deleted from the notation of "nationality" on his identification card. But if a Gentile wife of a Jewish man told the census taker she was Jewish, no attempt would be made to determine if she had actually converted to Judaism.[32] To overcome this criticism, a draft Population Registry Bill in 1963 empowered registration clerks to ask for documentary evidence of religious affiliation whenever they saw fit to do so.[33]

(2) *Quasi-Jewish subgroups.* The second classification of controversial cases of Jewish ethnic anomie in Israel is a consequence of
the state's policy of opposition to intermarriage and civil marriage.
Is a marriage between two people an intermarriage when one
clearly satisfies the aforementioned directives of Jewish identification and the other, despite affiliation with a self-identified Jewish
subgroup, does not? For instance, some Israeli rabbis, because of
what they consider to be deep historical and religio-cultural divergences, have refused to recognize as Jews, and therefore do not
officiate at weddings or sanction marriages involving, three old and
small subgroups that have thought themselves Jews for centuries:
the Samaritans, the Karaites, and the B'nei Israel.

The Samaritans had been separated from the Jewish mainstream in the fourth century B.C.—at which time they were regarded as heretics—and they were barred from sharing in the
rebuilding of the Temple in Jerusalem after the return from
Babylonian exile. Taking their name from Samaria, the district
they once occupied, Nablus (the biblical "Shechem") is their
traditional center and nearby Mount Gerizim is their holy place.
The Samaritans hold sacred only the Torah—and in a version of it
that differs slightly from the Massoretic text. The Chief Rabbi of
Jerusalem in 1841 was the first to relent, issuing a certificate
attesting that the Samaritans were a genuine branch of the Chil-
dren of Israel. Yitzhak Ben Zvi, the second President of modern
Israel, was instrumental in having them covered in the Law of
Return's immigration policy despite the fact that in the past the
Samaritans often denied their Jewish identification whenever it
was politically convenient, claiming instead to be descendants of
Canaanite and Phoenician origin.

The Karaites—a sect that began in Persia in the eighth century
A.D.—have not been acknowledged as Jews by the rabbinate because they too do not accept the Mishna and the Talmud. Furthermore, in Russia they had succeeded in exempting themselves
from restrictive measures against Jews by claiming Mongol descent. The B'nei Israel—a group in isolation for eighteen centuries
in the Bombay area of India—trace their origins to seven Jewish
families which had been shipwrecked nearby in the second century
B.C. after having fled ancient Israel and the conquering legions of
the Syrian King Antiochus. Rabbis have refused to sanction their
marriages to Israeli Jews on the grounds that while they were in

isolation many of them had maintained loose divorce procedures and had been married to non-Jews and improperly converted proselytes. In October of 1961, the Supreme Rabbinical Council of Israel modified the formal rabbinical position taken in 1915 that "it was forbidden to marry them and this ban applies until the coming of the Messiah," decreeing now that the B'nei Israel are Jews beyond question. Yet differential treatment has persisted in Israel despite vehement protests by the B'nei Israel, for a directive was issued to all rabbis in Israel instructing them to trace back as far as possible the ancestry of any B'nei Israel wishing to marry an Israeli Jew.[34]

(3) *Apostates*. The third classification of controversial cases, the most publicized of all, has already been referred to in connection with cases of population registry and the census. Nevertheless, the problem of the Jewish identification of apostates, particularly those who have converted to Christianity, warrants some separate and more detailed treatment, not only because of its serious implications for marriage but also as it relates to Israel's immigration policy under the Law of Return. The most crucial case so far has been that of a Jewish-born Catholic monk, Brother Daniel, who, after the establishment of the new State, claimed the right to automatic entry and citizenship. He insisted that he had changed only his Jewish religious affiliation but had not relinquished his Jewish nationality by his apostasy.

The status of the apostate among Jews historically and horizontally has been neither clear nor consistent. Rashi had stressed that even though the apostate sinned by his act he still remained a Jew, whereas Rabenu Tam was not quite so lenient, asserting that one should rejoice at the death of an apostate.[35] Katz[36] makes an important distinction between forced apostates (*anusim*) and voluntary apostates (*mumar* or *meshummad*) in the Diaspora during the Middle Ages as follows:

It is true that in times of persecution whole groups were sometimes baptized, either forcibly or with consent under threat of force. Such converts, however, not being genuine, made every effort to return to the Jewish fold. . . . The Jewish community was well aware of the existence of *anusim*, *i.e.*, forced converts. In prayers for the welfare of the Jewish community these were specially mentioned. It was deemed especially meritorious to assist them in their attempt to escape from Christianity. . . . The general trend prevailing in their (halakhists) discussions was to designate the . . . *mumar* or *meshummad* as a "sinning Jew" who, by his baptism, neither lost his Jewish identity nor exempted himself from any obligation incumbent on a Jew by virtue of his birth. . . . That the apostate might return, and was indeed obliged to do so, was never even questioned. Doubts arose only as to whether, having returned, he could be fully rehabilitated. . . . The principle that the apostate remained a Jew was upheld even in the case of one who persisted in his apostasy. . . . The popular view did not, however, accept the view that baptism did not affect the Jew's character qua Jew. Indeed . . . the practice won acceptance that the repentant convert must undergo a ceremony of purification in the ritual bath in the same way as a proselyte. This practice . . . is first mentioned in the thirteenth century. . . . We have a vivid description, dating from the thirteenth century, of a type of convert who was neither Jew nor Christian, but adopted the way of life of either community according to convenience. R. Me'ir of Rothenburg tells us that "there came a Jew who had been baptized and then repented, not with his whole heart, but hypocritically, like those utterly worthless folk who wander round the countryside, appearing now as Jews, and now conducting themselves according to the customs of idolaters (*i.e.*, Christians)." That some of the converts were at heart Jews or quasi-Jews is borne out by the fact that they tried to gain access to such means of salvation as the Jewish religion had to offer. We learn of converts who contributed to Jewish charity, and wished to be owners or part-owners of the Scroll of the *Torah* used in the synagogue service. . . .

Later, in the Eastern European *shtetl*,[37] the reluctance of Jews to accept the loss of even voluntary apostates persisted, as described in the following reconstruction of a typical community:

Every possible pressure is brought to avert such a catastrophe. . . . Rabbi, friends, exhort the renegade to reconsider before it is too late. If all fails, the convert, the *meshummad*, is dead to the group. Yet nothing is final, no relationship is irrevocably broken. He can always repent and return. If he does not, then his children may—and sometimes do. Even if they do not, they will still be somehow vaguely regarded as Jewish. A "real Jew" is known by his "Jewish heart," his "Jewish head," his scrupulous fulfillment of all the mitsvos. But there is also a saying, "a Jew always remains a Jew." If you are born of Jewish parents, if you have any Jewish blood in you, then you have some bond with Klal Israel (*i.e.*, the "all of Israel").

The outcome of Brother Daniel's case at least temporarily resolved the issue concerning apostasy and Jewish identification in

Israel. In December of 1962 a Supreme Court decision made a distinction between the traditional rabbinical position, such as represented by Rashi, and the secular one of the Jewish state. The majority of the court ruled that Brother Daniel and other apostates might still be considered Jewish as the term is rabbinically understood. But the Law of Return is secular legislation and must be interpreted accordingly. On that basis Brother Daniel could not be regarded as a Jew, for there is one element common to all Jews, from the extreme Orthodox to the complete freethinkers: they do not sever themselves from the historic past as is implicit in the conversion to Christianity or any other non-Jewish religion.[38]

(4) *Children of mixed ethnic parentage.* The fourth and final classification of controversial cases in Israel was also referred to in the first classification but not given a sufficiently intensive analysis to bring out all aspects of the dilemma of ethnic anomie. We have seen that according to the traditional rabbinical position, children of mixed ethnic parentage are Jewish by matrilineal descent, or by conversion to Judaism if their mother is Gentile. Modern secular Israel, except for a temporary deviation after 1958, has adhered to this rabbinical directive. The children of intermarriages contracted in the Diaspora (as in the case of approximately one thousand refugee Jewish men from Communist Poland who had married Gentile women and had migrated to Israel with their unconverted wives and children), and of "liaisons" across ethnic lines in Israel where intermarriages cannot be performed are affected by the seemingly clear-cut policy and directive. Yet two aspects of mixed ethnic parentage perpetuate the problem of identification. First of all, in many cases involving Arab Moslem fathers and Jewish mothers, a conflict exists between the Moslem norm that calls for patrilineal ethnic descent and the Jewish norm which dictates, as we have observed, matrilineal ethnic descent, with both sides claiming the children. Ironically, if the father in such cases is Jewish and the mother Moslem, neither can normatively claim the children unless, of course, a conversion by one or both parents obliterates the problem. The second aspect of mixed ethnic parentage not resolved by present policy and directives is embedded in the prevalent pattern of patronymy found in Jewish and other cultures. In those cases where the father is Jewish and the mother is not, the children, although legally non-Jewish, nevertheless bear a Jewish surname and are therefore sociologically identifiable as Jewish.[39]

American Cases

The founding of the new state of Israel and the inevitable eruption of dramatic cases of Jewish ethnic anomie has not precluded the continuing production of similar, though less ostentatious cases in the Diaspora. Comparing Jewish identificational problems in Israel with those in the United States, S. Herman [40] reported at the Fourth World Congress of Jewish Studies in the summer of 1965 his impression that Americans were better able to express their Jewish identity because they were more clearly marked off from the omnipresent Gentiles. The Israeli Jew, on the other hand, is rarely reminded of his Jewishness and is therefore less consciously aware of it than is his American counterpart.

The Christian Jews (or Hebrew Christians), both as individuals and as an organized subgroup, are a perennial source of dilemma on the American scene,[41] more to others than to themselves. It is an ongoing debate in American Jewish communities whether or not the Black Jews and the "Royal Order of Ethiopian Hebrews" are authentically Jewish.[42] The most controversial and publicized American case of Jewish ethnic anomie in recent years concerned Michael Hernstadt of Westchester County, New York, the product of a Jewish-Catholic intermarriage. Not a Jew according to Jewish law because his mother was Gentile, but subject to Jewish patronymic identification nonetheless, Mr. Hernstadt was baptized an Episcopalian. The illusion of his non-Jewish self-image was sociologically shattered in 1960 when the exclusive Scarsdale Golf Club refused to allow him to escort a young Gentile woman to the annual Holly Ball. The rejection was admittedly based upon the fact that the club considered Mr. Hernstadt Jewish despite his Episcopalian affiliation.[43] On this writer's own campus a debate between two faculty members brought forth still another type of case of Jewish ethnic anomie, reported as follows: [44]

Mr. Stanley Feingold (Political Science), speaking at Hillel House yesterday, explained why he does not believe in God and therefore has rejected Judaism. What was billed as a discussion turned into a debate when Mr. Feingold confronted Professor Bernard Brown (Physics) on the topic "How the Jewish Intellectual Responds to Judaism." Basing his rejection of Judaism on the tenet that a Jew must believe in God, Mr. Feingold said: "I reject the concept of a supernatural deity and therefore Judaism and all other faiths based on this. The existence of

God is a matter of moral indifference to me. A relationship to God does not equip me for a good life or help me solve my problems. . . ." Professor Brown said he found Mr. Feingold's definition of a Jew based purely on religion and that this idea of Judaism only developed as a reaction to political and social pressures. *"No matter what you say, I know you are a Jew,"* Professor Brown told Mr. Feingold. [Italics ours.]

An Existential Typology of Ethnic Anomie

We come now to the ultimate goal of this essay, namely, to propose a new typology that will consolidate the various expressions of ethnic anomie involving Jews. If successful, it may be utilized as a fresh starting point for further research and analysis. Our effort here fits into what Glazer [45] once characterized as a good part of the sociology of the Jews in "efforts to understand a social type . . . by trying to grasp what is essential to the phenomenon, what is logically implied by its nature. . . . It creates an arsenal of concepts and hypotheses to guide the more empirical-minded sociologist in a concrete investigation; and it synthesizes in general conclusions the information that accumulates from empirical investigation and historical research. . . ."

The rudiments of our typology are traced back in part to the pioneering social psychologists Cooley, Mead, Waller and others of the sociological school of social psychology,[46] all of whom viewed the social self in terms of the internalized responses of others. We see ourselves as others, especially the significant others, see us. But the more direct ancestor of our typology is the famous operational research definition of a Jew formulated by Herskovits [47] in 1927, a specific application of the aforementioned social psychological generalization. In his efforts to overcome the frustrations inherent in utilizing the standard criteria of Jewish identification—race, religion and nationality—Herskovits defined a Jew as "a person who calls himself a Jew or who is called Jewish by others." There were for the social psychologists as well as for Herskovits the self-image of the personality on the one hand and, on the other, the group's perception of the personality and its identity. This existential view of identity that claims it is whatever and whoever people think it is [48] has been employed ever since Herskovits' formulation in various American sociological studies of ethnic (especially Jewish) studies.[49]

Effective as this operational existential definition has been, it has had two major shortcomings. First, it falsely assumes that the two variables—the self-image and group recognition—always vary in value in the same direction. A Jew, in other words, so identifies himself *and* is so recognized by others; a non-Jew does not identify himself as Jewish *and* is not recognized as such by others. There is no allowance here for the possibility that under the contemporary social conditions of anomie, each variable may at times vary in value independently of the other. To be (or not to be) identified with a given ethnic group and to be recognized (or not to be recognized) as a member of that group by others does not exhaust the possibilities of identification. Persons may also be self-identified with the group but not be recognized as members by others, and some may not identify themselves with the group but be socially recognized as members.

A second deficiency of the Herskovits definition is that it fails to take into consideration what is inherent in a multigroup society. *Two or more groups* may be competitively involved in identificational and group recognitional claims and rejections.

To resolve both shortcomings, the following sixfold existential typology is offered. It is a scheme for the analysis of ethnic anomie that can be applied to the Jew of ambiguous status, or to any other ethnically peripheral and enigmatic persons and subgroups in modern society. It presumes a minimum of two groups with which such persons or subgroups are either self-identified or self-alienated, and, in turn, the persons or subgroups face either recognitional acceptance or rejection by each of the two groups:

Peripheral Individuals and Subgroups

| | Group 1 | | | Group 2 | |
	Self-identification	Self-alienation		Self-identification	Self-alienation
Group acceptance	a(c)	e(f)	Group acceptance	a c	e f
Group rejection	d f	b c	Group rejection	d(f)	b(c)

That is, for some ambiguous Jews there is a preponderance of (a) bi-group self-identification and group acceptance. At the other end of the spectrum others mostly experience (b) bi-group self-alienation and group rejection. In the middle range there are four variations of ambivalent identification and group recognition. Some peripheral people undergo (c) self-alienation and rejection by one group, and self-identification with and acceptance by the other; (d) self-identification with, but rejection by, both groups; (e) self-alienation from, but acceptance by, both groups; and lastly, (f) self-identification with, but rejection by one group, and self-alienation from, but acceptance by the other.

Conclusion

Application of this typology need not be limited to ambiguity among Jews, for ethnic anomie is now widespread in urban and mass societies and affects virtually all races, religious groups, and nationalities. In fact, the broader application should be encouraged; it may reveal the weaknesses in the typology that are not apparent in a particularistic application of it. This, in turn, could lead to its refinement as an instrument of sociological analysis.

Notes ▶

1. See, for example, Ruby Jo Reeves Kennedy, "What Has Social Science To Say About Intermarriage?" in Werner J. Cahnman, ed., *Intermarriage and Jewish Life*, New York, The Herzl Press and the Reconstructionist Press, 1963, pp. 19–37.

2. Milton M. Gordon, *Assimilation in American Life: The Role of Race, Religion and National Origins*, New York, Oxford University Press, 1964, pp. 19–25.

3. J. Milton Yinger, *Toward a Field Theory of Behavior: Personality and Social Structure*, New York, McGraw-Hill Book Co., 1965, p. 188.

4. Hendrik M. Ruitenbeek, *The Individual and the Crowd: A Study of Identity in America*, New York, Mentor Books, 1964, pp. 93ff.

5. Sophistication in this respect in American sociology began with Park's concept of the "marginal man." See Robert E. Park, "Human Migration and the Marginal Man," *American Journal of Sociology*, May 1928, pp. 881–93, reprinted in his *Race and Culture*, Glencoe, The Free Press, 1950, pp. 345–56.

6. William Graham Sumner, *Folkways*, Boston, Ginn and Co., 1906, p. 12.

7. The key references in the discussion that follows are Daniel J. Levinson, "The Study of Ethnocentric Ideology," in T. W. Adorno et al., *The Authoritarian Personality*, New York, Harper and Brothers, 1950, Chap. IV, pp. 102–50; Kurt Lewin, "Self-Hatred Among Jews," *Contemporary Jewish Record*, Vol. IV, 1941, pp. 219–32; Everett V.

Stonequist, *The Marginal Man*, New York, Charles Scribner's Sons, 1937; Joseph H. Fichter, *Social Relations in the Urban Parish*, Chicago, The University of Chicago Press, 1954, pp. 56–7, 59–67.

8. Park is believed to have derived his concept of the marginal man both from suggestions in the writings of Sombart and Simmel on the status and role of strangers and from his own personal observations of people who had become ethnically peripheral. To Park the emancipated Jew was the typical marginal man. In addition to the Park and Stonequist citations above, see John F. Cuber, "Marginal Church Participants," *Sociology and Social Research*, Sept.–Oct. 1940, pp. 57–62; Everett V. Stonequist, "The Marginal Character of the Jews," in Isacque Graeber and Steuart H. Britt, eds., *Jews in a Gentile World*, New York, Macmillan, 1942, pp. 296–310; Everett Hughes, "Social Change and Status Protest: an Essay on the Marginal Man," *Phylon*, First Quarter, 1949, pp. 58–65; David I. Golovensky, "The Marginal Man Concept: An Analysis and Critique," *Social Forces*, Vol. 30, March 1952, pp. 333–39; David Riesman, "Some Observations Concerning Marginality," in his *Individualism Reconsidered*, Glencoe, The Free Press, 1954, pp. 153–65; Aaron Antonovsky, "Toward a Refinement of the 'Marginal Man' Concept," *Social Forces*, Oct. 1956, pp. 57–62; Bernard Rosenberg and Gilbert Shapiro, "Marginality and Jewish Humor," *Midstream*, Spring 1958, pp. 70–80.

9. One contemporary sociologist views the concept as having as many as five meanings: powerlessness, meaninglessness, normlessness, isolation, and self-estrangement. See Melvin Seeman, "On the Meaning of Alienation," *American Sociological Review*, Vol. 24, No. 6, Dec. 1959, pp. 783–91.

10. See Eric and Mary Josephson, eds., *Man Alone: Alienation in Modern Society*, New York, Dell Publishing Co., 1962, pp. 12–15, 55.

11. *Ibid.*, pp. 13–14. See also Robert M. MacIver, *The Ramparts We Guard*, New York, The Macmillan Company, 1950, pp. 84–92; Jan Hajda, "Alienation and Integration of Student Intellectuals," *American Sociological Review*, Vol. 26, No. 5, Oct. 1961, pp. 758–77.

12. Melville J. Herskovits, "When Is a Jew a Jew?" *Modern Quarterly*, Vol. IV, No. 2, 1927, pp. 109–17. See also his "Who Are the Jews?" in Louis Finkelstein, ed., *The Jews: Their History, Culture and Religion*, New York, The Jewish Publication Society of America, Vol. II, 1960, pp. 1489–1509.

13. *Invitation to Sociology: A Humanistic Perspective*, Garden City, Doubleday and Co., 1963, pp. 102–3.

14. See, for example, Moshe Navon, "What Is a Jew?" *The National Jewish Monthly*, Dec. 1958, pp. 11, 13; Morris N. Kertzer, *What Is a Jew?*, New York, Collier Books, 1960 (revised edition);

Morris Adler, "What Is a Jew?" *Harper's Magazine*, Jan. 1964, pp. 41–5; Margaret Mead, *Israel and Problems of Identity*, New York, Herzl Institute Pamphlet #3, 1958, 27 pp. The constant probing for the criteria of Jewish identification has also invaded Jewish humor. For example: "Four conscientious Jews were discussing earnestly the question 'What is a Jew?' The first attempted to prove, at great length, that the Jews are not a nationality. . . . The second enthusiastically established to his own satisfaction that the Jews are not a religion. . . . The third grasped the first opening to argue vigorously that the Jews are not a race. . . . The fourth listened patiently to the heated debate, and then observed, 'I am surprised at you men. You are all using a negative approach and trying to prove only what the Jews *are not*. We should be more positive in our approach to such a subject.' 'All right,' the others conceded, 'so what is *your* idea on the matter?' The fourth discussant thought for a moment. Then he announced with the cadence of conviction, 'A Jew is a man who is discussing "what is a Jew."'" See *The Jewish Digest*, July 1965, p. 70. The anomic patterns of American society are also beginning to provoke members of other ethnic groups to ask the same introspective question about themselves. In an editorial entitled "What Is a Negro?" *Ebony*, Vol. VIII, No. 6, April 1953, p. 112, the conclusion was that "because of the many conflicting definitions and descriptions which fail properly to describe the American Negro, he can best be explained by what he is not."

15. The Jewish concept of a "Chosen People" has no peer in this respect, although many contemporary Jewish professional spokesmen have been quick to stress that the concept is misunderstood and misused. A typical defensive statement is that "no concept of Judaism has been more consistently misunderstood than that of the Chosen People. It has been confused with false pride and national chauvinism. It has been mistakenly identified with the pernicious doctrine of racial superiority. For the Jew, the concept of the 'chosen' people meant that more was expected of him than of others and that his actions would be judged by higher standards. It was a form of *noblesse oblige*, imposing upon him moral responsibilities, the need of stressing holiness, righteousness, and other spiritual values. . . ." See Morris Silverman, ed., "Note on the Chosen People," in *Sabbath and Festival Prayer Book*, New York, Rabbinical Assembly of America and United Synagogue of America, 1946, p. 483.

16. Raphael Patai, *Israel Between East and West*, Philadelphia, Jewish Publication Society, 1953, p. 119.

17. Nathan Ausubel, *History of the Jewish People*, New York, Crown Publishers, 1953, p. 25.

18. Beth Mikra: *Bulletin of the Israel Society for Biblical Research*, Vol. 2 (1962) and Vol. 3 (1963).

19. For example, it is to Gentile sailors that the Biblical Jonah announces "I am a Hebrew." See Book of Jonah, Chapter 1, verse 9.

20. Kertzer, *op. cit.*, pp. 21–2.

21. See, for example, Reinhard Bendix, "Society and Religion in Ancient Palestine," Chapter VII in *Max Weber: An Intellectual Portrait*, Garden City, Doubleday and Co., 1962, pp. 200–56; Avraham Harman, *Agricultural Settlement: Israel Today*, No. 2, Jerusalem, Israel Digest, Jan. 1960, pp. 3–4 (second edition).

22. Diaspora, a Greek word meaning "dispersion," was originally applied to the Jews who, after the Babylonian captivity, were scattered throughout the world. It now refers to all Jews outside Israel.

23. Oscar Handlin, "Group Life Within the American Pattern," *Commentary*, Vol. VIII, 1949, p. 411.

24. Irving Malin, *Jews and Americans*, Carbondale, Southern Illinois University Press, 1965.

25. In the medieval period (from the tenth to the fourteenth centuries), for instance, "Jews and Gentiles lived in such close proximity, there was always the possibility that individuals might change from one religion to the other. The only way of preventing such occurrences was by maintaining a rigid standard of mutual exclusiveness. . . . However, Christianity kept its doors wide open for the whole of the Jewish community (although in practice it was only individuals who crossed the threshold) and . . . Jewish teachers adopted the same attitude towards Christians, the only difference being that the likelihood of all Christians converting to Judaism was even more remote. . . . One of the most characteristic features of the social situation was the readiness of either community to welcome as members those outside it, on condition that they changed their religion." See Jacob Katz, "Apostates and Proselytes," Chapter VI in *Exclusiveness and Tolerance: Jewish-Gentile Relations in Medieval and Modern Times*, New York, Schocken Books, 1962, pp. 67–81. The Marranos of Spain, forced to be baptized as Roman Catholics, nevertheless secretly retained their Jewish identification and many Jewish religious practices for centuries. For a recent analysis of another cryptic Jewish group, see Daniel M. Friedenberg, "The Conversos of Soller," *The Jewish Digest*, July 1965, pp. 15–22.

26. See Marshall Sklare, ed., *The Jews: Social Patterns of An American Group*, Glencoe, The Free Press, 1958, p. 324. See also Solomon Liptzin, *Germany's Step-children*, Philadelphia, Jewish Publication Society of America, 1944, for analysis of "Jewish Christians" (Chapter III) and "Jewish Aryans" (Chapter XII).

27. Herskovits, *op. cit.*, pp. 1489ff.

28. Claris Edwin Silcox and Galen M. Fisher, *Catholics, Jews and Protestants*, New York, Harper and Bros., 1934, pp. 19–22.

29. These controversies in Israel have had nothing to do with citizenship which is available to all ethnic groups; rather they have been concerned with the nature and composition of Jewish ethnicity and identification.

30. Navon, *op. cit.*, pp. 11, 13.

31. *The New York Times*, Jan. 4, 1960.

32. Lawrence Fellows, "Rabbinate Yields on Israel Census," *The New York Times*, May 30, 1961.

33. *The Jerusalem Post*, Jan. 15, 1963.

34. For a descriptive account of these and other "quasi-Jewish" subgroups, see Schifra Strizower, *Exotic Jewish Communities*, London, Thomas Yoseloff, 1962.

35. See Max Goody, "Ideology of Conservative Judaism," *The Torch*, Winter Issue, 1964–65, p. 9.

36. Katz, *op. cit.*, pp. 68–75.

37. Mark Zborowski and Elizabeth Herzog, *Life Is With People*, New York, Schocken, 1962, pp. 231–2.

38. See Aharon Lichtenstein, "Brother Daniel and the Jewish Fraternity," *Judaism*, Vol. 12, No. 3, Summer 1963, pp. 260–80.

39. Navon, *op. cit.*, p. 11; see also Harry Simonhoff, *Saga of American Jewry*, New York, Arco Publishing Co., 1964; Lawrence Fellows, "A Harried Couple," *The New York Times*, Oct. 29, 1961; *The Jerusalem Post*, May 13, 1963; Brooks Atkinson, "Mrs. Eitani's Case," *The New York Times*, Jan. 19, 1965; *The Jerusalem Post Weekly*, June 25, 1965 and Aug. 20, 1965.

40. *The Jerusalem Post Weekly*, July 30, 1965.

41. See Sklare, *op. cit.*, p. 415; Silcox and Fisher, *op. cit.*, pp. 274–8.

42. See Howard Brotz, *The Black Jews of Harlem*, New York, The Free Press of Glencoe, 1964.

43. *The New York Times*, Jan. 15, 1961; Jessie Zel Lurie, "A 'Brother Daniel' in Scarsdale," *The Jerusalem Post*, Feb. 5, 1963.

44. *The Campus* (The City College of New York), March 22, 1962.

45. Nathan Glazer, "What Sociology Knows About American Jews," *Commentary*, Vol. 9, No. 3, March 1950, p. 277.

46. See, for example, G. H. Mead, *Mind, Self and Society*, Chicago, University of Chicago Press, 1934; Willard Waller, *The Family*, New York, The Dryden Press, 1938.

47. Herskovits, *op. cit.*, pp. 109–17.

48. Yitzhak Baer and Ben-Zion Dinur, *Religion and History:* Lectures delivered at the Ninth Convention of the Israel Historical Society, Dec. 1963, published by the Society, Jerusalem, 1964.

49. See W. L. Warner's Yankee City Series; Stanley K. Bigman, *The Jewish Population of Greater Washington in 1956,* Wash., D.C., The Jewish Community Council of Greater Washington, 1957; Charles R. Snyder, *Alcohol and the Jews,* Glencoe, The Free Press, 1958; *Who's Who in World Jewry-1965,* New York, David McKay, 1965.

II MINORITIES IN VARIOUS SOCIETIES

Oने of the traditional major weaknesses in the sociology of social problems—including minority problems—has been the lack of a comparative, or cross-cultural, approach. Typically, we have tried to understand a given problem in our society with hardly more than passing reference to similar problems in different societies.

Nevertheless, there is now a very noticeable shift in some specialties of American sociology toward a world perspective. The study of minority problems is involved in this movement, partly because of the potentially greater theoretical insight that a cross-cultural approach affords. But in another sense, the development of a wider perspective has been unavoidable. Westernization and urbanization can be seen as a vast culture complex which has been diffused into the continents of Asia, Africa, and Latin America sufficiently since World War II to create new multigroup societies and exacerbate the inevitable struggles for power and equality between ethnic groups. This phenomenon cannot be ignored by Americans.

All over the world one can find societies divided and embittered along one or more ethnic lines, such as race in South Africa and Rhodesia, religion in India, nationality in Cyprus and Canada, and language in Belgium. But it is the race problem that has become of paramount importance. Most Westerners, including Americans, think of the problem in the broad sense as essentially a struggle for equal status on the part of dark-skinned natives and peasants in underdeveloped areas. In the view of some students, this definition of the problem is probably already obsolete. The question no longer is whether African, Asiatic, or Latin American can achieve equality, but rather whether Western whites will lose it. In short, there is no assurance that mankind, after three hundred years of white or European dominance, will move safely toward race equality.

It would be a caricature of the crudest kind to define every ethnic problem in the so-called underdeveloped societies as a confrontation between exploiting European-derived whites and resentful native blacks. In the first reading of this section, for example, the deep-rooted religious antagonism between Hindu and Moslem in India and Pakistan is explored with compassion by the Indian scholar, Mr. Khushwant Singh.

3 ► WHY HINDU AND MOSLEM SPEAK HATE

KHUSHWANT SINGH

► THE SUMMER of 1947 was not like other Indian summers. Even the weather had a different feel in India that year. It was hotter than usual, and drier and dustier. And the summer was longer. No one could remember when the monsoon had been so late. For weeks, the sparse clouds cast only shadows. There was no rain. People began to say that God was punishing them for their sins.

Some of them had good reason to feel that they had sinned. The summer before, communal riots, precipitated by reports of the proposed division of the country into a Hindu India and a Moslem Pakistan, had broken out in Calcutta, and within a few months the death roll had mounted to several thousand. Moslems said the Hindus had planned and started the killing. According to the Hindus, the Moslems were to blame.

The fact is, both sides killed. Both shot and stabbed and speared and clubbed. Both tortured. Both raped.

From Calcutta, the riots spread north and east and west: to Noakhali in East Bengal, where Moslems massacred Hindus; to Bihar, where Hindus massacred Moslems. Mullahs roamed the Punjab and the Frontier Province with boxes of human skulls said to be those of Moslems killed in Bihar. Hundreds of thousands of Hindus and Sikhs who had lived for centuries on the North-West Frontier abandoned their homes and fled toward the protection of the predominantly Sikh and Hindu communities in the east. They traveled on foot, in bullock carts, crammed into lorries, clinging to the sides and roofs of trains.

Along the way—at fords, at crossroads, at railroad stations—

From *The New York Times Magazine*, September 19, 1965. © 1965 by The New York Times Company. Reprinted by permission of the publisher and author.

they collided with panicky swarms of Moslems fleeing to safety in the west. The riots had become a rout. By the summer of 1947, when the creation of the new state of Pakistan was formally announced, 10 million people—Moslems and Hindus and Sikhs— were in flight. By the time the monsoon broke, almost a million of them were dead, and all of northern India was in arms, in terror, or in hiding.

The summer of 1965 has been very much like that of 1947— only hotter and dustier and with even less rain. And both in India and in Pakistan people have been talking the language they did in 1947, the language of hate.

Pakistanis say that Indians never accepted the independent Moslem state of Pakistan and had been plotting for its destruction; that the Hindus who murdered Gandhi for protecting the Moslems have reduced Nehru's ideal of a secular state to a mockery: it is not a secular but a seculiar state, they jibe in a pun on the word peculiar; that India's 50 million Moslems live in fear of their lives, and hundreds of thousands have been forced by Hindu thugs to flee to Pakistan; that in the matter of Kashmir the Indians have dishonored their promise to hold a plebiscite and flouted resolutions of the United Nations; that Hindus insulted the Moslems by stealing the Hair of the Prophet from the shrine in Srinagar.

And now, they say, when the Moslems of Kashmir have risen in revolt against Hindu oppression, Indians have falsely accused Pakistan of abetting the rebellion and used it as an excuse to execute their sinister design of destroying Pakistan. Pakistanis regard this conflict as a struggle for survival as an independent Moslem nation. Their leaders have declared it to be a jihad—a holy war against the infidel.

Indians say that Pakistanis have always harbored ill will against India, particularly the Hindus; that, whereas the saintly Gandhi laid down his life for the cause of Hindu-Moslem unity and an enlightened Nehru gave Indian Moslems more than an equal status in India, Pakistan declared herself an Islamic state and thus reduced her 12 million Hindus and Christians to second-class citizens; that Moslem *goondas* were encouraged to organize pogroms against Hindus and Christians, thus compelling in the last 18 years, more than 5 million to leave Pakistan for India.

Indians insist on repeating that the people of Kashmir, both Moslem and Hindu, joined India of their own free will and all the trouble created in that state is by Pakistani infiltrators. Indians say they are fighting for an ideal, for the triumph of right over wrong. Their leaders have proclaimed it as a *dharmayudha*—a righteous war.

The conflict is in some respects a continuation of the civil strife of the summer of 1947. An important difference is that, while in 1947 the armies of the two nations were neutral and often performed missions of mercy, now it is the two armies that are locked in mortal combat.

In 1947, the Moslems fought the Sikhs and Hindus with knives, spears, brickbats, bottles full of acid and antiquated muskets. Now Saber jets, Mystères and Vampires contend for mastery of the skies, Sherman and Centurion and Patton tanks roll across the dusty plains and heavy guns shell cities on either side. But the contending parties are animated by the same passions which inflamed the minds of the contenders in 1947.

The Pakistani Army is entirely Moslem. Its morale is built on the Moslem's age-old contempt and hatred of the Hindu. India's Army has a few—no more than a handful—of Moslem officers. It is chiefly composed of Sikhs, Gurkhas, Mahrattas Rajputs, Dogras and Jats—all within the embrace of the Hindu social system and all, with the possible exception of the Gurkhas, fiercely hostile toward the Moslems.

War cries which were yelled across the rooftops in 1947 again echo on the battlefields of the Punjab. Pathan and Punjab Moslems go into action crying the name of Mohammed's son-in-law, "Ali, Ali." Sikhs who spearheaded the drive across the international frontier toward Lahore entered the fray beating their war drums and crying *"Sat Sri Akal!"* ("God is Truth!")

"What, in your opinion, is the root cause of the hostility between the Hindu and the Moslem?" I asked a group of Indologists assembled this month at Claremont, Calif., for the 11th International Congress for the History of World Religions.

Dr. Wilfred Cantwell Smith, director of the Center for Study of World Religions at Harvard and an acknowledged authority on Islam, replied: "Speaking ideologically, the Moslems feel it is their destiny to rule. They do not feel they can discharge their religious obligations except in an Islamic state, the Dar-ul-Islam. This notion has the sanction of the Moslem religious law, the Shariat. According to the Shariat, the Dar-ul-Harab (literally, 'realm of war') imposes a responsibility on the Moslem community living in a sovereign Moslem state to go to the help of Moslems who live outside, especially in neighboring states under non-Moslem rule."

"Would you then conclude that the Pakistanis have gone into Kashmir and now into India because they feel it is their religious duty to rescue Kashmiri and Indian Moslems from non-Moslem rulers?" I asked.

"I am not willing to answer that question," replied Dr. Smith firmly.

Dr. R. N. Dandekar, one of India's leading Hindu scholars, was more forthright. He said:

"The chief difference between Hindus and Moslems is their attitude toward people of other religions. Moslems are fanatics. They can think of nothing except in terms of Islam. Hindus are tolerant of other faiths and are ever willing to compromise with them and live in amity with those who profess them."

He elaborated his point: "India has been the home of many different religions—Hindus, Moslems, Christians, Sikhs, Buddhists, Jains, Zoroastrians and Jews. But for practical purposes you can divide India's 500 millions into just two communities, Moslems and others. Hindus, who form 80 per cent of the population of the country, have been able to come to terms with all other religious communities except the Moslems. Moslems have always stayed outside the mainstream of Indianism. Very few joined the freedom movement against the British. Of the thousands of Indian terrorists who were hanged by the British, you cannot name more than half a dozen Moslems."

"Their bodies are in India, but their hearts are in Arabia," added Dr. T. R. V. Murti, professor of Hinduism at the Benares Hindu University. "It is hard to believe that nine out of 10 Moslems on the subcontinent are converts from Hinduism and are Indians by race, language and way of living."

"I would not go so far as to accuse them of extraterritorial loyalty," protested Prof. A. K. Saran of the Lucknow University. "Hindus and Moslems belong to two culture worlds. And the Moslems can never forget that for 700 years before the British occupied India, they ruled over the Hindus."

This is exactly what Mohammed Ali Jinnah, the founder of Pakistan, used to say—Hindus and Moslems are not one people with different religions; they are two separate and distinct nations.

Although Moslems belong to the same races and speak the same languages spoken by other Indians of the region in which they live, their customs and way of living differ in some respects. A Moslem child is given a distinctively Moslem name such as Mohammed Ali. Sikhs and Hindus of northern India, particularly Jats, Rajputs and Gurkhas, often have similar names; for example, my own surname, Singh. Even Christians in most parts of India retain their Hindu names; only conversion to Islam requires a change.

A Moslem boy is circumcised and learns verses of the Koran from a mullah. A Hindu boy has his head shaved and if he belongs to one of the three upper classes of Hinduism, he wears a sacred thread and is taught Sanskrit texts by a *pandit*.

The dietary laws of Hindus and Moslems are different. Hindus worship the cow. The Moslems eat it. Hindus, if not vegetarian, eat pork. Moslems are seldom vegetarian, and like the Jews, consider the pig unclean. Moslems only eat the flesh of an animal slain by being bled to death. Hindus prefer to decapitate their goat; Sikhs go further and consider eating meat of an animal slain in the Moslem fashion to be sinful. There are certain differences in the style of dress of the two peoples. Hindus wear Gandhi caps and dhotis. Moslems prefer wearing fezzes or caps made of lamb's skin and usually wear loose-fitting pajama trousers.

Hindu women wear saris and sport a little red dot on their foreheads. Moslem women prefer the Punjabi *salwar-kameez* or the baggy *gharara*. Moslem women are often veiled. Hindu women never veil themselves.

Hindus worship a multiplicity of gods, read many sacred texts and venerate innumerable avatars. Moslems worship the one and only Allah, honor Mohammed as His one and only Prophet and read the Koran as the only true revelation of God; Hindus go to many places of pilgrimage and wash off their sins in India's many sacred rivers. For the Moslems the only places of pilgrimage are Mecca and Medina, or if he is a Shia Moslem, Karbala in Iraq.

When a Hindu falls ill he consults a Hindu *vail* learned in the Ayur-Vedic system of medicine. When a Moslem falls ill he consults a Moslem hakeem, learned in the *yunani* or Greek system of medicine. When a Hindu dies, he is cremated and his ashes immersed in a river or the ocean. When a Moslem dies, he is buried with his face turned toward Mecca.

Moslems look upon Hindus as mean, cunning and cowardly, fit only to be baboos (clerks) or banians (shopkeepers). They dismiss Hindu scholars as sanctimonious gas bags. "The only language a Hindu understands," say the Moslems, "is the language of the sword."

Hindus look upon Moslems as dirty, incapable of hard work and grasping. "Give them Kashmir and they'll be asking for something else," say the Hindus. "Their mentality is that of the Arab Bedouin. They are not the sons of the desert, but its fathers because wherever they go they create a desert. Look what they did to Hindustan!"

In every Indian city there is a Moslem locality distinct from the Hindu. Even villages where the two live together are more often than not known by the religious character—Moslem village, Hindu village, Sikh village.

History casts a long and dividing shadow between Hinduism and Islam. And the shadow is of religion, not of race or language. Arab traders are known to have come to India from time immemorial. Dhows laden with products of the desert—dates and aromatic herbs—took advantage of the easterly winds and sailed across the Indian Ocean. Their arrival on the west coast of India, stretching from the Rann of Cutch down to Cape Comorin, was as familiar to the people of the region as the flocks of monsoon birds which flew over from the African coast as heralds of the summer monsoon. These Arabs spent the rainy season in India exchanging their wares for Indian textiles and spices and sailed back to their homes before the winter set in. Some, however, stayed and settled in India.

After the Prophet Mohammed converted the Arabs to Islam, these traders introduced their new faith into India. Mosques sprang up along the western coast. There is evidence to prove that these early Arab Moslems were made more than welcome by the local Hindus, who gave them daughters in marriage. Descendants of these ancient traders are still found in large communities in Malabar, the present day state of Kerala. They are known as *moplahs* from the Malayalam word *mapilla*, meaning son-in-law.

The amicable relationship between the Hindu and the Moslem changed abruptly when, instead of the peaceful Arab trader, India began to be invaded from the northwest by Moslem armies. Early in the 8th century the 17-year-old Mohammed Bin Qasm overran Sind. From 1080, Mahmud of Ghazni began his invasion of India. He destroyed Hindu temples as centers of satanic idolatry. He put thousands of Hindus to the sword and made a pastime of raising pyramids of skulls of infidels.

Mahmud's destructive zeal reached its full frenzy in Somnath in Gujerat, reputed to be the richest temple of India. Mahmud slew its Brahmin priests, smashed the idols with his own hands and looted the temple coffers of their silver, gold and diamonds. He carried the sandalwood portals studded with precious stones back to Afghanistan as trophies. Ever since then the name of Mahmud has stunk in the nostrils of the Hindus. It is significant that in the month following the communal massacres of 1947 an unusually large number of boys born to Pakistani Moslem parents were given the name Mahmud.

Mahmud of Ghazni was only the first of a long line of Moslem idol-breakers. His example was followed by Mongols, Turks and Persians. And they killed and destroyed in the name of Islam. Not a single Buddhist, Jain, or Hindu temple in northern India escaped their iconoclastic zeal. Some temples were converted to mosques; idols and figurines had their noses, breasts or limbs lopped off; wall paintings were charred beyond recognition.

Even the Mogul Dynasty which ruled India for 200 years and gave it its most beautiful monuments, such as the Taj Mahal at Agra, had its quota of Hindu-baiters. Baber, who conquered India in 1526, raised a ghoulish mountain heap of 60,000 heads of Hindu Rajputs he had defeated in battle. The last great ruler of the dynasty, Aurangzeb, is reputed to have ordered governors of provinces to snip off the pigtails of Hindus and send them to Agra to be weighed. He imposed a tax, the *jiziya*, on all his non-Moslem subjects and forced many to be converted to Islam.

There were peaceful interludes in these centuries of persecution, the most notable being the reign of Akbar, who ruled India from 1556 to 1605. Akbar abolished discrimination against subjects of different faiths, elevated Hindus to high positions and entered into matrimonial alliances with Hindu Rajput princes. Akbar's name is honored with the title Akbar the Great. But Aurangzeb, who is praised by Moslem historians for his piety and the firmness with which he dealt with his non-Moslem subjects, is abominated by the Hindus.

It is little wonder that the Hindus began to look upon Moslems as tyrants and shunned those Indians who accepted Islam as traitors with extraterritorial loyalties. It took many long years of suffering and humiliation before the Hindus were able to hit back. One was Sivaji, the Mahratta. He defied the Moguls in central and southern India and ultimately triumphed over them. Even today, if you were to ask any Hindu who are the great heroes of Indian history, without doubt he would put Sivaji first. Y. B.

Chavan, India's Defense Minister, is often portrayed as Sivaji leading his men to battle.

Before the Sikhs and Mahrattas triumphed in India they had to suffer at the hands of two more Moslem invaders. In 1739, the Persian Nadir Shah looted Delhi and massacred more than 100,-000 men, women and children. He took with him the Peacock Throne, India's famous diamond, the Koh-i-Noor ("mountain of light") and thousands of slaves. Although he was indiscriminate in his looting and slaughter, it is only the non-Moslems who refer to his advent with bitterness and use the term *nadirshahi* or utter lawlessness.

The Afghan, Ahmed Shah Durani, followed Nadir Shah and sacked Delhi more than once. His wrath was largely directed against the Sikhs. Twice he blew up their temple in Amritsar and filled the pool surrounding the shrine with the entrails of cows. (The Sikhs do not venerate the cow as the Hindus but are strongly opposed to its slaughter.) The Sikhs returned the compliment by defiling mosques. They forced Afghans they had taken prisoner to wash the floors of the mosques with the blood of pigs.

The British attitude toward the Hindu-Moslem problem changed from time to time. For some years after the mutiny of 1857, in which Moslems had taken a greater part than the Hindus, the policy was distinctly anti-Moslem and pro-Hindu. After the foundation of the Indian National Congress in 1885, which began to agitate for freedom and was largely composed of Hindus, the policy became pronouncedly anti-Hindu and pro-Moslem.

The British encouraged Moslem separatism. Under the guise of neutrality they gave Moslems more privileges in services such as the police and the army than their numbers entitled them to. The British encouraged separate educational institutions—Islamic schools and colleges were matched by Hindu and Sikh schools and colleges. In public places such as railroad stations there were separate restaurants for Hindus and Moslems. Even drinking water booths bore signs—Hindu water, Moslem water.

Intercommunal riots became a normal feature of Indian life. Seldom did a Hindu or Sikh religious procession, passing a mosque, fail to spark a brawl. And every year, at the Moslem festival of Bakr-id commemorating Abraham's attempted sacrifice of his son, tension mounted high. Moslems made it a point to sacrifice a cow instead of a ram or a goat. And they took good care to decorate the cow and march it through streets where Hindus lived before taking it to the slaughter house.

The hostility so generated affected all sections of society, even the intellectuals. An anecdote of the time illustrates the rivalry between Hindu and Moslem scholars to prove the superiority of their respective ancient civilizations.

It is said that archeologists excavating the ruins of an old Hindu temple found a rusted steel wire. A Hindu pundit immediately declared this to be evidence that the ancient Hindus had a telephone system.

This spurred Moslem archeologists to excavate around the site of an old mosque. They could find nothing. But not to be outdone, a Moslem ulema declared this to be evidence that the ancient Moslems had known everything about wireless telegraphy.

The British Government set the scene for political separatism when it gave Moslems and, later, other religious minorities, separate electorates in elections to legislative bodies. This policy encouraged political parties which represented only the interest of their respective communities. With separate electorates, the British gave Moslems special privileges and thus kept them from joining the nationalists. Another reason for the Moslems keeping aloof from the nationalists was the fact that some of the leading figures in the movement, for instance, Bal Gangadhar Tilak of Maharashtra and Lajpat Rai of the Punjab, were also associated with Hindu revivalism. British patronage and suspicion of Hindu nationalism gave birth to the Moslem League, which in 1940 demanded an independent Moslem state, Pakistan.

There is little doubt that secular India has done better by her religious minorities than Islamic Pakistan. Indian Moslems hold a position of eminence. The Vice President of India, Dr. Zakir Hussain, two members of the Cabinet, a Governor of a state, many ambassadors, generals and senior civil servants are Moslems. Pakistan's record on this score is a very dismal one.

The stream of Hindu and Christian refugees has flowed incessantly from Pakistan into India. Sometimes it is a mere trickle; at other times, as last year when Hindus were alleged to have stolen the Hair of the Beard of the Prophet and there was fierce rioting, it became a flood. In their turn the refugees and right-wing Hindu elements organized anti-Moslem riots in India. In cities such as Jubbulpore, Aligarh, Jamshedpur and Calcutta, Hindu hoodlums took heavy toll of Moslem life. The police failed to bring them to book because no Hindus would give evidence against their coreligionists.

And once more the nightmare of 1947 is recalled. For months before the present fighting convoys of refugees trekked across the East Bengal frontier, men bearing marks of violence on their persons, women washing the blight of rape under floods of tears, children stricken dumb with terror.

In India as in Pakistan there are refugee camps, some housing more than 50,000 people. The Pakistanis have published a report on the maltreatment of Moslems in India. It has a long catalogue of case histories. Some fled because they were beaten, others because they were robbed or their women attacked. Most fled because of fear.

Earlier this year the Government of India commissioned me to write a report on Hindu and Christian refugees coming out of East Pakistan. I interviewed scores of them as they crossed the Indian borders in Assam, Tripura and West Bengal.

"Why did you leave Pakistan?" I asked them. A few said they had left because they were beaten or robbed. Some said they suspected their women would be abducted. But most of them had just one answer; they left because they had *bhoy*—fear.

4 ► APARTHEID IN SOUTH AFRICA

ALAN PATON

The prevalent policy of race relations in South Africa, better known by the name "apartheid," offers the world a classic example of a statistical minority—two million Afrikaners—who comprise a sociological majority, or dominant group, in a nation of 17.5 million people. Apartheid is also of significance to students of minority problems in the United States because it disrupts the naive notion that the trend of all race relations is toward equality and integration.

In the middle of the seventeenth century a heterogeneous lot of European colonists, mainly Dutch and French Huguenots, found themselves on the southern tip of Africa, a continent still unexplored by whites. In two generations they became a people of Africa, or Afrikaners, and subsequently, known by the name of Boers, they fought against the British Empire and created a nationalistic movement. By 1948, when these Nationalists won a parliamentary majority, they were ready to make South Africa into an Afrikaner-dominated society by the imposition of further restrictions against non-whites who were beginning to lay claim to their own nationalism.

Alan Paton, perhaps the best known of all contemporary South African writers and vehemently opposed to the policy of apartheid, now analyzes the pattern of race relations and describes the Afrikaner Nationalists who are responsible as "blind as Samson was."

. . .

From *The New York Times Magazine*, April 10, 1960. © 1960 by The New York Times Company. Reprinted by permission. This article first appeared under the title "As Blind as Samson Was."

Kloof, Natal, South Africa.

In this article I am attempting to depict the white South African who unreservedly supports apartheid, his life, his beliefs, his behavior, his thoughts of the future. It is written under the shadow of the terrible happenings at Sharpeville, Transvaal, where more than seventy African demonstrators were shot dead by the police, and of the turbulence that has followed—a tragic series of events that has been the direct consequence of the apartheid legislation known as the Pass Laws. For this tragedy the Afrikaner Nationalist blames agitators, Communists, liberals, the English press and the savagery of the African people. He blames anybody, everybody, but himself. If he does not change, and quickly, the catastrophic end is near.

I distinguish in this article between the Afrikaner and the Afrikaner Nationalist; but I do not intend this to conceal the truth that the great majority of Afrikaners are Nationalists who support apartheid. Nor do I wish to conceal the truth that most English-speaking South Africans support apartheid in one form or another, and that therefore they are unable to offer South Africa any alternative. If the white voter wants apartheid, who can give it to him better than the Afrikaner Nationalist?

▶ I OUGHT TO be able to write about the Afrikaner Nationalist and his *apartheid* policies. He is my boss. He tells me where I may live, to what parts of South Africa I may travel, to what schools and universities my children may go, with what kind of person I may eat or drink in any public place.

He tells me what books I may not keep in my house, and what kind of people may not live with me; he tells me what kind of persons I may not marry, and what kind of children I may not adopt. He is now considering what kind of beaches I may or may not visit, what picnic places I may or may not frequent; and he may soon tell me, although he has so far shrunk from it, what kind of guests I may have in my home.

If I should break any of his laws by way of protest, I am subject to a fine of £300 ($840) or imprisonment for three years or a thrashing of ten lashes, or any two of these (though I personally would not be lashed, having reached the age of 50). If I should incite others to break these laws by way of protest, I am subject to a fine of £500 ($1,400) or imprisonment for five years or a thrashing of ten lashes, or any two of these.

So long as I do not incite, however, I can still write freely and publish freely, though few of us think this liberty will last. However any writing which is critical of the Government and of *apartheid* is frowned upon, especially if it is published abroad. The Afrikaner Nationalist regards it as treachery to South Africa, and by South Africa he means, simply and unequivocally, the South Africa of which he is the boss. He knows no other.

The extent of his control over me is disguised because he lets me vote; he lets me, if I wish and am able to, send one of my own group, the one-million white, English-speaking group, to Parliament. But his control over other South Africans is absolute. He allows the one and a half million "colored" * people to have only four white representatives in Parliament, though his own Nationalist group of one and a half million has more than a hundred.† But, beginning in June 1960, he will not allow any representation in Parliament for the ten million Africans. He argues that Africans have their own territories, and there they may have their own self-government under tribal authority. And that is true, too, just as it is true that any representative of tribal authority would lose his job in five minutes if he failed to carry out *apartheid* policy.

The Indian group of half a million also has no representation in Parliament. If the Indians were given communal representation, they would probably abstain from using it on a spectacular scale. Quite apart from that, the Afrikaner Nationalist does not want Indian representatives in Parliament. He just cannot forgive the Indians for having come here, or the British sugar farmers for having brought them.

This Afrikaner ruler of mine is, to all outward appearances, made of steel. He goes on his way in the face of mounting world disapproval. Only three governments in the world think that *apartheid* is his own business. All the new African nations have condemned it. At this very moment, ordinary consumers in many Western countries are boycotting South African goods. *Apartheid* is, without rival, the best known, the most hated, of all the national policies of the world. Yet the Nationalist goes on. He shows no signs of trimming his sails.

Why does he behave like this? What sort of man is he?

* By "Colored" people we mean those of mixed white and other blood. The Africans form a separate group.

† There are two million Afrikaners, and it is estimated that at least three-quarters of them are Afrikaner Nationalists. By various electoral devices, not all due to the Nationalists, this Nationalist group controls two-thirds of the seats in the lower house of Parliament and 86 per cent of the seats in the Senate.

What does the Afrikaner Nationalist believe? He believes that God made separate peoples, and that He wants them to stay separate. He often blames visiting sailors for the existence of a million and a half colored people. But we never had that many visiting sailors. In any case, white men still break the fierce Immorality Act. Hardly a day passes but that some white man—some white man's family—is ruined because he has been caught breaking this iron law.

The Afrikaner Nationalist believes that God sent the Afrikaner to Africa, and gave him a civilizing mission. The great Voortrekker Monument at Pretoria—so coldly regarded by all non-Nationalists—commemorates the triumph of civilization over barbarism.

The Afrikaner Nationalist believes that God has called him to guide and control the destinies of all the people of southern Africa. He will make the laws and others will obey them. Nevertheless, he wants all the other groups in the country to develop harmoniously along their own lines. There is, however, one condition. All must accept *apartheid* as the rule of life.

The Afrikaner Nationalist has an exalted view of the state. Afrikaner churchmen regard with distaste those Christians who speak of the possibility of disobedience to the state. They regard it as lamentable to think of God and the state as in opposition. God is over the state, and the state is, by divine appointment, over man. Our Prime Minister, Dr. Hendrik Verwoerd, has publicly stated his belief that it is by God's will he rules.

The Afrikaner Nationalist has, therefore, an exaggerated view of what can be done by law. He thinks a new heaven and a new earth can be built by law, and by a new earth he means an earth where racial mixture is forbidden. He does not hesitate to use his power to crush any person who stands in his way, and he does not think this improper, for his authority is derived from God.

Men being human, fierce beliefs are seldom held in purity. These certainly are not. Afrikaner Nationalists are not just people doing God's will. Being human, their moral aspirations are remarkably compatible with their human wishes. They like to be boss. In the past, they liked to be boss because it brought great material advantages. For the same reason, they want to stay boss, but now is added a more terrible incentive—the fear that if they don't stay boss, Africa will spew them out.

It doesn't help—yet—to talk to a Nationalist about sharing

power; sharing power means the same to him as losing it. He thinks in racial groups, he thinks in terms of racial power; that is his whole philosophy and politics. To him, the sharing of power means death.

In a way, he is a tragic figure. He is the African who is afraid of Africa. He is the African who never identified himself with Africa. If Africa ever rejects him, it will be because he rejected Africa.

This is doubly tragic because he actually called himself the "Afrikaner," the "man of Africa." He never called himself a "European," as did almost all other white people in Africa. But today he is reminding Europe that he is the sole bastion of European civilization in Africa.

He even refuses to grant the black African the use of the word "African." The black African used to be a "kaffir," today he is a "native" or a "Bantu." But he, like the Afrikaner, wants to be called a "man of Africa."

Even the majority of the English-language newspapers refuse to use the word "African"; they always refer to "natives." They do this partly because our rulers don't like the word "African," partly because the newspapers don't like it themselves. The word "native" sounds calm and peaceful, and conjures up a picture of dusky belles in tropical glades; the word "African" is masculine and vast and continental and a bit frightening.

Apartheid is changing in character. It had to, because of the pressure of the outside world. A few years ago, *apartheid* was simply and plainly being boss. Our late Prime Minister, Mr. J. G. Strijdom, always called it by its simple Afrikaans name, *baasskap*, which means "boss-ship." But Dr. Verwoerd calls it "separate development."

In other words, *apartheid* is the way to give everyone a chance; one uses *baasskap* to separate utterly every white group from every non-white group, in trains, buses, cinemas, restaurants, offices, factories, residential areas, schools, universities; and even to separate white English children from white Afrikaner children in the schools; even to separate black Zulu from black Mosutho and black Xhosa in schools and urban townships.

When people are properly separated, friction will cease; that is the great theory. Black people will not be humiliated by white power; white people will not be terrified by black power, and will therefore act more justly. Each group will develop its separate institutions. There will be peace and cooperation, whereas now there is only fear and discord.

Let us recognize honestly that there are idealistic Afrikaner Nationalists who have turned with relief to the goal of "separate development." It is something positive to work toward. It is a goal infinitely more virtuous than that of *baasskap*.

Yet let us recognize also that it is a fantasy. That veteran Afrikaner theologian, Professor B. B. Keet, calls it a pipe dream. And so it is, not only because it is a fantasy, but because one seeks refuge in the pipe when reality is too hard for one. You can argue with an idealistic Nationalist, and almost get him to the point of seeing that "separate development" is a dream, and that for better or for worse we all have a common destiny, and he will grow more and more cornered, until he says with desperate intensity, he whose goal and end and passion is his people's survival, "We would rather die."

And will he die? And who will die with him? These are the questions I am pondering.

Of all the racial groups in the world, the Afrikaner Nationalist group is the most closed to others, the most turned-in upon itself, the most powerful in group opinion. It is willing to absorb any white person, but only on one condition—namely, that the Nationalist doctrines—above all, *apartheid*—are accepted. It does not readily accept Jews, Roman Catholics, or Freemasons; it rejects absolutely liberals, internationalists, universalists, integrationists and any person of color. It ostracizes any Afrikaner who has deviated. Therefore, it is regarded coldly by almost 90 per cent of the people of South Africa. And, God help us, it is hated by many.

But its isolation is more terrible than that, for its doctrines are hated by the overwhelming majority of the people of the earth. Money is poured out like water to prove to the world that *apartheid* is noble, but no one believes, except in sad places like Algeria, Mississippi and Notting Hill. Many Nationalists hate to travel abroad; they would rather travel in the Rhodesias, Kenya, Mozambique, the Congo. But each year their own continent grows more and more closed to them.

The Nationalist does not like this isolation, but he seems powerless to do anything about it. He would like world approval—who would not?—but the world seems to be demanding his very soul. So he stands with his back to the wall.

There is one thing about him that I am totally unable to

comprehend, and that is that he does not appear to see the havoc he inflicts on others in his headlong journey to a goal that isn't there.

A colored man commits suicide because he is ordered to move out of his house, not to make room for a bridge or a highway, but because of his color. A white man commits suicide because he cannot face prosecution under the Immorality Act. A white family goes to Europe because otherwise they could not keep their adopted colored child. A white wife and her children flee from the husband and father who has been declared to be colored, but, bitterest of ironies, the fleeing children are now colored, too. An African student wins a fine scholarship overseas but is not allowed to go; sometimes, not always, it is because he is known to be against *apartheid*.

So it goes on and on and on, until the heart could break. But the Nationalist's heart doesn't break. Why can't he see what he is doing? Or does he just not care! And if he doesn't care, can't he see how it looks to the outside world?

Like many others, I cannot comprehend it at all. I can only suppose that if one is a Nationalist, collective man overwhelms individual man. The Nationalist is not a man in the individual sense, he is group man, collective man. He has no meaning apart from his group. On the one hand, he despises individualism; on the other, he despises interracialism and internationalism. Any passion for human rights he regards as sentimentality. When he talks of freedom, it is his own that he means.

Therefore, as an individual, he is known only to individuals of his own group, or to those rare strangers who can enter the gate. These testify to his warmth, his hospitality, his generosity, his thoughtfulness, his care for others. Alas, these are not his virtues as collective man.

What made him thus? What so turned him in upon himself? My own forefathers, the British, must bear some of the responsibility. When the Afrikaners trekked north to escape British rule, it was the British who followed after them, especially when the world's richest gold deposits were found in Johannesburg. It was the British who conquered the two Afrikaner Republics in 1902 in the tragic Boer War. It was the British who entertained the foolish plan of Anglicizing the Afrikaners.

It was the British who, above all others, took the divergent elements of Afrikanerdom and fused them into a lonely and narcissistic people. Not even Britain's magnanimous restoration of self-government after the Boer War, not even Botha's and Smuts' magnanimous acceptance of it, were able to undo what had been done. The Nationalist remains obsessed with his past.

But there was another great factor also—the Africans, the other men of Africa. The Afrikaner loved Africa, but he could never come to terms with its people. Its people were not his fellow-Africans; they were the "black danger," the "black sea." They outnumbered him and, though he conquered them, he never ceased to fear them. His fear of them is the determinant of all his policies. This fact one must always remember.

All of us are determined by our past, but, if we are to grow up, there comes a time when we must take responsibility for ourselves. Today the world says to the Afrikaner, "We no longer want to hear about the past and what others did to you; we want to hear about the future and what you will do to others."

And the world is outraged by the answer.

It sometimes happens when some new edict of the Nationalists is published, that their opponents are not so much angry as baffled. The Minister of Bantu Education, Mr. Willie Maree, has just issued a public edict that his white officials must not shake hands with African teachers. They must bow to each other or clasp their own hands to each other, or do something equally absurd.

Why does a Minister do such a stupid thing? Why does he do it at the same time as his Government pours out money to prove to the world that *apartheid* is only brotherhood in disguise? One is forced to the conclusion that something is operating in this particular Minister against which he seems powerless. This particular white man of Africa fears other men of Africa so much that he fears to touch their hands, and he will not let other white men touch them, either. And he is a leader of Afrikaner Nationalism.

This triviality is not really trivial. It shows the true nature of *apartheid*, which in its essence is a rejection of one's fellow man. The Nationalist has rewritten the second great Commandment, and because his world is in two parts, the commandment is in two parts also:

Thou shalt love thy white neighbor as thyself, provided he accepts apartheid.

Thou shalt love thy non-white neighbor as thyself, provided he does not live next door.

The Nationalist believes in justice for black men, but it must be over there. He believes in opportunity for black men, but it must be over there. The people of the earth are learning fast that there is only one world, but he still thinks there are two. And if there are not two, he will make a law.

What does the Nationalist think of the future? He looks at it with foreboding, but then, he always did. Yet the foreboding has never been so great as now, because the future, so to speak, has never been so near. It has been standing out there for three centuries, but now it is knocking at the door.

The Nationalist comforts himself that the Afrikaner has always had to struggle, that the new crisis is nothing new. But in his heart he knows that this crisis is the last of all.

The Nationalist fanatic says, "God made us, and if He will destroy us, His will be done." Some observers think all Nationalists are like that, and that, like blind Samson, they will pull down the house upon themselves and their enemies.

In crisis, there is only one refuge for the group man. That is to call the group together and bar the doors and load the guns. That is what the Prime Minister, Dr. Verwoerd, is doing now. That is what every Nationalist Prime Minister did before him. The Nationalist knows no other politics. The Nationalist will never be able to come to terms with Africa; he understands Africa only so long as he is boss. His love for South Africa is deep and fierce, but how he would hate it if he were not the boss.

There is one hope, and one hope only, for the future of the white people of South Africa, and especially for the Afrikaner, and that is to come to some kind of terms with the other thirteen million; to negotiate, to discuss; to increase, not to decrease, representation; to open the door, to unload the guns; to stop these stupidities, like not shaking hands; to renounce the evil laws that result in violence and death, to foreswear *apartheid.*

· · ·

5 ► RACIALISM IS AN AFRICAN SICKNESS, TOO

GEORGE H. T. KIMBLE

Racialism is not the private property of European whites and their descendants. In Asia and Africa, for instance, non-whites have often uncritically accepted the whites at their own valuation of natural superiority. Once this uncritical acceptance of white superiority has been broken, the easiest emotion to arouse is the opposite one of xenophobic racialism—an intense hatred of whites and all things Western. As Professor Kimble, a geographer and African specialist, makes so clear in the piece that follows—racialism can characterize the thinking, feeling and behavior of subgroups among non-whites as well.

► IT IS BEGINNING to look as though those of us who wagered there was nothing wrong with colonial Africa that independence wouldn't cure miscalculated the odds. For almost everywhere independence is proving to be a time of frustration: of quick starts and slow going, of rising expectations and flagging efforts, of fine promise and indifferent performance.

Particularly frustrating is the resurgence of racialism—a distemper of the body politic long abhorred by most of Africa's leaders and long affirmed by them to be of non-African origin—because it not only diverts the attention of people from the high priorities of independence but also weakens their will to pursue them. The seemingly endemic strife in Algeria between Arab and Berber, or in the Congo between virtually all the larger tribal

From *The New York Times Magazine*, October 11, 1964. © 1964 by The New York Times Company. Reprinted by permission of the author and publisher.

groups, is one example. The massacre last winter of some 10,000 Watusi by the Bahutu and the flight of 150,000 more into neighboring territories is another.

Such outbreaks have made many people aware that there is more to racialism than antagonisms and prejudices based on color, as is primarily the case in the United States. Color, of course, is part of the problem in Africa, and not only in those places where the colors run from jet black to pale pink. A lightly pigmented skin is held by many indigenous Africans to carry class, just as it does in parts of Latin America and elsewhere.

The tribal troubles have also made many people aware that there is a good deal more to the problem than antagonisms and prejudices based on "race" as defined by the scientist. Granted that "well-developed and primarily heritable physical differences" (the words are taken from UNESCO's now classic report, "The Race Concept") have been at the root of some recent manifestations of racialism. To many Africans, as to many Americans, differences of stature, carriage, facial features, texture of hair and "looks" generally are as provocative of prejudice as differences of color. There can be little doubt, for instance, that the height and patrician bearing of the Watusi had something to do with the way the smaller, coarser-featured Bahutu felt about them.

What the "good deal more" of racialism is exactly is hard to define, but, almost certainly, it is to be looked for in the domain of cultural, rather than physical, anthropology. Consider some of the common ingredients. Education is one. Not the least of the things education confers upon the African is status, which continues to be a divider of men. Onetime equals become separated; those with education come to think of themselves as superior and, like the Pharisee, find it easy to thank God they are not as other men, and prove it by carrying briefcases and other symbols of learning on every conceivable occasion.

Christianity is another common ingredient. In part, this is because it has come to be associated in the minds of many Africans with education, but, more important perhaps, because many Christian missions have based their enterprise on the Biblical admonition to "come out from among them and be . . . separate." And it must be confessed that, whether from Christian conviction or less lofty motives, many European and American missionaries have practiced a species of apartheid as thoroughgoing as any found in the Republic of South Africa. Some of them have succeeded in getting their converts to do the same. I have been at mission stations where African callers were expected to use the back door—and did—and where the native Christians were not on speaking terms with the non-Christians.

The colonial presence has also been an important ingredient of racialism—and not merely the color-based version of it, of which, heaven knows, there is still far too much in Africa. From the start it was apparent to the African that the colonizers had abilities and skills that were out of his world. They had cures for many of the more troublesome diseases and, on the whole, they enjoyed much better health. They knew how to cope with flood and drought and other natural hazards. They ran businesses, plantations and mines; they maintained law and order over large areas with small forces. They lived well and securely.

Perceiving the advantages of such things, many Africans fell to imitating the colonizers, on the assumption that to do as a man does is to be as a man is. For Ivory Coast Africans to say, "We Frenchmen do this and that," and say it with a Parisian accent became as fashionable as the blue serge suits they liked to dress in. For many British West Africans, to talk of Beethoven, Brahms, Burns and the Brontës became "nobility's true badge." Some, less interested in nobility than nourishment, found status in consuming the colonizer's canned foods and bottled drinks.

Saner thinking, it is true, has come to prevail in most areas, but there are still many educated Africans who, while professing to be free from all taint of cultural snobbishness, to say nothing of cultural prejudice and hostility, continue to treat their less fortunate compatriots as "lesser breeds without the Law." Few professionally trained Africans have much interest in practicing their skills in the bush. And some of the worst student behavior I have encountered in a generation was on the campuses of West African colleges where no effort was made by many students to conceal the contempt they felt for their servants, and where no concern was shown for the illiterate villagers around them.

Not all the ingredients of racialism are imports. Some are domestic in origin. Thus, belief in the inherent inequality of people is encountered in many African societies. The Watusi, it seems, have always considered themselves to possess "a natural superiority," as Dr. Jacques Maquet, a leading authority on them, calls it.

And, until recently, they clearly had no difficulty in convincing the Bahutu of it, for although outnumbered about six to one, they kept them in a vassal-like servitude.

Many other stock-keeping groups have traditionally held similar opinions about themselves and found nothing self-evident about the equal right of all men to life, liberty and the pursuit of happiness. Centuries before the European entered his world, the Bushman of the Kalahari was the hunted as often as he was the hunter. The only liberty he knew was the liberty to escape capture; the only time he could pursue happiness was when he was not himself being pursued.

There also seems to be a belief among some Africans that inequality can be acquired as well as inherited. For instance, the Rer Manyo group of Somalis, who live by fishing, are looked down upon by their stock-raising Somali neighbors: the very words "Rer Manyo" are derogatory, signifying "common occupation." And there is little coming and going between the two, since overtures by the Rer Manyo are likely to be blocked by the taunt: "Speak not to me with the mouth that eateth fish."

Again, in the Teita Hills of Kenya, the man who abandons the old tribal ways, for whatever reason, is apt to find himself ignored, or even spurned and despised, by his more conservative peers. The farther he wanders from his village, the lower his standing becomes until it will be said of him: "He is no longer one of us; he is a man of such-and-such a place, so why should we have anything to do with him?"

Mohammedanism (which after all these centuries must surely be thought of as an indigenous religion) is also a divider and subjugator of men. For all its egalitarianism, it does not take kindly to opposition; in the past, many African people who refused to accept it found themselves segregated, enslaved or worse. In the Sudan, the Mohammedans of the north continue to speak of the so-called pagans of the south as an "inferior race," or as "*abeed*," a term of contempt meaning slaves.

How widespread is the occurrence of racialism? Some of the worst expressions of it continue to be supplied by the "settler" countries. In the Republic of South Africa, for example, discrimination against the man of color continues to have the full weight of the law behind it, as well as the sanction of the Dutch Reformed Church, to which most of the country's rulers belong.

At the same time, influential voices are being raised against the separate development of Bantu and non-Bantu, and even some militant Afrikaners are coming to see that the one battle apartheid will never win is the last. In Southern Rhodesia, the bars to equality have been slowly coming down for quite a while, but it is still easy for the aspiring African to trip on them. Segregation is still openly countenanced; promotion in business and industry is still hard to come by; and silence is still likely to descend upon the church or club meeting where an African is put up for membership.

In such recently freed settler countries as Algeria, the Congo and Kenya, the bars are all down but, as we know only too well in our country, the habits of generations die slowly and revive easily. It is one thing to "legalize" equality; it is another thing to live with it, let alone love it.

Not all settler countries have been badly racked by racialism, however. The Portuguese have never had much discriminatory legislation on their books, and many of their nationals appear to be color-blind. In the course of roughly 100,000 miles of African travel, I encountered fewer overt signs of racial prejudice in Angola and Mozambique than anywhere else. Furthermore, only in these two countries did I find Europeans and Africans working as equals in field and factory.

With racial prejudice declining in most, though by no means all, of the settler countries, it would be nice to think that it will soon be a thing of the past everywhere. But this appears to be unlikely for two reasons.

First, in every country of Africa rapidly growing numbers of people are learning new skills, taking over responsibilities formerly held by Europeans and other non-African groups, and earning incomes that were undreamt of until a few years ago. As with the front runners of every land, many of these people are coming to fear that the only way to keep what they have won is to prevent others from winning it, and that one of the best ways of doing this is to strew the course of the late starters with as many obstacles as possible.

This several countries are doing with great effectiveness. In the Sudan, for instance, the distance between the Mohammedan north and the non-Mohammedan south is steadily being widened. More and more manufacturing enterprises, including the processing of such "southern" crops as sugar, papyrus, cotton and tobacco, are being concentrated in the north. Some of those originally established in the south are being closed down. To make matters tougher still for the southerner, the Sudanese Government is actively encouraging northerners to settle in the south—often on the southerner's expropriated lands and with the help of loans the like of which few southerners have ever heard of.

Then, again, the southerner finds himself in increasing subjection to the northerner socially. Northerners now living in his midst have their own clubs and associations in which southerners are denied membership. Northerners who do try to fraternize with them are likely to be relieved of their jobs for refusal to adjust to northern norms of behavior.

Second, increasing numbers of Africans are finding nationalism to be a broken cistern, and are going back to (if they ever left) the ancient wells of tribalism. While few social organizations are more equality-minded than the average African tribe, not many tribes feel much obligation to practice equality toward any but their own kind. Once outside his tribal borders, a man is likely to find himself among people who feel no greater obligation to practice the equally nonracial principles of fraternity and liberty.

In many countries the old intertribal animosities and prejudices are today being exacerbated by the fact that, for one reason or another, some tribes have been more successful than others in the bid for power, and they like the fruits of their success too well to be willing to share them. It is not just that, in the eyes of many Kenyans, Jomo Kenyatta has far too many Kikuyus in positions of influence. It is that, in the Congo, it is now exceedingly difficult for the Central Government to exercise any authority in the provinces except through a tribally approved representative; to cope with this demand, it has been compelled to carve the country up into more than 20 "tribal" provinces, each of them as suspicious of its neighbors as they are of the Central Government.

It is also that almost everywhere, appointments—from bodyguard and booking clerk to college instructor and board member—are being made more and more on the basis of tribal connection rather than competence.

The mounting price of African racialism—whatever its guise—is clear for all to see. In the ledger of the older countries, such as the Republic of South Africa, the debit entries include the hardening of "positions," the loss of touch and dialogue, separate and unequal facilities, and international ostracism. At no time since the days of Hitler has racialism inspired such hatred, or imposed such disabilities and indignities.

In the newer countries, the debits include loss of face with the outside world; loss of (or at least, lessened) confidence in the integrity of the governments' leaders; loss of capital; loss of consensus (where it existed); loss of economic momentum; mounting inefficiency and an eager search for scapegoats, leading to new witch hunts, new oppression and mounting disillusionment among the common people. Many African students on American campuses no longer find pleasure in poking around our cupboards for skeletons; they now see that they have skeletons of their own, and barely enough cupboards to keep them in.

More private capital has left the new countries in the past five to six years than has entered them. Within six months of the announcement by the British Government of its intention to free Kenya, upwards of $50 million of "white" capital was withdrawn to Europe. In some countries there has been a similar flight of "nonwhite" capital.

Again, there is no longer much talk in countries like Ghana of equal rights for all people, irrespective of color, creed or class, and none at all of the rights of little people, indigenous or alien, not to be oppressed by big people. On the whole, it is now safer for a man to call himself a Ghanaian than a Fanti man or Ashanti man; safer still, to call himself a Nkrumah man.

What, if anything, can be done about it? The trouble with racialism, as with most other kinds of sin, is that it is more easily talked about than treated. But even to talk about it is to do something, for, as our own civil-rights campaigners have shown, talk itself may, upon occasion, be therapeutic, both for the sinned-against and the sinning. Certainly there can no longer be any question that the more racialism is talked about, the sooner it will come to be seen, and treated, for the evil thing it is. Indeed, the treatment is already in hand.

In country after country, Africans of many shades of opinion and color are laboring to improve the living standards of the lowly; to dispel the conceit of those who would have all men come to a knowledge of the truth as it is in the local leader; to expose the folly of those who would build a society on the shifting sands of privilege or wealth; and, not least, to teach the need for tolerance.

But treatment is one thing and cure is another. To be well-to-do is not necessarily to be unselfish. To be well-informed is not necessarily to be nice to live with; and to educate a child in the exercise of tolerance gives no guarantee that the man he becomes will allow himself to tolerate his tribal neighbor, his political opponent, let alone live in peace with all men.

Maybe, what most of us, Africans and Americans alike, need rather more than a change of thought is a change of heart—at any rate, the thing Dr. Robert Hutchins spoke about some years ago: "A deep sense of our own unimportance and a deep conviction of the importance of others." For isn't the converse of this the very root of racialism?

6 ▸ INDIANS AND COLOUREDS IN RHODESIA AND NYASALAND

FLOYD AND LILLIAN DOTSON

The attempt of European-derived statistical minorities in Central as well as South Africa to retain and even reenforce their dominant status over African, colored and Asiatic minorities culminated in 1965 with the illegal establishment of an independent Rhodesia. In the article that follows, Drs. Floyd and Lillian Dotson, a husband and wife team of American sociologists, show how the Indians and Coloreds—although assigned to the same inferior status by the whites of Rhodesia and Nyasaland (now Malawi)— "see these matters differently." The Dotsons conclude that the traditional dominance of the Europeans in Central Africa is being eroded and will soon crumble—a prediction that others have also applied to the pattern of dominance and minority status among the divergent ethnic groups of South Africa.

▸ IN CENTRAL AFRICA the European has been—and still is for the moment—the dominant ethnic group. To the European mind, Indians and Coloureds in the area constitute a natural unit, enough alike to be suitably lumped together for many social and administrative purposes. There are 'Asian and Coloured' hospitals

From *Race: The Journal of the Institute of Race Relations*, V, 1 (July, 1963), 61–75. Reprinted by permission of the author and publisher.

The data presented here were gathered during the course of a two-year study (1959–61) of the Indians of Rhodesia and Nyasaland. This project was sponsored by the Rhodes-Livingstone Institute for Social Research and supported by a research grant from the United States Educational Commission (Fulbright program).

and schools.[1] They are admitted to or excluded from other public facilities, such as municipal halls, theatres and swimming baths on the same basis.[2] They have the same status under the national defence legislation and receive the same reduced pay—i.e. about two-thirds of the European rate—while serving in the armed forces. They are entitled to the same benefits—again suitably adjusted to their status—under the existing welfare legislation. They were, when these were in force, subject to the same legal restrictions with respect to alcohol and the possession of firearms. In keeping with these practices they are often categorised together, without differentiation, in the official statistics.

That Indians and Coloureds are not in fact identical receives recognition, it is true, under many circumstances. In the larger towns, where more than one school would be desirable anyway, they have separate schools. Nor are they necessarily expected to live in the same residential area, although if they happen to do so no objection is raised by the Europeans. Europeans, of course, know perfectly well that these people differ in origin and customs. But how radically they differ and how little they have in common is only dimly appreciated since little interest is shown in these differences. It is enough in the European's eyes that both Indians and Coloureds are anomalies in a society otherwise structured on a bifurcation of European and African. And it is upon this negative and derivative principle rather than upon anything positive which they might be presumed to have in common that they are assigned equivalent status.

That is the European view. That Indians and Coloureds see these matters differently will be developed in some detail below. Their view of each other, together with enough background material to make these perspectives intelligible, is the main burden of this paper. Yet in the end neither Indians nor Coloureds in Central Africa can be understood except *vis-à-vis* the dominant European, and it is this theme to which we will briefly return in our conclusion.

It might be assumed—as we ourselves did until we learned better—that most Coloureds in the Federation are of South African origin. This assumption is plausible: a large proportion of the European population came from (or via) South Africa, and a distinctive Coloured 'community' had formed there long before the settlement of the territories now constituting the Federation. Movement of these people northwards, however, was discouraged by immigration policies adopted early by Southern Rhodesia and by a lack of economic opportunities in Northern Rhodesia and Nyasaland. There are, and always have been, some South African Coloureds in the area, but the overwhelming majority are of local origin. According to the 1956 census, nearly 90 per cent of the current Coloured population were born in the Federation, in contrast to a mere 6 per cent born in South Africa.[3] This does not mean, however, that most Coloureds are first-generation crossings. The miscegenation process began immediately upon settlement and apparently was greater in the early period than now in terms of the relative numbers of people involved. Within the recognised Coloured community—in other words, that covered by the census statistics—well over half (56.6 per cent) of the persons reported have parents who are both Coloured, and another 22.2 per cent claim one Coloured parent. We personally know young Coloured adults with children of their own who have (or had) parents who were Coloured, rather than European, Indian or African. In short, there is already emerging a third generation, distinctly Coloured in origin and orientation.[4]

Europeans and Indians began coming to Central Africa to settle at about the same time, but in greatly unequal numbers. Both Europeans and Indians made—and to be accurate, are still making —their contributions to the Coloured population. Which race has made more, in proportion to its numbers, is an intriguing question.[5] It is less significant sociologically, however, than an understanding of the circumstances and organisation under which contact took place. For the sake of contrast, we will touch briefly upon the European side of this picture first, although by definition we are more interested in Indian-African relations.

What types of Europeans during the early period of settlement were attracted into sexual arrangements with African women, and what those arrangements were, would make a fascinating study from several points of view. Unfortunately, the necessary facts for anything like a complete picture cannot now be resurrected in full detail. That some of the pioneers abstained, either from fastidiousness of taste and hygiene or from moral principles, or a happy combination of both, can be taken for granted. Nevertheless, the incidental evidence which we have collected upon this point convinces us that the number of European men who lived for any length of time amongst the Africans without contracting such relationships was probably rather small.

Among lower-class adventurers of the type so vividly portrayed for early Nyasaland by Johnston, such contacts may be safely assumed to have been all but universal.[6] But, while Johnston does not say so, they were certainly not confined to this class. Coloureds in Central Africa have customarily assumed the name of their father, and among the most common names of the older generation of Coloureds appear those of pioneer officials and administrators of the first rank. One of these gentlemen, who lived for many years in a remote area, is said to have fathered something like eighteen Coloured children—enough, in any case, for him to establish a private school for them. Members of this family are now leaders in several Coloured communities. Two Coloureds of our acquaintance in Nyasaland, now men in their mid-forties and early-fifties, are said to be the sons—by different mothers—of a bishop once stationed there.

Presumably there was often a certain structure and order to these relationships in the earliest period and in the remote areas. No evidence of which we are aware, however, leads us to believe that there ever existed in Central Africa the kind of dual family system—one household mothered by a native woman, the other by the European wife—which was commonplace in Latin America and which was common enough in the pre-Civil War South of the United States. Given the particular time and place, the very presence of European women in Central Africa—not necessarily one's own wife, but any woman within one's face-to-face community—seems to have strongly inhibited public acknowledgement of interracial sexual attachments. Eurafricans are in the main products of casual and mercenary encounters.

The pattern was different among the Indians, where a semi-permanent arrangement was common until a few years ago. This statement, as we will see, needs to be qualified to account for an important difference between Hindus and Muslims. But Muslims predominated in the early period, and so there is a certain rationale for considering 'Indians' and 'Muslims' as synonymous for the moment.

One of the few early (1905) descriptions of Indians in Southern Rhodesia contains a brief but relevant comment on this point. The observer is the Civil Commissioner of the Fort Victoria District. He is reporting on the some fifty to sixty Indians there (all but three of whom are male) who live by a cattle-and-grain trade with the Africans. After a fairly lengthy description of their business operations and mode of life, he goes on to say:

I have only to add that practically all the Indians in the Victoria District (there are no other coloured foreigners) are in the habit of keeping native women, whom, I believe, they obtain under the lobola system, and there is gradually springing up a race of bastards, who, it is possible, may in the future be a source of trouble and inconvenience to the Government.[7]

Our own interview data does not go back so far. Yet what we know of the situation in Northern Rhodesia and Nyasaland thirty to forty years ago presents the same essentials. A Hindu informant —a shoemaker by caste and trade—considered settling in Nyasaland in the early 1930s. He decided not to, primarily, it would seem, because the European population was too small to support much trade in shoes. But as he now tells the story, there were other reasons:

As you know, Nyasaland was originally settled mostly by Muslims. These people were very mean-minded. They thought in terms of pennies and tickeys, not even in terms of shillings, let alone pounds. Their stores were mud-and-wattle affairs, with a few pieces of cloth hung over a pole for the trade. These Muslims didn't even employ a houseboy. What they did was to hire a young African girl instead. This girl was half houseboy and half wife. That way of living didn't appeal to me.

Indians came to Africa for strictly economic reasons: the romantic attractions of sport and adventure which so powerfully operated as motives among the Europeans were in their case almost entirely absent. In spite of the fact that they might live for the greater part of their lives in Africa, they have not until recently seen themselves as being permanently rooted there. Like the modern suburban commuter who tries to combine the advantages of city employment with country residence, the Indian tried to combine the opportunity of making money in Africa with a traditional family and village life in India. Any number of middle-aged men in Central Africa have for most of their lives shuttled back and forth between India and Africa, ideally on a three-years-in-Africa, one-year-in-India basis. This meant in practice that a man left his wife and children in the care of his *khutumb* (extended family) in India. It is only within the last ten years or so, and then only through fear of the permanent exclusion of their families if they delayed bringing them, that Indian women have been brought to Central Africa in any considerable numbers.[8]

The one important exception to this rule were the Hindus of the higher castes. These, too, maintained close ties with India through periodic visits, but religious and caste imperatives demanded that they bring their wives to Africa as soon as it was economically feasible to do so. For this group, to live apart from one's wife for long periods of time was to take risks which could not be contemplated of not fulfilling one's religious and filial obligations through progeny. For this reason, most of the 'pioneer' women in the Indian community are found among the Hindus.

We do not know all that we should like to know concerning sexual relations between Africans and Hindus. This is a delicate question, which they discuss as reluctantly as do Europeans. To what extent, for example, have their notions of ritual pollution through intimate contact with social inferiors inhibited sexual relations with Africans? It certainly has not prohibited them altogether—that much we do know—but it has doubtlessly helped to define them as thoroughly unrespectable. Open arrangements, of the kind prevailing amongst the Muslims, were not countenanced; those contacts which did occur seem to have been in the main with prostitutes—temporary or professional. Thus, for rather different reasons, relationships with African women among Hindus are more comparable to those of Europeans than to those of their Muslim countrymen.

To return to the Muslims, a semi-permanent relationship resembling marriage seems to have been all but universal amongst them, particularly in rural areas. It is to these unions that most Indo-Africans owe their origin.

To Europeans, these relationships are described as 'marriages'— at least by implication, since the African woman is called a 'wife'. If it turns out that the man in question had (or has) a wife in India, then Islamic law and custom supporting the legitimacy of polygynous marriages is invoked as an explanation.

That in point of fact these arrangements were never accepted as legitimate is apparent on two grounds. First, marriage in India amongst Muslims is governed by caste to a degree not essentially different from that of Hindus; by definition, a really legitimate marriage would have to be with a woman of one's own caste. Second, looking at the matter from the standpoint of practice rather than theory, African 'wives' were invariably 'divorced' as soon as the Indian wife arrived in Africa from India.[9]

So much for history. Let us now turn to current attitudes and relations. We will try to look at this matter through the Coloured's eyes first, then the Indian's.

The problem of identity—of both the self and of others—is a relatively simple one for members of well-defined ethnic groups who have a common social and cultural origin. For such people— and that includes most of us—the social world falls into a clear-cut 'in-group' and 'out-group' ethnic pattern. But to the person of mixed parentage this problem of identity is a very serious one. It is no exaggeration, perhaps, to say that it is his basic problem. If I am of mixed 'blood' in Central Africa then what am I, in terms of model and aspiration—African, European, Indian or Coloured? And if the last category is the answer which I come up with, what does this mean concretely as a set of values and a way of life?

Posed on the cutting edge of experience, this question rises to consciousness as a matter of individual choice and decision. However since self-conception is a product of a specific social past, the 'choice' is largely illusory. The self-conception that the person of mixed parentage acquires hinges in fact mainly upon the group to which he is *allowed* to belong—within which he is accepted. People of mixed parentage in Central Africa live—with widely different degrees of success, it is true—like Africans, Europeans and Indians, as well as self-consciously as Coloureds. The recognised and socially-labelled Coloured community is composed of the latter, not the sum total of persons of mixed 'blood'.

The great majority of those persons of mixed parentage who do not live as Coloureds live like Africans. Whoever their father was, they were typically born and reared in their mother's village. They know no other life and they are accepted on some basis there. No one has any real idea how large this group is since it is not reflected in any existing statistics, but it must be of considerable proportions. We would guess that it may be as large as the recognised Coloured community. Considering the respective size of the European and Indian populations, the great majority of these mixed-blood Africans must be Eurafrican. On the other hand, it is probably true that more Indo-Africans in proportion to their numbers live as Africans. Physically, the only strikingly non-African characteristic which they usually possess is their abundant straight hair; thus, as American Negroes would say, they can more easily 'pass' as Africans. Furthermore since Indo-Africans tend to be discriminated against both within the Coloured community and by Europeans, there are fewer advantages for them than for Eurafricans in being recognised as Coloured.

Whether or not children with either European or Indian fathers who are born of African mothers living in the villages eventually come to be a part of the recognised Coloured community seems to depend in most cases upon what happens to them at school age. A teacher at a Coloured school in Southern Rhodesia describes the typical manner in which such a child there enters the Coloured community:

One of our most serious problems in this country is the Coloured child who comes to primary school for the first time without knowing English. These children were born out in the villages—the chances being nine out of ten that their European father has disowned them. So they grow up with their African mother and are essentially like Africans; they don't know English, for example, only the African language. Then at school age, a couple of African women will bring them into town one day and present them to the school here as a Coloured child, and then of course we have to take them in. It's not the child's fault, of course, but it's really tragic.

Alternatively, a child recognised by a welfare officer as seriously neglected and ill-used may be institutionalised by him, and thus in effect brought into the recognised Coloured community. Such action, however, is emphatically not encouraged at the policy level; welfare officers do not systematically comb the villages looking for Coloured children. Welfare and educational institutions for Coloureds are distinctly better than anything provided for Africans and are always strained to capacity. For this reason the regulations explicitly state that such institutions are intended only for children from families who are living in the European manner. However, since people are usually more humane in the concrete instance than their formal rules, these regulations are often ignored in practice.

That some Coloureds live as Indians in households headed by an Indian father can be attested to on the basis of half-a-dozen cases from our interview sample. Since our sample of some 300 families is, after all, only a small fraction of the total Indian population in the Federation, there are no doubt many more than we know about personally.

Living as or being reared as Indians does not mean, however, that these people are fully assimilated into the Indian community. With one possible exception, all those who have come to our attention are definitely not. This does not of course prove that such cases of complete assimilation do not exist; if such Coloureds were successfully 'passing' as Indians, presumably neither we nor most other people would be aware of it. That such cases do exist in considerable numbers is claimed by one of our informants, a young Hindu professional:

As you know, there are a lot of African Muslims in this area [Nyasaland]. Perhaps partly for this reason, the [Indian] Muslims are often willing to absorb their Coloured children and take them into the Muslim community, unlike the Hindus, who usually disown them. Some of these families try to protect their Coloured members and keep the fact that they are Coloured from the rest of the Indians.

It seems certain, however, that if such cases do exist—as they probably do—they are far too few to constitute a sociologically significant tendency. Typically, children who were given some sort of recognition while the father was living with their mother were abandoned when that mother was 'divorced'. Rather than the Indian family closing ranks to protect the children, more commonly, it seems, the Indian community closed ranks to protect the father. Speaking of this situation, a Coloured teacher told us:

After his Indian wife arrived from India, he [the father] didn't want to have anything to do with his Coloured children. Often, too, the other Indians in the community helped him out in this. In a great many of these cases we have great difficulty in finding out who the Indian fathers of these children are because the Indian community itself protects the father's identity, although they know perfectly well what the facts are.

Sociologically, the most significant fact with respect to Indo-Africans living within the recognised Coloured community is that they become thoroughly Europeanised in cultural values and mode of living, not Indianised. This is true even though, as in first-generation crossings, they may be at the same time familiar with either Indian or African culture, or both. Such people, for example, speak English among themselves, although they may know both Gujarati and an African language in addition to English. This cultural orientation to the European model is in part the work of the school, a thoroughly European institution. But the school is only the most obvious of the forces pushing the Indo-African in the European direction. In so far as one can speak meaningfully of a Coloured 'culture', that culture is European in origin and content. By the act of identifying oneself as 'Coloured', one thereby sets a course which, as one makes the interminable series of choices and decisions which constitute living, moves one inevitably in the European direction culturally.[10]

Nevertheless, where Indo-Africans are numerous enough to constitute a significant proportion of the Coloured community, they tend socially to form a distinctive and self-conscious group. This seems to be in the main a result of discrimination by Eurafricans. Trying to cash in on their presumed closer connexion to the dominant Europeans, Eurafricans attempt to subordinate the Indo-Africans. The resulting inter-group conflict has resulted in much bitterness. Attempts, for example, to organise the Coloured community in the Blantyre-Limbe region for political action foundered on this division during the period of negotiations for the 1960 constitutional changes in Nyasaland. Split on the issue as to whether a Eurafrican or an Indo-African should represent them at the conference, the Coloureds wound up with no representation at all.[11]

This social conflict, however, does not negate in any way what we have just described as the European orientation of Indo-Africans. Eurafricans try to identify themselves as much as possible with Europeans and in so doing try to deny this identification to Indo-Africans. But it does not follow that Indo-Africans try to identify themselves in a similar way with the Indian community. This difference between the two groups shows up very significantly in the terms by which they wish to be known publicly: Eurafricans want to be called Eurafricans: Indo-Africans dislike being called 'Indo-Africans' and wish to be known as 'Coloureds'.

These identities are of course sociologically explicable on the basis of the alignment of power within the country as a whole. Sociologists have long been aware that disadvantaged minorities, unless in active and open conflict with the dominant group, tend to hold evaluations of the dominant group, of other minorities and of themselves which reflect fairly closely the evaluations of the dominant group.[12] For example, 'self-hatred', based upon this principle, is a widely observed phenomenon among Negroes and Jews in the United States and, to a much lesser extent, among other minority groups as well.

A glimpse of the complicated social world of Central Africa, as seen by an Indo-African, is vividly revealed in one of our interview protocols. This particular informant is a man now in his fifties and a leader in his community. He was reared in the home of his Indian father and was sent to India for several years of education. After observing of the Africans that 'they have a natural hatred for us',[13] Mr. —— went on to describe the other components of the population in highly personal terms:

This country owes everything to the Europeans. They are the ones who came out here and built up the country. Generally, I get along well enough with Europeans, but if you invited me to your house I really wouldn't be anxious to go. If I went, I know I would be treated courteously enough while I was there, but I really wouldn't feel at home.

As far as the Indians are concerned, I have already explained to you how I feel about them. [He had said in great detail, that they were only interested in money, that they used to be exceedingly dirty, and that they were so dishonest that they couldn't be trusted under any circumstances.] Since I speak their language fluently, I can go to an Indian house and converse and get along well enough. But since they are, as I have said, completely unprincipled, I really don't like them.

On the other hand, if I go to another Coloured person's house, then at last I feel at home.

'Dirty', incidentally, seems to sum up in one convenient negative image of rejection what most people remember about the Indians of Nyasaland thirty years ago.[14] Significantly, when we asked a young Eurafrican—a man of some education from a socially stabilised family—what he remembers about the Indians as they were during his boyhood, all he could reply was:

When I was growing up here in Blantyre, we didn't have much to do with the Indians. My parents told me to stay away from them because they were dirty.[15]

To define the Indian's attitude toward the Coloured, one must take into account several variables: Hindus tend to be more negative than Muslims; older people are more negative than younger people; the culturally and politically conservative are more negative than the liberal-minded and Westernised. These are tendencies, and obviously in any given case one may have various combinations of these determining factors.[16] Yet in spite of these variations, it is safe to say that the prevailing attitude of all Indians is negative, the difference simply being one of degree. Coloureds and Indians are much too different in basic attitudes and values to be very compatible and these differences are such that in the Indian mind the Coloured is defined as hopelessly inferior.

The unreconstructed Hindu finds a rationalisation for his prejudices in his religious philosophy, which helps to provide him with his view of the world. To him, miscegenation is 'unnatural' in the primary sense of the word, being against God and nature. The following ideas, which come from an older Hindu of the *Patidar* (higher agricultural) caste, are unusual only in that they are so candidly expressed:

I can't change my skin [pinching up the skin on the back of his hand demonstratively]. I was born with this skin; I have had it all my life, and I will die with it. But if God had not intended for me to have this colour of skin, then He would have given me something different. He made the different races as they are, and if He had wanted them to be anything else then He would have made them different. But He didn't. So that must be the way He wanted them to be.

If you mix milk with water, you get something that may look like milk, but it really isn't milk. Nor is it water.

In another interview, we pointed out to this informant that not all Coloured children (as he had implied) were the responsibility of Europeans—that some were fathered by Indians. How, given the presumed repugnance for miscegenation which he attributed to Indians, could this fact be explained? To this observation, he replied:

Yes, that is true. But those children have Muslim fathers. They're all Muslims. You will never find a Hindu behaving in that fashion. You see, when the Muslims came to India, the only people they could convert were those of the lower castes. They are the kind of people from whom you can expect such behaviour.

To conclude from such remarks that Muslims are free from ideas and values concerning miscegenation which have their origin in the caste-structured society and culture of India would be grossly misleading. We have already pointed out that 'legitimate' marriage with Africans is prevented amongst Muslims—formal Islamic law to the contrary—by customary 'caste' regulations. With these prohibitions go deeply-ingrained negative attitudes toward inter-group mixing which, if not quite of the same intensity, are no different in kind from those held by Hindus. And of course for good reasons, since these notions are ultimately derived from Hindu culture.

A more rational ground for prejudice against Coloureds—and the one most freely admitted to Europeans—is that of the dangers of moral contamination of the young if the two groups are too intimate. This fear is rational to the extent that it is based upon facts: the Coloureds are confused and disorganised and moral standards among them are notoriously low. Few parents with middle-class pretensions—Coloured parents included—care to have their children consistently exposed to the kind of behaviour which constitutes the norm within the Coloured community.

Laxity and excess with respect to alcohol and sex are obvious facts of Coloured behaviour which are seized upon by Indians to illustrate their repulsion, but these are only surface manifestations of a radically different orientation to the world, of cultural ethos. Indians are puritanical in principle and practice; they are abstemious, parsimonious, hard-working, future-oriented, group-minded and pious—if not pious in the literal sense (which they often are) then in terms of their attitude toward their group's values as something sacred to be maintained at all costs. Sociologically, it is worth noting, these characteristics demand for their perpetuation strong controls and intensive socialisation.

Coloureds, by contrast, are everything in these respects which Indians are not. They are individualistic, hedonistic, and present-oriented; they tend to live for the day and typically they have only a minimal sense of individual or communal responsibility. Sociologically, these characteristics are at one and the same time a product and an index of weak group controls and goals.[17]

To Indians, Coloureds thus represent the social and cultural abyss awaiting them if they fail to maintain their ethnic virtues. An unequivocal statement of this widespread fear appears in our interview protocols from—on the face of it—an unexpected source. One of the few Indian Muslim 'pioneers' who has retained his African wife on principle told us:

I am married to an African woman, and my children are Coloured. But I won't have a Coloured person within half a mile of this house. That is one thing I have told my children time and time again. No Coloureds in this house! The local Coloured population completely lacks character—utterly. They might just as well be animals, because they act like animals.

We have a saying—it's kind of a joke—that such people worship *ing*. We say that because all the bad things which people do who don't have any character end in 'ing' in English. There is, for example, smok*ing*. And drink*ing*. And danc*ing*. And then, [just a bit hesitantly] there is that bad word which begins with 'f' and ends with 'ing.' All these things people do who don't have any character, and the Coloured people do them all.

This man, it must be pointed out in the interests of accuracy, is unusually pious. He is also extremely conservative politically and he is certainly old-fashioned and rigid generally in his views. Nevertheless, it is safe to say that hundreds of younger people, who would never dream of saying anything so crudely 'reactionary' to a European, share negative evaluations of Coloureds which differ only in intensity and not in kind from his.

This fear of moral contamination has been a major factor in the Indians' resistance to mixed Indian-Coloured schools: a resistance which has a long history but is not willingly acknowledged. Indians have sent their children to these schools only as the alternative to having no schools at all. On this matter, it is true, Indians have won some concessions: in the larger cities there are usually both Indian and Coloured schools at the primary level, with only a few Coloured children of Indian parentage in the Indian school. In one such urban community the Indians resisted the admission of Indo-Africans for fifteen years; the Government finally insisted that such children be admitted, as the price of its continued support.[18]

The objection to mixed schools on the grounds of moral contamination is reinforced by concern with status. Indians, with the possible exception of a few self-conscious liberals, deeply resented being classified by Europeans as equal in status to Coloureds. This facet of the matter appears clearly in a case which came to our attention towards the end of our investigations.

It had been recently decided, in a Northern Rhodesian town which is large enough to have separate schools at the primary level, to consolidate the available personnel from the so-called 'top primary' classes (post-Standard V students who are still below school-leaving age) and to hold such classes in the Coloured school. However, the education officials did not present this as a *fait accompli* to the Indians: they consulted the leaders and asked for community approval. This issue touched off a bitter row within the community. Approval for the official plan was won only by a small majority and then only on the ground that this was the best that they could hope to get.

A leader of the opposition in this case, when he was introduced to us for the first time, asked very aggressively, 'What do you think of the way the Europeans treat us?' Then he launched into a discussion of this school issue and concluded:

Why couldn't our children have been sent to the European secondary school, where there is plenty of room for them? Why do they have to be sent to the Coloured school? If that isn't an insult, then I can't think of one!

Why not, indeed? Why could not the Indian children have gone to the European rather than to the Coloured school?

The short but much too simple answer to this question would be because the European is prejudiced. Yet if the data presented in this paper are not seriously in error, the Indian and the Coloured are prejudiced too. What, then, is the essential difference?

The essential difference is that the European in this situation is dominant. Being dominant, he has the luxury of living out his prejudices, of expressing freely without restraint from other groups his socio-cultural 'nature'. The subordinate groups may be as prejudiced as he; yet we note in this situation how their prejudices are either brushed aside or made to fit somehow into the formal institutional order laid down by the dominant group. Indians and Coloureds go to the same school, like it or not. The European, having the power to do so, arranges his school on his own terms.

There are excellent theoretical reasons for doubting whether any society composed of widely divergent ethnic groups can exist without one of these groups clearly dominant over the others.[19] The historical dominance of the European in Central Africa is currently being eroded and will not last much longer. What the emerging pattern of dominance and subordination amongst the various ethnic groups in that part of the world will be in the future is the future's secret. What we can say with certainty is that when the African comes to be the ethnic as well as the numerically dominant group, the European, the Indian and the Coloured will live there on *his* terms, or not at all.

Notes ►

1. 'Asian' is standardised as the official term of reference in Central Africa. Since in point of fact virtually all 'Asians' are Indian in origin, it seems more straightforward to simply call them 'Indians', as

we do here. Some Muslims, it is true, prefer the term 'Asian' to 'Indian' on nationalistic grounds. Some of these Muslims go so far as to refer to themselves as 'Pakistani', in spite of the fact that virtually all of them are from territory now included within the present boundaries of India rather than Pakistan. Both Hindus and Muslims in Central Africa are predominantly from Gujarat, or from contiguous territory such as Kathiawar.

2. The legal status of these traditional discriminatory practices has changed drastically within recent years, and additional changes are constantly being made. Northern Rhodesia opened theatres and cafés to all races by legislative fiat in 1960. In 1961, the Southern Rhodesian courts went so far as to declare the municipal swimming baths of that territory open to all races.

3. The 1961 census gives a total of 14,100 for the Coloured population of the Federation—an increase of 29.9 per cent over the 10,855 recorded for 1956. The great majority of recognised Coloureds lived in Southern Rhodesia (10,560); Northern Rhodesia (2,050) and Nyasaland (1,490) divided the remainder between them.

4. The official 1956 statistics (the latest for which these percentages are available) give a European father and an African mother for 14.3 per cent of the total Coloured population; a European father and a Coloured mother provided an additional 6.1 per cent, making a subtotal of all those with European fathers of 20.4 per cent. First-generation Indo-Africans (those with an Indian father and an African mother) accounted for only 4.2 per cent of the recognised Coloured population of the Federation, but the distribution of these by territory was very uneven. In both Southern Rhodesia and Northern Rhodesia, first-generation Indo-Africans were few in number and minute as a proportion of the total (2.2 and 3.4 per cent respectively), but in Nyasaland they constituted no less than 18.0 per cent, as against 12.1 per cent for first-generation Eurafricans. These territorial variations are of course to be explained for the most part by the great differences in the proportions between Europeans and Indians in these three territories. In 1956, there were nearly 180,000 Europeans in Southern Rhodesia as against only 5,000 Indians. In Nyasaland, there were 8,500 Indians (10,630 in 1961) and 6,700 Europeans (8,750 in 1961). The basic difficulty with all official statistics for the Coloured population is the fact that only a fraction—and a completely unknown fraction at that—of the people of mixed parentage are recognised Coloureds. The official statistics are doubtlessly reasonably accurate for the recognised Coloured community. But they certainly seriously underestimate the actual numbers of first-generation Eurafricans and Indo-Africans in the Federation.

5. We attempted to work out an 'index of racial responsibility' for the Coloureds, using population statistics corrected for age and sex at various census dates. We gave up the idea when it became apparent that such an index would probably be more misleading than helpful, considering all the unknown factors involved. One—but only one—of these unknowns is the strong possibility that proportionately more Eurafricans than Indo-Africans are socially recognised as Coloureds.

6. Sir Harry H. Johnston, *British Central Africa*, London, Methuen, 1897, pp. 19–22.

7. National Archives, Salisbury, Item T2/2/18.

8. According to the 1946 census in Northern Rhodesia, there were 2.9 married males to each married female among the Indians. In 1956, this disparity narrowed down to a ratio of 1.4. In Nyasaland, the 1945 census data showed a ratio of 2.2 for married Indians 15 years of age and over, and in 1956 it was 1.2. In Southern Rhodesia, the ratio in 1956 was 1.1. Data on marital status of Indians are not available for 1946 in that territory, but even if they were, they would not be particularly relevant because immigration of adult Indian males has been cut off there since 1923.

9. We are, of course, using the term 'legitimate' here in its sociological rather than strictly legal sense. Yet even legalistically, most of these unions could not be considered legitimate; by the Koran, a Muslim male must marry either a Muslim woman or a Christian—a heathen, by implication, is fit only for concubinage.

The fact that a good number of Africans in Central Africa are Muslims might in theory help to promote legitimate intermarriage between the two races. Up to the present this remains theoretical, since in practice marriage is controlled by customary regulations of Hindu origin. It may very well be, however, that in the future, as Africans gain power and prestige and the temptation to intermarriage consequently becomes greater, this Koranic provision will be invoked with greater and greater frequency. In situations of change, people use whatever elements of their culture they can to help them meet the new demands.

10. We are, of course, making here an implied distinction between 'culture' and 'social structure' which should not be misunderstood. The fact that Coloureds as a group are thoroughly Europeanised culturally does not mean that they are becoming Europeans socially, or that they are accepted by Europeans as equals, or even as 'like us'. American Negroes are culturally American—they are certainly nothing else—and yet socially they constitute a highly distinctive group in American society.

11. *Nyasaland Times*, 19 July 1960.

A report in the *Central African Mail,* 17 April 1962, indicates that this conflict persisted. According to the newspaper's correspondent in Limbe, Indo-Africans were openly supporting Dr. Banda's Malawi Congress, while some Eurafricans were supporting Sir Roy Welensky's United Federal Party.

12. Cf., among others, Kurt Lewin, *Resolving Social Conflicts,* New York, Harper, 1948, pp. 186–200, and George E. Simpson and Milton J. Yinger, *Racial and Cultural Minorities,* New York, Harper, 1953, pp. 192–195, 304–307.

13. This statement needs to be interpreted against such background facts as illustrated in the following incident, reported by a Coloured teacher of South African rather than local origin:

When I was in ——, the principal of the Coloured school was a bloke by the name of ——. Blank's grandfather was one of the early Governors of the territory and he was very proud of it. When his own mother came to his house, she would go to the back door and kneel down and clap her hands in the African manner to get attention. Then she would be let in at the back door. I used to say to him 'My God, man, how can you do it? Even if she is an African, she is your own mother!' Since I am an outsider, I can see these things in a way which the local people cannot.

Significantly enough, the Federally-built Chichere school for Coloured in Blantyre—a modern and thoroughly exemplary institution—was the first government establishment to be attacked by Africans at the time of the 1959 Emergency in Nyasaland.

14. The belief that Indians are peculiarly unclean in their mode of life is still widely and firmly held by Europeans. As with all derogatory stereotypes of 'out-groups', this serves as a boundary-maintaining mechanism.

15. For a factual discussion of current hygienic standards among Indians in Central Africa, see F. Dotson and L. Dotson, 'Cultural Values and Housing Needs', *Social Research and Community Development, Based on the Fifteenth Conference of the Rhodes-Livingstone Institute for Social Research,* edited by Raymond Apthorpe, Lusaka, Rhodes-Livingstone Institute, 1961, pp. 58–66.

16. Thus, for example, a well-educated and liberal-minded middle-aged Hindu may be much less prejudiced against Coloureds than many younger Hindus are, and much less than the great majority of Muslims.

17. These, it should be noted, are really *class* rather than *ethnic* phenomena. What are perceived as specifically Coloured characteristics in Central Africa are characteristics of disorganised, frustrated and

severely depressed bottom-rung classes everywhere in the modern Western world. For a vivid picture of this class as it exists in the United States, cf. Genevieve Knupfer, 'Portrait of the Underdog', *Public Opinion Quarterly*, vol. xi, Spring 1947, pp. 114–122.

18. The Government did not demand at the same time that Eurafrican children be admitted to European schools as the price of their continued existence.

19. The role of the dominant in race relations has yet to receive the attention which we think it deserves. We hope shortly to publish further on this matter from a strictly theoretical point of view.

7 ► EMERGING PATTERNS OF ETHNIC STRAIN IN ISRAEL

JUDITH T. SHUVAL

At the juncture of the continents of Africa and Asia, the small state of Israel offers the sociologist an opportunity to study those aspects of a new immigrant-receiving society that have been conducive to the development of ethnic strain and prejudice. Despite certain cohesive features such as a common religious and national background and a high level of ideological commitment and collective solidarity, there has been, according to Israeli sociologist Dr. Judith Shuval, increasing evidence of a reduction of this solidarity. In the following essay Dr. Shuval describes the emerging divisive elements in the social structure and she attributes them partially to the heightened solidarity and visibility of specific ethnic groups among immigrants.

Introduction

It may seem at first glance paradoxical to study problems of ethnic relations and strain within the framework of Israeli society. In a country composed overwhelmingly of Jews who for generations have suffered various forms of religious and ethnic prejudice the world over, is it not striking that elements of prejudice should reveal themselves in the new state established by and for the very victims of such hostility? We shall not suggest here that anything even approaching the more virulent forms of anti-Semitism exists in Israel. What we shall describe and attempt to analyze here are

From Judith T. Shuval, "Emerging Patterns of Ethnic Strain in Israel," *Social Forces*, 40, 4 (May, 1962), 323–30. Reprinted by permission of the author and the University of North Carolina Press.

some elements of strain between ethnic groups and growing evidence of certain forms of scapegoating. Only rarely have these assumed extreme forms of expression; they generally manifest themselves on the level of exclusiveness and unwillingness to maintain social relationships with certain groups, stereotyped perception of ethnic group members, verbal hostility, tendencies to categorization and generalization in relationship to certain groups. However, the really important sociological point would seem to be the evidence for the *universalism* of certain types of prejudice which apparently appear even in a society as manifestly opposed to such phenomena as Israel, by its very nature, must be.

This paper will discuss some aspects of the social structure of Israeli society which, under certain circumstances, are conducive to the development of strained ethnic relations and manifestations of prejudice. The background we shall describe may serve as a potential field for such prejudice although we assume that of itself it does not bring about such phenomena. However, in a situation of structured strain, where there is a need for the displacement of hostility, the potential to ethnic prejudice may well transform itself into a reality. We shall present this general problem in three parts: 1) Background to the structure of ethnic relations; 2) Structured strain in the social system; 3) Evidence for ethnic hostility.

Background to the Structure of Ethnic Relations

COHESIVE FEATURES OF THE SOCIAL SYSTEM

Before proceeding to a discussion of some of the structural characteristics of the society which may be conducive to the development of strain or hostility between ethnic groups, let us consider some of the cohesive features of the social system which have contributed over the past years to its solidarity and which operate against many of the divisive elements to be described below.

The most outstanding cohesive feature of Israeli society, which is evident to the most casual observer, is the common religious and ethnic background of virtually all Israelis. Simply being Jews provides an ascriptive common historic and religious background which acts as a powerful cohesive bond for all. This is true despite the many subcultural variations associated on the one hand with the unique cultural forms developed by each group in its country of origin and which vary considerably from each other, and on the other with differences in degree and quality of adherence to traditional religious forms.

In addition to general identification as Jews, there is a strong element of identification with the relatively new State of Israel and its ideals. The ideal of "the ingathering of the exiles" is taken at face value and all groups of Jews, however diverse their origins, are viewed as having a rightful place in the society. Actually the value system surrounding the ideal of "the ingathering of the exiles" has served as the major obstacle to the growing particularistic orientation to specific ethnic groups [1] which will be described below.

This ideal has fostered a basically universalistic orientation toward the different ethnic groups comprising the population: it has emphasized equality of rights and duties, minimized status differentials, tended to play down or ignore signs of strain or evidence of negative stereotypes.

Despite considerable political differentiation, there has been a strong cohesive ideal of social justice and equality in Israeli society. This has expressed itself, until quite recently, in a relatively narrow range of social and economic classes, simplicity in style of life which has been associated with the strong pioneering ideal, highly developed social rights and benefits for all workers.

Over and above the positive cohesive elements described, there has been a negative factor which has undoubtedly contributed in no small measure to the solidarity of the society: the common enemy. Prior to the establishment of the State in 1948, the latter role was filled in large measure by the British; after 1948 the Arab states became the common enemy. Even after the War of Independence consciousness of a common enemy, particularly in the light of recurring border and diplomatic incidents, served to keep the population constantly aware of a major political danger to the very existence of the State, and such consciousness acts to promote general solidarity.

DIVISIVE FEATURES OF THE SOCIAL SYSTEM

1. *Weakening of over-all solidarity.* The elements of social solidarity described function counter to the development of strain between ethnic groups or manifestations of ethnic prejudice. How-

ever, it is our feeling that there has been a weakening of this solidarity in recent years as well as the development of a number of structural features in the social system which may be conducive to the growth of ethnic strain and prejudice.

If the solidarity described above is viewed as a function, at least partially, of the striving toward the achievement of two major common goals, namely, the establishment of the State and its defense against an outside enemy, then the reduction in solidarity becomes clear in the light of the basic achievement of these goals. Although the economic and political *maintenance* of the State continue to serve as major problems of concern to the leadership, the population as a whole does not view these with the same urgency as it did the earlier problems of *establishment* and *defense* of the then new State. Furthermore the number of alternative ways of achieving economic stability are considerable and these serve to recruit adherents thus emphasizing particularistic political or economic orientation rather than over-all solidary identification with the State as a whole.

The achievement of the major goals resulted, as in the case of all revolutionary movements, in a certain routinization of functions which were previously often performed on an idealistic or voluntary basis. The establishment of large bureaucratic systems is a *sine qua non* of a modern state and these appeared in Israel with surprising speed. The outstanding examples of cases where a routine bureaucracy took over functions that were previously performed largely by people motivated by collective, nonroutinized goals are the army and the government offices. The very nature of the bureaucratic official is such as to encourage job-specific orientation and the attainment of immediately defined goals rather than solidary identification with the broad goals of the society as a whole.

With the gradual stabilization of the country's economy and with the general lowering in the level of collective orientation has come an attenuation of the equalitarian ethic which was pervasive prior to the establishment of the State. Channels of mobility being relatively open in Israeli society, it was not long before higher achieved status positions were much sought after. The relatively narrow range of the class system which characterized the pre-state period, gave way to a considerably wider hierarchy of status groups.

2. *Increased "visibility" of ethnic groups.* Allport has empha-sized the need of visibility of individuals or groups as a prerequisite for the focusing of hostility or prejudice on them: "Visibility and identifiability aid categorization".[2] The greater this differentiation and visibility, the easier it becomes for one or more of the sub-groups to become a target for others.

The mass immigration to Israel which began immediately after the state was established contributed greatly to a high level of ethnic differentiation. Jews immigrated from a wide variety of national and cultural origins bringing with them a rich back-ground of culture patterns, values and norms. Specific languages and dialects were often spoken by the different groups. In addition certain groups were distinguishable by characteristic physical traits, such as skin color or physical build. This general combina-tion—distinguishing culture patterns, language, and, in many cases, characteristic physical traits—brought about a fairly high level of visibility and identifiability of the various ethnic groups making up the post-state population.

Although the general trend of acculturation is to attenuate the visibility of the different ethnic groups over time,[3] there are certain rather strong counter-trends which serve to heighten ethnic in-group solidarity and even to accentuate the identifiability of ethnic subgroups. During the earliest period immigrants are in the coun-try, identification with their own ethnic group serves as a source of emotional security in a strange and unfamiliar social situation. It is not uncommon during this period to find particularly strong ad-herence to traditional forms of behavior and cultural patterns as a means of attaining a measure of continuity with the past in a new situation. Such inward focusing serves to emphasize the solidarity of the ethnic in-group and to draw the boundaries with out-groups more distinctly.

An additional source of solidarity for certain of the ethnic groups may lie in the perception of a measure of hostility toward them by other elements of the population. In a sense we are putting the cart before the horse in presenting this argument now; however, there is undoubtedly a certain circularity in the process: hostility toward certain ethnic groups serves to heighten their feelings of solidarity, and increases their visibility as a result of intensified interaction with members of their own group and consequent adherence to traditional cultural forms.[4]

An additional factor which acts to heighten identifiability is the relatively high correlation between ethnic origin and socioeconomic status. In general we find in Israel that persons of Oriental or North African origin are concentrated at the lower end of the socioeconomic hierarchy while Europeans cluster more at the top. Needless to say this correlation is not perfect, but it is undoubtedly sufficient to add the identifiable characteristics of class position to those ethnic characteristics discussed above, and the combination results in an even higher level of visibility than that determined by ethnic or class membership alone.[5]

The historic and sociological reasons for the correlation of ethnic membership with socioeconomic status need not concern us in full here. Suffice it to note two major complexes of factors which have contributed to this situation. A. The generally lower educational and socioeconomic background in their countries of origin of immigrants from Near Eastern and North African countries as compared to those stemming from European origins. This low level is a function on the one hand of the relatively depressed social and economic conditions in these countries in general, and on the other of the particular position occupied by the Jewish population in these societies. B. Prolonged contact with the wider cultural framework in their countries of origin has resulted in the Oriental Jews acquiring a more passive orientation to life problems in general and the latter expresses itself in reduced aspirations for social mobility.[6] So that not only are these people relegated to the lower rungs of the socioeconomic hierarchy by virtue of their poor educational and occupational background, but they also tend to remain in that position with greater frequency than equivalently ranked Europeans because of their relatively limited aspirations for social mobility.

The close relationship between socioeconomic class position and ethnic origin has resulted in certain ecological patterns which also serve to heighten identifiability. Particularly in the unplanned urban centers, ethnic groups tend to cluster in certain neighborhoods which gradually assume an ethnic label. As in the case of other countries where ethnic ghettoes are found in the larger urban communities, this clustering is a function of economic factors determining the price and quality of housing as well as social factors associated with a need for the security which comes from living in proximity to members of one's own ethnic ingroup.[7]

Structured Strain in the Social System

The reduced solidarity of the over-all social system with its accompanying change in the value system, and the increased visibility of the specific ethnic groups, are in themselves insufficient to result in ethnic tension or manifestations of prejudice. However, given certain situations, particularly those involving a measure of strain in the social system and the need for focusing displaced aggression, the former conditions would seem likely to provide a set of acceptable target groups toward which hostility could be directed, as well as a value system which would be more likely to accept expressions of prejudice. We shall first present material concerning structured strain among immigrants who make up the majority of the Israeli population, and then proceed to the same problem among oldtimers since, as we shall attempt to show, it would be a mistake to assume that such strain expresses itself only with respect to the immigrants in the population.

STRUCTURED STRAIN AMONG IMMIGRANTS

Any changeover from one society to another inevitably involves a certain amount of strain for the individual; however, some overcome the inherent difficulties more easily than others. The type of strain we shall describe here appears to us to be of a fairly pervasive sort which is built into the immigrant role and which must be met virtually by all.

A certain amount of occupational dislocation is an almost inevitable consequence of mass immigration. This is particularly true when the economic structures of the country of immigration and emigration differ basically. In the case of Jewish immigration the problem is intensified by the fact that in almost all of the countries of origin Jews were clustered in certain specific categories of occupations. These were not always available in Israel, or even when they were available, the requirements for admission were frequently such as to prevent or delay entry of the immigrant into his familiar type of work, thus bringing about a certain loss of status, frustration, and the strain that accompanies them. Although this problem impinges chiefly on the breadwinner, other members of the family for whom the latter serves as their principal status symbol, may also be subjected to no small measure of strain as a result of such occupational dislocation. And even if the immigrant succeeds in finding a job that suits his ability and experience, he must nevertheless learn a set of new work roles, values, and expectations which are associated with the job in the new society.

All this is in the case of the breadwinner acquiring some sort of a job, even if it is one where he suffers a loss of status. The problem is compounded in the case of unemployment. Although the Israeli economy has made considerable efforts to combat unemployment, there has nevertheless been a problem of maintaining jobs for all. Although not excessive, a certain measure of unemployment exists and what is perhaps no less of a problem, a measure of underemployment among those employed by the various public works enterprises. The type of strain and frustration characteristic of unemployment are too well known to require elaboration here.[8]

The immigrant often finds his traditional value system to be in conflict with the values of the new society. This may be particularly true of people who emigrated from traditional societies which were relatively little affected by processes of westernization, but even for European immigrants the differences in values between their countries of origin and Israel are considerable. The problem of value conflict is made graphic if one considers the problem of the immigrant child in the Israeli school system faced by at least three social groups demanding conformity to different sets of norms: his family, his teachers and other official representatives of the Israeli value system, and his peers.

For many immigrants, coming to Israel resulted in the break-up of extended family systems. Oriental Jews in particular, for whom life within the framework of the extended family system has been traditional for generations, suffered by this change. Although the post-state immigration differed from pre-state immigration in that whole families often came together, it was not always feasible to settle the entire family group in proximity to each other, and this often resulted in families being spread in different parts of the country rather than concentrated in one location as a social unit.[9]

Even those immigrants who were not accustomed to living in extended family groups generally found themselves socially isolated with few members of their families or familiar friends living in their vicinity. It thus became almost a necessity for immigrants to strike out anew in the creation of the type of networks of relationships that lend stability to social life. This process is made particularly difficult in development centers which are characterized by extreme ethnic heterogeneity of the population.

STRUCTURED STRAIN AMONG OLDTIMERS

Since we are concerned here with the development of ethnic relations within the social context of the post-state period, we shall focus our discussion on the strain which impinges on oldtimers in Israel specifically as a result of the mass immigration. Clearly there are other, more general forms of strain which affect oldtimers, e.g. poverty, frustrated mobility aspirations, family problems, etc., but we shall not discuss these here. The latter are not directly relevant to the specific development of ethnic prejudice in Israel since there is no particular reason to believe that they changed fundamentally after the state was established.

With the passage of time, more and more of the ambitious, socially mobile immigrants have succeeded in establishing themselves economically and socially in the new society. During the post-state period of broad economic development, those with educational backgrounds or occupational skills have moved up the rungs of the social hierarchy to occupy positions of status and prestige. In so moving they have managed to bypass and overtake certain oldtimers who, for any number of reasons, have been unable to forge ahead as rapidly. The latter, if they are basically motivated by mobility aspirations or if they are for some reason dissatisfied with their present status position, may well feel a sense of frustration as they see these newcomers overtake them.

The status of "oldtimer in Israel" (vatik) no longer serves as an absolute criterion to obtain rights and privileges as was the case before the mass immigration. In the earlier period the longer a person was in the country the greater his rights with respect to jobs, housing, social benefits of all sorts, and prestige in the community. Although the criterion of "vetek" still remains, the mass immigration brought with it a new and separate criterion of rights and privileges in the society, i.e. "immigrant status". The ascribed status of "immigrant" automatically gives one considerable rights and privileges in obtaining more convenient loans, housing, medical treatment, jobs, and many other social benefits. An element of strain appears in the oldtimer role when a new criterion for the obtaining of such rights and privileges is introduced and coexists with his own. This is not to say that the rights of the oldtimer have been curtailed in any way, but that whereas formerly his status was the principal if not sole one granting such privileges, a new one has now been introduced. This form of strain is felt mostly by those oldtimers who have been in the country for a fairly long period of time but not long enough to acquire the rights and privileges of "real" oldtimers: this is the middle group which is caught between the rights and privileges of the "real" oldtimers on one hand and of the newly arrived immigrants on the other.

Evidence for Ethnic Hostility

As already noted, we shall not propose that ethnic relations in Israel are *extremely* strained or even that a real potential of serious ethnic strife necessarily exists. Nevertheless it is our feeling that if we accept Allport's definition of ethnic prejudice as "an antipathy based upon a faulty and inflexible generalization . . . directed toward a group as a whole, or toward an individual because he is a member of that group",[10] such prejudice may quite definitely be said to exist in Israel. It is directed principally against Jews of Oriental origin, but it has been our observation that more and more in recent years hostility has been focused specifically on the North African groups, and more particularly on the Moroccans. The remainder of this paper will present impressionistic and systematic empirical evidence to back up this generalization.

It should be noted before proceeding that almost no prejudice in Israel is institutionalized within a formal framework. There are no quotas in the schools; if Oriental groups are under-represented, as indeed they are in the secondary schools and in the universities, this may be attributed almost entirely to their relatively low socioeconomic status and more limited mobility aspirations and not to any policy on the part of the education institutions.[11] There is no formal discrimination in job opportunities. Public housing is distributed on a first come, first serve basis. If there has been clustering of ethnic groups in certain newly planned neighborhoods, this can generally be explained by the fact that these groups immigrated together and became eligible for new housing at the same time. Nor is there any difference in the quality of the housing made available to different ethnic groups.

Most of the prejudice in Israel appears within an informal social framework. There is frequent dropping of remarks concerning the undesirable physical or social traits of various ethnic groups. Stereotyped images of ethnic groups, particularly Oriental ones, are becoming more and more prevalent. There is a lack of willingness to associate informally with members of certain ethnic groups and this has resulted in considerable ethnocentrism in social relationships. We have found it quite rare to observe real friendship relations between Europeans and North Africans, or between Europeans and Near Easterners. True there may be a measure of association between members of these groups in the work situation but it is our impression that there is little carry-over into the less formal, more affective area of leisure time relationships.

An indirect but nevertheless meaningful way to estimate the prevalence of ethnic prejudice is the extent to which members of Oriental groups accept and internalize prevailing attitudes of others toward them. We have found indications that the stereotype of North Africans concerning their own group corresponds in its over-all structure to the stereotyped image others in the society carry of them. The process by which this internalization takes place is familiar from the work of G. H. Mead.[12] Not only is the negative stereotype accepted and internalized in considerable measure, but a marked rejection and hostility against members of their own group is revealed by North Africans. Such a self-hatred provides indirect evidence for the existence of prejudice in the society since it clearly represents the North Africans' reflection of the attitudes of others toward them.

Against this general background, the ethnic riots which occurred in Wadi Salib in 1959 are not too surprising a social phenomenon. True, this was the most extreme form of expression of strained ethnic relations that occurred up to that date. However, when we consider the isolated event within its total social context, it may be said, without attempting in any way to condone it, that it was an understandable and not altogether unexpected externalization of long-existent feelings of ethnic strain. We do not believe that riots of this sort are likely to be a frequent occurrence in the near future; however, when the pent-up ethnic strain accumulates sufficiently, a spark may understandably set off a chain of events similar to that witnessed at Wadi Salib.

We shall now present some systematic empirical evidence for the existence of hostility toward certain ethnic groups. The data are drawn from a study carried out in 1959 of 1511 settlers in four Israeli development centers:[13] Kiryat Gat, Ashkelon, Beer Sheva,

Kiryat Shmona.[14] A systematic sample of families was drawn from the list of residents in each community; men and women were interviewed alternately in a predetermined system.

Among other questions posed, residents were asked "On the basis of your experience living here, which ethnic group would you most and least prefer as neighbors?" Actually the positive and negative dimensions of the problem were presented separately, with the positive coming first. At the moment, however, we shall focus on the second dimension: groups disliked as neighbors.[15] Table 1 presents the frequency with which each over-all ethnic

Table 1. Rejection of Ethnic Groups as Neighbors in Terms of Ethnic Origin of Respondents

Country of Origin of Respondents	Percentage Indicating Dislike of Neighbors from the Following Countries of Origin:			
	Europe	North Africa	Near East	No Opinion *
Europeans....	10	33	22	35 (502)
North Africans..	11	33	25	31 (722)
Near Easterners..	7	37	27	29 (278)

* The relatively high percentage of "no opinion" may likewise be attributed, at least partially, to the ideological norm mitigating against expressions of ethnic prejudice.

group is mentioned by the other ethnic groups as disliked in the neighborhood context. It is clear from this table that all three ethnic groups in these communities express most hostility toward North Africans as neighbors: about a third of the total population, and an equal percentage of each of the ethnic groups viewed alone, rejects North Africans as neighbors. Although the Near Easterners are fairly close runners-up in lack of popularity (approximately a quarter of the population rejects them as neighbors), it is quite clear that most hostility is focused by members of all groups on North Africans. When the data are broken down to the specific ethnic groups making up the over-all groups considered collectively in Table 1, it becomes clear that fully a quarter of the population rejects Moroccans specifically. These data give us our first major systematic clue concerning the dimensions of the prejudice focused on North Africans.[16] In the light of the ideological sanctions discussed earlier, which would mitigate against the overt expression of hostility against specific ethnic groups, we would suspect that the prevalence of ethnic prejudice is considerably more widespread than is suggested by these data.

What reasons can be suggested for the singling out of North Africans as the major target of hostility? It is our feeling that the major explanation falls in the realm of the relatively great visibility of the North African group viewed against a general background of structured strain in the society, as already discussed. Over and above the more general ethnic characteristics leading to visibility, there are two unique factors which make the North Africans more visible than most of the other ethnic groups: a) the comparatively large *size* of this group in the immigrant population, b) the relatively heavy concentration of the North Africans in the lower rungs of the socioeconomic hierarchy. When taken together, these two factors make for a relatively large, highly visible group, easily identifiable by its ethnic-cultural traits as well as by its class position.

Needless to say the "visibility" argument only indicates why a specific group is chosen out of all the other available groups as the *target* of prejudice; it indicates nothing as to why hostile feelings were prevalent in the first place since we clearly do not assume that the target group provides adequate justifiable cause for the aggression expressed toward it. On the contrary: prejudice by its nature represents an exaggerated, over-generalized form of hostility which, although it may be based on a certain measure of veridical perception, is essentially not founded on objective characteristics of the target group. The explanation we would offer refers back to the discussion of structured strain in the society which apparently generates sufficient "free-floating anxiety" to require an acceptable target for displacement of aggression.

Not only are the North Africans singled out now as the major target for ethnic hostility, but there is evidence that prejudice toward them has been growing over the years. Without attempting to project this problem into the future, we may say that the data point to a developing pattern of prejudice toward North Africans. The data reported on in this paper are drawn from a study carried out in 1959. In Table 2 we present material from two additional similar (although not identical) studies carried out in 1950 and 1953 in which comparable material was gathered. The

Table 2. Hostility Expressed Toward North Africans
in 1950, 1953 and 1959

Year of Study	Question Posed	Percentage Replying "North Africans"
1950	"Which ethnic groups in this community do you particularly dislike?"	5 (1880)
1953	"What is the country of origin of the neighbors you like least in this community?"	19 (806)
1959	"On the basis of your experience living here, which ethnic group would you least prefer as neighbors?"	34 (1502)

1950 study is based on a sample of 1880 housewives in a representative group of old and new housing developments in Israel. The 1953 material is based on a sample of 806 men and women residents of Bet Mazmil, an immigrant housing development in the suburbs of Jerusalem.[17] Table 2 presents the percentage of respondents in each of three studies who spontaneously indicated "North Africans" in reply to the relevant question posed. It will be noted that, although the questions presented differ slightly from each other, all three probe essentially the same dimension of attitude, i.e. rejection of a specific ethnic group as neighbors.

The percentage rejecting North Africans has risen systematically over the nearly ten-year period from a low of five percent to a third of the population. The earliest study was carried out at the height of the immigration from North Africa so that there had been little time for a social attitude toward such a newly arrived group to crystallize. The 1953 study took place when the bulk of the North African immigration was already in the country, and one can see how prevalent the negative attitude had become. By 1959 a hostile attitude was expressed by fully a third of the population. As noted earlier, we have reason to suspect that the still prevalent ideological norm acts as a brake to the full expression of hostile feelings on the part of an even larger segment of the population.

Notes ►

1. The term "ethnic group" as used in the present study refers to Jews from different countries of origin who often differ considerably

from each other with respect to traditional cultural forms as well as with respect to their forms of religious expression.

2. Gordon W. Allport, *The Nature of Prejudice* (Cambridge, Mass: Addison-Wesley Publishing Co., 1954), p. 129.

3. The official ideology has almost always emphasized this trend and has tended to ignore the counter-trends discussed below.

4. It should also be noted that another quite frequent reaction to hostility is self-hatred, that is, rejection of members of one's own group. However, this form of behavior is less relevant to our problem than a reaction involving heightened identification. Gordon W. Allport, *op. cit.*, pp. 148–152.

5. See for a discussion of this problem, Judith T. Shuval, "Patterns of Intergroup Tension and Affinity", UNESCO, *International Social Science Bulletin*, Vol. VIII, No. 1, 1956, pp. 87–90.

6. See on this problem Judith T. Shuval, *Immigrants on the Threshold*, Chapter X, "Occupational Aspirations", in publication.

7. There is little evidence in Israel for the existence of formal restrictive covenants, although the author has heard of occasional informal agreements having the same general effect.

8. Hans Zeisel and Marie Jahoda, *Die Arbeitslosen von Marienthal* (Leipzig: S. Hirzel, 1933).

9. There has been a growing awareness of the social difficulties stemming from this separation and in recent years attempts have been made to avoid this problem.

10. Gordon W. Allport, *op. cit.*, p. 9.

11. In effect quite the reverse is true: every official effort is made to encourage non-European elementary school graduates to continue their education. This policy even expresses itself in giving scholarships to somewhat less qualified students of Oriental origin.

12. George H. Mead, *Mind, Self and Society* (Chicago: University of Chicago Press, 1947), pp. 135–226.

13. Development centers are planned urban communities settled mainly, but not exclusively, by immigrants. These are generally located in as yet undeveloped areas with the intention of providing an urban center in these areas for the surrounding agricultural communities.

14. The number of people interviewed was as follows: Kiryat Gat, 343; Ashkelon, 357; Beer Sheva, 443; Kiryat Shmona, 368.

15. We shall present the material on the positive aspect of this problem in subsequent publications.

16. It should be borne in mind, by way of limitation, that the data presented here, are drawn from four communities consisting mostly, though not entirely, of immigrants who arrived after the establishment of the state in 1948. The prevalence of prejudice among segments of

the population who are in the country for a longer period of time remains to be studied. The author is presently engaged in one such study, but results are not yet processed.

17. See for a report of the 1953 study Judith T. Shuval, "Patterns of Intergroup Tension and Affinity", UNESCO, *International Social Science Bulletin, op. cit.*, pp. 75–123. Reports of the 1950 study appear in typewritten form in the files of the Israel Institute of Applied Social Research, Jerusalem (Hebrew).

8► THE BRITISH SAY THEY AREN'T PREJUDICED

C. ERIC LINCOLN

As a consequence of the large migration of non-whites into the United Kingdom from the Commonwealth countries in recent decades, many British cities now have, for the first time in modern history, racial tensions not unlike those found in urban settings in American society. Yet Professor C. Eric Lincoln, a sociologist specializing in American Negro-white relations, perceived a deep-seated reluctance on the part of British whites to recognize the similarities between the British and American situations. In the article that follows, he describes his visit to the United Kingdom and offers a sociological insight into the attitudes and rationalizations which he detected there.

►"THEY'RE NOT like you, sir. You're an American. It's not that they're black, so much—they can't help that, I suppose. But if you'll pardon me, sir, they're filthy dirty. Most of them have tuberculosis. They spit in the street and they have venereal disease. Up in Birmingham and some other places, why, they're taking over the country."

The speaker was a very proper London taxi driver. He was talking about Britain's "dark million," the growing nonwhite population coming from the Commonwealth countries of Asia, Africa and the Caribbean.

When my taxi pulled up in front of the American Embassy in Grosvenor Square, he said with an air of triumph as he opened the cab door: "You see, sir, I told you. You're an American. I could

From *The New York Times Magazine*, November 14, 1965. © 1965 by The New York Times Company. Reprinted by permission of the author and publisher.

tell right off. The American colored are different from the nig-nogs we get here from the West Indies."

I tipped him and turned to go, but he called out after me: "God bless you, sir. I hope everything will turn out well for your people. And God bless your Dr. Martin Luther King! He is a great man!"

That very day in Selma, Ala., American Negroes were still stunned from a savage attack made on them by Sheriff Jim Clark's forces the day before. But in Britain, I mused ruefully, we are "different—and God bless Martin Luther King!"

A few days later I had lunch with a young M.P. at the House of Commons. "How do you assess the color problem in Britain?" I asked him.

"Well, first of all," he assured me, "it isn't at all like the racial problem in America. The British people, as you no doubt know, have absolutely no history of racialism. Our problem is primarily a physical problem—a problem of space and housing—particularly of housing. Many of our own people have been waiting years for housing. It's a matter of housing and jobs and trying to physically absorb a million immigrants into a situation that is already overcrowded."

Six months later, the same M.P. was reluctant to discuss the problem at all. In the interim the Labor Government had published a white paper on the subject and clamped down on the number of Commonwealth immigrants to be allowed into the country. Three years earlier, the Labor party had strongly opposed the then Conservative Government's restrictive legislation but has since found its stand electorally embarrassing. Some Labor politicians are afraid that an even mildly liberal policy on immigration will cost them five or 10 or even more seats at the next election.

Again and again throughout my visits in Britain I was to hear variations of the same theme: "We aren't prejudiced. We just don't have the facilities." Even the "coloreds" with whom I talked were reluctant to identify their problems with those of the Negro in America. "Our problems are different from yours," one young Jamaican professional told me.

What are the problems that are so "different"? The fundamental problem is that Britain, for the first time in modern history (there were some Africans with the Roman legions in the Roman occupation of nearly two thousand years ago), has an influx of nonwhites in sufficiently large numbers to become conspicuous in London, Birmingham, Manchester, Bradford, Sheffield and a half dozen other cities and towns.

As a result racial incidents have multiplied—and keep multiplying. While the frustrated Negroes in the Los Angeles ghettoes were rampaging in an orgy of burning and pillaging, crosses were being burned in front of "immigrant" homes in Britain. Further, a chapter of the night-riding Ku Klux Klan has allegedly been exported to these racially divided islands. "Coloreds" have been beaten and threatened. For all its "differences," the problem, or at any rate the way the problem is expressed, seems familiar. In at least one instance, in the Midlands industrial city of Wolverhampton, a white mob armed with sticks and bottles laid siege to a colored residence in support of a white family involved in a trivial dispute over a footpath.

The enormity of the Los Angeles riots had a sobering effect on the British. Both the press and the people generally were noticeably restrained in their comments on the racial crisis in California. Perhaps they saw in the carnage of Los Angeles an example of what could happen in Birmingham, Manchester or even London.

The "duskies" or "coloreds" so far constitute only 2 per cent of the population. Yet their presence has inspired troubles—political, psychological and economic—far out of proportion to their numbers, and this in a country with a long history of racial tolerance. For a hundred years and more, Hindus, Africans, Malays, Chinese, West Indians and countless other breeds have given dash to the majestic drabness of British officialdom, and their sons have been educated in the best British schools. In seaports such as Cardiff, Liverpool and Southampton, Negro sailors and their families have lived for generations.

After the last war, the United Kingdom opened its gates to the people of every Commonwealth nation, recognizing them as citizens of Britain and allowing them to vote after a residence of six months. It was the nonwhite countries that stood to benefit most —India and Pakistan with their teeming millions of unemployed and steadily rising birth rates, the crowded West Indies with a sick economy.

As early as 1952 Britain was already in trouble because of her policy of open immigration. Leaders from some of the towns where immigration was heaviest appealed to the Government for help in assimilating the colored migrants. The Colonial Office took the position that it could assume no responsibility for the migrants as they were British citizens who, just as any other citizens, were the responsibility of their local governments. Not until race riots (minor by American standards) occurred in Nottingham and in London's Notting Hill and Paddington in 1958 were the British shocked into an awareness of the increasing complexity of the race problem.

At that time there were only 200,000 coloreds in the country. Now there are well over a million, including an estimated 535,000 Pakistanis and Indians (and a few thousand Chinese and Africans) and 660,000 West Indians. Birmingham alone has a colored population of more than 70,000 (in a total population of 1,115,000). In some of the smaller cities the nonwhite population is 30 to 40 per cent of the total.

In an effort to control this rising tide, restrictions on immigration were established by the Conservative Government under the Commonwealth Immigrants Act of 1962. Control is exercised by a system of "employment vouchers" originally issued in three categories: "A," for applicants with jobs waiting in Britain: "B," for applicants skilled in a trade or profession short of workers; and "C," for veterans who have served the British Government in war and for all others who do not fall into the first two categories.

Physicians from India, nurses from the West Indies and a few other skilled persons have no problems in getting "A" vouchers. Further, the transport and hospital services are particularly dependent upon low-paid colored labor, admitted on "A" or "B" vouchers, to fill jobs as drivers, conductors, orderlies, nurses' aides and internes. While the labor unions are hostile toward nonwhites, for the most part, there is no objection to their working the late mill shifts that white workers do not want, or doing menial labor such as street-cleaning.

Last year some 20,000 Commonwealth citizens were permitted to come to Britain to work, and were accompanied or joined by 50,000 dependents. However, this was only part of the story. The 1962 Commonwealth Immigrants Act has many loopholes; thousands of other coloreds—particularly Indians and Pakistanis—entered illegally. Traffic in forged vouchers and other such devices is brisk, and there appeared to be no way to close all the gaps. The problem reached the stage, in fact, where high-level consultations were held with Commonwealth Governments.

Then last August, Herbert Bowden, leader of the House of Commons, announced that while Britain recognized "the valuable contribution" of Commonwealth immigrants, "nearly everyone appreciates that there is a limit to the number of immigrants that this small and overcrowded country can absorb." Therefore, he said, the Labor Government would reduce the number of permits from 20,000 a year to 8,500 and eliminate provisions for admitting immigrants in category "C" of the voucher system. Thus Labor—which had fought immigration controls when the Conservatives proposed them—in effect joined the Opposition. Furthermore, a public opinion poll indicated that the Government's "get tough" policy had the approval of three of four voters, and that more than 50 per cent of the voters thought that restrictions against colored immigration should be even more severe.

Although many Britons wish the coloreds would quietly go back where they came from, the coloreds have come to stay. (But not all of them: the Pakistanis and the Indians frequently stay only long enough to buy land at home and then return there.)

It is the West Indians who generally plan to remain. Many of them consider themselves "black Englishmen," and they do not conceive it strange that they should want to live in London. They work to buy houses and then send for their families. A house is not only a status symbol; in an economy where housing is tight it can also be the way to wealth.

Housing is hard to come by. In the London community of Brixton I talked with a Jamaican who had just bought a house. He had saved for four years, and then he had borrowed all he could get from his friends. He said that the agent had substantially overcharged him, but that he knew he was paying a color tax and accepted it, since he could do nothing about it. What he didn't know was that the house had a white "sitting tenant" who insisted on his right to continue occupying his apartment at the same rent.

The new landlord was beside himself with rage and fear. Every room in his house would have to bring in a certain income if he was to meet the inflated notes he was obligated to pay. The white tenant could find nowhere to go at the rent he was paying. Everybody was unhappy (except possibly the real estate agent, who had made a killing).

Many coloreds who have been stuck with white sitting tenants have resorted to "Rachmanism," a kind of harassment practiced by Peter Rachman, the late and infamous white slum landlord. His techniques ranged all the way from playing the radio full blast after midnight to encouraging the committing of indecencies in tenement halls and doorways. The whites (already primed to believe that the coloreds were filthy) would move out and their rooms be let quickly to coloreds willing to pay inflated rents.

Colored landlords who have adopted these techniques defend themselves by arguing that if they could buy at true market prices there would be no urgency to dispossess "sitting" whites.

Another source of friction is lower-class white resentment of the thrift and industry shown by the colored newcomers. The Asians are condemned for "sending money out of the country without paying taxes on it," and for working double shifts and upsetting the labor market. The West Indians are resented for buying houses (even at inflated prices) when native whites still need housing, and for buying flashy cars on the installment plan when all the whites in the neighborhood are walking.

A hostile Briton is inclined to make no distinction among nonwhite immigrants. (One civil servant referred to them all as "niggers," and said he'd "just as soon throw in the Maltese, the Cypriotes and the Greeks as well.") "Coloreds" and "immigrants" are the polite terms. At other times they are referred to as "wogs," "nignogs," "wallah-wallahs," "coolies," "blacks" and "darkies."

Some white Britons do have orders of preference—or at least orders of denigration—where nonwhites are concerned. Some prefer the Indians, others the Africans. Generally, it seems that West Indians are both more readily accepted ("They're like us except they're black") and more readily rejected ("They're nothing but savages"). The West Indians speak English and are thoroughly grounded in English values. They play cricket and become homeowners, and they are intensely loyal to the British Crown and to the British way of life insofar as they understand it and are permitted to become a part of it.

The Pakistanis, on the other hand, keep to themselves, refuse to learn the language, and have dietary and religious practices strange to Britons. Therefore legends about their personal habits quickly gain currency. They have been accused of bringing in tuberculosis, and while they may not have the disease when they arrive, the incidence among Pakistanis living in Britain is many times that of the national average. Health authorities attribute the high rate to an unaccustomed climate, improper diet and generally poor living conditions. In an effort to save money and because housing is hard to find, as many as 20 to 30 male Pakistanis may live together in one house, using the beds in shifts.

The immigrants, particularly the West Indians, are also held responsible for a high rate of venereal disease. This may be true; many are far from their families and, being excluded from respectable social contacts, turn to prostitutes for feminine companionship. It is hard to tell whether the immigrants are resented more for their venereal diseases or for their association with white prostitutes.

You can recognize a West Indian community by the gay, tropical blue, red and yellow paint on the facades of the old Victorian houses. No less picturesque are the West Indians themselves. They come off the planes or down the gangplanks in brilliant silk shirts of greens and reds, and impossible straw hats set at jaunty angles. On Saturday nights they have "commercial" houseparties (known as "house rent" parties among Negroes in America), and with their guitars and steel drums soon set the neighborhood athrob with Caribbean rhythms.

Their white neighbors (who don't go to the parties) say they are wild and rowdy. The policemen who do go (at the request of the neighbors) say the coloreds are no noisier than the Irish. And when it comes to criminal activity, fewer colored immigrants are involved, in proportion, than whites.

Prejudice against coloreds in public facilities has led the Labor Government to introduce a race-relations bill reminiscent of the 1964 Civil Rights Act in the U.S. It would outlaw discrimination "on grounds of color, race, or ethnic or national origins" in hotels, restaurants, pubs, theaters and public housing. However, it is conspicuously silent on employment and private housing.

Segregation in the schools has never been tolerated. The Ministry of Education recently directed a circular to local authorities recommending that the proportion of immigrants in any school or class be held to a third of the total, lest "serious strains arise." And in an effort to reassure English parents concerned by the great influx of immigrants Anthony Crosland, the Minister of Education, said: "We want to maintain standards for English children as well as coping with the special problem of the immigrant children."

While Britain's colored leaders welcome the Government's recognition of the color problem, they feel that the proposed antidiscrimination legislation does not go far enough. Some are convinced that the colored immigrant's salvation is in his own hands, and depends on his own enterprise, such as a new savings bank that opened recently to provide immigrant mortgages. The consensus is that the British immigrants could learn a lot from American Negro business and financial leaders who have had to organize their own institutions in order to become independent of prejudiced whites.

A new organization called the Campaign Against Racial Discrimination—CARD—grew out of a conference with the Rev. Dr. Martin Luther King last December. It is headed by David Pitt, a physician from Trinidad, and Mrs. Selma James, Jewish wife of C. L. R. James, a long-time Trinidad Socialist and political writer.

Mrs. James explained that CARD was committed to "co-ordinating the work of existing organizations and acting as a clearing house for information about the fight against discrimination in Britain." She emphasized that it was not an affiliate of Dr. King's Southern Christian Leadership Conference, and was not committed to any philosophies "other than its own." More than 25 immigrant organizations representing Africans, West Indians, Pakistanis, Indians and English sympathizers are already affiliated with CARD.

A more militant organization is the Racial Adjustment Action Society led by Michael De Freitas, a West Indian Negro who was a close friend and admirer of the late Malcolm X. Like Malcolm, Michael (also known as Michael X) is a Muslim and unstinting in his denunciation of the ruling whites. His movement is said to have a membership of around 50,000 and to be growing fast.

Under the influence of R.A.A.S., 500 West Indian, Indian and Pakistani spinners joined in a sit-down strike at a mill in Preston, Lancashire, last May. Many political eyebrows were raised at this unprecedented show of color solidarity among these three diverse racial and religious groups. It could be a sign of the times.

It would appear that the battle has been joined in Britain and that, like the United States, she has come full circle from studied ignorance of a problem to intelligent awareness and, finally, to confrontation and action. Make no mistake about it. White Britain's most desperate fear is that the "dark million" will grow to *two* "dark millions." And then perhaps to *three!* Who can say? But that is not the issue. The issue there as here is whether the Anglo-Saxon with all his social and political sophistication can learn to live comfortably with diversity.

A British columnist complains: "Many want to keep Britain white not because they hate other races, but because they love Britain; not because they despise the strange from distant lands, but because they cherish the familiar in their own." What a strange sound to come from old John Bull, who for 400 years of conquest never seemed to have thought much about it.

9 ► INTEGRATION AND PLURALISM VIEWED FROM HAWAII

J. MILTON YINGER

As the final piece in this section on minorities in various societies, we have chosen an essay by Professor J. Milton Yinger on the relation of ethnic integration to pluralism in Hawaii—one of the new states of American society. This provides us with an opportunity to examine a heterogeneous ethnic situation that subscribes to the American creed. It serves the twofold purpose of concluding our sampling of minority-group life throughout the world and providing us with a transition toward our next section on ethnic differentiation and inequality in American society.

J. Milton Yinger is Professor of Sociology and Anthropology at Oberlin College. In collaboration with his colleague, George E. Simpson, he is the author of the well-known study, Racial and Cultural Minorities: An Analysis of Prejudice and Discrimination. *More recently he has published* Religion, Society, and the Individual. *This article is based on one of a series of lectures given by the author at Town Hall, Los Angeles, and Pomona College with the support of the John Randolph Haynes and Dora Haynes Foundation.*

► IN AN ARTICLE in the *Encyclopedia of Social Science*, Edward Sapir describes in a delightful way the mutually contradictory functions of fashion. In the changing, mobile societies where

From *The Antioch Review* (Winter, 1962–63), 397–410. Copyright 1962 by The Antioch Press, Yellow Springs, Ohio. Reprinted by permission of the author and publisher.

This article first appeared in a modified form in *A Minority Group in American Society* (New York: McGraw-Hill, 1965).

fashion prevails, many persons are torn between a desire to be different, to stand out in the crowd, and a desire to belong, to feel the security of group acceptance. Fashion, which is custom in the guise of departure from custom, is an effort to negotiate between these two desires. A woman is dismayed at the thought of appearing in public in a hat that is not stylish at the given time and place —with a brim too wide or not wide enough, with feathers and dangles when simplicity is the mode. Thus she seeks to belong, to be like the others. The only thing that would dismay her more than excessive difference would be to discover that she is wearing a hat exactly like another's. To put the problem in terms of our theme, she wants integration, but she also wants pluralism. Or, in Sapir's words, she seeks the invigorating but comforting feeling of "adventurous safety."

Lionel Trilling has somewhere expressed the same idea by noting the tension between the desire for non-conformity and the desire to belong securely to a group. We resolve the issue by deciding to be non-conformists together.

Thus the topic of this paper has wide applicability. It is my concern, however, to refer only to its relevance for the study of minority groups. Let us define integration as a situation in which the members of a society, regardless of their race, religion, or national origin, move freely among one another, sharing the same opportunities and the same privileges and facilities on an equal basis. Thus defined, the term carries to some degree a connotation of assimilation: the loss of separating group identities, with differentiation only on an individual basis.

Pluralism, of course, means something quite different. Membership in distinctive ethnic, religious, or cultural groups is accepted and even applauded. Pluralistic societies pride themselves on the freedom granted to diverse groups to preserve their different cultural heritages, support various religions, speak different languages, and develop independent associations. This freedom is qualified only by the requirement of loyalty to the prevailing political and economic systems.

It is scarcely necessary to document the assertion that strong networks of private associations, based on the ideal of pluralism, do not weaken the cohesion of a democratic society but actually strengthen it. Such networks serve both to relate an individual, through groups that are close and meaningful to him, to the large, complex society, and also to protect him from excessive encroachments on his freedom by that society. A totalitarian state begins at once to try to destroy private associations—free trade unions, independent churches, autonomous news agencies, or lingual and cultural groups different from the majority—because they are bulwarks against domination by the state.

If these propositions are correct, they raise serious questions in connection with current trends in the United States: Does a democratic society require integration among its diverse peoples; or are minority groups actually an expression of legitimate pluralism? Does the process of desegregation threaten the balance of integration and pluralism? Has "segregation" been made into a loaded word that supports an attack on a desirable pluralism? Can we agree on the criteria by means of which it is possible to distinguish between undemocratic discrimination and valuable cultural differentiation?

I have no hope of answering these questions definitively, but if I can raise them in a useful way, we may be led to a productive reexamination of the issues involved. Perhaps the basic task is to explore the place of minority groups in complex societies and to distinguish them from pluralistic groups.

Although we shall be concerned only with the United States, the issues involved are international. In fact, excepting only war and the threat of war, perhaps no other topic arouses more interest around the world than the treatment of minority groups. South Africa's policy toward the Bantu minority (this is not a numerical term, of course; the Bantu make up seventy percent of the population of South Africa) is a subject for serious conversations in the United Nations. Problems connected with Algerians in Paris, Jamaicans in London, and Puerto Ricans in New York receive widespread attention in their own and their host countries and throughout the world. Periodic anti-Semitism continues to be used as a weapon by the Soviet government. The Prime Minister of Ghana jails his opponents and denies them civil liberties, thus converting them from a political opposition into a minority group. Communist China carries on an active campaign to stamp out what it calls "regional nationalism"—ethnic, religious, and lingual groups that show less than full enthusiasm for the central government. The dominant Singhalese of Ceylon oppose any separatist or pluralistic tendencies among the Tamil. One could go on. There are few societies in the world today without minority groups —groups that are singled out by the rulers or individuals, or both, for discriminatory treatment. Needless to say, the United States is prominent on the list of such societies, both because of her serious minority problems and because of her position as leader of the free world.

Recently, a great deal has been said about the injury done to America's international position by the undemocratic treatment of minorities. Without wanting at all to minimize that problem, which is exceedingly important, I seek here to explore the consequences of discrimination for the internal life of the nation.

I believe it is no exaggeration to say that how America deals with the minorities question is the most significant internal problem before us at this point in history. It would be overly dramatic to suggest that an issue has its moment on stage, as a democratic society struggles to become a fully unified nation; but a case can be made for reading history that way. We have moved from the struggle for independence, to conflict over universal manhood suffrage and representation, to the battle for unity, to the problem of the place of the worker in an industrial society, to the issue of setting a subsistence floor under the whole economy, to the task of joining the world made suddenly small. None of these issues, particularly, of course, the last, has been resolved; but the institutional framework for their resolution has been invented. And in this context we are coming to see that the full solution of each of the previous great issues depends to an important degree on the wise incorporation of minority groups into national life. This problem, of course, is not new, for we have been a nation of minorities from the beginning. But if our minorities are "Old American," as most of them are, serious attention to their place in society is not old. It would not be much of an exaggeration to say that twenty-five years ago the nation was largely unmindful of what this democratic society had to offer to persons of Negro, Mexican, Indian, or Oriental descent. Yet today the issue presses in on us. Our complacency is broken. A truly massive migration, a revolution of rising expectations—applying not simply to the Congo, to China, or to Egypt, but to our own minorities—war and cold war emphasis on our democratic leadership, and many other forces have made the minorities question unavoidable. Slowly we have developed new ideas and inventions in human relations; but the process is painful. It is not easy to get rid of an old institution.

In the study of the relation of integration to pluralism in the United States, one's attention is easily drawn to Hawaii. Among the images that cross the minds of mainlanders when they think of this cosmopolitan state, perhaps none stands out more vividly than the picture of diverse racial and cultural groups living peacefully side by side—indeed interacting freely with one another—while yet maintaining some sense of their separate identities. How accurate is this picture? What can we learn from the Hawaiian experience that has relevance for other parts of the country? Do we find there both integration and pluralism?

Recently, such questions as these were in my mind as I left for six months of research and teaching in Hawaii. I had never been to the Islands, but I was acquainted with the picture drawn in anthropological and sociological literature, a picture not uncomplicated by travel brochures, novels, and the glowing accounts of friends.

From the mainland, of course, Hawaii performs some subtle functions in our harried lives. It carries some of the load of our erotic imagery—the Polynesian maiden by the limpid pool—and offers some relief from our mingled fears and guilt over tense intergroup relations in the rest of the nation. On the islands these functions are somewhat less obvious. To some degree the imagery has to be pushed back to Tahiti (and in Tahiti, perhaps, to Bora Bora). And the intergroup relations picture is more complicated than it appears at first glance.

I need take little time describing the population of the state. Roughly speaking, it is one-third Caucasian (a group that now includes the Portuguese and most of the Puerto Ricans), one-third Japanese, one-sixth Hawaiian (a royal mixture, for only a small proportion of this one-sixth is full-blooded Polynesian), eleven per cent Filipino, six per cent Chinese, and in small proportion Korean, Samoan, and Negro. It is the only state in the union with a non-Caucasian majority.

To say that these groups live in perfect harmony would be an exaggeration. There are some ethnic prejudices and discriminatory practices, expressed largely in a kind of ethnic hierarchy. I shall not undertake here to offer an explanation for the ranking, except to say that it is based to an important degree on the chronology of migrations to the Islands. Each succeeding wave of migrants, with the exception of mainland Caucasians, has entered the status structure at the bottom. The groups that came to Hawaii earlier, therefore, have moved up to higher status levels in a way similar to the rise of European immigrants in the United

States. Chronology alone, of course, does not account for the present rough correlation between ethnic group and class position. The occupational and class origins of the migrants are involved, and variation in cultural preparation for life in a literate and technologically developed society must be considered. Racial prejudice as such plays only an unimportant part in producing the status patterns.

The result of these and other influences has been to place most Filipinos and Negroes near the bottom at the present time, along with some Puerto Ricans. Equally disadvantaged are most of the full-blooded Hawaiians who struggle with a problem not unlike that of many American Indians. They are unable to live by their aboriginal ways and yet are blocked by their own values and by the biases they meet from participation in the larger society. They feel some resentment, particularly toward the Japanese, who have moved rapidly ahead of them.

Above these groups are the part-Hawaiians and the Japanese, many of whom are moving with great speed up the educational, occupational, and income ladders. The Chinese, earlier migrants to the Islands, are further ahead still. One can occasionally detect a patronizing tone in their references to the Japanese, but on the whole they are friendly toward them. The high status of the Chinese, in turn, is slightly qualified by a touch of "anti-Semitism," for in Hawaii, as in lands of the Western Pacific, the business successes of the Chinese have sometimes led to their identification as "the Jews of the Orient."

The Caucasians (somewhat resentfully, the Haoles) are no longer the clearly dominant group. Most of the large business operations are still in their hands, but the overwhelming power of the Big Five has been dispersed since the war. The average income of the Chinese is now a little higher than that of the Haoles. Statehood has increased the importance of the political process and strengthened the position of the non-Caucasians.

The older generations of some of these groups, particularly the Chinese, Japanese, and Haoles, have taught their children some sense of separation if not of overt prejudice against other groups. This is partly the result of a desire to preserve distinctive cultural heritages and partly an expression of disdain for those who have not yet shown much talent for status improvement in an urban world. At the University of Hawaii, where I secured responses to a lengthy questionnaire from 500 persons, most students feel vaguely guilty about their tendencies toward categorical judgments. They have become self-conscious about their stereotypes; and most of them freely cross racial and ethnic lines in their friendship choices. Yet the results of the ethnocentric aspects of their training are still apparent, with reference, for example, to Filipinos. There are few Filipino students at the University. Although they are now moving up the status ladder, they are relative newcomers to the Islands; most still occupy low status jobs in the plantation areas. Since many of the University students are from Honolulu, they have little direct contact with Filipinos. This does not prevent a large proportion, however, from "knowing" that Filipinos are quick-tempered, revengeful, impulsive, musical, and quarrelsome. These adjectives were selected from a long list more than four times as frequently as one would have expected as a result of random choice. Yet it should also be said that over half of the students would welcome a Filipino as a close friend and less than ten per cent expressed strong hostility.

Although these observations qualify the view that Hawaii is a state almost lacking in intergroup hostility, the total picture remains one of relatively little stereotyping and discrimination. The light animosities that do exist are based more nearly on class differences than on race or ethnic origin. They are projected downward, for the most part, to the lower prestige groups. The Caucasians, however, are not universally applauded. An undertone of resentment is well expressed by the story of Japanese workers, furiously shovelling the hot lava that was pouring down the mountain from a volcano, trying to prevent it from rolling into a village. A Haole observer, who stood nearby to watch the spectacle, remarked to a friend: "That lava looks hot as hell." "Oh, those Haoles," said one Japanese worker to another, "they've been everywhere."

For many Caucasians in Hawaii, racial and ethnic lines are utterly unimportant. But there are patches of exclusiveness and old-fashioned prejudice. Although many professional positions are filled by persons of Oriental descent, there are some high-level business positions not fully open to non-Caucasians. There also remain a few segregated streets and golf, canoe, and business clubs. To some degree these represent the continuation of the old order when the Territory was a plantation with white overlords and Oriental and Polynesian field hands—to put it, of course, all too simply. That order is gone, but not all the ideas have changed.

Some younger Caucasians also defend these segregated patches with a somewhat plaintive feeling as they see how things are going —"we can't let the upstarts take over everything."

One would draw a false picture if he did not include these things. Yet they truly seem incidental. The impressive fact is that the state, only a short way removed from near-feudalism, is very nearly integrated—residentially, economically, educationally. This does not mean there are no class differences, for the class range is as wide in Hawaii as elsewhere. Nor does it imply that ethnic lines do not to some degree correlate with class. It means that categorical barriers against a group simply on grounds of group membership are rare. Even intermarriage is common. Between 1957 and 1959, one-third of all marriages in Hawaii were between persons of different ethnic or racial groups. Thirty-five per cent of the babies during that period were born to couples of mixed racial or ethnic origin. Another generation or two of this and it will be the wise child who knows his own great-grandfathers.

It is also important to emphasize that despite the low level of prejudice and the extent of integration among its many groups, Hawaii has not destroyed the sense of group identity. Perhaps the keenest impression that one gets in the state is the remarkable blend of integration and pluralism. Many Buddhist temples have established Sunday schools, and the children sing "Buddha loves me, this I know." But some Buddhist priests return to Japan to study the classic ways of their particular sect in order to preserve it without contamination in the new land. The University is a blend of all the peoples in the state, although class and ethnic factors are involved in the distribution; yet there are Chinese and Caucasian and Japanese sororities such as would be banned on some mainland campuses. When beauty contest time arrives, there are several candidates from each group who delightfully uphold the value of pluralism, and there are "cosmopolitans" to uphold the value of integration. And then not one but seven winners are chosen. Considering the number of lovely girls in Hawaii, no other arrangement is thinkable.

This, then, is the outstanding fact. Despite patchy discrimination, Hawaii has an amazing amount of unity in diversity. Somehow the state has preserved distinctive groups with visibly different subcultures, yet maintains integration among them. It is perhaps too early to know whether this is a purely temporary state of affairs, the fortunate balance of forces at a moment in time, or a surface phenomenon that hides deep rifts or, oppositely, hides powerful forces toward uniformity. However this may be, the Hawaiian situation at the present can be of great significance to the whole country, not because it will cause us on the mainland to change, but because it shows us a pattern of what can take place. Even though its causal importance is small, Hawaii can be an effective symbol at a time when America is experiencing in acute form the age-old problem of integration versus pluralism. How does a democratic society maintain a sense of unity at the same time that it permits, or perhaps even encourages, diversity? Does the idea of pluralism support some forms of segregation? If not, can distinctive cultures and points of view be maintained to enrich the nation and broaden the public debate? But if so, can certain forms of segregation be prevented from supporting undemocratic discrimination?

This is truly a difficult and paradoxical question. It is not always easy to distinguish between segregation (arbitrary and discriminatory separation) and legitimate pluralism. We want to support pride in one's group, the protection of its contribution to the national life, a meaningful tie to one's parents. Yet these can be related to a separatism that splits a society in serious ways. Let me undertake to state in a formal way a few basic principles that may help us to answer this question: When is a line of distinction undesirable segregation as contrasted with legitimate pluralism?

A line of distinction is undesirable segregation, not legitimate pluralism, when it is related in hidden ways to other lines of separation. A men's club, justified on the grounds that one has a right to pick his friends, often has covert or even obvious significance in politics and the higher job market. To be excluded from the club is to be kept, not just from a friendship circle, but from important economic and political participation. Housing segregation, often justified on much the same grounds, is frequently—one can almost say, I think, universally—related to segregation in schools, parks, and jobs. Above all, housing segregation separates the child from accessibility to the larger culture which he must master if he is to improve his situation.

Let me ask the question again: When does a line of distinction become undesirable segregation; when is it legitimate pluralism? When the separation is systematic or total it is undesirable segregation. It is one thing, for example, for a city to have a few lily-white neighborhoods. It is another thing to have massive ghettoization. That a non-Caucasian finds it difficult or impossible to buy a house in some areas of Makiki Heights in Honolulu may represent an unfortunate snobbishness, but its significance is vastly different from almost total exclusiveness in a city. Patches of segregation may be acceptable in a democracy, in the name of individual freedom (freedom even to be snobbish, however much one may think another impoverishes his life thereby). Systematic segregation, however, which allows minority-group members few escape hatches produces vastly more difficult problems, for the minorities and for the total community.

A third answer to the same question: When the segregation is designed to keep certain groups out, rather than to get or keep persons with certain characteristics in; that is, when it is exclusive rather than inclusive, it is an undesirable separation. Those who defend a white neighborhood do not say we want to get all whites, or all those whites who are of a given educational and economical level, in. They say: we want to keep non-whites out.

And finally, segregation is unacceptable when it is not based on some generally recognized cultural or functional distinction. When engineers are kept out of the AMA or non-Catholics from the Newman Club, no one objects. Exclusion of well-qualified Negroes from the Metropolitan or Cosmos Club in Washington, however, can scarcely be explained in cultural or functional terms.

These principles are neither exhaustive nor mutually exclusive, but together they may be helpful in making the moral decision so critically necessary today. Perhaps they can be summarized in these words: Separation is legitimate in a democracy when it is freely chosen and not coerced, when it does not deny any group access to the mainstreams of the culture while giving others an advantage, when it does not so warp the personalities of some—by denying them hope and the opportunity to learn the skills and values of the society—that not only they but the whole nation suffers.

There is probably substantial, but not complete, agreement among Americans on these principles. There is less agreement on how they can and should be applied to our current situation. It is relatively easy to apply them to Hawaii, where, for a number of reasons associated with the history of the Islands—a story I cannot examine here—their relevance is easy to see. It is vastly more difficult to apply these principles to minority-majority relations on the mainland, where we struggle painfully with problems associated with arbitrary segregation and discrimination based largely on race. There are some, of course, who resist the current process of change because they know that the white man is superior or because they want to preserve some advantage. But there are others who are troubled by the problem of pluralism. They ask, without understanding perhaps, but also without malice: "Why can't Negroes (or, less urgently, other non-whites or ethnically different groups) be content with 'their own' schools, residential areas, churches, and work situation?" And in the background we hear a small but growing number of Negroes—many of them members of the Black Muslims—answer: "Indeed, why not?" Their response is aggressive and divisive, however, not pluralistic. The answer we seek is complicated, but two aspects stand out:

First, the country cannot afford to allow them to "be content with their own . . ." because this implies a continuing separation from the mainstream of American culture. And it is just this separation that has produced such grave problems among Negroes as we face today. The separation began when their ancestors were torn from their homelands, deprived of any chance to maintain their cultures, and had their family patterns disrupted. The disasters of slavery were perpetuated by the semi-feudal system that followed—a system that has only recently been weakened. One of America's important tasks is to bring more Negroes, and the members of other disprivileged groups, into full participation in the total culture. Until we do, we shall continue to suffer such painful consequences of their isolation as a heavy crime rate, the loss of skills, the relative lack of educational disciplines and values, and carelessness with public and private property.

These consequences were kept down, or at least affected the total society less severely, so long as most Negroes were isolated and helpless on the plantation. This has led some persons to argue, with nostalgia, that those were better times. Perhaps they were, if one fears conflict more than he approves justice. To many, however, it seems better to struggle for justice even at the cost of some conflict. This issue is academic in any event, for Negroes have left the farm; they are dreaming the American dream; they are no longer docile. We could not have developed a mobile, industrial, urban society without this happening. Our clear choice now is to bear the costs of frustrating the drive toward equality of colored Americans or to do everything possible to speed their absorption, with full hope and opportunity, into all aspects of national life.

The second aspect of my answer to the question "why cannot they be content with their own . . . ?" is closely related to the first. Negroes do not have a distinctive tradition and culture. They are not a "group" in any meaningful definition of the term. The slavery experience smashed their native heritage but gave them only particles of a new one. As old Americans, they share the full culture, to which they have contributed richly, or they invent a new one. And this we certainly know: An impoverished, frustrated, angry collectivity invents a poor culture. Built on isolation and resentment, it is more likely to be an attack on the established way of life, a contraculture that denies the old values without having anything to put in their place, than a creative new culture.

The continued separation of racial minorities is not pluralism in anything more than a numerical sense. For a group to play a part in a meaningful pluralism, its members must share a viable tradition. It is not enough to be bound together by a distinction which has lost its historic significance; and it certainly is not enough to be identified by an arbitrary distinction that has no basis in cultural history or contemporary choice.

Even the kind of pluralism found in Hawaii today should not be looked upon as sacrosanct. One's cultural and national origins still affect life in significant ways despite a great deal of interaction across ethnic lines. But this may not be the case for many more generations. It is not easy to maintain a style of life, however dignified and valuable at its point of origin, in the vastly different setting of a cosmopolitan city in another society. The decline of distinctive traditions, however, need not be a loss. What would impoverish Hawaii and the whole nation would be the loss of contributions from each of the separate groups to the new and heterogeneous culture of modern society. Perhaps our emphasis should be not on historic pluralism, with its tendency toward rigidity and orientation to the past, but on a *contemporary pluralism*. By that phrase I seek to emphasize the contribution of many historic traditions to a new diverse culture; but I seek also to stress the value of freedom for individuals and new groups to choose from the variety and to create new cultural syntheses.

Hawaii has moved a long way from segregation and prejudice toward historic pluralism. Indeed, the complex intermingling of peoples takes her close to contemporary pluralism. The developments there during the last half century clearly show that diversity of race and culture need not be a barrier to integration. When the tests we have proposed are applied to the lines of separation in Hawaii, these lines are shown to be substantially if not completely legitimate by democratic standards. Separate social groups do not serve, to a strong degree, covert economic and political functions; separation is not massive or total; separate groups tend to be inclusive rather than exclusive; and they are based in most instances on significant cultural differences.

Race relations on the mainland, however, fail the tests we have proposed at almost every point. The separation is an expression, not of pluralism, but of discrimination. The task of a democratic society, therefore, is to make possible and to insist upon, not to prevent, the entry of Negroes and other disprivileged minorities into full participation in American life.

From our various perspectives, it is difficult to see the full complexity of this task. Some liberals, playing down the harm done by segregation and discrimination, make the minority-group members the heroes of the piece while dominant-group members are the villains. There are indeed minority-group heroes—persons of amazing accomplishments in the face of great odds. But there are also heroic white men. Is it not better to see us all in our common humanity—members of a species that has none too good a heart or head—struggling with grievous problems? If the social evils of segregation and discrimination are as monstrous as the liberals say—and I believe they are—then they must create some monstrous facts—as unhappily they do.

The conservative emphasizes those very facts. What *he* fails to see are the social practices and institutions that created and preceded those facts. He takes them simply as given. He sees a school deteriorate, as sometimes happens, when it is flooded with children from impoverished, segregated backgrounds with no educational tradition. He knows the comparative rates of crime. There is no need to deny such facts. But we do need to ask where they came from and how they can be removed. When we see a small Negro or Puerto Rican or Mexican child, we know that destructive patterns are not preordained in him. Yet we are caught in a vicious cycle so long as we use the contemporary facts to justify refusal to change the very conditions which produced those facts. I do not want to minimize the difficulties. Every step toward integration is painful, because we must enlarge the circle of interaction and participation of persons who have not—for want of opportunity—absorbed the full range of the community's values. But it is futile to say: pull yourself up by your own bootstraps and then we will integrate. The social steps have to be taken first, as an act of faith, if you will.

Happily, the act of faith is supported by many facts. Many minority-group persons, caught in deeply disprivileged circumstances, have nevertheless broken out, with the support of an exceptional parent, a friendly businessman, a superior mind, a religious faith—the sources of such an accomplishment are numerous. So deep is the commitment of most minority-group members to American values that every small gain yields surprising dividends. This may not long be the case. In the midst of a world-wide struggle for freedom, their hopes have been aroused as never before. A continued frustration of their aspirations will lead to an increase in extremist views and resentful actions. This is the time to move decisively.

III ETHNIC DIFFERENTIATION AND INEQUALITY IN AMERICAN SOCIETY

THE PREVIOUS section made abundantly clear the world-wide distribution of hostility and the growing struggle for power between ethnic dominant and minority groups. In each instance of ethnic differentiation and inequality, the ramifications are extensive, ranging far beyond the immediate participants. Aside from the self-evident social repercussions that weaken and divide a society, minority problems—especially in the United States, where democratic ideals and beliefs form the American creed—provoke political controversy and stimulate ethical and moral dilemmas. All Americans may be equal, but it seems that some are in fact "more equal" than others.

It was in this fashion that Gunnar Myrdal, the eminent Swedish social scientist, decided in 1944 to conceptualize American society's problem in Negro-white relations as "an American dilemma"—a conflict in values. True, there is an American creed—a system of general ideals, beliefs and norms governing human relations that finds its fullest voice in the Declaration of Independence, the Preamble to the Constitution and the Bill of Rights. Moreover, the American Judaeo-Christian heritage embodies such concepts as the essential dignity of the individual, the fundamental equality of all, and the inalienable rights of every person to freedom, justice and fair opportunity. But in conflict with this American creed there is an unofficial but nonetheless powerful second creed implicit in secondary legislation and explicit in the writings of the philosophers of racism and ancestor worship. According to this creed, America belongs to the "real" Americans—the "Wasps" (White Anglo-Saxon Protestants)—and not to Negroes, Puerto Ricans, Jews, and most foreigners. It is in such issues as the civil rights movement and the drive to liberalize immigration legislation that the various creeds come into sharpest conflict.

In its role as a leading world power, the United States has learned that this dilemma generates very serious international as well as internal criticism. Rivals of this society in the power struggle have always been quick to seize upon American minority problems and to exploit them to their own advantage.

A rare comprehensive view of American ethnic groups is offered as the first article of this section by Professor Nathan Glazer, one of the most eminent sociological specialists in ethnic relations and problems. His view of ethnic integration and pluralism should be compared with Professor J. Milton Yinger's in the last piece of the previous section.

10► THE PEOPLES OF AMERICA

NATHAN GLAZER

► THE HISTORY of ethnicity and ethnic self-consciousness in this country has moved in waves; we are now in a trough between two crests, and the challenge is to describe the shape and form of the next crest. That there will be another crest it is hardly possible to doubt. Since the end of European mass immigration to this country forty years ago we have waited for the subsidence of ethnic self-consciousness, and often announced it, and it has returned again and again. But each time it has returned in so different a form that one could well argue it was not the same thing returning at all, that what we saw was not the breakthrough of the consciousness of common origin and community among the groups that made America, but rather that ethnicity was being used as a cover for some other more significant force, which was borrowing another identity.

During the early years of the depression, ethnicity withdrew as a theme in American life. Both those who had urged the "Americanization" of the immigrant and the creation of "cultural pluralism" now had more important concerns. Immigration was matched by a counter-emigration back to the countries of origins; one episode of American history it seemed had come to an end. Then with the rise of Hitler the ethnic texture of American life began to reassert itself. First Jews; then Germans; then Czechs, Poles, Italians, and even the "old Americans," remembering their origins in England, all were spurred to action and organization by Hitler and the great war that he began. Samuel Lubell has traced how the support for

From *The Nation*, 201, 8 (September 20, 1965), 137–41.

This article subsequently appeared in *The State of The Nation* (Englewood Cliffs, N.J.: Prentice-Hall, Inc.). Reprinted by permission of the author and publisher.

Franklin D. Roosevelt in the great cities shifted from class to ethnicity, as the international conflict developed and various groups responded to, or against, Roosevelt as he displayed his sentiments and allegiances.

In 1945 this great crest began to withdraw. True, there was the continuing impact on ethnic groups of the confrontation with Russia and communism, but with the passage of time this began to lose its ethnic coloration. Catholics in general were more anti-Communist than others, Poles still more so, Jews much less so. But the international conflict was so sharply colored by ideology rather than national antagonism, that with the passage of time it no longer served to set group against group (as it had in the Hitler years). Soviet opposition to Israel and Soviet anti-Semitism; the rise of a measure of cautious Polish independence; de-Stalinization in Russia—all these developments softened the sharp conflicts which had created a powerful resonance among immigrants and their children in this country.

The Eisenhower period marked thus a new trough, and it was possible to conclude that the workings of the melting pot had been retarded only slightly by the Neolithic tribal ferocity of Hitler and the counter-reactions he evoked. But now a new wave began to gather force, a wave that had nothing to do with international affairs. Will Herberg interpreted the increased religious activity of the postwar years as a half-embarrassed means of maintaining group identity in a democratic society which did not look with favor on the long-continued maintenance of sharply distinguished ethnic groups. The "triple melting pot" theory of Ruby Jo Reeves Kennedy, along with her data on intermarriage, suggested that old ethnic lines were being replaced by new religious lines. The chameleon-like force of ancestral connection, one could argue, was being transmuted into the forms of religion. Those who were concerned for religion could of course take no comfort in this analysis, even if the religious denominations benefited from higher collections and new buildings. If our major religions are replacing ethnic groups, one could not yet herald the creation of a homogeneous and undivided American group consciousness in America, but at least our divisions no longer paralleled those of old Europe —something which had deeply troubled our leaders from Washington to Woodrow Wilson—but the more acceptable divisions of religion, which ostensibly had an older and more respectable lineage and justification. Thus, if Herberg could still discern the forces of ethnic identity at work in the new clothes of religious denomi-nationalism, at least they no longer expressed themselves openly.

But once again an unabashed ethnicity reasserted itself, in the campaign of John F. Kennedy and his brief Presidency. In his cabinet, for the first time, there sat a Jew of East European origin, an Italian American, a Polish American. If the Jews were no longer being appointed primarily to represent a group, there was no question that this was the explanation for the appointment of an Italian American and a Polish American. The Catholic President was reminded by everyone that he was an Irish President. He was the first President to be elected from an immigrant group that had suffered discrimination and prejudice, and that still remem-bered it—and those of us from later immigrant groups, who had experienced the lordly position of the Irish in the cities of the East, discovered only with some surprise that the Irish did re-member their days as a degraded minority. Those who stemmed from the new immigration now realized that the Irish shared very much the same feelings of resentment at past treatment, of gratification in present accomplishment and recognition. But the old Americans too responded to the realization that they had an Irish President, as well as a Democratic, Catholic, and intellectual President. Certainly it is hard to explain otherwise the mutual antagonism that rapidly sprang up between the new Adminis-tration and such a large part of the big business establishment, the seat of the old Americans, the "WASP" power. The Adminis-tration's policies were not antagonistic to big business. There was of course the President's violent response to the steel price rise, but was not that, too, a reflection—at least in part—of old ethnic images and conflicts? No one who spoke to anyone close to those events could doubt it.

I would suggest a gentle recession, if not a trough, in the period since President Kennedy's assassination. Two events to my mind suggest the retreat of an open and congratulatory ethnic self-assertiveness, and they are related. One is the new concern with the poor, which complementarily marks all the non-poor as mem-bers of the same group, with the same social task laid upon them; and the second is the steady radicalization of the civil rights movement and Negro opinion, and this increasingly places all the whites in the same category, without distinction. And once again a symbolic political event marks the recession of ethnic self-con-sciousness: the accession of President Johnson, who, like President

Eisenhower, comes from a part of America that was relatively unaffected by European immigration.

I have marked recurrent crests and troughs of ethnic self-consciousness by political events, but the political events have of course paralleled social events. The crisis of the depression erased for the moment ethnic memories and allegiances. The agony of the European peoples reawakened it. Prosperity and the rapid rise of the new immigrant groups to upper working-class and middle-class status again reduced their sense of difference. The security that came with long sustained prosperity made it possible for the descendants of despised immigrants to again take pleasure in their origins and their differences. One of the less observed effects of affluence is that it leads people to their real or hopefully reconstructed origins. In Europe and among Americans who look to the European upper classes this may mean acquiring crests, forebears, and antiques. Among the American descendants of European peasants and artisans, it meant, in a surprising number of cases, a new interest in the culture of the old country. But in the most recent period, the rise of the joint problems of poverty and the assimilation of the Negro raises a new set of questions. For the moment, ethnic self-assertiveness is in eclipse and even in bad odor. And the eclipse is directly related to the new problems.

Michael Harrington put the matter quite directly, when he said in a recent speech that the accumulated wisdom of the great European immigrant groups in this country has become irrelevant, for it will not help the current poor and it will not help the Negroes. In varying degrees, we are hearing the same from Louis Lomax, from James Baldwin, from Nat Hentoff, and from other supporters and defenders of Negro militancy. Inevitably the next wave of ethnic self-consciousness must reflect one of the most remarkable and least expected consequences of the Negro revolution—the growing estrangement between European ethnic groups and the Negroes. Its beginnings were studied by Samuel Lubell in the early postwar period, and we have seen the estrangement develop to the point where the fear of the white backlash—and this meant generally the backlash from recent white immigrant groups in the cities—became one of the major issues of the Goldwater-Johnson campaign. The separation, first the barest of lines, has deepened through conflicts over the adoption and administration of fair employment laws, fair housing laws, measures to combat *de facto* school segregation. The patterns under which and through which the European ethnic groups have lived—the trade unions and branches of industry dominated by one or a few ethnic groups, the ethnically concentrated neighborhood with its distinctive schools and churches and organizations—all have come under increasing attack. And thus the distinctive social patterns of the North and West, which the immigrant and the ethnic groups helped create, are now being slowly but surely turned into a Southern-like confrontation of white and black. The varied, more balanced, and more creative ethnic conflicts of the North are now in danger of being transformed into the monolithic confrontation of the South.

In the South, Northern variety never developed. One great division dominated and smothered all others, the division between black and white. In this area, the European immigrant of the later 19th and early 20th century never penetrated. All he had to offer generally was unskilled labor, and in the South the unskilled labor was the work of Negroes. The white immigrant laborer refused to enter an area in which the laborer was degraded not only by his work but by a caste system, where wages were low, and racial conflict hindered trade union development and social legislation. The immigrant worked in the parts of the country where work had greater respect and was better rewarded. If he entered the South, it was more often as a merchant than as a worker.

But in the Northern cities, where almost half the Negroes now live, it was not inevitable that the same line of division should be imported from the South. The entry of the Negro into the Northern cities in great numbers during and after World War I and again during and after World War II raised a critical question: was he the last of the great immigrant groups? Would his experience parallel that of the Irish and the Poles and the Jews who had arrived as exploited and unskilled workers and had moved upward, at varying speeds, into middle-class occupations, the professions, business? How would those who were themselves children and grandchildren of recent immigrant waves view him? How would he view himself and his prospects? Against whom would he measure his circumstances? And would the inevitable conflicts between the poorer and the more prosperous resemble the conflicts between Yankees and Irish, Irish and Italians—or would they take the form of the far more deadly and longer established conflict between black and white? I feel the answers are still not given. They will be shaped both by the established ethnic groups and the

Negro migrant. But I fear the answer from both sides will be . . . yes, the Negro is different.

It is impossible for the history of ethnic self-consciousness to escape from the impact of Negro urban migration, for all the waves of immigration have affected the self-consciousness of waves that came before. The old Americans reacted to the first great waves of immigrants of the forties and fifties of the 19th century with an exaggerated sense of their own high status and aristocratic connections. The early immigrants from each group withdrew from later immigrants, but were generally forced together with them because the old Americans imposed a common identity on them. The history of ethnic self-consciousness, it is clear, has not worked itself out independently of social and economic and political events. If anything, it has been a reaction to these events: the rise of one group, the occupancy of the bottom by another, the political conflicts of Europe, the sequence of immigration in each town and city and section. All these have helped mold ethnic self-consciousness, and its reflection in social activity, in political choice, in economic history.

But on the whole this self-consciousness, whatever its stages, has been marked by optimism and hope. I have described the Kennedy mood among the more recent and more sharply defined American ethnic groups as self-congratulation. Indeed it was that, though each of the groups might have found some basis for resentment rather than pride. The Irish had reached the heights of political success, and the Jews were prosperous, but both were still in large measure excluded from the pinnacles of economic power —the great banks, insurance companies, corporations. The Italians still were remarkably poorly represented in high political posts, and had a much smaller share in every establishment—economic, political, cultural—than the Jews, who had come at the same time and were less numerous. The Poles were even poorer. And yet such invidious comparisons—which the census made clear—were rarely made. All the new groups seem to have escaped from the difficult period of second generation self-depreciation and exaggerated Americanism. All seemed to wear ethnic connection with self-assurance. Certainly the growing prosperity of Europe, the increased trade with Europe, the wide acceptance of its consumer goods here, the large influence of European culture, all made the acceptance of one's ethnic connections easier—for by doing so, after all, one was no longer acknowledging poor relations. It was

fascinating to remark upon the change in the image of the homeland among the more self-conscious and better educated descendants of the immigrants. Ireland was no longer the home of pota-
toes and cabbage, but of Joyce and the Abbey theatre, good Irish
whiskey and Georgian architecture, horse-racing and tweeds. Italy
became the land of chic, while Israel and Poland, if they could not
compete in the arts of affluent consumption, became now para-
gons of political independence and heroism. Every group fortunately found something to admire in the old (or new) country,
and found it easy to acknowledge the connection that had once
been obscured.

But if this characterizes the most recent mood of ethnic self-
consciousness, it is now challenged by the new Negro militancy
and the theory on which it is reared. The self-congratulatory
expressions are strangled in the throat. For a while, in the forties
and fifties, when Jewish and Catholic groups worked effectively
with Urban League and NAACP, with Negroes proud of having
achieved middle-class status, the older ethnic groups and their
representatives could present themselves as models and elder
brothers—in community organization, group defense work, in cultural and political activity. But the radical Negro mood, and its
growing reflection among intellectuals, turns all whites into exploiters, with old Americans, old immigrants, and new immigrants
lumped together. The success of the ethnic groups—limited as it is
for many—now becomes a reproach. Their very history, which
each group has been so busy writing and reconstructing, now
becomes an unspoken (and sometimes spoken) criticism of the
Northern Negro. Both sides see it, and rush to explain themselves.

What after all is the history of the American ethnic groups but
a history of group and individual adaptation to difficult circumstances? All the histories move in the same patterns. The immigrants arrive; they represent the poorest and least educated and
most oppressed of their countries in Europe and Asia. They arrive
ignorant of our language and customs, exploited and abused. They
huddle together in the ghettos of the cities, beginning slowly to
attend to their most immediate needs—organization for companionship, patterns of self-aid in crisis, churches for worship, schools
to maintain the old culture. American society and government is
indifferent to their needs and desires; they are allowed to do what
they wish, but neither hindered nor aided. In this amorphous
setting where no limits are set to group organization, they gradu-

ally form a community. Their children move through the public schools and perhaps advance themselves—if not, it may be the grandchildren who do. The children are embarrassed by the poverty and ignorance of the parents. Eventually they, or the grandchildren, learn to accept their origins as poverty and ignorance are overcome. They move into the spheres of American life in which many or all groups meet—the larger economy, politics, social life, education. Eventually many of the institutions created by the immigrants become a hindrance rather than a necessity; some are abandoned, some are changed. American society in the meantime has made a place for and even become dependent on some of these institutions, such as old-age homes and hospitals, adoption services and churches—these survive and perhaps flourish. More and more of these institutions become identified with the religious denomination, rather than the ethnic group as such.

Note one element of this history: demand on government plays a small role; response by government plays a small role. There is one great exception, the labor movement. But even the labor movement, which eventually found support in public law and government administrative structure, began its history as voluntary organization in the amorphous structure of American society, and achieved its first triumphs without, or even against, government.

Does this history have any meaning for the American Negro? This is the question that Jews and Japanese, Irish and Italians, Poles and Czechs ask themselves. Some new immigrant groups—Puerto Ricans and Mexicans—think it does have a meaning for them. They try to model their institutions on those of earlier immigrant groups. They show the same uncertainties and confusions over what to do with the culture and language they have brought with them. The militant Negro and his white allies passionately deny the relevance or even the truth of this history. It is white history; as white history it is also the history of the exploitation of the Negro, of the creation of privilege on the basis of his unpaid and forced labor. It is not history he can accept as having any meaning for him. His fate, he insists, has been far more drastic and frightful than any other, and neither Irish famines nor Jewish pogroms make the members of these groups brothers in understanding. The hatred with which he is looked upon by whites, he believes, has nothing in common with the petty prejudices that European immigrant groups have met. And the America of today, in which he makes his great and desperate effort for full equality, he asserts, has little in common with the America of mass immigration.

A subtle intervention of government in every aspect of social life, of economy, of culture, he insists, is necessary now to create justice. Every practice must now be scrutinized anew for its impact on this totally unique and incomparable group in American life. The neighborhood school, the civil service system, the personnel procedures of our corporations, the practices of small business, the scholarship systems of our states, the composition and character of our churches, the structure of neighborhood organization, the practices of unions—all, confronted with this shibboleth, fail. The Negro has not received his due, and the essence of all of them is therefore discrimination and exclusion, and the defense of privilege. It is no wonder that ethnic self-consciousness, after its brief moment of triumph, after its legitimization in American life, now turns upon itself in confusion. After all, it is these voluntary churches, organizations, hospitals, schools, and businesses that have become the pride of ethnic groups, and the seat of whatever distinctiveness they possess. It is by way of this participation that they have become part of the very fabric of American life. But the fabric is now challenged. And looked at from another perspective, the Negro perspective, the same structure that defends some measure of uniqueness by the same token defends some measure of discrimination and exclusion.

It is impossible for the ethnic groups in America, who have already moved through so many protean forms, to be unaffected by the civil rights revolution. For this raises the question of the status of the largest of American minority groups, the one most closely bound up with American history from its very beginnings. Chinese and Japanese, perhaps Puerto Ricans and Mexican Americans can accept the patterns of development and gradual assimilation into American society that are exhibited in the history of the great European immigrant groups. For a while, some of us who studied this history and saw in its variety and flexibility some virtues for a mass, industrial society, which suppresses variety and flexibility in so many areas, hoped that the American Negro, as he entered the more open environments of Northern cities, could also move along the paths the European immigrant groups had followed.

We now wonder whether this hope was illusory. Whether it was the infection of Europeans with the virus of American racial prejudice; or the inability to confine the direct and violent conflict in the South; or the impact of slavery and Southern experience on the American Negro—it is clear, whatever the causes, that for one of the major groups in American life, the idea of pluralism, which has supported the various developments of other groups, has become a mockery. Whatever concrete definition we give to pluralism, it means a limitation of government power, a relatively free hand for private and voluntary organizations to develop their own patterns of worship, education, social life, residential concentration, and even their distinctive economic activity. All of these inevitably enhance the life of one group; from the perspective of the American Negro they are inevitably exclusive and discriminatory.

The general ideas that have justified the development of the ethnic group in America have never been too well explicated. We have tended to obscure the inevitable conflicts between individual group interest and national interest, even when they have occurred, rather than set down sharp principles to regulate the ethnic groups. If an ethnic group interest clashed with a national interest, we have been quite ruthless and even extreme in overriding the group interest. Thus two World Wars radically diminished the scale and assertiveness of German-American group life. But we have never fully developed what is permitted and what is not. Now a new national interest is becoming defined—the final liquidation of Negro separation, in all areas of our life: the economic, the social, the cultural, the residential. In every area, Negro separation, regardless of its causes, is seen as unbearable by Negroes. Inevitably this must deeply mark the future development of American ethnic groups, whose continuance contributes, in some measure, to this separation. Recently in this country there has been a positive attitude to ethnic distinctiveness. Oscar Handlin and others have argued that it does not divide the nation or weaken it in war; rather it helps integrate the immigrant groups and adds a rich strand of variety to American civilization. Now a new question arises: what is its effect on the Negro?

Perhaps, ironically, the final homogenization of the American people, the creation of a common nationality replacing all other forms of national connection, will now come about because of the need to guarantee the integration of the Negro. But I believe the group character of American life is too strongly established and fits too many individual needs to be so completely suppressed. Is it not more likely that as Negro demands are in varying measure met, the Negro too will accept the virtues of our complex society, in which separation is neither forbidden nor required, but rather tolerated? Perhaps the American Negro will become another ethnic group, accepted by others and accepting himself.

11 ▸ RACE, ETHNICITY, AND THE ACHIEVEMENT SYNDROME

BERNARD C. ROSEN

Any intelligent observer easily detects significant differentials in upward social mobility between American ethnic groups, but it is no easy matter to provide satisfactory explanations. In the following report of his research findings, Professor Bernard Rosen points out that the disparity between ethnic groups in rates of vertical mobility can be viewed, in part, as a function of their dissimilar psychological and cultural orientations toward achievement.

Convergence of historical and ethnographic data suggests that group differences in motivation, values and educational-occupational aspirations existed before immigration to the United States. The origins of these differences were in dissimilar socialization practices, traditions and life situations. Professor Rosen's current attitudinal and personality data reveal that these differences still exist for the most part.

▸ THE UPWARD mobility rates of many racial and ethnic groups in America have been markedly dissimilar when compared with one another and with some white Protestant groups. For example, among the "new immigration" groups which settled primarily in the Northeast, the Greeks and Jews have attained middle class status more rapidly than most of their fellow immigrants. In general, ethnic groups with Roman Catholic affiliation have moved up less rapidly than non-Catholic groups. And the vertical

From *American Sociological Review*, 24, 1 (February, 1959), 47–60. Reprinted by permission of the author and publisher.

mobility of Negroes, even in the less repressive environment of the industrial Northeast, has been relatively slow.[1]

The reasons offered to explain these differences vary with the group in question. Thus, differences in group mobility rates have sometimes been interpreted as a function of the immigrant's possession of certain skills which were valuable in a burgeoning industrial society. In this connection, there is some evidence that many Jews came to America with occupational skills better suited to urban living than did their fellow immigrants. Social mobility seems also to be related to the ability of ethnic and racial groups to organize effectively to protect and promote their interests. Both the Greeks and the Jews were quicker to develop effective community organizations than were other immigrants who had not previously faced the problem of adapting as minority groups. For the Jews, this situation grew out of their experiences with an often hostile gentile world; for the Greeks, out of their persecutions by the Turks. The repressiveness of the social structure or the willingness of the dominant groups to permit others to share in the fruits of a rich, expanding economy has also been given as an explanation of differential group mobility. This argument has merit in the case of Negroes, but it is less valid in a comparison of the Jews with Southern Italians or French-Canadians. Finally, it has been suggested that groups with experiences in small town or urban environments were more likely to possess the cultural values appropriate to achievement in American society than were ethnic and racial groups whose cultures had been formed in rural, peasant surroundings. Here, again, it has been noted that many Jews and a small but influential number of Levantine Greeks had come from small towns or cities, while most of the Roman Catholic immigrants from Eastern and Southern Europe (and Southern Negroes before their migration to the North) came from rural communities.[2]

As valid as these explanations may be—and we believe they have merit—they overlook one important factor: *the individual's psychological and cultural orientation towards achievement;* by which we mean his psychological need to excel, his desire to enter the competitive race for social status, and his initial possession of or willingness to adopt the high valuation placed upon personal achievement and success which foreign observers from Tocqueville to Laski have considered an important factor in the remarkable mobility of individuals in American society.

Three components of this achievement orientation are particularly relevant for any study of social mobility. The first is a psychological factor, *achievement motivation*, which provides the internal impetus to excel in situations involving standards of excellence. The second and third components are cultural factors, one consisting of certain *value orientations* which implement achievement-motivated behavior, the other of culturally influenced *educational-vocational aspiration levels*. All three factors may affect status achievement; one moving the individual to excel, the others organizing and directing his behavior towards high status goals. This motive-value-aspiration complex has been called the *Achievement Syndrome*.[3]

It is the basic hypothesis of this study that many racial and ethnic groups were not, and are not now, alike in their orientation toward achievement, particularly as it is expressed in the striving for status through social mobility, and that this difference in orientation has been an important factor contributing to the dissimilarities in their social mobility rates. Specifically, this paper examines the achievement motivation, values, and aspirations of members of six racial and ethnic groups. Four of these are "new immigration" ethnic groups with similar periods of residence in this country who faced approximately the same economic circumstances upon arrival: the French-Canadians, Southern Italians, Greeks, and East European Jews. The fifth is the Negro group in the Northeast, the section's largest "racial" division. The last, and in some ways the most heterogeneous, is the native-born white Protestant group. Contributing to the fact that these six groups have not been equally mobile, we suggest, are differences in the three components of the achievement syndrome: their incidence is highest among Jews, Greeks, and white Protestants, lower among Southern Italians and French-Canadians, and lowest among Negroes.

Research Procedure

The data were collected from a purposive sample of 954 subjects residing in 62 communities in four Northeastern states: 51 in Connecticut, seven in New York, three in New Jersey, and one in Massachusetts. The subjects are 427 pairs of mothers and their sons; 62 pairs are French-Canadians, 74 are Italians, 47 are Greeks, 57 are Jews, 65 are Negroes, and 122 are white Protestants. Most subjects were located through the aid of local religious, ethnic, or service organizations, or through their residence in neighborhoods believed to be occupied by certain groups. The subject's group membership was determined ultimately by asking the mothers in personal interviews to designate their religion and land of national origin. The interviewers, all of whom were upper-classmen enrolled in two sociology classes, were instructed to draw respondents from various social strata.[4] The respondent's social class position was determined by a modified version of Hollingshead's Index of Social Position, which uses occupation and education of the main wage-earner, usually the father, as the principal criteria of status. Respondents were classified according to this index into one of five social classes, from the highest status group (Class I) to the lowest (Class V).[5] Most of the mothers and all of the sons are native-born, the sons ranging in age from eight to 14 years (the mean age is about 11 years). There are no significant age differences between the various groups.

Two research instruments were a projective test to measure achievement motivation and a personal interview to obtain information on achievement value orientations and related phenomena. Achievement motivation has been defined by McClelland and his associates as a redintegration of affect aroused by cues in situations involving standards of excellence. Such standards usually are imparted to the individual by his parents, who impart the understanding that they expect him to perform well in relation to these standards of excellence, rewarding him for successful endeavor and punishing him for failure. In time he comes to have similar expectations of himself when exposed to situations involving standards of excellence and re-experiences the affect associated with his earlier efforts to meet these standards. The behavior of people with high achievement motivation is characterized by persistent striving and general competitiveness.

Using a Thematic Apperception Test, McClelland and his associates have developed a method of measuring the achievement motive that involves identifying and counting the frequency with which imagery about evaluated performance in competition with a standard of excellence appears in the thoughts of a person when he tells a brief story under time pressure. This imagery now can be identified objectively and reliably. The test assumes that the more the individual shows indications of connections between evaluated performance and affect in his fantasy, the greater the degree to which achievement motivation is part of his personality.[6] This projective test, which involves showing the subject four ambiguous pictures and asking him to tell a story about each, was given privately and individually to the sons in their homes. Their imaginative responses to the pictures were scored by two judges; the Pearson product moment correlation between the two scorings was .86, an estimate of reliability similar to those reported in earlier studies using this measure.

Following the boys' testing, their mothers were interviewed privately. The interview guide included several standardized questions designed to indicate the mother's achievement value orientations, her educational and vocational aspirations for her son, and the degree to which she had trained him to be independent.

Findings and Interpretation

Achievement Motivation. Empirical studies have shown that achievement motivation is generated by (at least) two kinds of socialization practices: (1) *achievement training,* in which the parents, by imposing standards of excellence upon tasks, by setting high goals for their child, and by indicating their high evaluation of his competence to do a task well, communicate to him that they expect evidences of high achievement; (2) *independence training,* in which the parents indicate to the child that they expect him to be self-reliant and, at the same time, grant him relative autonomy in decision-making situations where he is given both freedom of action and responsibility for success or failure. Essentially, achievement training is concerned with getting the child to *do things well,* while independence training seeks to teach him to do things *on his own.* Although both kinds often occur together and each contributes to the development of achievement motivation, achievement training is the more important of the two.[7]

Two bodies of information—ethnographic studies of the "old world" or non-American culture and recent empirical investigations of the training practices used by Americans of various ethnic backgrounds—strongly indicate that the six groups examined here, in the past and to some extent today, differ with respect to the degree to which their members typically emphasize achievement and independence training. Ethnic differences in these matters were first studied by McClelland, who noted that the linkage between independence training and achievement motivation established by recent empirical studies suggests an interesting parallel with Weber's classic description of the characterological consequences of the Protestant Reformation. Weber reasoned, first, concerning salvation, that an important aspect of the Protestant theological position was the shift from reliance on an institution (the Church) to a greater reliance upon self; it seemed reasonable to assume that Protestant parents who prepared their children for increased self-reliance in religious matters would also tend to stress the necessity for the child to be self-reliant in other aspects of his life. Secondly, Weber's description of the personality types produced by the Reformation is strikingly similar to the picture of the person with high achievement motivation; for example, the hardworking, thrifty Protestant working girl, the Protestant entrepreneur who "gets nothing out of his wealth for himself except the irrational sense of having done his job well." [8]

The hypothesis deduced from these observations was put to the test by McClelland, who questioned white Protestant, Irish-Catholic, Italian-Catholic, and Jewish mothers about their independence training practices. He found that Protestants and Jews favored earlier independence training than Irish and Italian Catholics.[9] These findings are supported and enlarged upon by data derived from questioning the 427 mothers in this study about their training practices. The mothers were asked, "At what age do you expect your son to do the following things?" and to note the appropriate items from the following list (taken from the Winterbottom index of training in independence and mastery):[10]

1. To be willing to try things on his own without depending on his mother for help.
2. To be active and energetic in climbing, jumping, and sports.
3. To try hard things for himself without asking for help.
4. To be able to lead other children and assert himself in children's groups.
5. To make his own friends among children of his own age.
6. To do well in school on his own.
7. To have interests and hobbies of his own. To be able to entertain himself.
8. To do well in competition with other children. To try hard to come out on top in games and sports.
9. To make decisions like choosing his own clothes or deciding to spend his money by himself.

An index of independence training was derived by summing the ages for each item and taking the mean figure. The data in Table 1 show that the Jews expect earliest evidence of self-reliance from their children (mean age 6.83 years), followed by the Protestants (6.87), Negroes (7.23), Greeks (7.67), French Canadians (7.99), and Italians (8.03). Both primary sources of variation—ethnicity and social class—are significant at the .01 level.

Data on the relative emphasis which racial and ethnic groups place upon achievement *training* (that is, imposing standards of excellence upon tasks, setting high goals for the child to achieve, and communicating to him a feeling that his parents evaluate highly his task-competence) are much more difficult to obtain. Achievement training as such, in fact, is rarely treated in studies of ethnic socialization practices. Hence, inferences about achievement training were drawn primarily from ethnographic and histor-

Table 1. Mean Age of Independence Training by Ethnicity and Social Class

| Ethnicity | Social Class * | | | $\bar{x}$ | N |
	I-II-III	IV	V		
French-Canadian	8.00	7.69	8.08	7.99	62
Italian	6.79	7.89	8.47	8.03	74
Greek	6.33	8.14	7.52	7.67	47
Jew	6.37	7.29	6.90	6.83	57
Negro	6.64	6.98	7.39	7.23	65
Protestant	5.82	7.44	7.03	6.87	122
$\bar{x}$	6.31	7.64	7.59		

Ethnicity: $F = 8.55$ $P < .01$
Social Class: $F = 21.48$ $P < .001$
Ethnicity $\times$ Class: $F = 6.25$ $P < .01$

* The three-class breakdown was used in an earlier phase of the analysis. An examination of the means of cells using a four-class breakdown revealed no change in pattern and did not warrant new computations.

ical materials, which are usually more informative about achievement as such than about relevant socialization practices.

The groups about which the most is known concerning achievement training, perhaps, are the Protestants, the Jews, and, to a lesser extent, the Greeks. These groups traditionally have stressed excellence and achievement. In the case of the Protestants, this tradition can be located in the Puritan Ethic with its concept of work as a "calling" and the exhortation that a job be done well. Of course, not all Protestants would be equally comfortable with this tradition; it is much more applicable, for example, to Presbyterians and Quakers than to Methodists and Baptists. Nonetheless, the generally longer residence of Protestants in this country makes it probable that they would tend to share the American belief that children should be encouraged to develop their talents and to set high goals, possibly a bit beyond their reach. The observation that Jews stress achievement training is commonplace. Zborowski and Herzog note the strong tendency among *shtetl* Jews to expect and to reward evidences of achievement even among very young children. The image of the Jewish mother as eager for her son to excel in competition and to set ever higher goals for himself is a familiar one in the literature of Jewish family life.[11] Careful attention to

Table 2. Mean Achievement Motivation Scores
by Ethnicity and Social Class

	Social Class					
Ethnicity	I-II	III	IV	V	$\bar{x}$	N
French-Canadian	10.00	10.64	8.78	7.75	8.82	62
Italian	8.86	12.81	7.54	10.20	9.65	74
Greek	9.17	12.13	10.40	8.75	10.80	47
Jew	10.05	10.41	10.94	11.20	10.53	57
Negro	11.36	9.00	8.23	6.72	8.40	65
Protestant	11.71	10.94	9.39	7.31	10.11	122
$\bar{x}$	10.55	11.26	9.01	8.32		

Ethnicity: $F = 1.23$ $P > .05$
Social Class: $F = 5.30$ $P < .005$
Ethnicity × Class: $F = 1.32$ $P > .05$

standards of excellence in the Greek home is stressed by the parents: children know that a task which is shabbily performed will have to be re-done. In this country, the Greek is exhorted to be "a credit to his group." Failure to meet group norms is quickly perceived and where possible punished; while achievement receives the approbation of the entire Greek community.

Among the Southern Italians (the overwhelming majority of American-Italians are of Southern Italian extraction), French-Canadians, and Negroes the tradition seems to be quite different. More often than not they came from agrarian societies or regions in which opportunities for achievement were strictly curtailed by the social structure and where habits of resignation and fatalism in the face of social and environmental frustrations were psychologically functional. Under such conditions children were not typically exhorted to be achievers or urged to set their sights very high. Of course, children were expected to perform tasks, as they are in most societies, but such tasks were usually farm or self-caretaking chores, from which the notion of competition with standards of excellence is not excluded, but is not ordinarily stressed. As for communicating to the child a sense of confidence in his competence to do a task well, there is some evidence that in the father-dominant Italian and French-Canadian families, pronounced concern with the child's ability might be perceived as a threat to the father.[12]

On the whole, the data indicate that Protestants, Jews, and Greeks place a greater emphasis on independence and achievement training than Southern Italians and French-Canadians. The data on the Negroes are conflicting: they often train children relatively early in self-reliance, but there is little evidence of much stress upon achievement training. No doubt the socialization practices of these groups have been modified somewhat by the acculturating influences of American society since their arrival in the Northeast.[13] But ethnic cultures tend to survive even in the face of strong obliterating forces, and we believe that earlier differences between groups persist—a position supported by the present data on self-reliance training. Hence, the hypothesis that the racial and ethnic groups considered here differ with respect to achievement motivation. We predicted that, on the average, achievement motivation scores would be highest among the Jews, Greeks, and white Protestants, lower among the Italians and French-Canadians, and lowest among the Negroes. Table 2 shows that the data support these predictions, indicated by the following mean scores: Greeks 10.80, Jews, 10.53, Protestants 10.11, Italians 9.65, French-Canadians 8.82, and Negroes 8.40.

A series of "t" tests of significance between means (a one-tail test was used in cases where the direction of the difference had been predicted) was computed. The differences between Greeks, Jews, and Protestants are not statistically significant. The Italian score is significantly lower ($P < .05$) than the score for the Greeks, but not for the Jews and Protestants. The largest differences are between the French-Canadians and Negroes on the one hand and the remaining groups on the other: the French-Canadian mean score is significantly lower ($P < .01$) than those of all other groups except Italians and Negroes; the mean score for all Negroes is significantly lower (P < .01) than the scores for all other groups except French-Canadians. A "Roman Catholic" score was obtained by combining Italian and French-Canadian scores, and scores for all non-Negro groups were combined to form a "White" score. The differences between group means were tested for significance (by a one-tail "t" test) and it was found that the "Catholic" score is significantly lower than the scores for Protestants, Greek Orthodox, and Jews (P < .01). The Negro mean score is significantly lower than the combined score of all white groups (P < .002).

A comparison of ethnic-racial differences does not tell the whole story. There are also significant differences between the social classes. In fact, analysis of Table 2 indicates that social class accounts for more of the variance than ethnicity: the F ratio for ethnicity is 1.23 (P > .05), for class 5.30 (P < .005). The small number of cases in Classes I and II greatly increases the within-group variance; when these two classes are combined with Class III the variance is decreased and the F ratio for ethnicity increases sharply to 2.13 (P < .06). Social class, however, remains more significantly related to achievement motivation than ethnicity. This finding is especially important in this study since the proportion of subjects in each class varies for the ethnic groups. There are relatively more middle class than lower class subjects among the Jews, Greeks, and Protestants than among Italians, French-Canadians, and Negroes. To control for social class it was necessary to examine the differences between cells as well as between columns and rows. A series of "t" tests of differences between the means of cells revealed that for the most part the earlier pattern established for total ethnic means persists, although in some instances the differences between groups are decreased, in others increased, and in a few cases the direction of the differences is reversed. Neither ethnicity nor social class alone is sufficient to predict an individual's score; both appear to contribute something to the variance between groups, but on the whole social class is a better predictor than ethnicity. Generally, a high status person from an ethnic group with a low mean achievement motivation score is more likely to have a high score than a low status person from a group with a high mean score. Thus, the mean score for Class I-II Negroes is higher than the score for Class IV-V white Protestants: the score for the former is 11.36, for the latter, 7.31; a "t" test revealed that the difference between these two means is significant at the .05 level, using a two-tail test. This relatively high score for Class I-II Negroes, the third highest for any cell in the table, indicates, perhaps, the strong motivation necessary for a Negro to achieve middle class status in a hostile environment. Generally, the scores for each group decrease as the class level declines, except for the Jews whose scores are inversely related to social status—a finding for which we can offer no explanation.

Achievement Value Orientations. Achievement motivation is one part of the achievement syndrome; an equally important component is the achievement value orientation. Value orientations are defined as meaningful and affectively charged modes of organizing behavior—principles that guide human conduct. They establish criteria which influence the individual's preferences and goals. Achievement values and achievement motivation, while related, represent genuinely different components of the achievement syndrome, not only conceptually but also in their origins and, as we have shown elsewhere, in their social correlates.[14] Value orientations, because of their conceptual content, are probably acquired in that stage of the child's cultural training when verbal communication of a fairly complex nature is possible. Achievement motivation or the need to excel, on the other hand, has its origins in parent-child interaction beginning early in the child's life when many of these relations are likely to be emotional and unverbalized. Analytically, then, the learning of achievement oriented values can be independent of the acquisition of the achievement motive, although empirically they often occur together.

Achievement values affect social mobility in that they focus the individual's attention on status improvement and help to shape his behavior so that achievement motivation can be translated into successful action. The achievement motive by itself is not a sufficient condition of social mobility: it provides internal impetus to excel, but it does not impel the individual to take the steps necessary for status achievement. Such steps in our society involve, among other things, a preparedness to plan, work hard, make sacrifices, and be physically mobile. Whether or not the individual will understand their importance and accept them will depend in part upon his values.

Three sets of values (a modification of Kluckhohn's scheme [15]) were identified as elements of the achievement syndrome,[16] as follows:

1. *Activistic-Passivistic Orientation* concerns the extent to which the culture of a group encourages the individual to believe in the possibility of his manipulating the physical and social environment to his advantage. An activistic culture encourages the individual to believe that it is both possible and necessary for him to improve his status, whereas a passivistic culture promotes the acceptance of the notion that individual efforts to achieve mobility are relatively futile.

2. *Individualistic-Collectivistic Orientation* refers to the extent to which the individual is expected to subordinate his needs to the group. This study is specifically concerned with the degree to which the society expects the individual to maintain close physical proximity to his family of orientation, even at the risk of limiting vocational opportunities; and the degree to which the society emphasizes group incentives rather than personal rewards. The collectivistic society places a greater stress than the individualistic on group ties and group incentives.

3. *Present-Future Orientation* concerns the society's attitude toward time and its impact upon behavior. A present oriented society stresses the merit of living in the present, emphasizing immediate gratifications; a future oriented society encourages the belief that planning and present sacrifices are worthwhile, or morally obligatory, in order to insure future gains.

Examination of ethnographic and historical materials on the cultures of the six ethnic groups revealed important differences in value orientation—differences antedating their arrival in the Northeast. The cultures of white Protestants, Jews, and Greeks stand out as considerably more individualistic, activistic, and future-oriented than those of the Southern Italians, French-Canadians, and Negroes. Several forces—religious, economic, and national—seem to have long influenced the Protestants in this direction, including, first, the Puritan Ethic with its stress upon individualism and work; then the impact of the liberal economic ethic (Weber's "Spirit of Capitalism") emphasizing competitive activity and achievement; and finally, the challenge of the frontier, with its consequent growth of a national feeling of optimism and manifest destiny. All of these factors tended very early to create a highly activistic, individualistic, future-oriented culture—the picture of American culture held by foreign observers since Tocqueville.[17]

The Jews, who for centuries had lived in more or less hostile environments, have learned that it is not only possible to manipulate their environment to insure survival but even to prosper in it.

Jewish tradition stresses the possibility of the individual rationally mastering his world. Man is not helpless against the forces of nature or of his fellow man; God will provide, but only if man does his share. Like Protestantism, Judaism is an intensely individualistic religion and the Jews an intensely individualistic people. While the family was close knit, it was the entire *shtetl* which was regarded as the inclusive social unit; and in neither case was loyalty to the group considered threatened by physical mobility. The Jews typically have urged their children to leave home if in so doing they faced better opportunities. *Shtetl* society, from which the vast majority of American Jewry is descended, vigorously stressed the importance of planning and working for the future. A *shtetl* cultural tradition was that parents save for many years, often at great sacrifice to themselves, in order to improve their son's vocational opportunities or to provide a daughter with a dowry.[18]

In some respects, Greek and Jewish cultures were strikingly similar at the turn of the century. The ethos of the town and city permeated the Greek more than most other Mediterranean cultures, although only a small proportion of the population was engaged in trade—with the important exception of the Levantine Greeks, who were largely merchants. The image of the Greek in the Eastern Mediterranean area was that of an individualistic, foresighted, competitive trader. Early observers of the Greek in America were impressed by his activistic, future-oriented behavior. E. A. Ross, a rather unfriendly observer, wrote as early as 1914 that "the saving, commercial Greek climbs. From curb to stand, from stand to store, from little store to big store, and from there to branch stores in other cities—such are the stages in his upward path." [19]

Though separated by thousands of miles, French-Canadian and Southern Italian cultures were similar in many respects. Both were primarily peasant cultures, strongly influenced by the Roman Catholic Church. Neither could be described as activistic, individualistic, or future-oriented. In Southern Italian society the closed-class system and grinding poverty fostered a tradition of resignation—a belief that the individual had little control over his life situation and a stress upon the role of fate (*Destino*) in determining success. The living conditions of French-Canadians, although less harsh, were sufficiently severe to sharply limit the individual's sense of mastery over his situation. In neither group was there a strong feeling that the individual could drastically improve his lot; for both groups the future was essentially unpredictable, even capricious. Extended family ties were very strong in both groups: there is the Southern Italian saying, "the family against all others;" the French-Canadian farmer in need of help will travel many miles to hire a kinsman rather than an otherwise convenient neighbor.[20]

Ironically, although Negroes are usually Protestant (however, not ordinarily of the Calvinistic type) and have been exposed to the liberal economic ethic longer than most of the other groups considered here, their culture, it seems, is least likely to accent achievement values. The Negro's history as a slave and depressed farm worker, and the sharp discrepancy between his experiences and the American Creed, would appear to work against the internalization of the achievement values of the dominant white group. Typically, the Negro life-situation does not encourage the belief that one can manipulate his environment or the conviction that one can improve his condition very much by planning and hard work.[21] Generally, family ties have not been strong among Ne-

Table 3. Mean Value Scores by Ethnicity and Social Class

| Ethnicity | Social Class | | | | | |
	I-II	III	IV	V	$\bar{x}$	N
French-Canadian	4.00	4.21	4.60	2.46	3.68	62
Italian	5.86	4.00	3.96	3.40	4.17	74
Greek	6.33	5.52	4.80	3.25	5.08	47
Jew	5.94	5.47	5.41	4.80	5.54	57
Negro	6.00	5.00	4.90	4.67	5.03	65
Protestant	5.86	5.50	4.97	3.54	5.16	122
$\bar{x}$	5.91	5.08	4.78	3.49		

$$\text{Ethnicity:} \quad F = 11.62 \quad P < .001$$
$$\text{Social Class:} \quad F = 33.80 \quad P < .001$$
$$\text{Ethnicity} \times \text{Class:} \quad F = 2.43 \quad P < .01$$

groes, although traditionally the mother was an especially important figure and ties between her and her children, particularly sons, may still be very strong.[22]

Another and more direct way of studying ethnic values is to talk with group members themselves; thus our personal interviews with the mothers. (Their sons in many cases were too young to give meaningful answers.) They were asked whether they agreed or disagreed with the following statements, listed here under the appropriate value orientation categories.

1. *Activistic-Passivistic Orientation.*

Item 1. "All a man should want out of life in the way of a career is a secure, not too difficult job, with enough pay to afford a nice car and eventually a home of his own."

Item 2. "When a man is born the success he is going to have is already in the cards, so he might just as well accept it and not fight against it."

Item 3. "The secret of happiness is not expecting too much out of life and being content with what comes your way."

2. *Individualistic-Collectivistic Orientation.*

Item 4. "Nothing is worth the sacrifice of moving away from one's parents."

Item 5. "The best kind of job to have is one where you are part of an organization all working together even if you don't get individual credit." [23]

3. *Present-Future Orientation.*

Item 6. "Planning only makes a person unhappy since your plans hardly ever work out anyway."

Item 7. "Nowadays with world conditions the way they are the wise person lives for today and lets tomorrow take care of itself."

Responses indicating an activistic, future-oriented, individualistic point of view (the answer "disagree" to these items) reflect values, we believe, most likely to facilitate achievement and social mobility. These items were used to form a value index, and a score was derived for each subject by giving a point for each achievement-oriented response. In examining the mothers' scores two assumptions were made: (1) that they tend to transmit their values to their sons, and (2) that the present differences between groups are indicative of at least equal, and perhaps even greater, differences in the past.

The ethnographic and historical materials led us to expect higher value scores for Jews, white Protestants, and Greeks than for Italians, French-Canadians, and Negroes. In large measure, these expectations were confirmed. Table 3 shows that Jews have the highest mean score (5.54), followed closely by Protestants (5.16), Greeks (5.08), and Negroes (surprisingly) (5.03). The

Italians' score (4.17) is almost a point lower, and the French-Canadian score (3.68) is the lowest for any group. The scores for Jews, Protestants, and Greeks do not significantly differ when the two-tail test is used (we were not able to predict the direction of the differences), but they are all significantly higher than the scores for Italians and French-Canadians. When Italian and French-Canadian scores are combined to form a "Roman Catholic" score, the latter is significantly lower ($P < .001$) than the scores for Jews, Protestants, or Greeks.

The prediction for the Negroes proved to be entirely wrong. Their mean score (5.03) is significantly higher ($P < .001$) than the scores for Italians and French-Canadians. Nor is the Negro score significantly different from those for Protestants and Greeks, although it is significantly lower than the Jewish score ($P < .05$) when the one-tail test is used. The skeptic may regard the relatively high Negro value score as merely lip-service to the liberal economic ethic, but it may in fact reflect, and to some extent be responsible for, the economic gains of Negroes in recent years.[24]

Social class also is significantly related to achievement values and accounts for more of the variance than ethnicity: the F ratio for class is 33.80 ($P < .001$); for ethnicity 11.62 ($P < .001$). Almost without exception, the mean score for each ethnic group is reduced with each decline in status. *Social class, however, does not wash out the differences between ethnic groups.* A series of "t" tests between cells across each social class reveals that Greek, Jewish, and Protestant scores remain significantly higher than Italian and French-Canadian scores. Negro scores also remain among the highest across each social class. Ethnicity and social class interact and each contributes something to the differences between groups: the individual with high social status who also belongs to an ethnic group which stresses achievement values is far more likely to have a high value score than an individual with low status and membership in a group in which achievement is not emphasized. For example, the Class I-II Greek score is 6.33 as compared with the Class V French-Canadian score of 2.46—the difference between them is significant at the .001 level. On the other hand, the score for Class I-II Italians, an ethnic group in which achievement values are not stressed, is 5.86 as compared with 3.25 for Class V Greeks—the difference between them is significant at the .001 level. Neither variable, then, is sufficient to predict an individual's score; and for some groups social class seems to be the more significant factor, for others ethnicity appears to play the greater role. Thus, for Jews and Negroes the mean scores remain relatively high for each social class; in fact, Class V Jews and Negroes have larger mean scores than many French-Canadians and Italians of higher social status.

Aspiration Levels. Achievement motivation and values influence social mobility by affecting the individual's need to excel and his willingness to plan and work hard. But they do not determine the areas in which such excellence and effort take place. Achievement motivation and values can be expressed, as they often are, through many kinds of behavior that are not conducive to social mobility in our society, for example, deviant, recreational, or religious behavior. Unless the individual aims for high vocational goals and prepares himself appropriately, his achievement motivation and values will not pull him up the social ladder. Increasingly, lengthy formal education, often including college and post-graduate study, is needed for movement into prestigeful and lucrative jobs. An educational aspiration level which precludes college training may seriously affect the individual's chances for social mobility.

Their cultures, even before the arrival of the ethnic groups in the Northeast, were markedly different in orientation towards education.[25] The Protestants' stress upon formal education, if only as a means of furthering one's career, is well known. Traditionally, Jews have placed a very high value on educational and intellectual attainment; learning in the *shtetl* society gave the individual prestige, authority, a chance for a better marriage. Contrariwise, for Southern Italians, school was an upper class institution, not an avenue for social advancement for their children, booklearning was remote from everyday experience, and intellectualism often regarded with distrust. French-Canadians, although not hostile to education and learning, were disinclined to educate their sons beyond the elementary level. Daughters needed more education as preparation for jobs in the event they did not marry, but sons were destined to be farmers or factory workers, in the parents' view, with the exception at times of one son who would be encouraged to become a priest. Greeks—generally no better educated than Italians or French-Canadians—on the whole were much more favorably disposed towards learning, in large part because of their intense nationalistic identification with the cultural glories of ancient Greece.[26] This identification was strengthened by the relatively hostile reception Greeks met on their arrival in this country, and is in part responsible for the rapid development of private schools supported by the Greek community and devoted to the teaching of Greek culture—an interesting parallel to the Hebrew School among American Jews. Finally, Negroes, who might be expected to share the prevalent American emphasis upon education, face the painfully apparent fact that positions open to educated Negroes are scarce. This fact means that most Negroes, in all likelihood, do not consider high educational aspirations realistic. And the heavy drop-out in high school suggests that the curtailment of educational aspirations begins very early.

To test whether and to what degree these differences between groups persist, the mothers were asked: "How far do you *intend* for your son to go to school?" It was hoped that the term *intend* would structure the question so that the reply would indicate, not merely a mother's pious wish, but also an expression of will to do something about her son's schooling. The data show that 96 per cent of the Jewish, 88 per cent of the Protestant, 85 per cent of the Greek, 83 per cent of the Negro (much higher than was anticipated), 64 per cent of the Italian, and 56 per cent of the French-Canadian mothers said that they expected their sons to go to college. The aspirations of Jews, Protestants, Greeks, and Negroes are not significantly different from one another, but they are significantly higher than the aspirations of Italians and French-Canadians (P < .05).

Social class, once more, is significantly related to educational aspiration. When class is controlled the differences between ethnic groups are diminished—particularly at the Class I-II-III levels—but they are not erased: Jews, Protestants, Greeks, and Negroes tend to have aspirations similar to one another and higher than those of Italians and French-Canadians for each social class. The differences are greatest at the lower class levels: at Class V, 85 per cent of the Protestants, 80 per cent of the Jews, and 78 per cent of the Negroes intend for their sons to go to college as compared with 63 per cent of the Greeks, 50 per cent of the Italians, and 29 per cent of the French-Canadians.

The individual, to be socially mobile, must aspire to the occupations which society esteems and rewards highly. An individual, strongly motivated to excel and willing to plan and work hard, who sets his heart on being the best barber will probably be less vertically mobile than an equally endowed person who aspires to become the best surgeon. Moreover, the individual who aspires to a high status occupation is likely to expend more energy in competitive striving—and in so doing improve his chances for social mobility—than someone whose occupational choice demands relatively little from him.

Since many of the boys in this study were too young to appraise occupations realistically, we sought to obtain a measure of ethnic group vocational aspiration by questioning the mothers about their aspirations for their sons, once again assuming that they would tend to communicate their views of status levels and their expectations for their sons. Ten occupations were chosen which can be ranked by social status; seven of our ten occupations (marked below by asterisks) were selected from the N.O.R.C. ranking.[27] The occupations, originally presented in alphabetical order, are given here in the order of status: Lawyer*, Druggist, Jewelry Store Owner, Machinist*, Bank Teller, Insurance Agent*, Bookkeeper*, Mail Carrier*, Department Store Salesman*, and Bus Driver*. The mothers were asked: "If things worked out so that your son were in the following occupations, would you be satisfied or dissatisfied?" To obtain aspiration scores for each mother, her responses were treated in three ways:

1. The number of times the mother answered "satisfied" to the ten occupations was summed to give a single score. In effect this meant giving each occupation a weight of one. Since the subject must inevitably select lower status occupations as she increases her number of choices, the higher the summed score, the lower the aspiration level. The basic limitation of this method is that it is impossible to know from the summed score whether the occupations chosen are of low or high status.

2. To correct for this, a second index was derived by assigning weights to the seven occupations taken from the N.O.R.C. study according to their position in the rank order. Thus the highest status position, lawyer, was given a rank weight of 1.0 and the lowest a weight of 6.5 (store salesman and bus driver were tied for last place). Here again, the higher the score, the lower the aspiration level.

3. A third method of weighting the occupations was devised by taking the percentage of the entire sample of mothers who said that they would be satisfied with a particular occupation, and using the reciprocal of each percentage as the weight for that occupation. (The reciprocal was first multiplied by one thousand to eliminate decimals.) The mothers ranked the occupations

somewhat differently than the N.O.R.C. ranking (assigning a higher status to bookkeeper and insurance agent and lower status to machinist and mail carrier). The assumption here is that the

Table 4. Mean Scores and Rank Position of Six Ethnic Groups Using Three Indexes of Vocational Aspiration *

| | Index of Vocational Aspiration | | | |
Ethnicity	Number Satisfied	Rank Weight	Reciprocal Weight	N
French-Canadian	6.60 (5)	14.43 (5)	119.90 (5)	62
Italian	5.96 (4)	12.66 (4)	104.55 (4)	74
Greek	4.70 (2)	7.78 (2)	73.51 (2)	47
Jew	3.51 (1)	6.02 (1)	59.48 (1)	57
Negro	6.95 (6)	16.18 (6)	138.74 (6)	65
Protestant	5.28 (3)	10.12 (3)	88.19 (3)	122

* Rank positions are shown by figures in parentheses.

higher the percentage who answered "satisfied," the higher the status of the occupation. A score for each mother was obtained by summing the reciprocal weights for each occupation chosen. With this method, the highest status occupation is lawyer (score of 11.0), the lowest bus driver (48.0). All ten occupations were used in this index. The higher the subject's score, the lower her aspiration level.

Although these indexes differ somewhat, they provide very similar data on ethnic group vocational aspirations. Table 4 shows the same rank ordering of groups for all three indexes, in descending order as follows: Jews, Greeks, Protestants, Italians, French-Canadians, and Negroes. A series of "t" tests of differences between group mean scores revealed differences and similarities much like those found for achievement motivation. Thus the Jews, Greeks, and Protestants show significantly higher mean scores (that is, they tend to be satisfied with fewer occupations and indicate satisfaction with only the higher status positions) than the Roman Catholic Italians and French-Canadians.[28] The mean score for Jews is significantly higher than the scores for Protestants and Greeks, but there are no significant differences between Greeks and Protestants, or between Italians and French-Canadians. The mean score for Negroes is significantly lower than the scores for all other groups except French-Canadians. In examining the aspirations of Negroes it should be remembered that most of these occupations are considered highly desirable by many Negroes, given their severely limited occupational opportunities, so that their aspiration level may appear low only by "white" standards. There are, however, these problems: are the Negro mothers (83 per cent) in earnest in saying that they intend for their sons to go to college? And, if so, how is this to be reconciled with their low vocational aspirations?

Social class, too, is significantly and directly related to vocational aspiration—a familiar finding—*but it is not as significant as ethnicity*. Analysis of variance of data for each of the three indexes reveals that ethnicity accounts for more of the variance than social class. For example, when the number of occupations with which the mother would be satisfied for her son is used as an index of vocational aspiration, the F ratio for ethnicity is 12.41 (P < .001) as compared with a ratio of 9.92 for social class (P < .001). The same pattern holds for data derived from the other two indexes. Although ethnicity and class interact, each contributing to the differences between groups, the effects of class are more apparent at the middle class (Classes I-II-III) than at the working and lower class (Classes IV-V) levels.

As the question was worded in this study, in one sense it is misleading to speak of the "height" of vocational aspirations. For all groups have "high" aspirations in that most mothers are content to have their sons achieve a high status. The basic difference between groups is in the "floor," so to speak, which they place on their aspirations. For example, at least 80 per cent of the mothers of each ethnic group said that they would be satisfied to have their sons be lawyers, but only two per cent of the Greeks and seven per cent of the Jews were content to have their sons become bus drivers, as compared with 26 per cent of the French-Canadians and 43 per cent of the Negroes. Again, 12 per cent of the Jewish, 22 per cent of the Protestant, and 29 per cent of the Greek mothers said that they would be satisfied to have their sons become department store salesmen, as compared with 48 per cent of the Italians, 51 per cent of the Negro, and 52 per cent of the French-Canadian mothers.

Summary

This paper examines differences in motivation, values, and aspirations of six racial and ethnic groups which may explain in part their dissimilar social mobility rates. Analysis of ethnographic and attitudinal and personality data suggests that these groups differed, and to some extent still differ, in their orientation toward achievement. The data show that the groups place different emphases upon independence and achievement training in the rearing of children. As a consequence, achievement motivation is more characteristic of Greeks, Jews, and white Protestants than of Italians, French-Canadians, and Negroes. The data also indicate that Jews, Greeks, and Protestants are more likely to possess achievement values and higher educational and vocational aspirations than Italians and French-Canadians. The values and educational aspirations of the Negroes are higher than expected, being comparable to those of Jews, Greeks, and white Protestants, and higher than those of the Italians and French-Canadians. Vocational aspirations of Negroes, however, are the lowest of any group in the sample. Social class and ethnicity interact in influencing motivation, values, and aspirations; neither can predict an individual's score. Ethnic differences persist when social class is controlled, but some of the differences between ethnic groups in motivations, values, and aspirations are probably also a function of their class composition.

Notes ►

1. Cf. W. L. Warner and L. Srole, *The Social Systems of American Ethnic Groups*, New Haven: Yale University Press, 1945; F. L. Strodtbeck, "Jewish and Italian Immigration and Subsequent Status Mobility," in D. McClelland, A. Baldwin, U. Bronfenbrenner, and F. Strodtbeck, *Talent and Society*, Princeton: Van Nostrand, 1958; M. Davie, *World Immigration*, New York: Macmillan, 1936.

2. Cf. N. Glazer, "The American Jew and the Attainment of Middle-Class Rank: Some Trends and Explanations," in M. Sklare, editor, *The Jews: Social Patterns of an American Group*, Glencoe, Ill.: Free Press, 1958; W. L. Warner and L. Srole, *op. cit.*; T. Burgess, *Greeks in America*, Boston: Sherman, French, 1913; T. Saloutos, "The Greeks in the U.S.," *The South Atlantic Quarterly*, 4 (January, 1945), 69–82; T. Kalijarvi, "French-Canadians in the United States," *Annals, American Academy of Political and Social Science* (September, 1942); F. L. Strodtbeck, "Family Interactions, Values and Achievement," in D. McClelland, *et al., op. cit.*; G. Myrdal, *An American Dilemma*, New York: Harper, 1944.

3. B. C. Rosen, "The Achievement Syndrome: A Psychocultural

Dimension of Social Stratification," *The American Sociological Review*, 21 (April, 1956), 203–211.

4. The interviewers were trained by the writer; efforts were made to control for interviewer biases. It should be remembered that the sample is not random at any point in the selection process. Hence, the reader is cautioned to regard the data presented here as tentative and suggestive.

5. A. B. Hollingshead and F. C. Redlich, "Social Stratification and Psychiatric Disorders," *American Sociological Review*, 18 (April, 1953), 163–169.

6. D. C. McClelland, J. Atkinson, R. Clark, and E. Lowell, *The Achievement Motive*, New York: Appleton-Century-Crofts, 1953.

7. M. Winterbottom, "The Relation of Need for Achievement to Learning Experiences in Independence and Mastery," in J. Atkinson, editor, *Motives in Fantasy, Action and Society*, Princeton: Van Nostrand, 1958; B. C. Rosen, "The Psychosocial Origins of Achievement Motivation," mimeographed progress report to the National Institute of Mental Health, 1957.

8. D. C. McClelland, "Some Social Consequences of Achievement Motivation," in M. R. Jones, editor, *Nebraska Symposium on Motivation*, 1955, Lincoln: University of Nebraska Press, 1955.

9. D. C. McClelland, A. Rindlisbacher, and R. C. deCharms, "Religious and Other Sources of Parental Attitudes Towards Independence Training," in D. C. McClelland, editor, *Studies in Motivation*, New York: Appleton-Century-Crofts, 1955.

10. Winterbottom, *op. cit.* Though primarily a measure of independence training, two items in this index—items 6 and 8—are considered measures of mastery training, a concept akin to our notion of achievement training. The failure to disentangle independence training from mastery (achievement) training has been responsible for some confusion in earlier studies of the origins of achievement motivation. (For an analysis of this confusion, see Rosen, "The Psychosocial Origins of Achievement Motivation," *op. cit.*) The two components were kept in the index in order to maintain comparability between this study and the earlier work on ethnic groups by McClelland reported above.

11. M. Zborowski and E. Herzog, *Life Is With People*, New York: International Universities Press, 1952.

12. P. H. Williams, *South Italian Folkways in Europe and America*, New Haven: Yale University Press, 1938; H. Miner, *St. Dennis: A French-Canadian Parish*, Chicago: University of Chicago Press, 1939.

13. It does not necessarily follow that the impact of American culture has reduced the differences between groups. An argument can

be made that for some groups life in America has accentuated differences by allowing certain characteristics of the groups to develop. We have in mind particularly the Greeks and Jews whose need to excel could find little avenue for expression through status striving in Europe.

14. Rosen, "The Achievement Syndrome," *op. cit.*, pp. 208–210.

15. F. Kluckhohn, "Dominant and Substitute Profiles of Cultural Orientations," *Social Forces*, 28 (May, 1950), 376–393.

16. For the most part, the value orientations examined in this study, their description, and the items used to index them, are identical with those which appear in Rosen, "The Achievement Syndrome," *op. cit.*

17. For a history of the development of the liberal economic ethic and its manifestation on the American scene, see J. H. Randall, *The Making of the Modern Mind*, Boston: Houghton Mifflin, 1926; J. K. Galbraith, *The Affluent Society*, Boston: Houghton Mifflin, 1958.

18. Zborowski and Herzog, *op. cit.*; B. C. Rosen, "Cultural Factors in Achievement," mimeographed, 1952; Strodtbeck, "Family Interactions, Values and Achievement," *op. cit.*

19. Quoted in Saloutos, *op. cit.*, p. 71. The writer is indebted to J. Gregoropoulos, a native of Athens, for many helpful comments on European and American Greek communities.

20. Miner, *op. cit.* See also Williams, *op. cit.*; Strodtbeck, "Family Interactions, Values and Achievement," *op. cit.*

21. We recognize that to infer a group's values from its life-situation and then to use these values to explain an aspect of that situation is to reason circularly. However, the temporal sequence between values and mobility has a chicken-egg quality which is difficult to avoid because values and life-situation interact. To some extent, knowledge of ethnic cultures prior to their arrival in the United States helps to establish the priority of values to mobility. In the case of the Negroes, however, relatively little is known about their several cultures before their transportation to this country.

22. E. F. Frazier, *The Negro Family in the United States*, Chicago: University of Chicago Press, 1939; see also Frazier's *The Negro in the United States*, New York: Macmillan, 1957, especially Chapters 13 and 24.

23. Of course, if Whyte is correct about the growth of the organization man and the importance of the "social ethic," agreement with this statement may indicate an asset rather than a handicap to social mobility. See W. H. Whyte, Jr., *The Organization Man*, New York: Simon and Schuster, 1957.

24. The relatively high value score for Negroes supports our conten-

tion that achievement motivation and achievement values are genuinely different components of the achievement syndrome. It will be remembered that the Negroes had the lowest mean motivation score. If achievement motivation and values are conceptually and empirically identical, there should be no difference between the two sets of scores.

25. For a comparison of ethnic group education and vocational aspirations, see R. M. Williams, Jr., *American Society*, New York: Knopf, 1951, Chapter 8; F. J. Woods, *Cultural Values of American Ethnic Groups*, New York: Harper, 1956, Chapters 5 and 7.

26. Attempts by Mussolini to create a similar bond between his people and ancient Rome, or even the more recent Renaissance, were unsuccessful. French-Canadians for the most part have long refused to be impressed by the "secular" achievement of European anti-clerical French society.

27. National Opinion Research Center, "Jobs and Occupations: A Popular Evaluation," *Opinion News*, 9 (September 1, 1947). We substituted store salesman for store clerk and bus driver for streetcar motorman. The position of the three occupations which did not appear in the N.O.R.C. survey are ranked according to their similarity to occupations in the survey.

28. Similar Jewish-Italian differences are reported in F. L. Strodtbeck, M. McDonald, and B. C. Rosen, "Evaluation of Occupations: A Reflection of Jewish and Italian Mobility Differences," *American Sociological Review*, 22 (October, 1957), 546–553.

12▸ CHILDHOOD INDOCTRINATION FOR MINORITY-GROUP MEMBERSHIP

JOSHUA A. FISHMAN

Learning to become a member of an ethnic minority is, like any other socialization process, a complex acquisition of attitudes and values, statuses and roles, that begins early in life. Part of this socialization process takes place informally in family and peer-group relationships and interrelationships. Another part of childhood indoctrination into minority-group membership is provided formally in schools established by minority groups.

Professor Joshua Fishman now explores this indoctrination with reference to the minority-group schooling of several ethnic groups, particularly, American Negroes, Roman Catholics and Jews.

▸ THIS PAPER deals with the minority-group child and the schools specifically set up for his education within the group. It attempts to examine the effects of such formal education on the attitudes and behavior of the child toward the values, customs, and individuals of the larger society. It also inquires into the effects of the school on his view of himself as an American and as a member of a specific ethnic group. It attempts to assess the extent to which the school contributes to his self-definition and his aspirations as a member of his own group, as well as of American society as a whole.

The school in America operates within a complex cultural envi-

Reprinted by permission of the author and *Daedalus*, published by the American Academy of Arts and Sciences, Brookline, Massachusetts (Spring, 1961), 329–49.

ronment. There exists an "American" society, in no way dependent on Jews or Catholics, Poles or Italians, Negroes or Orientals. The core of that society is white, Protestant, middle class, and it attracts all other particles to it. This is the culture into which immigrants are assimilated, and it forms the one accepted set of standards, expectations, and aspirations, whether they pertain to clothing, household furnishings, personal beauty, entertainment, or child-rearing.

Yet this does not mean that there is a single core group. Certainly, the white, Protestant, middle-class Americans cannot be said to share a single clear-cut set of cultural patterns. There are important rural-urban, North-South-West, Episcopalian-Lutheran-Baptist, and other differences. Psychologically, however, the term "core culture" still makes sense, particularly when it is used from the point of view of any given minority. It is no more difficult to speak of American than of French or Russian national characteristics. The American cultural constellation is not a fixed one, but it is certainly there as a structural, dynamic, meaningful whole.

The present discussion deals with only one theatre of activity, the life of the minority-group child, and with only one instrument, his school. There are infinitely more complex and diversified social processes that affect both school and child, but it is nevertheless useful to concentrate on a specific set of problems and to build on a single set of assumptions. The assumptions posit a compelling American core culture, toward which the minority-group child has ambivalent feelings. He is attracted to it, surrenders willingly to it, desires to participate fully in it. The imperfect congruence between his aspiration and the possibility of his being absorbed generates ambivalence whenever he is rejected. Nevertheless, the minority-group child is ever ready to swallow his pride and try once more. This core culture, therefore, establishes the direction and intensity of America's impact on the minority-group child and on his feelings of belonging. We are here attempting to examine the effects that schools established by minority groups have upon these attitudes.

It will be useful to say something about the concepts of retentionism, separatism, integrationism, and biculturism that figure in the discussion that follows. By "retentionism," I mean the attempts by the minority group, either through the school or by any other means, to retain unique values and behavior, either in an altered or adapted form, or under the maximal self-determining conditions which a given minority group has attained.

By "separatism," I mean a tendency not to interact with the American core. Separatism is exclusive; it posits the superiority of the in-group, and the inferiority or undesirability (often in moral or ethical terms) of the core group. Separatism is a matter of degree, however, and the above definition merely indicates its extreme forms.

By "integrationism," I mean a tendency to maximal interaction with the American core. Integrationism posits the preferability of the "core" group to that of the minority in-group. Integrationism looks toward the incorporation of the member of the minority group in the "core." Although integrationism is regarded by its opponents as a euphemism for "a will to disappear," it is not necessarily that. When it is weak, it may not even mean a denial of separatism, since the two may co-exist within the same individual or group.

By "biculturism," I mean an orientation toward a maximally creative and positive involvement in the value-behavior complex of both the minority and the core. Biculturism involves selection from both systems and a synthesis of the elements selected. Biculturism results from the interaction of two healthy cultural systems within a single individual or group, with neither system dominating the other. It also represents a nonextreme and unfinished solution, one that must be worked out, bit by bit, over time. It is not an immediately available system which provides ready-made solutions to all present and future problems, as do the extremes of separatism or of integrationism.

These remarks will be limited to only three of the American minority groups, the Negroes, the Catholics, and the Jews. These are the groups on which most psychological and sociological research has been concentrated; studies of their schools extend over more than three decades. Furthermore, these are the largest minority groups, and their success in the bicultural rearing of their children, therefore, will strikingly affect the course of other, smaller minorities. What is more, since they constitute a quarter or more of the American population, their experiences are of great importance for the entire structure of life in the United States. Finally, these three groups differ radically as to their relation to the core, their internal organization, and their retentionist interests and activities. It will be useful to note whether these differences affect the retentionist outcomes of stimuli derived from school experiences. If not, it is possible that all American minority groups display strong psychological and social similarities in relation to the core.

The problems of Negroes in the United States are in many ways markedly dissimilar from those of other American minority groups. Instead of the removable stain of immigrant status, they carry the indelible stain of pejorative pigmentation. Their former bondage sets them apart from even the most disadvantaged white-skinned minorities, while their liberation has left a still sensitive scar in American social, political, and economic life. They constitute the only American minority with whom memories of white fratricide and of interracial homicide are alike associated. Severe sexual taboos and dislocations in status surround their acceptance into white, Protestant, middle-class society. Their deliverance is still a long way off.

Negro secular schools, staffed and supported by the Negro community specifically to foster a positive biculturism, do exist at all rungs of the educational ladder.[1] Negro religious schools may also aid the same purpose. Unfortunately, there have been few studies of children or young people attending either type of schools.

The only parochial setting in which Negro children have been fairly intensively studied is the segregated public school. This school differs from those of other minority groups, first because it is neither maintained, directed, nor, indeed, positively regarded by the community it serves, and second, because its curriculum and standards are limited by the very community which imposes inferior status on the Negro. As a result, the segregated public school has often functioned under conditions inverse to those governing other minority-group schools: both the direct and the indirect stimuli for keeping segregated schools come from the outside, not the inside.

Nevertheless, the similarities in striving among America's minority-group children are such that findings based on the segregated Negro schools do not differ significantly from those based on the voluntarily segregated institutions sponsored by other groups. One may ask about segregated Negro education some of the questions we ask about Catholic and Jewish schools. To what extent do they succeed in bolstering pride and security in one's group? To what extent do they succeed in communicating to their students the accomplishments of Negro culture in this country and elsewhere?

To what extent do their students develop positive self-feelings and identifications with being Negro, as well as the ability to interact positively with white society without denying the values and achievements of their own group?

An early series of studies and more recent ones as well [2] have consistently pointed toward the high premium placed on light pigmentation by Negro nursery-school children attending both voluntarily and involuntarily segregated, semisegregated, and mixed schools. All Negro children, from the lightest to the darkest, tend to report their own pigmentation as lighter than it actually is, and light-skinned Negro children still frequently identify themselves as white at ages when darker Negro children have accepted the actuality, though not the desirability, of their negroid features. Light-skinned nursery-age children are preferred as friends, are oftener assigned desirable characteristics, and report fewer difficulties later in connection with being Negro when they are aged ten to twelve. The Northern Negro child permits himself white self-ascriptions more frequently and until a later age than the Southern Negro child.

These attitudes and preferences certainly do not spring from stimuli originating in the school. The Negro child derives them from adult Negro values, and the latter, in turn, are derived from the core society and the core values, toward which the values of the American Negro are oriented. These values are not bicultural, and they permeate the Negro child's attitudes to himself and others.

A number of studies over a long span of years have reported that the attitudes of Negro children (attending segregated and semi-segregated schools) toward white children are more favorable than the attitudes of the white children toward them.[3] This preference has been found to increase with the age of the Negro children. Negro children have also been found to be critical or nonaccepting of other Negroes in some of the areas mentioned by white children, for example, in their mechanical and intellectual ability.[4] Several investigators have concluded from such data that American children reflect the social attitudes of the society of which they seek to be a part, regardless of the race, color, or creed of the particular group of which they are members.[5] Differences are only in degree, not in kind. The fact that the attitude of segregated Negro high-school students toward Negroes was, before the Supreme Court decision of 1954, more positive than was previously reported [6] may have wide-reaching implications if it can be related to other social processes in both the Negro and the white communities. One related factor was the recorded improvement in white children's attitudes to Negroes in the same communities. The upheaval and dislocation after the Supreme Court decision may have negated the mutually facilitating process that was possibly in operation.

Two other studies of great theoretical interest compare Negro children attending schools of various degrees and types of segregation. Both are more than a decade old, so that further investigation would be needed to make sure that their conclusions still obtain. A comparison of attitudinal adjustment toward Negroes and whites on the part of Negro students in mixed and segregated high schools in Ohio [7] found that the least significant difference between these two groups of students was in their attitudes toward "other" pupils (these were predominantly white in the mixed schools), although even specific attitudes to Negroes were not reliably different. A highly provocative study compared the attitudes of children living in all-Negro communities in Oklahoma with those of Negro children residing in various biracial communities of the South and North.[8] The investigator concluded that an individual growing up in an all-Negro society would have virtually the same attitudes toward whites as would any other American Negro. On the other hand, the individuals reared in the all-Negro communities were found to have much more favorable attitudes toward Negroes. This last finding recalls a much earlier one pointing to certain general benefits to personality accruing to children who attended segregated rather than mixed schools in Cincinnati.[9] Actually, the balance of benefits as between the two types of schools was precarious. The segregated group showed more social participation but less versatility in play, a greater tendency toward self-criticism, but also a greater interest in skilled professions, and, therefore, perhaps less inclination to leave school and try to get a job.

This research overwhelmingly supports the conclusion that the attitudes of American Negro children educated in segregated schools to their own group and to others, including the dominant white group, their vocational aspirations, their concepts of right and wrong, their hobbies and interests, to an overwhelming extent are influenced by the attitudes and behavior of significant core groups and by the attitude-forming media which the core society controls. Similar findings for Negro children attending nonsegregated schools are also plentiful. Although new conditions are now appearing, their general effect will probably make Negro children even more responsive and more exposed to the standards, strivings, and values of the core society. If this is really true for the Negro child (whose social distance from the core, to begin with, is greatest and is "legally" reinforced) and for the segregated school (at which attendance is enforced by external authorities), then the implications for children in other minority-group schools are unmistakable.

The American Catholic minority is quite different. Its schools, unlike those of the Negroes, are directly maintained by strong forces arising from within, rather than as a result of exclusion from without. Attendance is mandatory rather than merely desirable—although a large area of "extenuating circumstances" is recognized as excusing nonattendance. Unlike the case of the Negro minority, the issue of self-directed separation versus greater integration in the American community is a live one among Catholics, with both alternatives actively competing. Unlike the Jewish community, there are no structurally safeguarded gradational subdivisions within the Catholic religious leadership that correspond to alternative retentivistic philosophies. Like the Jewish minority, American Catholics come from a variety of European backgrounds. Two important factors in the development of American Catholic institutions, however, have been the numerical superiority and the superior status of Catholics of Irish derivation. Certain uniquely Irish-Catholic experiences in the "old country," as well as specifically Irish experiences on their arriving in America after the potato famines, have all left a stamp on the course of Catholicism in the United States.

Though they are the largest and best organized religious-cultural group in this country, Catholics have influenced American values and institutions far less than their thirty-odd million might have led one to predict. This is probably attributable to two opposing forces: the engulfing appeal of American secular life, on the one hand, and the tenacious in-breeding of Catholic energies through a huge network of educational, social, cultural, and economic institutions paralleling those of the core society, on the other. Although non-Catholic Americans have pointed to the separatist-retentionist power of this latter complex of forces (not to mention some people's dread that Catholics might dominate American life), Catholic leaders have even oftener recognized the constantly debilitating influence on Catholics of the dominant forces in American society as a whole. Recent changes in Catholic voting behavior, the rising rate of Catholics' marrying non-Catholics, the extremely high rate of their attendance at non-Catholic institutions of secondary and higher education—these are facts not to be overlooked in discussing the success of Catholic retentionist efforts in contemporary America.

A large-scale, thorough study of boys attending Catholic high schools [10] revealed the preponderant influence of the home and neighborhood over church and school in establishing interests and attitudes. Nearly half the two thousand boys studied in twenty schools throughout the country declared that their schools had not influenced their vocational choices, and fully two-thirds considered that their teachers did not understand their problems. Only 12 percent named the priest as their source of intimate counsel, while 56 percent believed that their parish provided insufficient social meetings for boys and girls. An athlete ranked first as their ideal or hero, while Jesus took third place. As to the aspirations they expressed, money ranked first, material possessions for pleasure ranked second, and eternal happiness and salvation third. Heading the list of their personal problems was the question of purity and sex. One-third reported they were unaware of what was sinful. Their primary sources of information on sex were companions (half of the boys), secular books (39 percent), secular magazines (32 percent), priests (26 percent) and "the street" (23 percent). A study of girls, while it revealed slightly less of a departure from the values of school and church, also showed a noticeably questioning attitude toward restrictions in reading, movies, and drinking.[11]

The ability of the Catholic parochial school to further retentionism may be measured in terms of religious understanding, belief, and practice, and of leisure-time and vocational interests. With respect to religion, Catholic educators have reported many findings that demonstrate the difficulties of their task. A series of interesting studies shows the lack of success as late as the eighth, ninth, and tenth grades in training children to recognize the central position of the Mass in Catholic worship: almost two-thirds of over a thousand parochial-school eighth-grade children investigated gave unsatisfactory replies.[12] By far the largest number of parochial-school children leave the Catholic school system after the eighth grade to attend public high, vocational, and technical schools. Those remaining in the ninth and tenth grades are a much more select group, at least as far as parental and home factors are concerned. Even so, studies of children in these two grades revealed that the gain in understanding and attitudes concerning the Mass was small, in spite of one or two years of difference in maturity and in instruction.[13] Even graduates of twelve- and sixteen-year programs of Catholic-sponsored study are described as retaining merely "a string of dogmas and moral precepts, threats and promises, customs and rites, tasks and duties [which are regarded as] imposed on unfortunate Catholics whilst the non-Catholic gets off free."[14]

A series of studies of the topics Catholic high-school boys remember in connection with retreats consistently points to purity and sex as of major interest, as compared with a negligible interest in God, ultimate ends, prayer, grace, and the sacraments. Reading interests during periods of retreat show a similar trend. Although in one study students attending Catholic schools were found to be more spiritually motivated in forgoing their own immediate satisfactions for the benefit of others, they did not differ at all from comparable students attending public schools in their readiness for such self-sacrifice.[15]

The familiar pattern of accepting direction from elsewhere than the school is also observed in leisure activities and vocational goals. The reading interests of Catholic high-school boys, for instance, are concentrated almost exclusively on sports, adventure and mystery stories. Indifference to Catholic publications of any kind is general.[16] Interest in religious vocations, as reported by a variety of investigators, or the influence of religion on any vocational choice is slight and steadily decreases as the children grow older.[17]

In intergroup relations, the successful inculcation of school-derived and school-supported views also seems negligible. Thus the attitudes to Negroes on the part of white, Catholic, parochial-school children in the South have been found to be negative; they showed no improvement with an increased length of school attendance, and differed not at all from those of Catholic children attending public schools. The phenomenon cannot be ascribed to the Negro's overwhelming non-Catholicism, since Catholic parochial-school children in the Southwest are even more intensely anti-Mexican (and the Mexicans are Catholic) than the students in the South are anti-Negro. Anti-Jewish sentiments among parochial-school children have also been chronicled. Thus it seems that the child arrives at the Catholic parochial school with already established attitudes and needs in relation to his total American environment, and that the school itself is not strong enough to change these attitudes, even when it regards change as desirable. A similar conclusion concerning the impact of Catholicism on the political, social, and economic attitudes of adult Catholics appears from the nationwide Catholic public-opinion surveys conducted by the Catholic University of America.

Perhaps the extent of intermarriage is the best criterion of the ability of the Catholic parochial school to regulate its students' integration with the general American community. Although even in the absence of intermarriage it may well prove impossible to maintain a dynamic minority-group community, it certainly seems improbable that such a community can be maintained if the group cannot control attitudes to intermarriage. The many studies (with only one to the contrary) which have disclosed that attendance at parochial school does not appreciably affect the Catholic child's attitudes toward intermarriage [18] must be taken as evidence that the retentionist effectiveness of the Catholic school, when face to face with the "indulgent" American Protestantism and nonviolent secularism of the twentieth century, is far less than obtained during earlier periods, when Catholics suffered actual persecution.

The tireless efforts of Catholic leaders to employ parochial education to transmit the deep philosophical and religious differences which separate Catholicism from American Protestantism and from secularism have been most consistently embarrassed by the strivings of Catholic parents, young people, and children. Although the educators protest that it is "surely not enough" for parochial schools "to boast that their graduates are fine Americans [since] this is not the divine standard by which they shall be judged," [19] they nevertheless suspect that they have often been forced to trade their "splendid educational heritage for a 'mess of North Central Association pottage.' " [20]

The Jewish school of whatever type can be no more effective in creative retentionism than the Catholic school. In fact, Jewish education, serving a numerically smaller and far less organized and unified group, functioning most frequently on a supplementary basis (on weekday afternoons or Sunday only), and concentrating on the short time span of late childhood and early adolescence, faces many problems unknown to Catholic education. In many ways the Jewish minority epitomizes values and trends found in the core, and it is the most urbanized group in a society tending to increasing urbanization. Its tradition of universal intellectual and higher-order conceptual interests dovetails with the core's increasing devaluation of manual drudgery. Its traditional educational emphasis brings it into contact with the very best of American and worldwide cultural and technical proficiency at a time when the core society itself is entering on a frenzied pursuit of higher and technical education. The shedding of Jewish traditional ways and beliefs has therefore been hastened in a period of unparalleled American pragmatism, secularism, and permissiveness in the personal, social, and economic spheres. Under such circumstances, the current which the Jewish retentivist school must battle is strong indeed.

There have been surprisingly few studies of the effects of Jewish schooling of any kind upon concurrent or later interaction with the "America-American-Americans" complex. In most Jewish educational circles there is a strong disinclination for objective studies of "outcomes"; such calculation is nontraditional, and in addition there is probably an unconscious recognition that the better the calculation, the less pleasant the truths revealed. Estimates of outcomes involving Americanism are doubly taboo. At one ideological extreme there is a hypersensitivity to the idea that perhaps anything less than a "perfect adjustment" to the American environment is obtained, particularly in view of the fact that something quite different from an adjustment to "American success" is desired in the first place. At the other extreme is a similar fear born of the realization that the biculturative efforts of the school cannot really compensate for the rebuffs the child receives from the core society.

In a group such as this, that needs at least eleven distinct types of schools, all for the purpose of indoctrinating its young for membership in a minority group, in accord with varying philosophies, one might expect somewhat differing results for retentionism. On the whole, however, a fragmented Jewish education can no more point to any signs of successful biculturistic retentionism than can a seemingly uniform Catholic education. In fact, the results are strikingly similar for both groups, even if, regrettably, we must rely on studies conducted over many years, with many disparate instruments.

A series of studies spanning twenty-five years by the only investigator to have done more than superficial work provides us with interesting and consistent results.[21] With respect to attitudes toward and knowledge of Jews and Jewishness, L. Lehrer has consistently found that there are only insignificant differences between children receiving a formal Jewish education and those without such an education, or among children differentiated as to the specific type of Jewish education received. Some minor differences in sex and age do approach significance, but their consistency from one study to another is low. It seems justifiable to conclude that the highly differentiated organizational-ideological sponsorship of Jewish education corresponds neither to dynamic differences in the parental societies from which Jewish school children come, nor, most emphatically, to the different milieus of Jewish children. Lehrer concludes that "no matter how divergent the various circles of the Jewish people in America, no difference is noticeable among their children in the . . . character of their national belonging. Apparently, the Jewish environment is so constructed that every circle leads to the same psychological state in early childhood." [22] Yet another quotation from Lehrer's work suggests a conclusion which seems as relevant today as it was over a decade ago, and as applicable to children attending non-Jewish minority-group schools as to those attending Jewish schools: [23]

In a community where Jewishness is restricted to an existence primarily on an ideological, intellectual plane and is insufficiently enriched by the natural forces that exist in a full way of life . . . a child who is detached from our social functioning will sense in us primarily our weak and discriminated status, a status from which it is imperative that he escape. This will lead him to seek proximity to others, to search for protection by identifying with those objectively stronger, not knowing that this mode of adjustment also opens the way for tragic disappointments and conflicts.

That the Jewish schools, therefore, wield insufficient forces for "attaching" the vast majority of children from "unattached" homes to Jewish social functioning is an undeniable fact.

Other studies point to the mild effect of Jewish education in establishing unique behavior or values. That such education does not appreciably affect traits of character and personality is shown by at least two early studies.[24] A comparatively recent one concludes that in choosing friends Jewish boys' behavior toward one another does not reflect the degrees or kinds of Jewish education their parents have selected for them.[25] A highly regarded recent investigation states that Jewish boys in attending synagogue and neighborhood centers strive for increasingly broader, "in common," non-Jewish friendships and activities as they grow older and as their socio-economic level rises.[26] This is also the finding of a companion study of both boys and girls in another city.[27] Some insignificant correlations between childhood Jewish education and early adult Jewish activities have also been reported.[28] A study comparing Zionist and non-Zionists college students reports that both groups failed to mention Jewish education (a background variable on which they differed significantly and in the expected direction) among the facts they believed had affected their current attitudes toward the Jewish group.[29]

Two studies point to interesting successes in retentionism. In one, the students of Yiddish secular schools who had obtained the highest scores on a scale reflecting the degree to which they heard and used the Yiddish language also defined themselves as Jews (not employing the "American" option) more frequently than did children with lower scores on this scale. These children, however, did not differ from the others with respect to leisure activities,[30] the number of intimate friends they claimed, or the public-school marks they achieved. They did differ significantly from the others in the frequency with which they expressed interest in Yiddish for its general cultural and group-survival values, rather than for family, secretive, or general educational values. The investigator concluded that the high scores on his bilingual scale were concomitants of specific in-group identifications, but that they had no concomitants in the child's general activities and interests beyond the control of the in-group. In the absence of reliable data concerning either the measure of bilingualism or its concomitants, as well as in the absence of any following study of the longitudinal permanence of the findings, this claim—although it may be valid —seems somewhat premature. Assuming its validity, we cannot but be impressed by its separatist connotations, as opposed to a biculturism that is truly open in both directions.

The same author also recently reported a large-scale study of the negative stereotypes concerning American values, practices, and persons subscribed to by students attending eleven separate ideological-structural types of Jewish schools.[31] Except for one type of school, no significant difference in their readiness to accept these negative stereotypes was noted between students attending different types of Jewish schools, whether the children were classified only by types of school or were further classified by age, length of attendance at the Jewish school, parental occupation, parental birthplace, or parental education. The one consistent exception involved the students of Orthodox all-day schools. These students showed a significantly greater willingness to accept such negative stereotypes. However, when these students were grouped by age, from eight to thirteen, their acceptance of negative stereotypes lessened steadily, with the result that by the time they were thirteen there was no longer any important difference between these students and all the others. Within the Orthodox all-day school, an analysis by years of study (holding age constant) also suggested a decreasing acceptance of negative stereotypes concerning American values, practices, and persons. The author concluded that American-Jewish children, regardless of the specific type of minority-group indoctrination they receive, seek acceptance by and participation in the American core society. For many Orthodox all-day school students, coming as they do from separatist homes and adult milieus, the school functions as a major agency for Americanization, acquainting them with American pastimes, cultural values, and societal opportunities. Again, the conclusions are probably exaggerated; but, if we grant their validity, the only retentionist successes to which they point are heavily tinged with exclusiveness and separatism at the direct expense of biculturism.

A few additional studies may be mentioned. A recent study compared the attitudes toward non-Jews on the part of Jewish children attending a "traditional" all-day school with those of other Jewish children (equated for age, sex, and parental socioeconomic status) attending public schools. This study substantiates the hypothesis advanced by an earlier investigation, that no significant differences would appear.[32] The two samples of pupils were also compared with respect to their in-group attitudes. No clear differences emerged between the two groups of children, so dissimilar in their Jewish experiences. Dissatisfaction with being Jewish was about equally prevalent. Although differently rationalized and verbalized, the dissatisfactions in both samples derived from the individual and social restrictions and from the penalties perceived as being the concomitants of Jewishness. In addition, both groups regarded the positive features of Jewishness in much the same manner; they overrated the importance of Chanukkah, for example, and underrated other features of Jewish tradition. This compensatory mechanism for feelings of inferiority because of the colorful pageantry of Christmas is a significant index of the source of values and aspirations for both groups. Just as "parochial" as opposed to "public" education for Jewish children does not seem to be the "controlling variable . . . in the etiology of positive and negative out-group feelings in young children," neither does it seem to be such a variable in ambivalent feelings toward membership in the Jewish group.

Yet another recent study, with somewhat different primary interests, considered not only the ideological affiliation but also the generational position among Jewish children.[33] Its findings agree with those of the studies previously reported. Jewish boys from the first to the third generation show an ascending "inner maladjustment" on a projective scale for measuring personality. Socioeconomic status and the ideological affiliation of the school or synagogue attended seemed to have little effect on these or subsequent scores. Scores on a structured measure of "social maladjustment" show an opposite trend, with the third-generation boys scoring best, and the first generation, worst. In connection with this last measurement, the author believes that boys born abroad, whose parents are not fully Americanized, may either feel somewhat insecure in their overt relationships with American society, or they may not as yet be endeavoring to adopt American norms of social adjustment. The third-generation boys, however, seek to appear as fully Americanized, as socially indistinguishable from the core group, as possible. In connection with the first measurements cited above, the author believes that the higher the degree of acculturation without acceptance by the dominant group, the greater the probability of "inner maladjustment" and marginal feeling. The generational trends were as clear among boys attending Orthodox schools of various structural types as among boys attending schools of other ideological and structural combinations.

Finally, it is appropriate to mention a study of those who continue their Jewish education past the normally terminal, elementary level.[34] These young people, attending Jewish supplementary high schools and teachers' seminaries in various cities, were asked to describe any crises they had experienced which had almost brought them to the verge of quitting. The respondents with the most intensely Jewish home environment most frequently named crises involving the attractions or demands of the surrounding, non-Jewish, cultural sphere. Subjects from less intensely Jewish homes, and, therefore, probably in no such conflict about the attractive features of the general American environment, usually attributed their crises to dissatisfaction with the Jewish school itself.

Many people are concerned about the marginal man, and in truth he represents a conspicuous problem in the participation of Jewish and other minority-group children in American core society, whether or not these children attend a minority-group school. The school is generally too weak to produce enduring conflicts or enduring retentionism. The reason for a marginal relation lies in the core society and its "look me over but don't touch me" invitation to the minority-group child. A vigorous biculturism could abolish this marginal relation, as could a vigorous separatism. The minority-group school, however, is too debilitated and timid for either of these ventures. It is certainly in no position to undertake the more difficult and the more initially disruptive of the two, a genuine biculturism.

This does not mean that the minority-group school accomplishes nothing, however. It exists in order to maintain certain minority values, which wage a losing conflict with core values; but this is only one level at which the effectiveness of minority-group schools can be evaluated. There is undoubtedly a second level, that of social relations, and here the school serves to maintain intragroup relations among minority-group children. It is one of the institutions of the minority-group community that preserves a relative amount of solidarity and intragroup feeling from childhood through marriage, and as such it affects choices in friendship, political opinions, levels of aspiration, and biases. The relation between school and neighborhood should perhaps be studied more carefully. The most effective minority-group school may prove to be one located in the more highly organized or more culturally intensive of the minority-group communities.

The foregoing studies are sadly insufficient as a research program for answering many significant questions about the minority-group child. Spread over a quarter of a century or more, they suffer from shortcomings in their design and in their statistical analysis; they reveal a bewildering proliferation of methods and lack the refinements of controls and independent checks—above all, they lack the interdisciplinary focus and enrichment that differentiate true research programs from fragmentary short-term excursions.

Nevertheless, these studies do serve as straws in the wind, and our confidence in them is bolstered by the consistent trend they show. The minority-group school is patently unable to rechannel the major strivings and the behavior of the child in relation to the "America-American-Americans" complex. Not only is the child's response to American values, goals, and opportunities beyond regulation or substantial modification by the school, but also this response is well established even before the child attends school. With these values, goals, and opportunities beckoning to the minority-group child as attractively (if not more so) as to the child with a core background, the ethical, ethnological, and logical arguments for biculturism run against insurmountable difficulties from an entirely different realm. Dynamic biculturism may exist in certain parts of the globe, but not in any setting like America's constellation of socio-psychological and politico-economic realities. These realities make it simpler for American minorities to maintain a "separatist" existence than a bicultural balance. A two-front compaign is beyond their logistic resources; a one-front campaign is frequently beyond their emotional and material longings, for it entails excluding one's self from the American dream.

The weakness of retentionism is perceived even by minority-group leaders. Thus, the basic needs of children and adolescents are chiefly met by activities and programs that have little if any in-group distinctiveness. These programs imply that, if the leadership must painlessly work toward its long-range retentionist goals, it must provide art, recreation, counseling, comradeship, medals, and newspaper publicity. The less central and less distinctive goals are played up because these, not the retentionistic goals, are of natural and immediate interest.

Retentionism as inculcated by the schools, therefore, has often had little to show for its pains other than an ability to retreat according to plan. The few reported instances of the successful inculcation by the schools of minority attitudes and behavior are striking indeed. Their common denominator is some type of ethnic exclusivism, rather than pluralism or a broadly conceived biculturism. Furthermore, a longitudinal study of them has unfortunately been entirely neglected. After all, our ultimate interest is not merely in the consequences of indoctrinating children, but in the mature adult; and at present we have very little from which to extrapolate the successes in retentionism beyond the meager studies of children reviewed above. A few investigations, however, do indicate a substantial consistency between childhood and adult patterns, and in these cases the findings and their implications confirm the conclusion that the schools have only a slight retentionist effect.

If, as it appears, the attitudes and responses of minority-group individuals to American core society do not originate mainly in the school, then we may turn briefly to the following factors, some of which, at least theoretically, may better determine such responses —indeed, may determine the nature of the minority-group school itself.

The compatibility of values and behavior. To what degree are the "modal" traits of personality, the "typical" values, goals, and customs of the minority group compatible with those of the core society? This question must be reexamined periodically, since such compatibility as may exist is itself a function of other variables mentioned below. Retentionism is probably facilitated when a minority and a core society, from the beginning, do not share similar values in terms of material success, attitudes toward centralized governmental intervention, political democracy, and characteristics such as aggressiveness, independence, and experimentalism. Ultimately, it may be more difficult for retentionism to operate successfully in areas where the values are maximally dissimilar or discrepant.

Participationism and separatism. Does the minority group reach out toward participation in the core society, or does it so structure its life that separatism is the conscious or preferred outcome? The minority-group school can probably function best against a separatist background. In fact, even the core school may find that under optimally separatist conditions it must accommodate the views of the minority. Participationism as well as separatism undoubtedly exist to some degree within any minority group. Their extent and influence must be mapped, and the effectiveness of the school studied in that light.

Change versus no change. Intimately related to the two considerations above is the attitude to changes in its own values on the part of the minority group. It would be misleading to claim that each group merely desires to maintain its own way of life. Societies vary tremendously in their attitudes toward change. The direction of change must also be considered, since the school that is subject to emphases on revitalization or nativism may receive from the society at large impulses different from those that operate when retentionism alone is at issue.

Vitality and exclusiveness. Minority groups differ in the degree to which they try to provide their members with structured activities in diverse areas of life. They also differ in the degree to which they succeed in attracting and holding interest in such activities. When the school is the only agent for retentionism, its effectiveness will be the less, and correspondingly, when it is a part of the whole constellation of adult and child activities in all spheres (recreational, cultural, social, religious, and economic), it is the greater.

Generational cleavage. To some extent this is a variable related to time. The cleavages in language, customs, values, and goals are probably least either soon after or long after the first exposure of the minority group to the American core society. This curvilinear relation affects the school, and the attitude of an in-group society to such a cleavage must therefore be ascertained before the effectiveness of the school can be gauged. When I. L. Child (1943) posited his rebellious, in-group, and apathetic types,[35] he was speaking of a society in the throes of a generational cleavage. Now that our minorities, to the third and fourth generation, have been exposed to American life, this typology may have less meaning. If it still has value, the proportions in each of his three types may show marked changes and thus may produce side effects with which the school must cope.

Contributions from abroad. A minority society which is continually receiving blood transfusions from abroad may be able to maintain schools exhibiting greater retentionism than one to which no new blood arrives. The new blood may consist either of ordinary immigrants or teachers, leaders, writers, or others coming from the "old country" to settle in or visit the "colonies" here. Books, music, periodicals, and financial subventions may also stiffen retentionism. Thus, communication with the old country, cultural envoys from the old country, even campaigns to help the old country—all may serve to strengthen emotional and behavioral bonds, just as the school does. On the other hand, if the old country has disappeared, the effect on the school can be shattering.

The status of the old country. The disappearance of the old country from the political or cultural map is the extreme instance of dislocation in origins. Wars, political and social changes, economic transformations, or any factors that make the home country different from what it was when the minority group lived there, will affect retentionism. Tensions between the home country and the United States, the appearance of new elites, extensive reforms in language—these are all disruptive factors which must affect the minority-group school here.

The "new country." The American mass media, not only in communications, but also in education, recreation, consumption, and production, are a potent force in reducing the distinctiveness of any segment of our population. Even if the democratic and self-determining values of the core group do affect the minorities, such values may be powerless against a uniformity that grows by mutual consent.

Demographic factors. The importance of numerical factors is self-evident, particularly if the group settles in highly urbanized surroundings and places a premium on participation. Since the minority-group school often serves a limited area and may therefore have a small enrollment, such further demographic factors as sex ratio, age distribution, population density, and the presence and status of other minority groups must be considered.

It would not be putting it too strongly to say that these factors (and any other larger societal factors) determine either the bicultural or retentionist success of the minority-group school. They interact, of course, and, in different groups at any time or in the same group at different times, they account for the variations in ascertaining school outcomes. If the school is to be a success, some need must be felt for the survival of the minority group. There must be some soil from which it can get nourishment—economic necessity, the social protection of the individual, religious convictions, or national pride. There must be some sociogenic or biogenic purposes it helps to serve better than do other groups in our complex society, in which multiple reference groups are so common. The school itself must build on these foundations, with greater or less success. It cannot normally be expected to provide those foundations.

In most sizable American minority groups, the trend of the variables mentioned above does not encourage the successful pursuit of creative bicultural retentionism. On the other hand, the American core society, even in the distant future, cannot be expected to assimilate physically the American Negro, Jewish, or Catholic societies. A triple or quadruple (or higher multiple) melting pot is here to stay. This represents the final problem—or tragedy—of the large American minority groups. Both psychologically and socially, the minorities are destined for a state of suspended animation. Having surrendered their own creative cultural props in the pursuit of the American ideal, they are left with the dilemma that the creators of the dream have themselves lost faith in it, and the dream itself cannot then be realized.

Notes ▶

1. Even more than in the case of other American minority groups, it is important to spell out the values of American Negro societies, with respect to both their congruences and conflicts with the American core values. There are a few studies which indicate that upper-, middle- and lower-class Negroes and whites have very similar values and child-rearing practices. On the other hand, the variants in Christian tenets, the folksongs and tales, the group values related to recent servitude, the ties with African groups now achieving or approaching nationhood, the "typical" views of self and of life that are related to being Negro—all these are known only intuitively, and are suggested here as elements in a specifically American-Negro cultural milieu.

2. K. B. and M. K. Clark, "The Racial Identification of Negro Pre-School Children," *Journal of Experimental Education* (JEE), 1939, 8: 161–163; "The Development of Consciousness of Self in Negro Pre-School Children," *Journal of Social Psychology*, 1939, 10: 591–599; "Skin Color as a Factor in Racial Identification," *ibid.*, 1940, 11: 159–169; R. M. Goff, *Problems and Emotional Difficulties of Negro Children*, New York, Teachers College, 1949; D. Senter and F. Hawley, "The Grammar School [and] Native New Mexicans," *Social Forces*, 1946, 24: 398–407.

3. E. Helgerson, "Race and Facial Expression in Choice of Playmate," *Journal of Negro Education* (JNE), 1943, 12: 617–622; D. H. Russel and I. V. Robertson, "Minority Groups in a Junior High School," *School Review*, 1947, 55: 205–213.

4. T. E. Davis, "Negro College and Grade School Students," JNE, 1937, 45: 525–533.

5. S. Gray, "The Wishes of Negro School Children," *Journal of Genetic Psychology*, 1944, 64: 225–227; W. I. Murray, "Social Sensitivity of Some Negro High School Pupils," JNE, 1945, 14: 149–152.

6. G. D. Mayo and J. R. A. Kinzer, " 'Racial' Attitudes of White and Negro Students, 1940, 1948," *Journal of Psychology*, 1950, 29: 397–405; Q. F. Schenk and A. K. Romney, "Differential Distance Attitudes among Adolescents," *Sociology and Social Research*, 1950, 35: 38–45.

7. R. W. Pugh, "Negro Students in Mixed and Separate High Schools," JNE, 1943, 12: 607–616.

8. M. C. Hill, "Race Attitudes in the All-Negro Community in Oklahoma," *Phylon*, 1946, 7: 260–268.

9. I. B. Prosser, "Negro Children in Mixed and Segregated Schools," JNE, 1934, 3: 269–273.

10. V. H. Fleege, *Self-Revelation of the Adolescent Boy*. Milwaukee, Bruce, 1945.

11. M. A. Dowd, "Changes in Moral Reasoning through the High School Years," *Studies in Psychology and Psychiatry*, 1948, 7: no. 2.

12. M. Brendan (Leger), "Mistaken Conceptions of Catholic School Children Regarding the Mass," *Catholic Educational Review* (CER), 1948, 46: 267–274.

13. M. B. Fannon, "Tenth Grade Students' Understanding of the Mass," CER, 1955, 53: 188; M. C. McGowan, "Understanding of the Mass among Ninth-Grade Negro Boys and Girls," CER, 1955, 53: 187.

14. Paul M. Baier, "Supernatural Life," CER, 1956, 56: 319–327; R. Morris, "The Institutionalizing of Religion," *American Catholic Sociological Review*, 1956, 17: 98–108.

15. M. S. Walz, "High School Students' Attitude to Self-Sacrifice," CER, 1950, 48: 401–402.

16. E. F. Donahue, "Reading Interests of Catholic Boys," CER, 1947, 45: 525–533.

17. M. A. Ketterer, "Motives of Catholic High School Boys in Choosing Occupations," CER, 1949, 47: 401; G. W. Holdbrook, "Attitudes of High School Girls toward Religious Life," *ibid.*, 1948, 46: 238; M. B. Luther, "Vocational Motivation of Adolescents," *ibid.*, 1950, 48: 400–401.

18. H. F. Hoover, "Attitudes of High School Students toward Mixed Marriages," CER, 1949, 47: 400; 1950, 48: 475; E. A. Leyden, "High School Pupils of Catholic and Mixed Marriage Families," *ibid.*, 1950, 48: 185–186; E. J. Vollmer, "Attitudes of Boarding and Day Students toward Mixed Marriage," *ibid.*, 1942, 47: 116; K. J. Watters, "High School Students' Attitudes toward Mixed Marriages," *ibid.*, 1949, 47: 115.

19. "Catholic Education and the 'American Way.'" *America*, 1954, 91: 535.

20. B. J. Sheil, "The Subtleties of Secularism," National Catholic Education Association *Bulletin*, 1948, 44: 6–12.

21. L. Lehrer, "The Psychology of the Jewish Child in America," *Yivo Annual of Jewish Social Science* (YAJSS), 1946, 1: 195–216; "American-Jewish Children," *Tsukunft*, 1935, 40: 513–518; "Teachers and Schools under Various Conditions," *Yivo Bleter* (Bulletin), 1936,

9: 76–106; "Children in Wartime," *Jewish Review*, 1943, 1: 31–50; "The Role of Jewish Symbols," YAJSS, 1951, 6: 37–72.

22. YAJSS, 1946, 1: 195–216.

23. *Yivo Bulletin*, 1936, 9: 76–106.

24. A. N. Franzblau, *Religious Beliefs and Character among Jewish Adolescents*. New York, Teachers College, 1934; M. L. Lurie and M. Weinreich (eds.), "Jewish Social Research," YAJSS, 1949, 4: 147–312.

25. M. Rosenbaum, "Indoctrination for Minority Group Membership," *Microfilm Abstracts*, 1949, 9: 168–170.

26. I. Chein and J. I. Hurwitz, *The Reaction of Jewish Boys to Being Jewish*. New York, National Jewish Welfare Board, 1950. Mimeo.

27. M. Radke, *Group Belonging of Jewish Children*. New York, American Jewish Congress, n.d. (1951?). Mimeo.

28. S. M. Blumfield, "Elementary Jewish Education and Interests," *Jewish Education*, 1937, 9: 143–147.

29. M. Radke, *The Meaning of Minority Membership to Jewish College Students*. New York, American Jewish Congress, n.d. (1951?). Mimeo.

30. J. A. Fishman, "Bilingualism in a Yiddish School," *Journal of Social Psychology*, 1952, 36: 155–165.

31. ————"Negative Stereotypes Concerning Americans," *Genetic Psychology Monographs*, 1955, 51: 107–182.

32. D. A. Golovensky, Ingroup and Outgroup Attitudes of Young People (Ph.D. dissertation, New York University, 1954).

33. V. Sanua, Personality Adjustment among Different Generations (Ph.D. dissertation, University of Michigan, 1956).

34. A. Eisenberg and S. Warkow, "Continuity of Higher Hebrew Study," *Jewish Education*, 1956, 26: 42–50.

35. I. L. Child, *Italian or American? The Second Generation in Conflict*. New Haven, Yale University Press, 1943.

13► THE TREATMENT OF MINORITIES IN SECONDARY SCHOOL TEXTBOOKS: CONCLUSIONS

LLOYD MARCUS

Systematic analyses of the content of the mass media a generation ago typically revealed that American minorities were stereotyped in fiction as villainous, and as engaged in menial and marginal occupational roles. Similarly, investigations of the content of textbooks for the humanities and social studies used in primary and secondary schools pointed to a pattern of condescension, error and neglect regarding the contributions to American society made by Negroes, Italians, Jews and other minorities. There was instead a preoccupation with minority-group maladjustment.

A generation later similar studies indicate insignificant change toward a more accurate portrayal of minority groups in fiction and non-fiction. The following conclusions in a recent content analysis of a sample of textbooks are the work of the Anti-Defamation League of B'nai B'rith, a Jewish agency which seeks, among its other services, to expose hostility directed against minorities in general and American Jews in particular.

► This study was designed to determine the nature of progress in textbook treatment of certain topics in intergroup relations since the publication of *Intergroup Relations in Teaching Materials*, a comprehensive study of the problem published by the American Council on Education in 1949.

From Lloyd Marcus, "The Treatment of Minorities in Secondary School Textbooks: Conclusions" (pamphlet), New York (1961), 59–60. Reprinted by permission of the author and the Anti-Defamation League of B'nai B'rith.

The current report is based on findings from 48 leading American junior and senior high school textbooks in the area of social studies. All 48 were analyzed for their presentations on the topics of Jews and Nazi persecutions of minorities, respectively. Twenty-four were selected in order to study portrayal of American Negroes and treatment of American immigrants and migrant groups. . . .

Although there has been marked, but very uneven, improvement in intergroup relations content since 1949, only a few books within each subject-area category (i.e., American history, world history, problems of American democracy) give a realistic and constructive portrayal of certain minority groups. No one book gives an adequate presentation of all four topics covered by this report.

A majority of the texts still present a largely white, Protestant, Anglo-Saxon view of history and of the current social scene. The nature and problems of minority groups in America are still very largely neglected.

I. *Treatment of the Jews continues to suffer from an overemphasis on their ancient past and on the theme of persecution.* Textbook accounts of the Crucifixion seldom involve Jews in the potentially harmful manner of older books; however, they are still too superficial to dispel misconceptions that may underlie some feelings of anti-Semitism. Much space is given to democracy's heritage from the ancient Hebrews and to the progress of the state of Israel. Jews are no longer referred to as a "race." Few texts present a varied, true-to-life picture of Jews in America today. Only a few describe past and present participation by Americans of Jewish faith and/or descent in the many phases of our national life in adequate manner.

II. *Nazi persecutions of minority groups are inadequately treated.* Approximately one-third of the 48 texts omit the topic entirely. More than three-quarters of them slight or minimize what the Nazis did to their victims. Several texts in the subject area of world history have excellent material on some aspect of the problem: Hitler's racist theories, the identity—both Jewish and non-Jewish—of his victims, the successive stages of brutality that culminated in mass murder. On the other hand, the number of victims or the international reaction and consequences of the Nazi assault on innocent people seldom get adequate space or fair presentation.

III. *The Negroes' position in contemporary American society is very largely ignored*. Textbook treatment of racial inequality, and attempts at its eradication, consist more of complacent generalizations than hard facts. In most cases, the 1954 Supreme Court decision on public school desegregation is presented without any consideration of the underlying principles and of the subsequent, ongoing attempts at compliance and evasion. The achievements of living Negro Americans are mentioned in very few books. Residential segregation by race is seldom discussed. American Negroes are portrayed, for the most part, in the eras of slavery and of Reconstruction. What comes through in most books is a stereotype of a simple, child-like, superstitious people. Neither scientific information about race nor historical data about the achievements of Negro Americans is utilized by the average book to give the reader a more valid perspective. With extremely few exceptions, photographs and other illustrations continue to show an all-white America, not an interracial and increasingly integrated nation.

IV. *Immigrants to the continental United States receive considerable attention in American history and social-problems texts.* A more sympathetic portrayal is generally accorded to the post-1880 immigrants from Southern and Eastern Europe than was reported in 1949. Similarly, the history of restrictive legislation is now seldom couched in terms that place an onus on the immigrant. But there is virtually no improvement in textbook treatment of the Asiatic immigrant, who is still shown, in most cases, as a strange, unassimilable outsider presenting a threat to the living standard of native Americans. Little attention is paid to America's increasingly significant Spanish-speaking immigrant and migrant groups. Little is said in favor of these groups; in several cases, negative stereotypes are still presented. A few textbooks continue to refer to all groups of immigrants as outsiders, but more accounts now reflect the realization that the United States is made better by the richly diversified heritage of its pluralistic citizenry.

14► ETHNOPHAULISMS AND ETHNOCENTRISM

ERDMAN B. PALMORE

There is an old and trite saying that "sticks and stones may break my bones, but words will never hurt me." If one can believe the only kind of hurt an ethnic group suffers is physical violence, and if one fails to see hurt or hostility in ethnic relations as a continuum of varying intensity, then derogatory terms, or ethnophaulisms, should be left out of any systematic study of minority problems. On the other hand, if verbal attack is recognized as a universal weapon debasing the ethnic out-group and enhancing the ethnocentrism of the in-group, then it differs only in degree from a lynching. The following analysis of ethnophaulisms by Dr. Erdman Palmore revolves around five simple but convincing and useful generalizations.

► IT SEEMS to be universal for racial and ethnic groups to coin derogatory terms and sayings to refer to other groups. Well over three thousand such terms and sayings are known today,[1] yet there is no systematic analysis of the phenomenon. Although it is frequently mentioned, there is no attempt to discover in it any pattern of generalizations,[2] nor is there even an accepted name for derogatory group nicknames. A. A. Roback has proposed the neologism "ethnophaulism" (derived from Greek roots meaning to disparage an ethnic group) to refer to group insults. Since there is apparently no other available word we will use "ethnophaulism" specifically to mean a racial or ethnic group's derogatory nickname for another.

Reprinted from Erdman B. Palmore, "Ethnophaulisms and Ethnocentrism," in *The American Journal of Sociology*, LXVII, 4 (January, 1962), 442–45, by permission of the University of Chicago Press. Copyright 1962 by the University of Chicago.

In view of the universality of ethnophaulisms and their close connection with ethnocentrism and prejudice, this analysis of the data attempts to discover patterns and generalizations that may make the sources and functions of ethnophaulisms understandable. The analysis is focused on the United States since the data from other countries are less systematic and comprehensive. Five generalizations may be made from the analysis.

1. *All racial and ethnic groups use ethnophaulisms to refer to other groups.*—Of American racial and ethnic groups, whites call Negroes "niggers" and Negroes call whites "pales"; the Spanish-speaking are called "spics" and the non-Spanish "gringos." Protestants call Catholics "mackerel-snappers," while Catholics call Protestants "prods." Occidentals call Orientals "yellow," Orientals call Occidentals "foreign devils." Gentiles call Jews "yids," Jews call Gentiles "goys." Whites call Indians "redskins," Indians call whites "palefaces." The English-speaking call the French "frog-eaters," the French call the English-speaking "anglishe" (pejorative of *Anglais*). The English-speaking call Italians "wops," Italians call the English-speaking "inglese" (connoting "an easy mark").

This proposition seems to apply also to all other known groups. Although some languages have not been systematically examined, it is probably safe to say that there is no known group which does not use ethnophaulisms.[3]

2. *There is a close association between the amount of prejudice against an out-group and the number of ethnophaulisms for it.*— This proposition seems valid for the dominant United States ethnic group, the white Anglo-Saxon Protestants (for the sake of brevity we will use the nickname "Wasp" for this group, from the initial letters of "white Anglo-Saxon Protestants"). Table 1 lists the ethnic groups in order of increasing prejudice entertained by Wasps, according to Bogardus' "Social Distance Scale."[4] The table also gives the number of ethnophaulisms listed in the *Dictionary of American Slang* used by Wasps for each group and shows an almost perfect rank correlation with the degree of prejudice (Kendall's tau = .95). Thus, it seems the greater the hatred of a group, the more ethnophaulisms express and reinforce it. An alternate interpretation would be that the more ethnophaulisms, the greater resulting prejudice—which then raises the question: Why are more ethnophaulisms used for one group than for another? This may be the old problem of the chicken and the egg.

Table 1. Rank Order of Prejudice by Wasps against Other Groups and Number of Ethnophaulisms

Racial or Ethnic Group	Rank Order*	No. of Ethnophaulisms
Canadians	1	1
British (English, Scotch, and Irish)	2	3
North Europeans (non-German)	3	4
Germans	4	9
South and East Europeans	5	9
Jews	6	15
Spanish-speaking	7	10
Oriental	8	18
Negro	9	56
Total		125

* Ranked by Bogardus' "Social Distance Scale."

Probably both interpretations are partly correct: a high degree of prejudice leads to the use of more ethnophaulisms and this in turn leads to more prejudice.

Nevertheless, it is not clear why there should be any association between prejudice and ethnophaulisms. One could speculate that greater hostility could be expressed and reinforced simply by repetition of a small number of ethnophaulisms or by using stronger ones. Nevertheless, here the number of ethnophaulisms is the important variable.

3. *When the out-group is a different race, most ethnophaulisms express stereotyped physical differences.*—This proposition seems to apply to the ethnophaulisms for Negroes, but not to those for Orientals. Two-thirds of the fifty-six ethnophaulisms for Negroes refer to stereotypes of physical difference, but only one-third of the eighteen ethnophaulisms for Orientals do so. Perhaps this is because the physical differences between Negroes and Caucasians are usually greater than those between Orientals and Caucasians.

The most common physical difference referred to is skin color (for Negroes: "blue," "blue-gum," "chocolate drop" or "chocolate bar," "dark meat," "darky," "dingie," "domino," "eight-ball," "ink," "lemon," "mocha," "nigger," "shine," "skillet," "scuttle," "seal," "shade," "shadow," "smokey," "smudge," "spade," "stove-lid," and "tar-pot").[5] Other physical ethnophaulisms refer to features of the head: hair (for Negroes, "burrhead," "fuzzy," "kinky-head," "moss," "nap," and "woolly-head"); eye ("slant-eye" or "slopie" for Orientals); nose ("hook-nose" used both by Orientals for Caucasians and by Gentiles for Jews); mouth ("satchel-mouth" and "shad-mouth" for Negroes); or shape of head ("jar-head" for Negroes and "flange-head" for Orientals). There seem to be no common ethnophaulisms for any other parts of the body. Perhaps the explanation is that skin type and head features are the most visible physical differences.

4. *When the out-group is of the same general racial type, most ethnophaulisms express stereotypes of highly visible cultural differences.*—Cultures differ as to food, language, or accent, common first names, and common occupations. Of the fifty-one ethnophaulisms applied to other Caucasian groups, 59 per cent refer to one of these differences. Twelve refer to food ("spiggoty" from spaghetti; "greaser" from greasy foods; "pepper" from peppery foods; "chili-eater"; "frog-eater"; "porker" sarcastically, from the Jewish prohibition on pork; "kraut," "sausage," and "limburger" for Germans; etc.). Eight refer to the language or accent ("yid" for Yiddish; "hebe" for Hebrew; "spick" from the phrase "No spicka da English"; etc.). Seven are corruptions of common first names ("ikey" and "kike," from the Jewish name Isaac; "abie," from the Jewish name Abraham; "mick," from the Irish name Michael; "paddy," from the Irish name Patrick). Three are derived from occupations common to the group ("cloak-and-suiter" from the common Jewish occupation of tailoring; "turf-cutter" from the Irish occupation of cutting peat; and "herring-choker" from the Scandinavian occupation of fishing). There are no ethnophaulisms for less visible differences such as family structure, education, or ideology.

5. *The derivations of most ethnophaulisms express some unfavorable stereotype.*—Of the 125 ethnophaulisms used by Wasps and listed in the *Dictionary of American Slang*, 105 (84 per cent) seem derived from unfavorable stereotypes, though in the case of several, the derivations are not obvious. The Negro term for whites, "ofey," is probably pig-latin for "foe." [6] Similarly, "ogfrey" for Frenchmen is pig-latin for "frog" (short for "frog-eater"). The terms "goy" and "goyim" for Gentiles come from ancient Hebrew and mean "uncivilized." "Sheeny" for Jew is probably derived from the German "schin" meaning a petty thief or miser. The ethnophaulism for Germans, "jerry," is from British slang for "chamber pot." "Monk" from monkey and "ring-tail" from "ring-tailed baboon" used for Orientals comes from the common notion that Orientals look like monkeys. The term "boogie" for Negroes

may be derived from the Southern slang for syphilis and thus reflect the myth that Negroes are venereally diseased; it is not derived from the type of jazz called "boogie-woogie" because the use of "boogie" to refer to both Negroes and to syphilis is much older than its use as a type of jazz. The epithet "cluck" for Negroes is probably derived from the slang word, "dumb-cluck." "Russian" for Negroes refers to Negroes who are "rushin" up North to get out of work. "Square-head" for Scandinavians may be based on the slang, "square," meaning dull, old-fashioned, or unsophisticated. "Dingbat" for Italians and for Chinese is derived from slang for vagabond or beggar. "Gook" for any foreigner comes from slang for dirt or slime.

Nevertheless, there are about twenty terms which have become derogatory but seem to be from neutral or even positive sources. The common first names which are the source of several ethnophaulisms mentioned above do not seem to have unfavorable connotations. "Pickaninny" is derived from the Portuguese for "very little"; "jig" and "jigaboo" may be related to the dance called "jig" and the Negro's supposed instinct for dance and rhythm; "wop" for Italians comes from the Spanish "guapo" meaning a tough brave man; "Bohunk" and "hunkie" come from corruptions of "Bohemian" and "Hungarian." None of these appear based on derogatory stereotypes.

Finally, there remain a few ethnophaulisms whose derivations seem to be unknown: "gange" or "kange" for Negroes, "kelt" or "keltch" for whites (Negro use), and "mockie" for Jews. Thus, although most ethnophaulisms used by Wasps seem derived from unfavorable stereotypes, the several contrary cases are a challenge for future research.

The above generalizations fit in well with the theory that labels used in a culture influence the perception and thinking of its members.[7] Thus the Wasp who is raised in a culture where such labels as "nigger" or "boogie" are common would be more likely to respond to a Negro in terms of pejorative stereotypes than if those labels were rare. According to this theory Shakespeare was wrong when he said, "What's in a name? That which we call a rose/By any other name would smell as sweet." It may well be that if a rose were labeled "stinkweed" it would be perceived as smelling less sweet.

In summary, five generalizations relating ethnophaulisms and ethnocentrism are supported by the evidence available from the

United States. Further research is needed to determine if they apply to other cultures and, if so, to show why. We may discover that ethnophaulisms are essential for the existence of such forms of ethnocentrism as chauvinism, pejorative stereotypes, scapegoats, segregation, and discrimination.

Notes ▶

1. Listed in A. A. Roback, *A Dictionary of International Slurs* (Cambridge, Mass.: Sci-Art Publishers, 1944) and in H. Wentworth and S. B. Flexner, *Dictionary of American Slang* (New York: Thomas Y. Crowell Co., 1960).

2. E.g., R. K. Merton, *Social Theory and Social Structure* (Glencoe, Ill.: Free Press, 1957), pp. 421–34; and W. G. Sumner, *Folkways* (Boston: Ginn & Co., 1940), par. 15. Wilmoth A. Carter lists nicknames in his "Nicknames and Minority Groups," *Phylon*, V (Third Quarter, 1944), 241–45, but he has not attempted systematic quantitative analysis.

3. See Roback, *op. cit.*, for lists of ethnophaulisms from more than twenty-three different languages. This would not apply to cultures which have no "slang" or nicknames: their group insults would be part of the "proper" language.

4. E. S. Bogardus, "Changes in Racial Distance," *International Journal of Opinion and Attitude Research*, I (December, 1947), 55–62.

5. Note the many negative connotations of "black" and "dark" in the English language: blackball, blackguard, blackhearted, blacklist, blackmail, darken (to make gloomy or sadden), darkness (wickedness or evil), etc.

6. The source for these derivations is the *Dictionary of American Slang*.

7. E.g., G. W. Allport, *The Nature of Prejudice* (Garden City, N.J.: Doubleday & Co., 1958), chap. x, and B. L. Whorf, *Language, Thought, and Reality* (New York: John Wiley & Sons, 1956).

15► A STUDY OF RELIGIOUS DISCRIMINATION BY SOCIAL CLUBS

HAROLD BRAVERMAN AND LOUIS KRAPIN

Many of the cruder forms of anti-Negro, anti-Semitic, and anti-Catholic hostility in American society—such as lynching and restrictions in employment, public accommodations and education —are no longer of the same magnitude as they were up until World War II. What persists with little diminution, nevertheless, is the genteel exclusion of some minority groups by social clubs. The extent of such discrimination against one prominent minority group—the American Jews—is alleged to exceed by far the restrictions the group now experiences in education, employment, housing and public accommodations. One reaction, as we see in the following study, is the emergence of the minority group's own social clubs.

► DISCRIMINATORY PRACTICES by social clubs, long recognized as a pervasive pattern among proverbially gregarious Americans, were dramatically and publicly challenged last summer by the U.S. Attorney General and several other important public figures who resigned from the Metropolitan Club, probably the most distinguished club in Washington, D.C.

In the spring of 1959 Dr. Ralph Bunche publicly challenged the action of the West Side Tennis Club in Forest Hills, N.Y. in refusing membership to his son. The Club is the scene of the most

From *Rights*, 4, 3 (January, 1962), 83–86. Reprinted by permission of the authors and the Anti-Defamation League of B'nai B'rith.

important national and international tennis matches held in the U.S.

In 1955, Mrs. Eleanor Roosevelt, invited to speak at a community Brotherhood Week function in Lancaster, Pa., cancelled her appearance at the last moment. She found that the club at which the meeting was to be held barred Jews from membership and as guests at all other times.

Why these public challenges? Clubs which discriminate on religious and racial grounds have traditionally taken, and won acceptance for, the position that the social club is an extension of one's own parlor. Since a man has a right to choose whom he will invite into his home, he thus also has the right to choose whom he will admit to his club.

Are these actions then a challenge to the right of privacy or a questioning of the nature of the social or private club? Attorney General Kennedy said it was the latter, explaining that the Metropolitan Club's restrictive policy, because it kept members from inviting certain foreign diplomats into the Club, created international political ramifications.

Dr. Bunche took a similar position. He contended that the West Side Tennis Club, because of its central place in the tennis world, was not merely a private sports club, but had a quasi-public character.

As for Mrs. Roosevelt, she questioned the morality of holding a Brotherhood Week observance in a club that at all other times excluded people whom it was willing to acknowledge as brothers on this one day only.

Are the positions cited here then a challenge to the right of privacy or are they indeed a challenge to those who, by their insistence upon social exclusiveness, seek to obtain or hold economic, political and other power advantages to which they may otherwise not be entitled?

If the latter, social discrimination (i.e., discrimination by clubs) assumes new dimensions. If the seat of power in any community discriminates against Jews, it may sound a note that will be taken up by others in the community. The industrialist will be confirmed in his negative view about Jewish plant managers; the plant managers in turn will find it more expedient not to employ Jewish subordinates. Lower echelon civic groups, ears closely attuned to the note from on high, will find sanction for similar exclusions. The university, upon whose board of trustees sit members of the discriminatory club, will not protest a quota system, the fraternities will mimic their elders in exclusionary practices. Thus may a new generation, while still in its formative years, be schooled in the ways and benefits of social discrimination.

Comparatively few of the exclusionary clubs are strategic elements in the power structure of a community; many more merely foster undesirable and undemocratic social practices. These latter groups may be only minor sources of irritation, singly, but they represent in their totality a formidable expression of anti-Semitic attitudes. They are the result of social and economic forces which have been operating on the American scene for many decades. They represent the attitudes of individual Americans and, in that sense, signify that education for democracy still has far to go.

Obviously, the Anti-Defamation League must be concerned with the irrational exclusion of Jews from clubs which by reasonable test are secular in purpose and program. For such exclusions represent a philosophy of racism. At the same time, ADL is aware that the practices of clubs which bar Jews has had its concomitant in the establishment by Jews of separate club facilities. Some of these, as the statistics on the following pages will show, also adopted exclusionary patterns.

The Sample

To determine the extent of religious discrimination by social clubs in the United States, the Anti-Defamation League surveyed a representative list of such clubs which could be reasonably termed a national cross-section. The criterion for selection was whether the clubs employed professional managers. A list of clubs maintained by a group of professionals in the private club field was used for the sample. The total number of such clubs was 1,332. For purposes of the study 44 Armed Forces clubs on the list were excluded, leaving a balance of 1,288 clubs with essentially civilian memberships.

The 1,288 clubs were situated in 46 states and the District of Columbia. Only four states—Alaska, Maine, New Hampshire and Vermont—were not represented in the survey group which was based on the list. The number of clubs in the other states ranged from one each in North Dakota and Wyoming to 159 in New York State.

The clubs on which information was sought were broadly of two types. First, city clubs which were defined as clubs physically situated within cities or towns; there were 369 such. In terms of distribution among the states, the number of city clubs ranged from one each in seven states to 59 in New York State.

The second major group on which information was sought was country clubs. There were 919 such clubs on the initiation of this survey. Country clubs were defined as those located in suburban and rural areas which had the accoutrements normally associated with country clubs—golf course, tennis courts, swimming pools, and other sport facilities.

The distribution of the country clubs among the states ranged from one in each of four states to 116 in the State of New York.

Aims of the Study

The first step was to obtain an evaluation of the status of each club. Three categories were established: (1) high prestige or power structure clubs; (2) those which enjoyed average acceptance in their community; (3) and those which were considered of little or no importance. This information was obtained by interviewing knowledgeable people and polling a cross-section of community opinion. At the same time, an estimate of each club's membership was sought.

Thereafter, a determination was made for each club as to whether it discriminated on the basis of religion.

An identification of "non-discriminatory" was made if the club accepted Christians and Jews without regard to religion in its membership policy and practice. For any clubs so identified, no further information was sought.

However, if the club were considered discriminatory on grounds of religion, it was studied further. Such clubs would be identified as "Christian" clubs if they either barred Jews or had a quota for Jewish membership. The reporters were asked to distinguish between those clubs that barred Jews absolutely and those that admitted Jews on a limited basis.

In the same way, identification was made of "Jewish" clubs which either barred Christians or had quotas for Christian members.

Finally, wherever a club was identified as a "Christian club" or a "Jewish club," the reporter sought to establish whether the restrictions were official (i.e., in the club's constitution or by-laws) or unofficial (i.e., informal, gentlemen's agreements, etc.)

The Final Study Group

Of the 1,288 clubs on which information was sought data were received on 1,152, or almost 90 percent. The remaining 136 included clubs that had gone out of existence, or about which, for a variety of reasons, information was not available.

The 1,152 clubs about which information was obtained were located in 46 states and the District of Columbia. Again, only four states—Alaska, Maine, New Hampshire and Vermont—were not represented. The 1,152 clubs were distributed from a low of one each in Nevada, North Dakota and Wyoming to a high of 149 in New York State.

Of the 1,152 clubs, 349 were city clubs. These city clubs were distributed from a low of one each in Idaho, Mississippi, Montana, New Mexico, North Dakota, Rhode Island and West Virginia to a high of 43 in the State of New York.

Information was obtained on 803 country clubs which were distributed from a low of one each in Idaho, Nevada, South Dakota and Wyoming to a high of 106 in New York State.

National Findings—City and Country Clubs Combined

1. Of the 1,152 clubs on which sufficient information was received for evaluation, 693 (or 60 percent) were deemed to enjoy top status in their communities. 372 clubs in the national group (or almost 33 percent of the total) had average acceptance in their communities. The remaining clubs, numbering 87 (or almost 8 percent of the national survey group), were evaluated as clubs which enjoyed little or no standing in their communities.

2. The total estimated membership of the 1,152 clubs in the survey group was almost 700,000.

3. Of the 1,152 clubs, 371 (or almost 33 percent) were non-discriminatory, erecting no religious barriers to membership.

4. 781 clubs (or 67 percent) practiced religious discrimination.

5. Of the 781 clubs which practiced religious discrimination, 691 were "Christian clubs" which either barred Jews completely or imposed a limitation upon the number of Jews that could join.

These 691 "Christian clubs" represented 88 percent of all the discriminatory clubs and 60 percent of all clubs examined.

6. Of the 781 discriminatory clubs, 90 were "Jewish clubs" which either barred Christian membership or imposed limitations upon Christians. Thus, the "Jewish clubs" represented almost 12 percent of all the discriminatory clubs, and almost 8 percent of all clubs studied.

7. Of the 691 "Christian clubs," 555 (or about 80 percent) barred Jews completely. The remainder, 136 (or about 20 percent), limited Jewish membership to small numbers.

8. Of the 90 "Jewish clubs," 85 (or about 95 percent of the group) barred Christian members completely; the other five admitted Christians in small numbers.

9. Of the 781 discriminatory clubs, 696 (or 90 percent) maintained their restrictions "unofficially"—without religious proscriptions in their constitutions or by-laws. The restrictive practices of these clubs was carried out informally through gentlemen's agreements, etc. The remaining 85 restrictive clubs were said to maintain their restrictions "officially"—by constitution or by-laws.

City Clubs

1. Of the 349 city clubs that were evaluated, 210 (60 percent) enjoyed top status in their cities and towns. 106 (more than 30 percent of the city clubs) had average acceptance in their communities while the remaining city clubs, numbering 33 (almost 10 percent of all the city clubs) were evaluated as groups that enjoyed little or no standing in their communities. It may be noted at this point that the status distribution of the city clubs is almost identical with the status distribution of all *City and Country Clubs Combined.*

2. The total estimated membership of the 349 city clubs was almost 300,000 or slightly less than half of the total estimated membership of *City and Country Clubs Combined.*

3. Of the 349 city clubs surveyed, it was found that 147 (over 40 percent) were non-discriminatory, erecting no religious barriers to membership.

4. 202 city clubs (almost 60 percent) practiced religious discrimination.

5. Of the 202 city clubs that practiced religious discrimination, 186 (or more than 90 percent of all discriminatory city clubs) were

"Christian clubs" which either barred Jews completely or imposed limitations on the number of Jews that could join. It may be noted here that discriminatory "Christian clubs" comprised more than 50 percent of all the city clubs examined.

6. Of the 202 discriminatory city clubs, 16 were "Jewish clubs;" 14 of these barred Christians completely while two accepted Christians in small numbers. Thus, "Jewish clubs" represented about 8 percent of all the discriminatory city clubs and about 5 percent of all the city clubs studied.

7. Of the 186 "Christian city clubs," 139 (or about 80 percent) barred Jews completely. The other 47 "Christian city clubs" limited Jewish membership to small numbers.

8. Of the 202 discriminatory city clubs, 183 (or 90 percent) maintained "unofficial" restrictions by means of gentlemen's agreements, etc. The remaining 19 discriminatory city clubs were said to maintain their restrictions "officially."

9. The 202 discriminatory city clubs were analyzed to determine how they were distributed in terms of status. We found that of the 202 discriminatory city clubs, 115 (or 55 percent) were reported as enjoying top prestige in the cities and towns where they were located. 63 of the discriminatory city clubs (32 percent) were identified as having average acceptance in their communities. The remaining discriminatory city clubs, 24 in number (or about 13 percent of the discriminatory group), were identified as being of little or no consequence in their communities. It should be noted that the total estimated membership of the discriminatory city clubs was over 200,000, representing almost a third of the total estimated membership of all the clubs we surveyed.

Country Clubs

1. Of the 803 country clubs evaluated, 483 (60 percent) were top status clubs. 266 (33 percent of the country clubs) had average acceptance while the remaining country clubs, 54 (or 7 percent), were evaluated as not having significant standing. Again, it is noteworthy that the status distribution of the country clubs in percentages is virtually identical with the status distribution of all *City and Country Clubs Combined* and with *City Clubs*.

2. The total estimated membership of the 803 country clubs was over 400,000, or more than half of the total estimated membership of all the clubs surveyed.

3. Of the 803 country clubs surveyed, 224 (28 percent) were non-discriminatory, erecting no religious barriers to membership.

4. 579 country clubs (72 percent) practiced religious discrimination. It should be noted that this percentage figure is appreciably higher than the proportion of city clubs (60 percent) that used religious criteria.

5. Of the 579 country clubs that discriminate along religious lines, 505 (or 87 percent of all the discriminatory country clubs) were "Christian clubs." It is worthy of note that the "Christian clubs" comprised almost 63 percent of all the country clubs in our study group.

6. Of the 579 discriminatory country clubs, 74 were "Jewish clubs;" 71 barred Christians completely, while three accepted Christians in small numbers. The "Jewish country clubs" represented about 12 percent of all discriminatory country clubs and about 9 percent of all the country clubs studied.

7. Of the 505 "Christian country clubs," 416 (or about 80 percent) barred Jews completely. The other 89 "Christian country clubs" (or about 20 percent) limited the membership of Jews.

8. Of the 579 discriminatory country clubs, 513 (about 90 percent) maintained their restrictions "unofficially." The other 66 country clubs were reported to have restrictions in their constitutions or by-laws.

9. The 579 discriminatory country clubs were analyzed for status distribution. We found that of the 579 country clubs, 352 (60 percent) were top groups. 182 (32 percent) were described as clubs with average acceptance in their communities while the remaining discriminatory country clubs, 45 in number (or 8 percent of the discriminatory group), were of low rank. The total estimated membership of the discriminatory country clubs was about 260,000, or somewhat over a third of the total estimated membership of all the clubs surveyed.

Regional Analysis

As we pointed out in our *National Findings—City and Country Clubs Combined*, our study of 1,152 clubs revealed that 781 (or 67 percent of the national total) practiced religious discrimination. 691 were "Christian clubs" that discriminated against Jews, while 90 were "Jewish clubs" which discriminated against persons of the Christian faith.

In order to determine whether there were any significant regional differences with respect to club discrimination, we analyzed our data in terms of five geographical areas, as follows:

1. *South and Southwest*: Alabama, Arizona, Arkansas, District of Columbia, Florida, Georgia, Kentucky, Louisiana, Mississippi, North Carolina, Oklahoma, South Carolina, Tennessee, Texas, Virginia, West Virginia.

2. *Far West*: California, Colorado, Hawaii, Nevada, New Mexico, Oregon, Utah, Washington, Wyoming.

3. *Mid West*: Idaho, Illinois, Indiana, Iowa, Kansas, Michigan, Minnesota, Missouri, Montana, Nebraska, North Dakota, Ohio, South Dakota, Wisconsin.

4. *North Atlantic*: Delaware, Maryland, New Jersey, New York, Pennsylvania.

5. *New England*: Connecticut, Massachusetts, Rhode Island. Here follow the findings:

1. The regional percentages of discriminatory clubs are: South and Southwest, 60 percent; Far West, 58 percent; Mid West, 73 percent; North Atlantic, 74 percent; New England, 68 percent. From these data, it appears that discrimination by clubs is significantly higher in the Mid West and North Atlantic states than in the other three regions.

2. Of the discriminatory clubs in the South and Southwest, 91 percent are "Christian clubs." In the Far West the percentage is 95. In the Mid West, the "Christian clubs" comprise 89 percent of all discriminatory clubs. In the North Atlantic states and New England, the proportions were 81 percent and 93 percent respectively.

3. The proportion of "Jewish clubs" among the discriminatory clubs varies little in four regions. In the South and Southwest it is 9 percent; in the Far West, 5 percent; in the Mid West, 11 percent; and in New England, 7 percent. But in the North Atlantic states, 19 percent of all the discriminatory clubs were "Jewish clubs."

The Athletic Clubs

It has long been believed that many major city clubs calling themselves "Athletic Clubs" (usually preceded by the names of their home cities) show a complete disregard for the maxim of fair play. The study provided an opportunity to evaluate the long-held suspicion that "Athletic Clubs" in large American cities frequently set up religious criteria for membership.

The survey group included 19 "Athletic Clubs" situated in 19 great cities. The total membership of these 19 clubs is over 50,000. Fourteen of them are regarded as prestige groups while five are said to have average acceptance in their communities.

Of the 19 "Athletic Clubs," only five are non-discriminatory as between Jews and Christians. However, of the remaining 14 clubs, seven bar Jews completely while seven impose a quota upon Jewish membership.

In short, 75 percent of the city "Athletic Clubs" examined have discriminatory barriers against Jewish members. And, contrary to the courage so commonly associated with athletic activities, these discriminatory clubs universally enforce their restrictions "unofficially"—i.e., by gentlemen's agreements and the blackball.

The Prestige Clubs

In order to understand better the potential impact upon Jews of club discrimination, the data were analyzed with particular attention to clubs that were evaluated as enjoying maximum prestige in their communities.

Of the 1,152 city and country clubs examined, 693 (60 percent) were accorded such distinction. Of these 693 top American clubs, 455 (66 percent) practice religious discrimination.

Of the 455 discriminatory clubs, 417 (more than 90 percent) discriminate against Jews.

To recapitulate in terms of the total prestige group of 693 clubs included in our study, 60 percent of the prestige group discriminated against Jews; 5 percent discriminated against Christians; and 35 percent were non-discriminatory in terms of religion.

Conclusions

1. Religious discrimination by clubs in the United States is extensive and pervasive. The fact that 67 percent of all the clubs studied practiced religious discrimination indicates a serious failure on the part of the American community, at the social level, to accept the individual on the basis of individual worth and merit.

2. If the thesis is accepted that many prestige clubs are factors in the power structures which influence greatly the political and

economic life of the community, then the fact that 60 percent of the prestige clubs of the United States discriminate against Jews has serious implications for the Jewish group.

3. It would appear that the extent of discrimination against Jews by clubs is far greater than the levels of discrimination against Jews in other areas such as education, employment, housing and public accommodations.

4. A consequence of the development of the institution of the "Christian club" has been the emergence of the "Jewish club." The fact that almost 8 percent of all the clubs studied were "Jewish clubs" that discriminated against Christians is eloquent testimony to the further institutionalization of religious prejudice. When, as and if Jewish community relations agencies conclude that the problem of the "Christian club" merits their attention, they will inevitably have to cope with the other side of the coin— the "Jewish club."

16► RACIAL INEQUALITY IN EMPLOYMENT: THE PATTERNS OF DISCRIMINATION

HERBERT HILL

A *hard core of ethnic stratification in American society, as well as elsewhere, is the inequality of economic opportunity between groups. Minorities rarely have equal access to the same training, occupational structure, income and financial security afforded dominant groups. Except for some American Indians, no American minority suffers more in this respect than do American Negroes, among whom unemployment runs almost twice as high as among whites.*

The long-term paradox behind this ratio is that at the start of the economic depression in the 1930's—and long before any meaningful civil rights movement—the unemployment rate for nonwhites was approximately equal to that of whites. And despite a wide demand for Negro white-collar workers, the median income of Negroes fell by 1965 to only slightly more than half the income of whites, lower than it was in 1955. Even when American Negroes are gainfully employed they are concentrated in the occupations with the lowest wage scales.

The next essay by Mr. Herbert Hill, Labor Secretary of the National Association for the Advancement of Colored People, emphasizes that while American Negroes have been making legal gains—as in the passage of the Civil Rights Act of 1964—they have been losing in their struggle for economic justice.

From "The Negro Protest," *The Annals of the American Academy of Political and Social Science*, Vol. 357 (January, 1965), 31–47. Reprinted by permission of the author and publisher.

TIMISTIC ASSUMPTIONS regarding the Negro's progress in ican society must be re-examined in the light of the Negro's current economic plight. The great mass of Negroes, especially in the urban centers, are locked in a permanent condition of poverty. This includes the long-term unemployed as well as the working poor, who know only a marginal economic existence and who increasingly are forced into the ranks of the unemployed.

The Unemployment Crisis

The Negro community throughout the United States is today experiencing a crisis of unemployment. Negroes now constitute a very large part of the hard-core, permanently unemployed group in American society. In Northern industrial centers one out of every three Negro workers was unemployed for varying lengths of time between 1958 and 1963, and a very high proportion exhausted all of their unemployment compensation benefits. More than 50 per cent of all the unskilled Negro workers in the country have been unemployed for substantial periods since 1958. Furthermore, it is evident that the unskilled Negro worker, forty-five years of age and over, who has lost his job, will never again work at productive gainful employment.

Of great significance is the fact that, since 1951, the differential in the average income of Negro and white workers has been increasing. By December of 1951, the Negro median wage was approaching 57 per cent of the white workers' average income. Since that time, however, the gap between the income of white and Negro workers has been growing steadily greater. In Michigan, for example, the ratio of average Negro income to white income dropped from 87 per cent in 1949 to 76 per cent in 1958, and has continuously deteriorated since that time.[1]

During the period of 1960–1961 in Chicago, Negroes, who constitute 20 per cent of the total labor force, were 43 per cent of Chicago's unemployed. This does not include the significant number of Negroes who, in Chicago, as elsewhere, have dropped out of the labor force and, therefore, are no longer counted among the unemployed.

During 1960–1961, white males in Chicago between the ages of 25 and 44 had an unemployment rate of only 2.2 per cent—minimal unemployment; however, in the Negro ghetto in Chicago, and in other urban industrial centers, unemployment has become a way of life. In thirty-one all-Negro census tracts, the unemployment rate was over 15 per cent, while only three white census tracts have a ratio that high. Labor force projections indicate that there will be 450,000 more workers in Chicago's metropolitan area in 1970 than there were in 1960. More than one-third of these will be Negro. Yet the trend of employment potentiality indicates that only 150,000 new positions will be created by 1970. The future holds only the prospect of increasing long-term unemployment for the Negro wage earner.[2]

As a result of automation and other technological changes in the economy, unskilled and semiskilled job occupations are disappearing at the rate of 35,000 a week or nearly two million a year. It is in these job classifications that there has been a disproportionate displacement of Negro workers.

The economic well-being of the entire Negro community is directly and adversely affected by the generations of enforced overconcentration of Negro wage earners in the unskilled and menial job classifications in the industrial economy. A continuation of this pattern will cause even greater crises in the years to come unless fundamental and rapid changes take place in the occupational characteristics and mobility of Negro labor in the United States. In March of 1964, the United States Department of Labor announced that Negroes constitute 20.6 per cent of the nation's unemployed, although Negroes comprise only 10 per cent of the population. To quote the *New York Times*, "Unemployment of these proportions were it general, would be a national catastrophe."

Months before the 1964 summer racial disturbances in New York City, a report was made public by Dr. Kenneth Clark, a well-known psychologist on the faculty of the City College of New York and Director of the Northside Clinic, a psychiatric center in Harlem.

This 615-page study known as the HARYOU report, sponsored by Harlem Youth Opportunities Unlimited (HARYOU), a research program jointly financed by United States government and New York City funds, was conducted for over eighteen months by a staff directed by Dr. Clark and was released under the subtitle: "A Study of the Consequences of Powerlessness and a Blueprint for Change." This highly significant report documented in great detail the pattern of life in Harlem and described the Negro's status in the nation's largest segregated community.

This report notes that unemployment in Harlem is more than double the unemployment rate in the rest of the city, that median income of Harlem residents is less than 60 per cent of the city's median, that even for those who work, "the menial and unrewarding nature of the employment of most of the Negro men and women living in this ghetto can only mean a marginal subsistence for their families."

In relation to future prospects for Negro employment, the report indicates that almost half of all Negro workers in New York City are concentrated in "dead end" jobs—in occupational classifications that will be eliminated as a result of technological innovation—and that Negro wage earners in large numbers are prevented from developing new employment skills. The Study warns "that the unemployment situation among Negro youth in Central Harlem is explosive," and notes an increasing "movement towards jobs of an even more menial and marginal nature." Dr. Clark's conclusions were confirmed by United States government figures which revealed that 26 per cent of male Negro youths were unemployed during July of 1964. The jobless rate among Negro male youth for all of 1963 was 25.4 per cent, nearly twice as high as the figure among their white counterparts.

The Negro in the South

There can be no doubt that in the Southern states there exists a rigid and systematic pattern of employment discrimination based on race. Industrial management and organized labor, as well as state agencies and the federal government, are responsible for the continued existence of the pattern of racial job discrimination. An immense industrial development has been taking place in the southeastern states since the end of World War II, but a most disturbing aspect of the rapid growth of manufacturing facilities in the South has been the serious inability of the Negro worker to register significant employment gains in the new Southern industrial economy.

Investigations indicate that in the textile industry, still the basic manufacturing industry of the South, Negroes are in a most marginal position. According to state government figures, the number of textile workers employed in South Carolina was 48,000 in 1918 and 122,000 in 1960, while the percentage of Negroes in the textile labor force fell from 9 per cent to 4.7 per cent over this period. On

July 6, 1961, the National Association for the Advancement of Colored People filed an extensive series of complaints against major textile manufacturing companies with the President's Committee on Equal Employment Opportunity. Three years later there is little change in the racial occupational pattern in the Southern textile industry. Negroes remain concentrated in menial and unskilled classifications and comprise about 2 per cent of the work force.

The Committee has very limited powers in carrying out the purpose of Executive Order 10925, which requires equal employment opportunities by all contractors doing business with the United States government. Its impotence becomes evident when confronted by the powerful financial and political forces in control of the textile industry.

On April 6, 1962, in an appraisal of the first year of operation of the President's Committee on Equal Employment Opportunity the NAACP stated:

The administration has relied for favorable publicity on a superficial approach called "Plans for Progress." The so-called "Plans for Progress"—voluntary agreements entered into by a few large corporations—may yield high returns in press notices but only superficial and token results for Negro workers in new job opportunities. The "Plans for Progress" have not produced the large scale job opportunities for Negro workers that have been so long denied them. It is our experience that major U.S. Government contractors operating vast multi-plant enterprises regard the signing of a "Plan for Progress" as a way of securing immunity from real compliance with the antidiscrimination provision of their government contract.

In January 1963, the Southern Regional Council [3] confirmed the judgment of the NAACP regarding voluntary compliance and concluded with the following statement regarding the operation of the "Plans for Progress" in the Atlanta area:

Most contractors felt—and readily stated—that the Plan was not applicable to them. A few said it would become applicable when the hiring of a Negro would be advantageous, i.e., when the Negro market demanded it. Some did not even know of the existence of the "Plans for Progress" while others who knew, and who did employ a few Negro janitors or porters on their staffs, felt they were thereby upholding the object of the Plan. To sum up, indications are that the interpretation of the voluntary and affirmative provisions of the program is being left to the individual signers themselves.

In heavy industry, the gains of Negro labor throughout the Southern states are most limited. Negro employment is negligible in such major industrial operations as the General Motors plants in Atlanta and Doraville, Georgia, and the Ford Motor Company plants in Atlanta, Memphis, Norfolk, and Dallas. The employment study made by the United States Commission on Civil Rights confirms our opinion that very little progress has been made by the Southern Negro in heavy industry. The Commission's findings are summarized in part in its published report as follows:

This Commission's investigations in three cities—Atlanta, Baltimore and Detroit—and a Commission hearing in Detroit revealed that in most industries studied, patterns of Negro employment by Federal contractors conformed to local industrial employment patterns. In Atlanta, the two automobile assembly plants contacted employed no Negroes in assembly operations. Except for one driver of an inside power truck, all Negro employees observed were in janitorial work— sweeping, mopping, carrying away trash. Lack of qualified applicants cannot account for the absence of Negroes from automotive assembly jobs in Atlanta. Wage rates are relatively high for the locality and the jobs are in great demand. The work is at most semi-skilled and educational requirements are extremely low.[4]

A major problem for Negro workers in Southern industry is the operation of separate racial seniority lines in collective bargaining agreements entered into by management and labor unions. Investigations of the status of Negro workers in pulp and papermaking operations, in chemical and oil refining, in steel and tobacco manufacturing, as well as in other important sectors of the Southern industrial economy, clearly indicate that Negroes are usually hired exclusively in classifications designated as "common laborer" or "yard labor" or "nonoperating department" or "maintenance department." These are the euphemisms for the segregated all-Negro labor departments established by the separate racial promotional lines in many labor-management contracts throughout Southern industry. As a result of these discriminatory provisions, white persons are initially hired into production or skilled craft occupations which are completely closed to Negro workers. The Negro worker who is hired as a laborer in the "maintenance department" or "yard labor department" is denied seniority and promotional rights into desirable production classifications and is also denied admission into apprentice and other training programs. In these situations Negro seniority rights are operative only within certain all-Negro departments, and Negro workers therefore have an extremely limited job mobility. Thus Donald Dewey, of Columbia University, reports that most Southerners believe that their economy is divided into "white" and "Negro" jobs.[5] The North Carolina Advisory Committee to the United States Commission on Civil Rights reports that, "North Carolina in common with states of its region, has traditions which more or less automatically assign Negroes to menial or unskilled positions." [6]

The pulp and papermaking industry is one of the fastest growing manufacturing industries in the South. Company management and the trade unions which have jurisdiction in this important Southern industry are responsible for a rigid pattern of discriminatory practices including separate racial promotional lines in union contracts which limit Negro workers to menial, unskilled job classifications at low pay and which violate their basic seniority rights. The two dominant unions in this industry are the United Papermakers' and Paperworkers' Union and the International Brotherhood of Pulp, Sulphite and Paper Mill Workers' Union, both affiliated with the AFL-CIO. In virtually every paper mill in the South where they hold collective bargaining agreements, these two unions operate segregated locals and include discriminatory provisions in their union contracts. A compelling example of the operation of segregated locals with separate racial seniority lines is to be found at the large manufacturing plant of the Union Bag-Camp Paper Corporation in Savannah, where thousands of persons are employed. This plant has the largest single industrial payroll in Savannah.

The tobacco industry is important in the Southern industrial economy, and here, too, we find a pattern of separate racial seniority lines in virtually all collective bargaining agreements between the major tobacco manufacturing companies and the Tobacco Workers International Union, AFL-CIO. In one of the largest manufacturing plants, that of the Liggett & Myers Tobacco Company in Durham, North Carolina, colored workers are employed in unskilled and janitorial jobs with limited seniority rights operative only in all-Negro designated classifications. Investigations made by the NAACP indicate that in this tobacco manufacturing plant, as in so many others, Negroes are initially hired only as sweepers, janitors, and toilet attendants and are promoted exclusively within the limited "Negro" seniority line of progression.

Negro railway workers throughout the South are the victims of a traditional policy of job discrimination as a result of collusion between railway management and railroad labor unions. In St. Petersburg, the Atlantic Coast Line Railroad, and, in Memphis, the St. Louis-San Francisco Railroad Company, for example, have entered into agreements with the Brotherhood of Railroad Trainmen to deny qualified Negro railway workers opportunities for promotion and advancement. These are typical of similar practices elsewhere.

The Brotherhood of Railroad Trainmen, an AFL-CIO affiliate, removed the "Caucasian Only" clause from its constitution in 1959. However, this was apparently for public relations purposes only, as the union continues in most cities to exclude qualified Negro railroad employees. Frequently, in collusion with management, Negro brakemen are classified as "porters" and then refused membership in the union under the pretext of their being outside its jurisdiction. This, however, does not prevent the Trainmen's Union from negotiating wages and other conditions of employment for these so-called "porters" who have no representation in the collective bargaining unit.

State Employment Services

Another extremely serious problem confronting Negro workers is the discriminatory practices of state employment services whose operation, in Southern states, is characterized by a pattern of racial segregation and discrimination. These states include Alabama, Florida, Georgia, Louisiana, Mississippi, North Carolina, South Carolina, and, partially, Virginia and Tennessee. Job orders are racially designated, and job referrals are made on the basis of race. Major industrial corporations operating with federal government contracts cannot possibly be in compliance with the President's Executive Order banning employment discrimination where such contractors in the South are using the facilities of the state employment services. The United States government is completely responsible for providing the operating costs of all state employment services. Federal funds are disbursed by the Department of Labor, which administers the Federal-State Employment Services program. It obviously makes no sense for the Administration to issue executive orders banning employment discrimination by government contractors while agencies of the federal government subsidize such discriminatory practices. The NAACP has repeatedly called upon the United States Department of Labor to take decisive action to eliminate the pattern of discrimination and segregation in the operation of state employment services.

Federal Support of Discrimination

Even in the North, the operation of the state employment services represents a serious problem to Negro workers. The state employment services receive funds and awards from the federal government based to a very large degree on the number of gross placements made during the year. This inevitably places operating personnel in the position of responding to arbitrary and discriminatory job requirements in referring workers for jobs and in selecting them for admission into training facilities. A further problem is the usual tacit assumption by local employment service personnel that there are "white" jobs and "colored" jobs. This is a result of the prevailing hiring pattern in many localities and the reluctance of state employment services to innovate changes in the established racial patterns.

Because the colored worker is extremely vulnerable to long-term unemployment as a result of the combined factors of racial discrimination and technological change, Negro workers more than any other group in the work force qualify for training under the Federal Manpower Development and Training Act. However, investigations made by the NAACP clearly indicate that Negroes, with some few exceptions, are being limited to programs that simply perpetuate the traditional concentration of Negroes in menial and unskilled jobs. Thus, in Portland, Oregon, there was an all-Negro training program for hotel waiters, and in Pensacola, Florida, there were all-Negro programs for chambermaids and waitresses. In Birmingham, Alabama, there are all-white training programs in electronics and arc welding, but Negroes are limited to training as laundry-machine operators and shirt-pressers. In Beaufort, South Carolina, there is a training program for Negro waiters, while in Greenville, South Carolina, there is an all-white program for general machine and tool machine workers. The *Courier-Journal*, Louisville, Kentucky, December 11, 1962, in a news report headlined "200 Retrainees Can't Get Jobs" states: "One course was held for Negro clerk-stenographers but it developed that employers in that area wanted only white clerical help."

On May 3, 1963, Clarence Mitchell, director of the NAACP Washington Bureau, in a strongly worded letter to Representative Carl D. Perkins, chairman of the General Subcommittee on Education of the House Committee on Education and Labor, protested against the racial practices of Manpower Development and Training Act (MDTA) programs. The Association requested the correction of policies which force Negroes to be shunted into training programs for "chambermaids, shirt pressers, service station attendants, waiters and waitresses." Although expressing support for the MDTA general program, the NAACP statement condemned practices "which foster racial segregation and also continue to promote the antiquated idea that the kitchen is the only place for colored wage-earners."

In addition to the pattern of racial segregation in the training programs conducted under the Manpower Development and Training Act in Alabama, Georgia, Mississippi, South Carolina, and other Southern states, reports from Northern communities indicate that because of the statutory requirement that there shall be "reasonable expectation of employment" as a basis for entry into training programs, unemployed low-skilled Negro workers are very frequently screened out of admission into desirable programs for skilled craft training. The consequences of the Manpower Development and Training Act for Negroes have been no training or segregated training or training for the lowest and least desirable job classifications. A continuation of this pattern will simply extend and deepen the job gap between white and Negro workers.

The Department of Health, Education, and Welfare each year distributes fifty-five millions of dollars of federal funds for education under the Smith-Hughes Act; a very large part of this is given to vocational training programs in which Negroes are totally excluded or limited to unequal segregated facilities. Vocational and trade schools in the Southern states receive a substantial part of these federal funds, but in most Southern urban areas where there has been a tremendous growth of manufacturing operations, we find that the limited programs offered in Negro vocational schools are obsolete in terms of modern industrial technology. Thus, while white students in vocational schools are preparing for advanced technology in electronics and for the automotive and aero-space industries, Negroes are limited to "home economics" and other traditional service occupations, and here also the federal government has a direct responsibility for helping to perpetuate the pattern that makes the Negro worker an unskilled worker and most vulnerable to large-scale permanent unemployment.

Apprenticeship and Vocational Training

For every 100 skilled workers that the nation had in 1955, it will need 122 in 1965 and 145 in 1975. However, all the available data clearly indicate that the nation's apprenticeship programs, as well as other training programs, are not even turning out enough new craftsmen to replace those who retire. Automation and other technological changes in the economy have greatly increased the demand for skilled workers, and, currently, the large appropriations for national defense also significantly increase the demand for skilled workers and technicians. It is now clear that in the next decade the entire American economy will be faced with a serious crisis because of the lack of skilled manpower.

A major factor contributing to the irrational, wasteful, and socially harmful operation of the nation's apprenticeship and vocational training programs is the color discrimination and racial exclusion which characterize training programs in major sectors of the economy in the North as well as the South. Discrimination in job-training programs is also greatly responsible for the very high rate of Negro unemployment.

For many occupations the only way a worker can be recognized as qualified for employment is to successfully complete apprenticeship training programs. This is true for the printing trades, among machinists and metal workers, in the various crafts in the building and construction trades industry, and many others.

Studies, such as that made by the New York State Commission Against Discrimination,[7] as well as by the National Association for the Advancement of Colored People, clearly indicate that no significant advances have been made by Negroes in those craft union apprenticeship training programs which have historically excluded nonwhites. An examination of the available data makes it evident that less than one per cent of the apprentices in the building and construction industry throughout the United States are Negro. In the ten-year period, 1950–1960, in the State of New York, the increase of Negro participation in building trades apprenticeship programs rose from 1.5 per cent to 2 per cent.

Open access to plumbing and pipefitting apprenticeship controlled by the Plumbers Union is a very rare experience for young

Negroes in the North as well as the South. Similarly, Negro youths are excluded from apprenticeship programs controlled by the Sheet Metal Workers Union, the International Brotherhood of Electrical Workers, the Lathers and Plasterers Union, the Boiler-makers, the Structural Iron Workers Union, and from other important craft unions operating in the construction industry.

Almost equally exclusive are the printing trades unions. In a survey made by the National Association for the Advancement of Colored People of the seven major New York City newspapers in 1962, we find that, with the exclusion of building services and maintenance personnel, less than one per cent of those employed on the major New York newspapers are Negro. Virtually all of the Negroes employed on these newspapers are in the "white collar" jurisdiction of the New York Newspaper Guild.

It is estimated that in New York City less than one half of one per cent of those currently employed in the newspaper crafts outside the Guild's jurisdiction are Negroes. This includes printing pressmen, compositors, photoengravers, stereotypers, paper-handlers, mailers, and delivery drivers. As far as apprenticeship training for these crafts is concerned, we have been unable to detect a single instance where Negroes have been recently admitted into a training program in the newspaper crafts in the City of New York or in other major cities in the United States.

In the study entitled *Made in New York: Case Studies in Metropolitan Manufacturing,* published by Harvard University in 1959, we are told that

Negro and Puerto Rican women who are on the lower rungs of the city's economic ladder have become important in the New York garment industry, but they work mainly in the more established branches and with few exceptions . . . they do not become highly skilled tailor system workers on dresses or "cloaks." As a result a shortage of skilled sewing machine operators is developing.

In most of these programs the role of the labor union is decisive because the trade union usually determines who is admitted into the training program and, therefore, who is admitted into the union membership.

Labor unions also exercise control over apprenticeship programs through hiring hall procedures in de facto closed shop situations. In these circumstances, craft unions have the power either to promote or to prevent the admission of individuals or of an entire class of persons. By means of a variety of formal and informal controls, craft unions are frequently the decisive factor in the recruitment process in many apprenticeship programs and often directly prevent Negro youth from becoming skilled craft workers via the established route of apprenticeship.

On the level of the small shop and local union, the tradition of racial discrimination has now become deeply institutionalized. A form of caste psychology impels many workers to regard their own positions as "white man's jobs," to which no Negro should aspire. These workers, and often their union leaders, regard jobs in their industries as a kind of private privilege, to be accorded and denied by them as they see fit. Often Negroes are not alone in being barred from such unions which have much of the character of the medieval guild, but Negroes as a group suffer the most from these practices. On the local level, the tradition which sustains discrimination is to be found among skilled workers in heavy industry as well as in the craft occupations, and in the North almost as commonly as in the South.

The Bureau of Apprenticeship and Training of the United States Department of Labor, in giving certification to an apprenticeship program, provides the legal basis for public subsidies to apprenticeship programs. The federal government, through grants-in-aid from the United States Office of Education of the Department of Health, Education, and Welfare, provides funds which subsidize apprenticeship training programs in many states. The federal government, therefore, is directly subsidizing discrimination in the skilled trades whenever a trade union or employer excludes Negroes and members of other minority groups from admission into a registered apprenticeship training program.

The Racial Practices of Organized Labor

The Report on Employment [8] of the United States Commission on Civil Rights indicated the significant extent of discrimination within organized labor, and stated that the "efforts of the AFL-CIO have proved to be largely ineffective" in curbing discrimination and that the impact of union discrimination, especially in skilled craft occupations, was a basic factor in contributing to the concentration of Negroes in menial, unskilled jobs in industry, their virtual exclusion from construction and machinist crafts, and accounted for the extreme vulnerability of Negro labor to long-term unemployment both of a cyclical and structural nature. The report urged passage of federal legislation for prohibiting discrimination by unions and stressed the inability of the AFL-CIO to take action on its own initiative against the broad pattern of union racist practices.

The course of events in the past decade, and especially since the merger of the AF of L with the CIO in 1955, clearly indicates that the social consciousness of the industrial unions with their sensitivity to the problems of the Negro wage earner has now all but totally vanished. Instead, trade unions are responding like other conservative institutions in American society to the intensified demands of the Negro for full equality. A significant indication of this conservatism was the refusal of the AFL-CIO Executive Council to support the August 28, 1963, March on Washington, the greatest Negro demonstration in the nation's history.[9]

Dr. Kenneth Clark, writing in the HARYOU report, states:

The status of Negroes in the power councils of organized labor in New York City is most tenuous, if not nonexistent. The persistent pattern of racial discrimination in various unions, including some which still enjoy the reputation of being liberal, reflects the essential powerlessness of Negroes to affect the conditions of their livelihood. HARYOU's difficulty in finding a suitable representative of labor for its Board of Directors highlighted the fact that there is no Negro who occupies a primary power position in organized labor in New York City. There are a few Negroes who are constantly referred to as representatives of labor, but upon careful examination it is found that these Negroes, for the most part, hold their positions at the pleasure of more powerful white bosses or leaders. Even in those unions where the bulk of all of the workers are Negroes and Puerto Ricans, the top overt or covert leadership is almost always white. There is evidence that under these circumstances the union leaders are not always above entering into sweetheart contracts, or other types of conspiracies with the bosses, to the disadvantage of the Negro and Puerto Rican workers.

Even some unions which boast of a "liberal" past are under attack for discriminatory racial practices now that large numbers of Negroes have entered their jurisdiction. On April 4, 1961, a complaint was filed by Ernest Holmes, a Negro worker, against the International Ladies' Garment Workers Union (ILGWU) with the New York State Commission for Human Rights, the agency that administers the state's fair employment practices statutes.

The ILGWU was accused of discriminatory practices involving Negro workers. Later investigations revealed that nonwhites in the New York garment industry were concentrated in the lowest-paid job classifications with very little job mobility, because, with some few exceptions, they were denied admission into the union's skilled craft locals, that the virtually all-Negro and Puerto Rican "push boys" unit known as 60A is in practice a "jim crow" auxiliary, and that not a single Negro was an International Union officer, or on the 23-man executive board, or permitted to serve in any significant leadership position.[10]

On May 18, 1963, in the case of Ernest Holmes, the ILGWU entered into a stipulation with the State Commission for Human Rights in which the Union agreed to admit Mr. Holmes into the Cutters' union, Local 10 of the ILGWU, to assist him in seeking employment, and to arrange for additional training as an apprentice cutter.

This is what the State Commission had ordered the ILGWU to do a year before when a finding of "probable cause" was issued by the investigating commissioner. The *New York Times*, July 2, 1962, in a report headlined "Union Told to Get Job for a Negro," stated:

A garment cutters' union has been ordered by the State Commission for Human Rights to arrange for employment of a Negro at union rates commensurate with his skill and to admit the Negro into union membership if his work is satisfactory.

The *Times* story also states:

With regard to the union, the decision found that "the evidence raises serious doubt as to its good faith to comply with the State Law Against Discrimination in the matter of his complaint; and that there was 'probable cause' to credit the allegations of the complaint."

On September 14, 1962, Ruperto Ruiz, Investigating Commissioner, New York State Commission for Human Rights, in a letter to Emil Schlesinger, attorney for Local 10, stated that the Commission had

repeatedly requested and for a period of eight months tried to obtain data pertinent to a resolution of the charges of discrimination against Amalgamated Ladies Garment Cutters Union—Local 10. These efforts were unsuccessful. The failure of representatives of that local to co-operate in the investigation despite their promises to do so left me no alternative but to find "probable cause to credit the allegations of the complaint."

It is of some significance to note that this was not the first encounter by the ILGWU with the New York State antidiscrimination agency. Eighteen years ago the ILGWU entered into an agreement with the New York State Commission Against Discrimination—the predecessor to the State Commission for Human Rights—that it would not bar Negroes, Spanish-speaking, or other persons from membership in the all-Italian locals (*Elsie Hunter* v. *Agnes Sullivan Dress Shop*, September 4, 1946). After the Commission called the union's attention to relevant portions of the State antidiscrimination law and informed the ILGWU that the existence of nationality locals was a violation of the statute, a conference was held on January 22, 1947, at the offices of the State Commission Against Discrimination in New York City. Frederick Umhey, executive secretary of the ILGWU, represented the Union, and Commissioner Caroline K. Simon, the State Commission.

This was an action brought by a Negro member of Local 22, International Ladies' Garment Workers Union, who was barred from higher paying jobs controlled by Local 89, an Italian local. The charge was dismissed after the union agreed to eliminate such exclusion practices. Today, eighteen years later, not a single Negro or Spanish-speaking person holds membership in the two Italian locals which have control of some of the highest paying jobs in the industry, and no action has been taken to comply with the state law forbidding such practices.

Currently, the Negro worker is confronted not with a trade union movement that is a force for social change, but, on the contrary, with a national labor organization that has become a very conservative and highly bureaucratized institution, defending the *status quo* which is now directly attacked by the Negro in virtually every area of American life.

Many trade unions lag behind the progress made by other institutions in the community. In East St. Louis, Illinois, and Tulsa, Oklahoma, for example, Negro children attend integrated schools during the day, but their parents attend segregated union meetings at night, if they are admitted into labor unions at all. Recently A. Philip Randolph, president of the Brotherhood of Sleeping Car Porters, called "for a crusade to desegregate the Southern AFL-CIO State Conventions and City Central bodies" and stated that "this is a problem probably not less significant or difficult than the desegregation of public schools in the South."

There is a deep distrust among many Negro wage earners and others within the Negro community toward trade unions. It is a distrust well founded in experience. For today, as in the past, there is a profound disparity between the public image presented by the national AFL-CIO and the day-to-day realities as experienced by many Negro workers. This is true in the North as well as the South. There are few exceptions, especially in the mass production industries where, historically, there has been a large concentration of Negro workers and in some unions such as the United Automobile Workers (UAW), the United Packinghouse Workers (UPW), and the National Maritime Union (NMU) where there is an ideological sensitivity to the "Negro question."

But for the Negro in major areas of the economy, in the building and construction trades, in the railroad industry, among the Seafarers and the Boilermakers and the oil and chemical workers and machinists, in pulp, tobacco, and paper manufacturing, in metal working, in the printing trades, and in many other industries highly unionized for a long period of time, trade union practices are characterized by a broad pattern of discrimination and segregation.

AFL-CIO affiliated unions engage in four basic categories of discriminatory racial practices. They are: exclusion of Negroes from membership, segregated locals, separate seniority lines in collective bargaining agreements, and refusal to admit qualified Negroes into apprenticeship training programs controlled by unions.

The Brotherhood of Railway and Steamship Clerks which operates many segregated local lodges in Northern as well as Southern cities is among the important international unions responsible for a broad pattern of segregation.

The United Brotherhood of Carpenters and Joiners, for over a half-century, has been among the most important of all the building trades unions, and, with very few exceptions, organizes Negroes and whites into separate locals insofar as it permits Negroes to join the union at all. In the South there seems to be no exception to this rule, and it is most often followed in Northern cities as well. In Memphis and Chicago, for example, Negro carpenters in segregated local unions found that members of the white locals refused to work on the same job with them.

The white locals are in control of the union hiring hall, and, because of frequent arrangements with municipal and county political machines, all hiring for major public as well as private construction projects is done through the "lily-white" union hiring hall. Quite frequently Negroes are excluded altogether from work in white neighborhoods. This means that Negro carpenters are restricted to marginal maintenance and repair work within the Negro community and that they seldom are permitted to work on the larger construction projects. The same practices are true for other building-trades unions in many cities throughout the country.

Discriminatory racial practices by trade unions are not simply isolated or occasional expressions of local bias against colored workers, but rather, as the record indicates, a continuation of the institutionalized pattern of anti-Negro employment practices that is traditional in important sectors of the American economy.

The pattern of union responsibility for job discrimination against Negroes is not limited to any one area of the country or to some few industries or union jurisdictions, but involves many labor organizations in a wide variety of occupations in manufacturing and construction on the railroads and in the maritime trades. An example of this is the Seafarers International Union (SIU) which operates union-controlled hiring halls on Great Lakes ports such as Duluth, Chicago, Detroit, Buffalo, and Cleveland. As a systematic practice this union will dispatch Negro workers for menial jobs only as "mess boys" and cooks in the galley departments of ships operating under SIU collective bargaining agreements. Over the years Negro members of the Seafarers International Union have repeatedly protested this practice, but to no avail, as the union continues discriminatory job assignments in its hiring halls.

On occasion one or two Negroes have been admitted into an all-white local union as token compliance within a state or municipal fair employment practice law, as with the International Brotherhood of Electrical Workers in Cleveland, the Bricklayers Union in Milwaukee, and the Railway Clerks Union in Minneapolis, but this is essentially a limited and strategic adjustment to community pressure and represents very dubious "progress."

Certainly the token admission of a few Negroes into an electrical workers union in Cleveland or Washington, D.C. can no more be regarded as integration than can the token admission of two or three Negro children into a Southern public school. There are also several instances where unions have removed the "lily-white" exclusion clause from their constitutions as public relations gestures only, but continue to exclude Negroes from membership by tacit consent.

As long as union membership remains a condition of employment in many trades and crafts and Negroes are barred from union membership solely because of their color, then trade union discrimination is the decisive factor in determining whether Negro workers in a given industry shall have an opportunity to earn a living for themselves and their families. This is especially true in the printing trades, the construction industry, and other occupations where labor unions exercise a high degree of control over access to employment.

The Need for a Federal Fair Employment Practices Law

The operation of state and municipal fair employment practices commissions is absolutely no substitute for a strong federal fair employment practices law.[11] With one or two exceptions, state and municipal fair employment practices commissions are drastically limited in their effectiveness by inadequate funds and inadequate staff. Most of these agencies are simply complaint-taking bureaus that often take years to resolve an individual complaint received from an aggrieved citizen. We know that, in practice, only a very small fraction of all individuals who are the victims of employment discrimination because of race or religion ever file complaints with state or municipal commissions; therefore, because of the complexities in eliminating discriminatory employment practices, the fundamental approach must be towards the initiation of affirmative action based upon the over-all pattern of employment discrimination. In addition, one must note the unfortunate inability of state and municipal fair employment practices commissions to eliminate discriminatory racial practices in many important areas of the active job market. Among these is the building and construction trades industry. The pattern of discrimination in this important sector of the economy was extensively studied for the New York State Advisory Committee to the United States Commission on Civil Rights by Dr. Donald F. Shaughnessy of Columbia University.[12]

The construction industry represents a segment of the economy which is not declining. General contractors and the employers associations believe that there is a severe shortage of both residential and nonresidential construction in New York City and other major urban centers. New York, with twice the population of Chicago, has over four times the need for office space. Data indicates that the construction demand is growing.

Dr. Donald Shaughnessy has pointed out that the fear of unemployment by construction workers must be set aside due to reliable estimates of forthcoming construction activity. New construction was scheduled to increase by 57 per cent between 1960 and 1964, and to double between 1970 and 1975, according to Commerce Department estimates. The volume of construction and new repairs is also expected to grow. Thus the skilled manpower necessary in 1970 will be 35 per cent above the present labor supply.

The *Wall Street Journal*, April 10, 1964, in a front page story, states: "Booming construction activity will provide strong support this year for the nation's economy." The report concludes by noting that "the general contractors who build highways, housing, office structures, and utility facilities generally agree they will have record volume." Although this industry is expanding, Negro workers have not been able to enter into the construction crafts. This occurs because, as Shaughnessy notes: "The economic characteristics of the industry have created a condition wherein the decision making power is concentrated in the local union."

It is the economic structure of the building industry which concentrates in the local unions the power to decide who obtains employment and who gets admitted to the craft. The men who are engaged in construction work are recruited from labor pools controlled exclusively by the various unions in the craft jurisdictions of building trades. The union is the sole employment agency, and the men who appear on the jobs are those whom the union has referred to the job site. Contractors are thus completely dependent upon local unions for their labor supply. This factor further increases the power of local craft unions to control the employment process.

A. H. Raskin in discussing this pattern writes that these practices go

far beyond the issue of discrimination. It brings into challenge the sub rosa closed shop arrangements many unions of skilled craftsmen have managed to retain, even though these have technically been illegal since the passage of the Taft-Hartley Act seventeen years ago.[13]

Rather than admit Negro members, the unions frequently encourage the use of out-of-town labor. Based upon direct interviews, Shaughnessy found that commuters travel as much as 120 miles per day from Connecticut and elsewhere to find steady employment in New York, when the available local union membership supply is exhausted. But local sources of skilled Negro manpower are deliberately ignored. During the spring and summer of 1963, there were approximately 1,200 plumbers with "travelling cards" from other cities working in New York City.

Thus, the New York State Advisory Committee of the United States Commission on Civil Rights stated in its 1963 report that

the building trades unions continue to maintain an effective shortage of labor. One way that shortage is preserved in the face of continuing high demand is the use of commuters like those from Bridgeport who represent an auxiliary source of manpower that can be cut off at any time.

Out-of-town construction workers commute over a hundred miles daily to jobs in New York City, while local Negroes and Puerto Ricans are denied employment and entry to union-controlled jobs and apprenticeship programs.

In the physical reshaping of New York City, as in other urban centers, there has been a tremendous increase in the rate of residential and nonresidential construction. Virtually all new construction work in New York City is performed by union labor operating under collective bargaining agreements with building trade unions that make contractors entirely dependent upon union-controlled hiring halls as the exclusive source of labor supply. With rare exceptions these union hiring halls are "lily-white" in New York and throughout the nation.[14]

During the summer of 1963, thousands of persons demonstrated at several public construction sites in New York City against the racial practices of the AFL-CIO building trades unions. The rights they were seeking through these demonstrations are nonnegotiable legal rights that exist at the federal level—Executive Orders 10925 and 11114; at the state level—New York Law Against Discrimination, Section 296 and the New York Public Works Law, Section 220-e; and at the city level—New York City Administrative Code, Section 343-8.01.

Despite repeated documentation and disclosures of discrimination in the construction industry by the United States Commission on Civil Rights, the Mayor's Action Panel, the New York City Commission on Human Rights, and the New York State Commission for Human Rights, as well as reports from the NAACP and the Urban League, public officials have refused, apparently for political reasons, to enforce these laws.

The state of Pennsylvania has had a fair employment practices law since 1955, and Philadelphia has had a municipal fair employment practices statute since 1948. However, at the present time there is a widespread pattern of Negro exclusion from the major building trades craft unions in the Philadelphia area, where there are vast construction projects. The Philadelphia *Tribune,* in its issue of February 12, 1962, stated: "Philadelphia labor unions have fostered a pattern of racial discrimination that is unsurpassed even in the Deep South." Mass demonstrations by civil rights organizations against the racial practices of building trade unions have also occurred in Philadelphia, Cleveland, Pittsburgh, Los Angeles, Newark, New Jersey, and other cities.

As is evident, the pattern of Negro exclusion from the major AFL-CIO building trades unions continues unabated even in cities and states where there has long been a fair employment practices law. This is significant as it indicates the serious inability of such agencies to reach the skilled craft occupations that are characterized by a pattern of discrimination and expanding job opportunities. Thus, today in the United States there are more Negroes with Ph.D. degrees than there are Negroes who are licensed plumbers or licensed electricians.

Year after year, thousands of nonwhite students graduate from vocational high schools in the major urban centers of the nation, but after satisfactorily completing their courses of study in a variety of craft skills, young Negro workers ready to enter the labor market are denied employment opportunities in the printing industry, among machinists, or in building and construction trades and are forced to take low-paying menial or unskilled jobs if they are to work at all. Many of them are forced completely to abandon hope for work in the craft for which they were trained. Is it any wonder that there are many school drop-outs each year among Negro youth in vocational training schools, who soon enough learn the realities of the racial practices of craft unions in New York City, Chicago, Philadelphia, and elsewhere and express their feeling of futility by leaving school at an early age?

Adoption of a federal fair employment practices law that would decisively intervene in breaking the national pattern of Negro exclusion in the building trades, the printing industry, the metal crafts, and other skilled occupations would have a significant effect in reducing the rate of school drop-outs among minority-group youth.

The Negro is now making the same demands upon organized labor that are being made upon all other institutions in American society, and it is certain that the attacks upon racism within trade unions will proceed with the same intensity as against other organizations that impose restrictions based on race and color.

In January 1961, the NAACP released a documented study entitled "Racism Within Organized Labor: A Report of Five Years of the AFL-CIO." This report concluded that during the five years which have passed since the AFL-CIO merger, there has been no systematic or co-ordinated effort by the Labor Federation to eliminate racism within local unions where anti-Negro practices are traditional. The NAACP report gave a detailed series of examples of the wide variety of anti-Negro practices and indicated the urgent need for action by the Federation's leadership.

The NAACP report received widespread public attention and was immediately attacked by spokesmen for the AFL-CIO but strongly defended by Negro trade unionists and by A. Philip Randolph—President of the Brotherhood of Sleeping Car Porters and conspicuously the only Negro Vice-President of the AFL-CIO —who stated that the NAACP survey was "factual and accurate," and "unquestionably a significant and useful document for those concerned with making organized labor the democratic force it should be." Randolph told a conference of Negro trade unionists:

We in the Negro American Labour Council can without reservation state that the basic statements are true and sound; the delegates of the Brotherhood of Sleeping Car Porters have presented these facts to convention after convention of the AFL for a quarter of a century.

Randolph later presented to the Executive Council of the Federation, detailed charges of anti-Negro practices together with specific recommendations to eliminate discrimination and segregation within affiliated international and local unions. The response of the AFL-CIO Executive Council was to censure Randolph and to reject his proposals.

Because the NAACP has now concluded, on the basis of the

factual record, that the national AFL-CIO and its affiliated international unions are either unable or unwilling to move decisively
against racist elements and to eliminate widespread anti-Negro
practices, the Association is attempting to develop a new body of
labor law on behalf of Negro workers.

This effort involves the federal courts as well as the National
Labor Relations Board (NLRB). On February 4, 1964, an NLRB
trial examiner ruled that Negroes who are required by their unions
to join racially segregated locals and to work under union contracts
that discriminate can have those unions found guilty of unfair
labor practices.

This ruling involving the AFL-CIO International Longshore-
man's Association in Brownsville, Texas, represented an important
step forward in the Negro workers' long fight against racial discrimination by trade unions. On July 2, 1964, the National Labor
Relations Board in a historic decision ruled that racial discrimination by labor unions is an unfair labor practice and that unions
may lose their certification as the collective bargaining agent as a
result of such practices.

The charges of discrimination were filed on behalf of members
of the all-Negro Local 2 of the Independent Metal Workers
Union. In 1962, when Ivory Davis, a Negro member of Local 2,
was denied admission to a company-sponsored apprenticeship
training course, the white local (Local 1) refused to process his
grievance. At the request of Local 2, the National Association for
the Advancement of Colored People entered the case on October
4, 1962, and filed a motion with the National Labor Relations
Board asking that Local 1's certification be rescinded. The NAACP
also asked that this motion be consolidated with unfair labor
practices proceedings previously instituted by the National Labor
Relations Board against Local 1.

For the first time in the Board's history, it has ruled that racial
discrimination by a union in membership practices—such as exclusion or segregation of Negroes—is a violation of the duty of fair
representation under Section 9(a) of the National Labor Relations Act. In this case involving Negro workers at the Hughes Tool
Company in Houston, Texas, a new principle in administrative
labor law was established that will have far-reaching consequences
if sustained by the federal courts.

The NAACP has other cases pending in state and federal district courts and with the NLRB in an effort to eliminate discrimi-

natory practices within organized labor and by employers. The intent of these cases is to establish a new legal standard of responsibility for trade unions to represent all workers within their jurisdiction fairly and equitably and without regard to considerations of race and color. New cases will be initiated in state and federal courts in addition to further complaints before the NLRB on behalf of aggrieved Negro workers in the near future.

The civil rights issue has emerged as the central question confronting the entire American society. It is evident that the AFL-CIO and all other institutions will be judged by the Negro on the basis of their actual day-to-day performance and not on the exercise of empty ritual.

Negroes may be winning the broad legal and social struggles for equality in the United States, but they are losing the battle for equal employment opportunity and economic justice. At the present time, the historic civil rights gains won by Negroes in the past twenty years are in danger of being destroyed by the growing crisis of unemployment and underemployment that directly affects the well-being of the entire Negro community and leads to acute social dislocation and despair.

The emergence of a large "underclass" of the Negro unemployed, the growth of a permanent Black lumpenproletariat, might very well alter the character of the Negro civil rights movement—a movement that in the past has operated in the classic tradition of protest and reform—and thus lead to developments that have the gravest implication for the whole of American society.

Notes ►

1. Herman P. Miller, *Rich Man, Poor Man* (New York: Thomas Y. Crowell, 1964), p. 88.

2. Harold Baron, "Negro Unemployment—A Case Study," *New University Thought*, Vol. 3, No. 2 (September–October, 1963), p. 43.

3. Southern Regional Council, *Plans for Progress: Atlanta Survey*, January 1963.

4. U.S. Commission on Civil Rights, *Employment*, 1961, Report No. 3, pp. 65–66.

5. Donald Dewey, "Negro Employment in Southern Industry," *Journal of Political Economy*, LX (August 1952), pp. 279–293.

6. *Equal Protection of the Laws in North Carolina: Report of the*

North Carolina Advisory Committee to the United States Commission on Civil Rights, 1962, Washington, D.C., p. 87.

7. New York State Commission Against Discrimination, *Apprentices, Skilled Craftsmen and the Negro: An Analysis* (New York, 1960); Herbert Hill, *The Negro Wage-Earner and Apprenticeship Training Programs* (New York: National Association for the Advancement of Colored People, 1960).

8. United States Commission on Civil Rights, *Report on Employment*, Washington, D.C., 1961.

9. For a discussion of trade union racial practices see Herbert Hill, "Labor Unions and the Negro," *Commentary* (December 1959), pp. 479–488; "Racism Within Organized Labor," *The Journal of Negro Education*, 1961, No. 2, pp. 109–118; and "Has Organized Labor Failed the Negro Worker?" *The Negro Digest* (May 1962), pp. 41–49.

10. See *Congressional Record—House*, January 31, 1963, pp. 1496–1499 (Testimony of Herbert Hill on Racial Practices of ILGWU). See also Herbert Hill, "The ILGWU—Fact and Fiction," *New Politics*, 1962, No. 2, pp. 7–27.

11. For an analysis of State FEPC laws, see Herbert Hill, "Twenty Years of State Fair Employment Practice Laws: A Critical Analysis," *Buffalo Law Review*, Vol. 13 (Autumn 1964), pp. 22–69.

12. D. F. Shaughnessy, "A Survey of Discrimination in the Building Trades Industry," New York City, April 1963. Dr. Shaughnessy's study was the basis for the "Report of the New York Advisory Committee to the U.S. Commission on Civil Rights" (August 1963).

13. A. H. Raskin, "Civil Rights: The Law and the Unions," *The Reporter*, Vol. 31. No. 4, September 10, 1964, p. 26.

14. See, *A Report of the New York Advisory Committee of the U.S. Commission on Civil Rights*, August 1963.

17 ► "THE WONDER IS THERE HAVE BEEN SO FEW RIOTS"

KENNETH B. CLARK

The race riot, one of the most dramatic and violent expressions of interethnic hostility, has a history in American society that coincides with the development of large urban communities and the consequent frustrations inherent in urban patterns of ethnic segregation. In the last article of this section Professor Kenneth Clark takes the especially violent 1965 race riot in Los Angeles as his point of departure for an analysis of the phenomenon and its function in race relations.

► IT IS ONE measure of the depth and insidiousness of American racism that the nation ignores the rage of the rejected—until it explodes in Watts or Harlem. The wonder is that there have been so few riots, that Negroes generally are law-abiding in a world where the law itself has seemed an enemy.

To call for reason and moderation, to charge rioters with blocking the momentum of the civil-rights movement, to punish rioters by threatening withdrawal of white support for civil rights may indeed ease the fears of whites and restore confidence that a firm stern hand is enforcing order.

But the rejected Negro in the ghetto is deaf to such moral appeals. They only reinforce his despair that whites do not consider equal rights for Negroes to be their due as human beings and American citizens but as rewards to be given for good behavior, to

From *The New York Times Magazine*, September 5, 1965. © 1965 by The New York Times Company. Reprinted by permission of the author and publisher.

be withheld for misbehavior. The difficulty which the average American of goodwill—white or Negro—has in seeing this as a form of racist condescension is another disturbing symptom of the complexities of racism in the United States.

It is not possible for even the most responsible Negro leaders to control the Negro masses once pent-up anger and total despair are unleashed by a thoughtless or brutal act. The prisoners of the ghetto riot without reason, without organization and without leadership, as this is generally understood. The rioting is in itself a repudiation of leadership. It is the expression of the anarchy of the profoundly alienated.

In a deeper sense such anarchy could even be a subconscious or conscious invitation to self-destruction. At the height of the Harlem riots of 1964, young Negroes could be heard to say, "If I don't get killed tonight, I'll come back tomorrow." There is evidence these outbreaks are suicidal, reflecting the ultimate in self-negation, self-rejection and hopelessness.

It was the Negro ghetto in Los Angeles which Negroes looted and burned, not the white community. When white firemen tried to enter the ghetto, they were barred by Negro snipers. Many looters did not take the trouble to avoid injury, and many were badly cut in the looting orgy. So one cannot help but wonder whether a desire for self-destruction was not a subconscious factor. Of the 36 people killed in the Los Angeles riot, 33 were Negroes, killed in the campaign to restore law and order. The fact of their deaths—the senseless deaths of human beings—has been obscured by our respectable middle-class preoccupation with the wanton destruction of property, the vandalism and the looting.

Appeals to reason are understandable; they reflect the sense of responsibility of Governmental and civil-rights leaders. But they certainly do not take into account the fact that one cannot expect individuals who have been systematically excluded from the privileges of middle-class life to view themselves as middle-class or to behave in terms of middle-class values. Those who despair in the ghetto follow their own laws—generally the laws of unreason. And though these laws are not in themselves moral, they have moral consequences and moral causes.

The inmates of the ghetto have no realistic stake in respecting property because in a basic sense they do not possess it. They are possessed by it. Property is, rather, an instrument for perpetuation of their own exploitation. Stores in the ghetto—which they rarely own—overcharge for inferior goods. They may obtain the symbols of America's vaunted high standard of living—radios, TV's, washing machines, refrigerators—but usually only through usurious carrying costs, one more symbol of the pattern of material exploitation. They do not respect property because property is almost invariably used to degrade them.

James Bryant Conant and others have warned America it is no longer possible to confine hundreds of thousands of undereducated, underemployed, purposeless young people and adults in an affluent America without storing up social dynamite. The dark ghettoes now represent a nuclear stock pile which can annihilate the very foundations of America. And if, as a minority, desperate Negroes are not able to "win over" the majority, they can nevertheless effectively undermine what they cannot win.

A small minority of Negroes can do this. Such warnings are generally ignored during the interludes of apparent quiescence and tend to be violently rejected, particularly when they come from whites, at the time of a Negro revolt.

When Senator Robert Kennedy incisively observed, after Watts, "There is no point in telling Negroes to observe the law. . . . It has almost always been used against [them]," it was described by an individual who took the trouble to write a letter to *The New York Times* as an irresponsible incitement to violence. The bedeviling fact remains, however, that as long as institutionalized forms of American racism persist, violent eruptions will continue to occur in the Negro ghettoes. As Senator Kennedy warned: "All these places—Harlem, Watts, South Side—are riots waiting to happen."

When they do happen, the oversimplified term "police brutality" will be heard, but the relationship between police and residents of the ghetto is more complicated than that. Unquestionably, police brutality occurs. In the panic probably stemming from deep and complex forms of racism, inexperienced policemen have injured or killed Negroes or Puerto Ricans or other members of a powerless minority. And it is certainly true that a common denominator of most, if not all, the riots of the past two summers has been some incident involving the police, an incident which the larger society views as trivial but which prisoners of the ghetto interpret as cruel and humiliating.

In spite of the exacerbating frequency of police racism, however, the more pertinent cause of the ghetto's contempt for police is the role they are believed to play in crime and corruption within the ghetto—accepting bribes for winking at illegal activities which thrive in the ghetto. The police, rightly or wrongly, are viewed not only as significant agents in exploiting ghetto residents but also as symbols of the pathology which encompasses the ghetto. They are seen matter-of-factly as adversaries as well as burdens. The more privileged society may decide that respect for law and order is essential for its own survival, but in the dark ghettoes, survival often depends on disrespect for the law as Negroes experience it.

Thus the problem will not be solved merely by reducing the frequency of police brutality or by increasing the number of Negro policemen. It will require major reorganization and re-education of the police and a major reorganization of the ghetto itself. To say as Police Chief William Parker did of the Los Angeles Negroes, "We are on top and they are on the bottom," is to prove to Negroes that their deep fears and hatred of established law and order are justified.

While the riots cannot be understood by attempts to excuse them, neither can they be understood by deploring them—especially by deploring them according to a double standard of social morality. For while the lawlessness of white segregationists and rebellious Negroes are expressions of deep frustrations and chronic racism, the lawlessness of Negroes is usually considered a reflection on all Negroes and countered by the full force of police and other governmental authority, but the lawlessness of whites is seen as the primitive reactions of a small group of unstable individuals and is frequently ignored by the police—when they are not themselves accessories. Moreover, rarely do the leaders of a white community in which white violence occurs publicly condemn even the known perpetrators, while almost invariably national and local Negro leaders are required to condemn the mob violence of Negroes.

As long as these double standards of social morality prevail, they reflect the forms of accepted racism which are the embers of potential violence on the part of both Negroes and whites. And it should be obvious also, although it does not appear to be, that the violence of the Negro is the violence of the oppressed while the violence of white segregationists seeks to maintain oppression.

It is significant that the recent eruptions in Negro communities have not occurred in areas dominated by more flagrant forms of racism, by the Klan and the other institutions of Southern bigotry.

They have occurred precisely in those communities where whites have prided themselves on their liberal approach to matters of race and in those states having strong laws prescribing equal opportunity, fair employment and allegedly open housing. (Some observers see a relationship between the defeat of the open housing referendum in California and the Los Angeles outbreak, but it would seem misleading to attempt to account for the riot by any single factor.)

It is revealing to hear the stunned reaction of some top political officials in Los Angeles and California who are unable to understand that such a thing could happen in Los Angeles. Here, they said, whites and blacks got along fine together; here, as reporters constantly pointed out, ghetto streets are lined with palm trees, some with private homes surrounded by tended lawns.

Americans are accustomed to judging the state of people's minds by the most visible aspects—the presence of a TV antenna indicates affluence and a neat lawn a middle-class home. The fact is a ghetto takes on the physical appearance of the particular city —in New York, rat-infested tenements and dirty streets; in Los Angeles, small homes with palm trees—but in many a small home live numerous families and in every house live segregated, desperate people with no jobs or servile jobs, little education, broken families, delinquency, drug addiction, and a burning rage at a society that excludes them from the things it values most.

It is probably not by chance that the Federal Civil Rights Act of 1964 and the Voting Rights Act of 1965 were followed by violence in the North. This was important legislation, but it was more relevant to the predicament of the Southern Negro than to Negroes in Northern ghettoes.

It may well be that the channeling of energies of Negroes in Southern communities toward eliminating the more vicious and obvious signs of racism precludes temporarily the dissipation of energy in random violence. The Northern Negro is clearly not suffering from a lack of laws. But he is suffering—rejected, segregated, discriminated against in employment, in housing, his children subjugated in *de facto* segregated and inferior schools in spite of a plethora of laws that imply the contrary.

He has been told of great progress in civil rights during the past 10 years and proof of this progress is offered in terms of Supreme Court decisions and civil-rights legislation and firm Presidential commitment. But he sees no positive changes in his day-to-day life. The very verbalizations of progress contribute to his frustration and rage. He is suffering from a pervasive, insensitive and at times self-righteous form of American racism that does not understand the depth of his need.

Not the civil-rights leaders who urge him to demonstrate, but the whites who urge him not to "in the light of present progress" contribute to the anger which explodes in sudden fury. He is told by liberal whites *they* contribute to civil-rights causes, *they* marched to Washington and journeyed to Selma and Montgomery to demonstrate their commitment to racial justice and equality.

But Negroes see only the continuing decay of their homes, many of them owned by liberal whites. He sees he does not own any of the means of production, distribution and sale of goods he must purchase to live. He sees his children subjected to criminally inefficient education in public schools they are required to attend, and which are often administered and staffed by liberal whites. He sees liberal labor unions which either exclude him, accept him in token numbers or, even when they do accept him en masse, exclude him from leadership or policy-making roles.

And he sees that persistent protest in the face of racism which dominates his life and shackles him within the ghetto may be interpreted by his white friends as a sign of his insatiability, his irrationality and, above all, of his ingratitude. And because this interpretation comes from his friends and allies it is much harder to take psychologically than the clear-cut bigotry of open segregationists.

It is precisely at this point in the development of race relations that the complexities, depth and intensity of American racism reveal themselves with excruciating clarity. At this point regional differences disappear. The greatest danger is an intensification of racism leading to the polarization of America into white and black. "What do they *want?*" the white man asks. "Don't they know they hurt their own cause?" "Get Whitey," cries the Negro. "Burn, baby, burn." At this point concerned whites and Negroes are required to face the extent of personal damage which racism has inflicted on both.

It will require from whites more than financial contributions to civil-rights agencies, more than mere verbal and intellectual support for the cause of justice. It will require compassion, willingness to accept hostility and increased resolve to go about the common business, the transformation and strengthening of our society toward the point where race and color are no longer relevant in discussing the opportunities, rights and responsibilities of Americans.

Negroes, too, are confronted with difficult challenges in the present stage of the civil-rights struggle. The bitterness and rage which formed the basis for the protests against flagrant racial injustices must somehow be channeled into constructive, nondramatic programs required to translate court decisions, legislation and growing political power into actual changes in the living conditions of the masses of Negroes. Some ways must be found whereby Negro leadership and Negro organizations can redirect the volatile emotions of Negroes away from wasteful, sporadic outbursts and toward self-help and constructive social action. The need for candid communication between middle-class Negroes and the Negro masses is as imperative as the need for painful honesty and cooperation between Negroes and whites.

These demands upon whites and Negroes will not be easy to meet since it is difficult, if not impossible, for anyone growing up in America to escape some form of racist contamination. And a most disturbing fact is the tendency of racism to perpetuate itself, to resist even the most stark imperatives for change. This is the contemporary crisis in race relations which Americans must somehow find the strength to face and solve. Otherwise we will remain the victims of capricious and destructive racial animosities and riots.

The key danger is the possibility that America has permitted the cancer of racism to spread so far that present available remedies can be only palliative. One must, however, continue to believe and act on the assumption that the disease is remediable.

It is important that all three branches of the Federal Government have committed themselves to using their power to improve the status of Negroes. These commitments must be enforced despite overt or subtle attempts to resist and evade them.

But this resistance must be seen not only in the bigotry of segregationists. It must be recognized in the moralizing of Northern whites who do not consciously feel themselves afflicted with the disease of racism, even as they assert that Negro rioting justifies ending their involvement in the civil-rights cause. It must be recognized in the insistence that Negroes pull themselves up by their own bootstraps, demonstrating to the liberal and white communities they have earned the right to be treated as equal American citizens. These are satisfying, self-righteous arguments but they cannot disguise the profound realities of an unacknowledged racism.

If it is possible to talk of any value emerging from the riots it would be this: They are signals of distress, an SOS from the ghetto. They also provide the basis for therapeutically ventilating deeply repressed feelings of whites and Negroes—their underlying fear and the primitive sense of race.

In the religiously oriented, nonviolent civil-rights movement in the South, courteous, neatly dressed Negroes carrying books fitted into the middle-class white image more adequately than the vulgar whites who harassed them. The middle-class white, therefore, identified with the oppressed, not the oppressor. But empathy given as a reward for respectable behavior has little value. Understanding can only be tested when one's own interests are deeply threatened, one's sensibilities violated.

These feelings of hostility must be exposed to cold reality as the prelude to realistic programs for change. If under the warmth of apparent support for civil rights lies a deeply repressed prejudice, no realistic social change can be effective.

It would be unrealistic, of course, to expect the masses of whites and Negroes who have grown up in an essentially racist society suddenly to love one another. Fortunately, love is not a prerequisite for the social reorganization now demanded. Love has not been necessary to create workable living arrangements among other ethnic groups in our society. It is no more relevant to ask Negroes and whites to love each other than to ask Italians and Irish to do the same as a prerequisite for social peace and justice.

Nevertheless, real changes in the predicament of previously rejected Negroes—changes compatible with a stable and decent society—must be made, and soon.

The Negro must be included within the economy at all levels of employment, thereby providing the basis for a sound family life and an opportunity to have an actual stake in American business and property.

The social organization of our educational system must be transformed so Negroes can be taught in schools which do not reinforce their feeling of inferiority. The reorganization, improvement and integration of our public schools is also necessary in order to re-educate white children and prepare them to live in the present and future world of racial diversity.

The conditions under which Negroes live must be improved— bad housing, infant mortality and disease, delinquency, drug addiction must be drastically reduced.

Until these minimum goals are achieved, Americans must accept the fact that we cannot expect to maintain racial ghettoes without paying a high price. If it is possible for Americans to carry out realistic programs to change the lives of human beings now confined within their ghettoes, the ghetto will be destroyed rationally, by plan, and not by random self-destructive forces. Only then will American society not remain at the mercy of primitive, frightening, irrational attempts by prisoners in the ghetto to destroy their own prison.

IV SELECTED AMERICAN MINORITIES

WITH THE noteworthy exception of Indians and Negroes, the greater part of the American people came to this country as immigrants. As the most recent phase of the overall process of migration, immigration is marked by the departure from one political unit, the nation-state, and the entry into another, with an accompanying change in jurisdiction. Immigrant-receiving countries such as the United States, Canada, Australia, New Zealand and many of the South American states, are typically newer, less densely populated and offer more economic opportunities and freedom of expression than do the emigrant-releasing countries.

After the period of colonization, old immigration (American society's first pattern of immigration) lasted until 1880. It drew people mostly from Northern and Western Europe. New immigration took over after a decade of transition and lasted from 1890 to 1930—the immigrants coming predominantly from Central, Southern and Eastern Europe. During the nineteenth century, and continuing into the twentieth, Asiatic immigration and immigration from other American countries became conspicuous—most recently in the refugee movement from Cuba. Beginning in the mid-1930's, displaced persons and refugees arrived from Central and Eastern Europe. Lastly, we mention the Puerto Rican migrants who, although technically not immigrants because of their American citizenship, nevertheless have faced problems of adjustment similar to those of immigrants in previous movements, especially new immigration.

In this section there are readings on the Chinese, Puerto Ricans, Mexicans and Roman Catholics—ethnic minorities whose problems are representative of those found in the broad spectrum of American immigration since the nineteenth century. The first piece, on the voluntary segregation of the Chinese in New York's Chinatown, is by Dr. Dan Y. Yuan, a sociologist who immigrated from Taiwan and studied and wrote in the role of a participant observer.

18► VOLUNTARY SEGREGATION: A STUDY OF NEW YORK CHINATOWN

D. Y. YUAN

► THE CHINESE population in the United States has exhibited a tendency to concentrate in segregated communities within the large cities. San Francisco's Chinatown ranks first numerically, that of New York City is second, and that of Los Angeles third. There are no Chinatowns to be found in cities under 50,000 population, nor are there Chinatowns in states having fewer than 250 Chinese.[1] In light of these statements, we may well ask ourselves the questions: Why do the Chinese tend to concentrate in a segregated community within a large city, and to what degree is it voluntary or involuntary segregation? It is the purpose of this paper to answer these questions.

This paper presents findings concerning a study of New York's Chinatown [2] and investigates the degree to which a Chinatown represents voluntary or involuntary segregation. Tentatively, therefore, a scale of intensity between voluntary and involuntary segregation is presented.

The Scale of Segregation

Voluntary Segregation:	(1) Strict voluntary
	(2) Voluntary
	(3) Voluntary involving involuntary factor(s)
Involuntary Segregation:	(4) Involuntary involving voluntary factor(s)
	(5) Involuntary
	(6) Strict involuntary

From *Phylon* (Fall, 1963), 255–65. Reprinted by permission of the author and publisher.

According to this scale, there are three forms of voluntary segregation and three forms of involuntary segregation. Segregation is an old phenomenon in human history and is universal. Segregation does not always mean "racial segregation." It may appear "in the usual class lines of a democratic society, or the castes of a stratified society; . . . the emergency use of force, as in concentration camps and restricted zones during war time. . . ." [3] The scale has been devised for all types of segregation and is not limited to race relations only. However, this study of New York's Chinatown emphasizes race relations.

Theoretically, is the suggested scale of segregation possible? Firstly, strict voluntary segregation is almost impossible in the field of race relations but is possible in other relationships. For example, one order of Catholic sisters voluntarily enters a segregated convent, prohibits contacts with the outer world and prays for the salvation of the entire world. The Catholic church does not force them to enter; it is their choice whether they do so or not.

Secondly, voluntary segregation is possible in race relations. Two examples are given below. One is that of the white people in the African colonies who voluntarily segregate themselves from the native population in order to preserve so-called white supremacy. E. E. Bergel calls this activity "self segregation." [4] Another example is given by Brewton Berry in his analysis of race relations, namely, the process of voluntary segregation which "is illustrated by the Mennonites, who have striven to isolate themselves from the general population in their determination to resist the forces of assimilation." [5]

Thirdly, there is voluntary segregation involving involuntary factors, of which the Chinese community in New York is a good example. This will be discussed later. Another example of this kind of segregation is the Jewish ghetto. The ghetto is a form of voluntary segregation in which there are also some involuntary factors.

Fourthly, involuntary segregation involving voluntary factors is also found in present-day race relations. Berry calls this a voluntary choice of (involuntary) segregation.[6] This can be illustrated by the segregated communities established voluntarily by Negroes in the South, where segregation is involuntary for them.[7] Frazier calls these communities "racial islands." [8]

Fifthly, there is involuntary segregation, which applies to Negroes in the United States. It is not their volition to be treated under the principles of the so-called separate but equal doctrine; they are involuntarily separated from whites through enforcement by the dominant group.[9]

Finally, there is strict involuntary segregation, which is not often seen today. One possible example would be slavery, for slaves are treated under separate and unequal principles.

After enumerating the possibilities of different kinds of segregation on the suggested scale, which indicates the degree of intensity from strict voluntary to strict involuntary segregation, we are ready to proceed with this study by suggesting to what degree New York's Chinatown is a voluntarily- or an involuntarily-formed community.

The Development of Chinatown

Effort was made in the analysis to exclude mutually the voluntary and the involuntary choice (factors). The involuntary choice of the Chinese preceded the voluntary development of New York's Chinatown. The period of defensive insulation is a period between these two, the last period being gradual assimilation. In short, the stages of the development of Chinatown may be illustrated in the following chart. The hypothetical stages are based on the analysis.

Hypothetical Stages of the Development of Chinatown

Involuntary choice (discrimination and prejudice toward the Chinese)	Defensive insulation (need for mutual help)	Voluntary segregation	Gradual assimilation
(1)	(2)	(3)	(4)

Generalizations

The Chinese people were welcomed to the United States. The social relationship between the Chinese, representing a minority group, and the Americans, representing a dominant group, is derived from the social interactions between them. In general, social interaction under a favorable situation may lead to friendship, but under unfavorable situations may lead to conflict and hostility. At first, the Chinese laborers were welcomed because of the demands for cheap labor after the discovery of gold in California. A pattern of demands and response developed, and as a result laborers from Canton Province, China, came to the United States. A sociological analysis of the historical data suggests that in general, a minority group, such as the Chinese, is welcomed by a majority group, if the minority group meets the needs of the majority group at that particular time.

Why did the anti-Chinese attitudes develop? Changing environment causes the changing of attitudes, and when the whites moved into the mining industry and began to compete with the Chinese, great hostility and conflict emerged. Racial discrimination and prejudice toward the Chinese developed because of this conflict and hostility. The Chinese became the scapegoat in the economic competition. On the basis of such facts, a second generalization can be stated. The prejudice or discrimination of a majority group towards a racial minority, such as the Chinese, often emerges because of the conflicting values between them. These conflicting values may be political, economic, ecological, or racial factors.

After the rise of anti-Chinese sentiments on the West Coast, some people tried to prevent the exclusion of Chinese laborers. For example, a book was written by George F. Seward, United States Minister to China, in 1881, one year before the adoption of the Chinese Exclusion Act, in which the author said: "I found, in brief, that the Chinese have been of great service to the people of the Pacific Coast; . . . that the objections which have been advanced against them are in the main unwarranted; . . . the fears of large immigration . . . are unnecessary. . . ." [10] His efforts were in vain. There was little choice (involuntary) for the Chinese but to find some means to survive in such an alien environment. The solution to this problem was similar to the pattern of voluntary mass-return to Japan of the Japanese in the United States previous to World War II. Thus, defensive insulation was employed by the Chinese. The applicable principle here is that when a minority, such as the Chinese, has been discriminated against, it has no choice but to develop some means of defense. In general, it will develop the means voluntarily.

When the Irish miners began to flow into the West, great hostility grew against the Chinese because of the competition. The Chinese, as a minority group, could not compete with organized labor. The Immigration Commission Report of 1910 stated that "vocationally there has been a clear tendency on the part of the

Chinese to withdraw from the competitive forms of labor and business and to enter less productive urban callings." [11] A comparison of the occupational distributions of the Chinese population between 1870 and 1920 indicates that the Chinese withdrew from competition with organized labor.[12] The following table shows this trend.

Table 1. Selected Occupations for the Chinese in the United States, 1870–1920

Occupation	Year	Number of Chinese	Percentage Increase or Decrease
Miners and Laborers	1870	27,045	− 99.45
	1920	151	
Domestic service workers	1870	9,349	+280.00
	1920	26,440	
Traders and Dealers	1870	779	+960.00
	1920	7,477	

SOURCE: David Te-Chao Cheng, *ibid.*, p 59.

Examination of the above data together with the previous historical analysis suggests that when majority and minority groups are in conflict, in general, the minority tends to withdraw from the field of competition in the long run, and shifts to more or less noncompetitive fields in order to survive.

Owing to the nature of the relationship which the first generation of a minority group establishes with the majority group, the adjustment of the Chinese has been primarily economic, and only secondarily, cultural.[13] The withdrawal from competition with organized labor has been one of the economic adjustments. This phenomenon has been generalized in the above proposition. The processes of "consciousness of kind" and "consciousness of difference," which operate among the Chinese people, were especially strong during the period of adjustment when anti-Chinese prejudice and discrimination were intensive. The Chinese became conscious of their own group-identification on the basis of either cultural or biological similarities. "On one basis or another, these groups [minority groups] are singled out by the society in which they reside and in varying degrees and proportions are subjected to economic exploitation, segregation, and discrimination." [14] Bierstedt points out that "it is the similarities that people recognize in one another that induce them to seek one another out and to form groups. . . ." [15] The strong prejudice against the Chinese strengthens the "we-feeling" among them. They realize that they must help each other in an alien country to which originally they did not belong. They must defend themselves against further rebuffs by the majority. Toynbee, in his analysis of the origin and growth of civilization, points out the importance of the pattern of challenge-response. The Chinese tend to develop voluntary segregation as their way of responding to the challenge of the environment.

This type of response suggests that because of the unfriendly situation—the prejudice towards them, the consciousness of kind, the "we-feeling," and the withdrawal from the field of competition—the Chinese people have need of mutual help. Several patterns of defense have been employed by them. As has been noted, they have shifted to non-competitive business. This withdrawal may be viewed as a kind of self-defense against greater hostilities which might occur if further competition were to continue.

Furthermore, due to the shift in their business to restaurant, laundry, and gift shop ownership, the Chinese have become urbanized. These businesses can be supported by only the greater cities, so a Chinatown flourishes only where large cosmopolitan populations desire "something different."

Protest is another type of defense. After the passing of the Chinese Exclusion Act, directed against Chinese laborers in 1882, the Chinese government protested.[16] These protests were only a gesture because of the weakness of China at that time.

It is said that a minority group voluntarily isolates itself in order to avoid insults. The Chinese moved from rural to urban areas where there was great hostility towards them because of competition. Some Chinese moved to the East Coast because anti-Chinese prejudice was strong along the West Coast. There was a tendency to integrate the "we-group" and gradually to establish segregated communities among large urban centers in which they could hold interaction with the majority to a minimum, and thus avoid conflicts, hostilities and insults. Nowadays, however, it is difficult to trace these defensive patterns because the old prejudices and discrimination towards the Chinese are no longer strong enough to make them aware of the necessity for self-defense.

This analysis, then, confirms indirectly the proposition, "To run away from prejudice and/or discrimination shown by a majority group toward a minority group helps the formation of voluntary segregation."

The principle which emerges from this analysis is that a minority, such as the Chinese, who have experienced rebuffs from the majority, develop a kind of defensive insulation that protects them against further rebuff. There are several patterns of defensive means: withdrawal against further rebuff, relocation (urbanization or ruralization), protest, avoidance, and so on. These patterns can be traced only when the prejudices and discrimination towards a minority are strong enough.

Regarding the development of voluntary segregation involving involuntary factors, the Chinese had no choice (involuntary factor) but to develop some kind of defensive means in order to survive in such an unfriendly situation, as has been noted above. But there are other possible reasons contributing to the formation of Chinatown, which may be summarized as follows: (1) Relatives like to live together. Under an unfriendly and uncertain situation, relatives live together for mutual help. This is an indication that "a strong system of group solidarity—subordination of the individual to the family, for instance—protects and supports the individual in such a way that breakdown of this solidarity intensifies insecurity." [17] The large family system is preserved in a country of "individualism," because of the necessity of observing group solidarity. The members of the groups help each other in many ways.

(2) Foreign-born minorities have language difficulties. The early Chinese immigrants were uneducated laborers; in the new country they had language difficulties. It is assumed that relatives and friends assisted one another in "interpreting" for those who did not understand English well. Even in 1920, seventy years after the first mass immigration, the percentage of illiteracy for the Chinese was high on the West Coast. Table 2 shows the percentages of illiteracy among those age twenty-one and over. Therefore, language barriers did slow down the process of assimilation; on the other hand, it contributed to voluntary segregation.

(3) The preservation of the Chinese way of life is one of the important factors which might explain why the Chinese live together. Like the reasons outlined above, the desire of the Chinese to preserve their early customs and folkways is related to their cultural background. The disposition of the Chinese to settle in segregated communities in an effort to cherish different traditions and peculiar folkways in the seclusion and security of their own communities is also true.

Table 2. Illiteracy Rates for the Chinese in the United States
According to the 1920 Population Census*

Sex	California			Oregon		
	Total No.	Illiterate		Total No.	Illiterate	
		No.	Percent		No.	Percent
Both Sexes	22,638	4,352	19.2	2,484	774	31.2
Males	20,437	3,590	17.6	2,273	704	31.0
Females	2,201	762	34.6	211	70	33.2

SOURCE: Eliot Grinnel Mears, *Resident Orientals on the American Pacific Coast* (Chicago, 1928), p. 423.
* For population 21 years and over.

Therefore, this analysis suggests, generally speaking, that the stronger the traditional culture, the greater the desire of the minority group to live together voluntarily.

(4) When the Chinese laborers transferred from mining to domestic service, they migrated to urban low-rent areas in the large cities and, year after year, the segregation of the Chinese community developed. It should be kept in mind that these laborers were uneducated, and the best chance for them to meet the challenge of the environment was to perform domestic services such as they probably had done in China.

"The first arrivals are the most important since they establish the standards of comparison with other races. An unfortunate feature arises when the later comers are of a higher social class." [18] It was the Chinese laborers who established the pattern of comparison. This pattern could be misleading, for the Chinese are often associated with hand laundries. There are not so many hand laundries in a city in China, but, as a result of economic competition, there is a large number of them in New York.

(5) Other possible factors in the formation of Chinatowns are the Buddhist religion, a strong Chinese nationalism, and racial discrimination against the Chinese. [19]

Group tensions is another factor in voluntary segregation. As in other immigrant minorities in the accommodation stage, the Chinese developed a segregated community within a large city. "The two extreme solutions for eliminating a given group conflict are (a) complete isolation, *e.g.*, geographic exclusion and (b) complete assimilation." [20] The first part of this theory is partly accepted by the majority in their policy-making towards the Chinese: "Let us exclude the Chinese laborers because with their cheap labor they may lower our living standards." However, this did not solve the problem of the Chinese laborers already in the United States. Therefore, when the Chinese tended to form Chinatowns, the majority groups tolerated the situation because they did not favor complete assimilation at that time. The voluntary segregation of the Chinese, who confined themselves to the Chinese community, was a means to abate conflicts and hostilities. It has been found that "sustained interaction between majority and minority is essential if the lines of communication and understanding necessary for an effective intergroup relations program are to be established." [21] Thus, voluntary segregation is a temporary "safety zone" between group conflicts and tensions. In other words, there is a positive relationship between the decrease in competitive interaction and group conflicts. This analysis, together with the others given above, suggests that a decrease in the frequency of interaction between the members of a majority group and a minority group, if not by force, in general will increase the degree of voluntary segregation and thus decrease group conflict and tensions.

A revised Bogardus Social Distance Scale was used to measure the social distances between the Chinese and four other minorities, namely, Jew, Italian, Puerto Rican, and Negro. It was found, in general, that the present-day Chinese students show the greatest amount of prejudice. The first-generation immigrants show the least prejudice; and in between there is the second generation. MacIver and Page pointed out that group prejudice is learned. The Chinese students have a wider range of social interaction and contacts with the majority than the first generation. They are quick to absorb the "American prejudice" toward other minorities. The first-generation Chinese, who confine themselves to a segregated community, understand less because of fewer contacts with outside groups, and fewer contacts with majority members from whom they could learn "American prejudice." The second generation expresses moderate group prejudice between the other two groups because they are at the "marginal stage." The analyses of the social distance test and the range of social interactions suggest that the more frequently a member of a minority group interacts with members of the majority group, the stronger his prejudice towards other minorities is apt to be.[22]

The first generation, the second generation, and the present-day students were asked to rate the degree of acceptance of the Chinese by the majority group in six areas, namely, work, school, politics, housing, public affairs, and social activities. The results reveal that the Chinese are accepted in school and are not accepted in politics. They are accepted partially in work and in housing, and are less accepted in public affairs and social activities. If the Chinese were fully accepted by the majority, there would be no need for them to develop a voluntarily segregated community in which their socio-emotional needs are met. This analysis suggests that the higher the legal, political, economic, and social barriers against assimilation, the more the minority group consolidates its advantages.

Nowadays, the prejudice and discrimination against the Chinese are not as strong as they were, and there is no necessity, therefore, for the Chinese to practice defensive insulation and voluntary segregation. It is interesting to note that in the great metropolitan area of New York, the Chinese population is about twenty-five thousand in addition to the eight thousand in and around New York's Chinatown. In other words, the great majority of the Chinese are living outside Chinatown, scattered all over the metropolitan area. They have not isolated themselves in order to avoid further rebuffs because they are accepted almost anywhere they choose. But New York's Chinatown still exists, and about eight thousand people voluntarily live there. This may be explained by the "institutionalization" of the voluntary segregation of Chinatown. The norms of the community sanction the leaving of people who do not want to stay. The original functions of voluntary segregation had been for defensive purposes; now, the main functions have been shifted to business purposes. The changing functions are possible because the norms of the community only push the deviant function to the existing degree of obedience. In other words, the changing function is a moving equilibrium. Even though the younger generations tend to move out, Chinatown will continue to exist as a "symbol" of voluntary segregation because it will become a commercial district in which not too many Chinese will remain as residents. With the change in its original function, New York's Chinatown tends to become a commercial district, or a "symbol" of voluntary segregation in place of the previous "defensive purpose."

Voluntary segregation does not curtail assimilation but delays the process to some extent. Since the situation for the Chinese has improved in the United States, and the younger generations are more or less "Americanized," the process of assimilation is quicker than it was. On the other hand, the more the tensions between the two nations lessen, the more the tensions between the Chinese living in America and Americans tend to decrease. And a decrease of tensions facilitates assimilation. In the social attitudes test, the results show that Chinese favor better intergroup relations, which relations also facilitate the acceptance of assimilation. The previous analysis indicates that Chinatowns will decline as the younger generations tend to move out. This is a good indication that the assimilation process is taking place. Therefore, in general, one can conclude that voluntary segregation of the Chinese does not curtail assimilation, but does delay the process to some extent.

Gradual assimilation is taking place, but complete assimilation is impossible until the resistance to intermarriage by both the majority and minority groups is removed. If the "color line" is crossed by interracial marriages, unequal treatment of a minority cannot be enforced. There are many ways to advocate intermarriage if improved race relations are desired. For example, Lee points out:

A decision of the California Supreme Court has affected the assimilation process within the last two years (1948–1950). The law forbidding intermarriage in the state is declared non-enforceable, and the increase in mixed marriages is marked. Los Angeles alone reported almost a hundred cases within six months after the decision was publicized.[23]

There is no segregation in Hawaii because intermarriage is accepted and regarded as an "honor." Originally, "the king [in Hawaii] secured the services of a number of white men. . . . These men . . . were given positions of honor and were given native women of chiefly rank to be their wives . . . their half-blood children by the Hawaiians were accorded high rank." [24] But we should not over-emphasize the correlation between intermarriage and desegregation because there is also a positive correlation between the decrease of prejudice and desegregation. For example, in French Martinique, segregation of color is not visible today because there is little or no prejudice.[25] Therefore, it can be suggested that the norm of a group disapproving interracial marriage indirectly contributes to voluntary segregation of that group. On the other hand, where the interracial marriage is accepted, voluntary segregation is difficult to maintain.

A Final Note

This analysis suggests, in general, that the segregated community of the Chinese in New York is one kind or form of voluntary segregation on the devised scale, namely, the "voluntary segregation involving involuntary factor(s)." Theoretically, voluntary segregation is distinct from involuntary segregation. In practice, however, it is difficult to tell one from the other, as seen in the case of the Chinese. It is interesting to note that Leo Kuper also had difficulty in differentiating between voluntary segregation and compulsory (involuntary) segregation in his case study of Durban, South Africa.[26] The suggested scale of segregation, further breaking down the component parts of both kinds of segregation, is aimed at solving the difficulties.

Race relations are no longer a domestic problem which can be solved at national leisure. During the last few years, the United Nations Educational, Scientific and Cultural Organization has done a series of projects to study "international tensions and the techniques for their relief."[27] The suggested scale of segregation might help to discover different approaches to solve different kinds or forms of segregation in our present-day "international" race relations. Any conclusions or generalizations formulated in this paper, nevertheless, are, and should be, tentative. The author can only express the hope that his study of what has already been done, though incomplete, may stimulate others to make further scientific inquiry into Chinese-American relations, which is one aspect of "international" race relations.

Notes ▶

1. See Rose Hum Lee, "The Decline of Chinatowns in the U.S.A.," *American Journal of Sociology*, LIV (March, 1949), 422–32.

2. This study was conducted in New York City in 1959. A questionnaire was given to 75 respondents. This paper is based on D. Y. Yuan's "Voluntary Segregation: A Study of New York Chinatown" (unpublished Master's thesis, The City College of New York, 1959).

3. "Segregation," *Dictionary of Sociology*, 1955 edition, p. 289.

4. Egon Ernest Bergel, *Urban Sociology* (New York, 1955), p. 89.

5. Brewton Berry, *Race and Ethnic Relations* (Boston, 1958), p. 274.

6. The term "segregation" used in race relations in the Southern

United States always implies "involuntary" segregation for the Negroes.

7. Berry, *op. cit.*, pp. 297–98.

8. E. Franklin Frazier, *The Negro in the United States* (Chicago, 1939), Chapter II.

9. Charles F. Marden, *Minorities in American Society* (New York, 1952), Chap. 9.

10. George F. Seward, *Chinese Immigration, in Its Social and Economic Aspects* (New York, 1881), p. vi.

11. Eliot Grinnel Mears, *Resident Orientals on the American Pacific Coast* (Chicago, 1928), p. 197.

12. David Te-Chao Cheng, *Acculturation of the Chinese in the United States, A Philadelphia Study* (China, The Fukien Christian University Press, 1948), p. 59.

13. For the adjustment of the Chinese in the United States, special interviews of the Chinese may be obtained from *Orientals and Their Cultural Adjustment* (Fisk University, Nashville, Tenn., 1946).

14. Charles Wagley and Marvin Harris, *Minorities in the New World* (New York, 1958), p. 17.

15. Robert Bierstedt, *The Social Order* (New York, 1957), p. 434.

16. Mary Roberts Coolidge, *Chinese Immigration* (New York, 1909) especially Chap. XVI.

17. Talcott Parsons, *Essays in Sociological Theory* (Glencoe, Ill., 1954), p. 285.

18. Mears, *op. cit.*, p. 334.

19. Assuming that "voluntary segregation involving involuntary factors" is the kind of segregation which applies to Chinatown, we need to find the most important reasons that would explain why the Chinese live together in Chinatown. A series of seven possible reasons was given and respondents were asked to rank them by importance. The most important reasons are listed above.

20. Robin Williams, *Reduction of Intergroups Tension* (New York, 1945), p. 46.

21. John P. Dean and Alex Rosen, *A Manual of Intergroup Relations* (Chicago, 1955), p. 7.

22. This proposition is based on the assumption that group prejudice is learned. Some sociologists like William I. Thomas argue that race prejudice is organic and instinctive. For details see William I. Thomas, "The Psychology of Race Prejudice," *The American Journal of Sociology*, IX (March, 1904), 611.

23. Rose Hum Lee, "A Century of Chinese-American Relationships," *Phylon*, XI (Third Quarter, 1950), 240–45.

24. Edward B. Reuter (ed.), *Race and Culture Contacts* (New York, 1934), p. 151.

25. Wagley and Harris, *op. cit.*, pp. 108–9.

26. Leo Kuper, *Durban, A Study in Racial Ecology* (New York, 1958).

27. Otto Klineberg, *Tensions Affecting International Understanding* (New York, 1950), p. vii.

19► THE ADJUSTMENT OF PUERTO RICANS TO NEW YORK CITY

JOSEPH P. FITZPATRICK

Puerto Ricans have been entering the mainland in significant numbers only since the 1940's, and their center of concentration has always been New York City, despite some dispersal to other cities in recent years. Like others who had come before them, Puerto Ricans in the United States have been seriously handicapped by poverty and difficulty in using the English language. Unlike others, however, Puerto Ricans have arrived mainly by air rather than sea. They have included a number of Negroes from a non-English-speaking culture, and they have been preponderantly female in sex ratio.

In the following article Professor Joseph Fitzpatrick, a Jesuit sociologist who has written extensively on the Puerto Rican migrant in New York City, discusses some of the crucial problems of adjustment confronted by these newcomers in the metropolitan community.

► IN ATTEMPTING to evaluate the role of prejudice in the adjustment of the Puerto Ricans in the next ten years, a number of factors affecting the life of Puerto Ricans on the mainland must be kept distinct, one from the other. First, it is important not to confuse prejudice against the Puerto Ricans with certain kinds of difficulties which are simply part of the problem of urban living for poor people whether they are Puerto Rican or not. There is danger both to Americans and to Puerto Ricans in identifying as

From the *Journal of Intergroup Relations* (Winter, 1959–60), 43–51. Reprinted by permission of the author and publisher.

prejudice something which is part of the routine of living in the modern city. Secondly, it is important not to allow certain temporary outbursts of prejudice which create temporary difficulties to blind us to the real issues in long-range adjustment. Thirdly, the major issues in long-range adjustment are partly cultural, and partly racial. It is in terms of these two factors, cultural integration and racial integration, that the real issue of prejudice must be examined.

Different people have different abilities to face change, to become adjusted to a strange world and a new way of life. In the history of American migrations, the adjustment of newcomers has generally been a three-generation process.[1] The person who migrates generally never becomes fully American. The child born in the United States of immigrant parents is the classic "second generation", the child who is caught between two cultures. He is living in the culture of his parents while he is in his home, and he is being taught a different culture in the school, the neighborhood, at work. He is neither completely old nor completely new. This is the difficult generation. Finally, the third generation, grandchild of the immigrants, is American. He reflects, perhaps, many of the influences of the older culture, but for all practical purposes, his culture is that of the United States.

There is no reason to believe that this process should take any longer for the Puerto Ricans than it took for earlier immigrants. There are many indications which I shall mention later that it may take less. The focus of our discussion is the relation of prejudice and discrimination to this process of adjustment: will the experience of these two difficulties in the case of Puerto Ricans hinder the process of adjustment?

Conflicts of Interest

When a large group of newcomers move into a city, a great many differences arise which I call *conflicts of interest*. In the study of migrations, I have been repeatedly impressed not only by the difficulties faced by the migrating peoples, but by the distress that immigration creates for people who are already there. No people likes to have its way of life upset, and large-scale migration always upsets it. Old and pleasant routines are interfered with; crowding increases discomfort; expectations are not met; economic advantages are threatened; people have to change their way of doing things, and ordinarily people do not like to change their way of doing things. This is not a pleasant experience. It is part of what I might call the "attrition" of social change and social development. It is a difficult experience for migrants and established residents which is part of the ordinary experience of newcomers and old-timers in a large and complicated city.[2]

It is wise not to confuse this with prejudice and discrimination. Prejudice certainly becomes involved, as we shall see. But the experience itself is a painful process in which resentment, antagonism and conflict are very understandable human reactions which may not be based at all upon prejudice against the group of newcomers.

The neighborhood is the main focus of this experience. For instance, the practice of converting apartments, readapting them into rooming houses or apartments and renting them to Puerto Ricans inevitably precipitates a conflict of interest. Prompted by a desperate need for housing, Puerto Ricans move in, to find themselves the object of bitter resentment on the part of older residents. Prejudice comes to play an important role, indeed, but the major role is a conflict of interests: the desire of a landlord to increase his profits; the need of Puerto Ricans for a place to live; and a concern of older residents for the preservation of their neighborhood.

It is a trying task in these situations to distinguish between an understandable conflict of interests and an outburst of prejudice and discrimination. Exploitation and manipulation may be at work by thoughtless landlords or financial interests. It seems to me that one great contribution that inter-group relations officials are making is precisely in helping the residents of changing neighborhoods to identify the real nature of the problem and to clarify the dynamics of the conflict. In this way, instead of older residents wasting their energy in hostility against newcomers, they may marshal their common strength against a common danger. If the initial situation is defined as prejudice, or if the situation deteriorates into prejudice and discrimination, the possibility of dealing with it peacefully may be lost.[3]

A second experience of this nature is associated with relocation. I am fully aware that re-development can sometimes be a polite word for getting rid of Puerto Ricans, Negroes and others whom comfortable citizens do not want around. But in a city like New York, slum conditions pile up and deterioration leads to drastic action. Since many of the Puerto Ricans are in the poor housing, they are displaced, relocated, subjected to a great many inconveniences, which make life extremely difficult for them. In a very understandable cry against this inconvenience, it is not uncommon to speak of discrimination and prejudice. These elements are present, but many other elements are present also: the turmoil that has been associated with the city's life for generations; part of the death and re-birth that have marked the city's history, the demolition and rebuilding that has been pushing immigrants around the city for more than a hundred years. A certain amount of perspective in this regard is a helpful thing to have. The experience is part of the conflict of interests which has always marked the life of immigrants.

A third experience of this nature is in the area of occupation. Newcomers become a threat to the jobs of older residents. In this situation Puerto Ricans are exploited.[4] However, it would not be wise to confuse exploitation with prejudice. A person who exploits another is not concerned whether he is English, French, Puerto Rican or Scandinavian. If he can find someone of whom he can take advantage, he is remarkably unconcerned about racial or ethnic backgrounds. In fact, some of the most effective exploiters of immigrants were members of their own ethnic group. The poverty of Puerto Ricans, their language handicap, their lack of sophistication about mainland city life, leave them, at this moment, particularly exposed to exploitation.

It seems to me that, in this regard, it is much more effective to minimize the factor of prejudice even though it may be there, and to guide the Puerto Ricans to a kind of positive action against the situation of exploitation in general. This will gradually be corrected by improved education, by social and economic advancement, by social and political organization and action.

These are some of the conflicts of interest, the trials that generally beset older residents and immigrants in a large and complicated city.

Conflicts of Culture

There is a second area of conflict—a conflict of culture. When people of two different ways of life meet, serious difficulties arise for both. Gradually, in the United States, the migrating groups have lost the old way of life from which they had come, and have adopted a way of life that is characteristic of the United States. This is the process, so familiar to us, of immigrant assimilation.

The really serious aspect of the conflict of cultures is the distress it causes for the migrant or immigrant himself—his bewilderment in a world he does not understand, his confusion in the presence of customs and expectations that are strange to him. What was right in Puerto Rico, for instance, becomes wrong on the mainland; what was wrong in Puerto Rico becomes right on the mainland; the things that gave a man or woman dignity and honor in a Puerto Rican village are greeted with ridicule in New York. Parents never fully understand their children; children never fully understand parents. Conflict between the generations may arise. Unless the family and the individual person are strong, life can become disorganized. Delinquency and mental breakdown may follow.

It is perfectly clear that Puerto Ricans are going through this distressing experience at the present time. There is no reason to believe that adjustment will be any slower among Puerto Ricans than among earlier groups; indeed, it may be much more rapid.

The conflict of culture affects the older residents in a different way. They find their own customs and way of life under pressure of strangers whom they do not understand. They fear the threat to their own values and traditions from people who are different. This is the fear, so common in the United States, that repeatedly leads to the judgment that immigrants are not assimilable; are therefore a threat to our social and political institutions. This is the fear that was reflected in the adoption of the quota system of restricting immigration. I am reluctant to call this simply a problem of prejudice, although prejudice is continually intertwined with it. It is a problem of cultural misunderstanding, of ethnocentrism, of dislike for others because they do not do things our way.

The Matrix of Prejudice

However, it is within the context of these two conflicts—of interest and of culture—that prejudice and discrimination fester and break out. These two kinds of conflict are used to rationalize and justify prejudice. Hatred or dislike for others; refusal to meet them or live with them; refusal to learn about the culture of others or to look searchingly into one's own; these are all rationalized as the means that one must take to protect his economic interests, and, more important, to protect his moral standards.

The judgment against the different culture of another group of people is almost always cast in moral terms. Their way of life is pictured as immoral, and admitting them to association with one's self is pictured as inviting the danger of moral corruption. These fears are projected into a sweeping judgment against the migrating people; general condemnations prevent people from seeing the admirable traits of the newcomers; the older residents try to isolate themselves from the stranger; discrimination is in full sway.

The New York Story

Against this background, we can examine the present situation in New York.

In the first place, New York is going through a period of rapid and difficult change. The migration of people into and out of the city has been creating a great deal of inconvenience and distress. People who have moved out and have to pay higher rents for what they call decent housing are inclined to blame their difficulty on the Puerto Ricans who moved into the neighborhood. More seriously, the people who would like to move out but who have to stay in the neighborhood blame their distress also on the Puerto Ricans.

Secondly, there is the general situation of crime in the city. This is an unfortunate situation that troubles everybody. Indeed Puerto Ricans probably suffer at the hands of the city's delinquents much more than the rest of the population. People do not feel safe, and the older New Yorkers compare the dangers of the city today with the peacefulness which they experienced in their neighborhoods twenty or thirty years ago. There is a natural tendency to look for some obvious target on which to pin the blame.

Finally, there is the conflict of culture we have discussed. People have moved in who have a way of life the older residents do not understand.

As a result of all this, the older New Yorkers look for a scapegoat and the scapegoat is obviously there. The whole situation becomes projected upon the Puerto Ricans. Add to this the dramatic convergence of crime within recent months and you have the present outburst of resentment.

What hope is there in the situation? A great deal, I think. In the first place, it would not be wise to allow the temporary difficulties of the present moment to obscure the important issues in long-range adjustment. Resentment such as that of the present is not new in New York. Actually the resentment against the Puerto Ricans cannot be compared in bitterness with the resentment that was shown to early groups of immigrants. If strength, perseverance and courage enabled the early immigrants to overcome more serious crises, there is every reason to believe that strength, perseverance and courage will enable the Puerto Ricans to overcome this one. What is more, a crisis like this will probably strengthen the solidarity of the Puerto Rican community. Strength against a common danger may be very helpful in giving greater stability to the position of Puerto Ricans in New York. Finally, the crisis will clarify for older residents and for Puerto Ricans a conflict which exists. Recognizing it more clearly, they will be in a better position to deal with it effectively.

Hopeful Aspects

Some aspects of the present migration indicate that the cultural adjustment of Puerto Ricans will be easier than that of earlier groups.[5] In the first place, there is a very strong emphasis today on "cultural pluralism", the importance of respecting the culture of newcomers, of not trying to Americanize them too rapidly. This stems from the realization that overhasty attempts to get previous immigrants to accept our way of life impeded the process of assimilation instead of advancing it. This has led to a second phenomenon related to the present migration, the extraordinary effort being made by teachers, public officials, social workers, priests and church officials to acquaint themselves with the background of the life of Puerto Ricans so that they may work more effectively with them. As far as I can determine, this has never happened before in any migration. It is one of those striking developments in human relations which is characteristic of our times.

Secondly, the fact that Puerto Ricans have been part of the United States has given them some familiarity at least with our way of life. This has become much more intense with the nature of the migration. It is assuming the characteristics of an experience in commuting rather than migrating. Movement back and forth between the Island and mainland has increased so much that the Island is almost a suburb of mainland cities. This increasing familiarity with American life should lead to more rapid under-standing of it on the part of the Puerto Ricans, and more facility in adjusting to it.

Thirdly, there is the important policy of the New York archdio-cese in attempting to provide all possible assistance to the Puerto Ricans to help them to become integrated into established par-ishes. The archdiocese is not following a policy of setting up separate parishes for the Puerto Ricans, but is making an extraor-dinary effort to train priests, sisters and lay workers to work with the Puerto Ricans as they seek to become active members together with older parishioners in existing parishes. Such a remarkable experiment in integration has never been attempted before. De-spite the understandable difficulties which this involves for newly arrived migrants, the policy should facilitate the long-range adjust-ment of the Puerto Ricans.

Finally, the experience of being scattered widely through the city may advance the adjustment of Puerto Ricans, or may slow it down. For instance, except in a few sections of the city, the Puerto Ricans have not been able to establish what is called an "immi-grant community", an area where everyone is Puerto Rican, where Island customs and way of life would be transferred to the streets of New York. In the past, the immigrants moved to areas of second settlement, newly-built homes available to low income people, where solid blocks of Irish or German or Jewish or Italian people could be found. This is no longer possible to a migrating group. Policies in low-cost housing projects, redevelopment and relocation are intermingling them with older residents over wide areas; they are moving into the interstices of the city where build-ings have begun to show the signs of age.

The Color Question

Another possible impediment to speedy adjustment revolves around the troublesome issue of color.[6] The adjustment of Puerto Ricans involves not only a question of cultural adjustment, but in many cases a question of racial adjustment for some Puerto Ricans who will be identified on the mainland as "colored".

The Puerto Ricans are the first group, migrating in large num-bers to mainland cities, who bring with them a tradition of widespread social intermingling and intermarriage of people of notice-ably different color. Two things may happen:

If this practice continues among the Puerto Ricans on the mainland, they may break the resistance to integration in main-land cities. If they can become established in mainland parishes and neighborhoods as a people that takes the intermingling of white and Colored for granted, we should expect that the older residents will also gradually come to take for granted the intermin-gling of the two. Should the Puerto Ricans succeed in doing this, they would have brought to the mainland the extraordinary bless-ing of advancing the practice of acceptance of people regardless of their color.

However, another development may take place. Recognizing the handicaps of color on the mainland, the Puerto Ricans may gradu-ally split into two groups: those who are taken as white becoming assimilated into the white community; those who will be consid-ered Colored becoming assimilated into the Negro community. If this happens, the Puerto Rican community will have become shattered; they will have lost their honorable tradition of non-discrimination; and the mainland cities will still be back where we would have been had Puerto Ricans never come.

The key factor in this problem is not the racial prejudice of mainland Americans. The existence of that and its manifestations are perfectly clear to everyone. The key factor in this will be the attitude of the Puerto Rican migrants themselves. It will involve their reflecting on the meaning of color in Puerto Rico; making explicit the values which have been implicit in customary behav-ior; and consciously facing the issue of color as they have never had to face it on the Island.

Two things are clear to anyone who is familiar with the culture of Puerto Rico: discrimination such as it exists on the mainland has not existed there; color is a matter of considerable anxiety for much of the population.[7] It is not easy for a mainlander to reconcile these two things. The reason for it seems to be the following:

Color and Class

In a two-class society of a traditional Spanish type, color became one obvious way of identifying a person as a member of the lower class. Once a person's identification with the lower class was clear, the factor of color did not mean much if it meant anything. It was only when a person developed aspirations for social advancement that color would become an issue. Obviously Colored features were a drawback to social advancement. However, if a Colored person was able, by his ability and his accomplishments, to distinguish himself, to become prominent, his higher class status would tend to overshadow his color. José Celso Barbosa, a Colored man, founder of the Republican Party in Puerto Rico, claims in his writings that he never felt any disadvantage due to his color. His picture hangs in a prominent place in the Ponce City Hall. In other words, his position and his role in society subdued acknowledgment of his color. Steward, in his study of 200 top families in Puerto Rico, indicates that a number of people in these top families had noticeable Negro or Indian features, but they were considered white. (Steward, J., *People of Puerto Rico*, p. 425.)

Puerto Ricans generally explain the difference between the role of color on the mainland and in Puerto Rico as follows: On the mainland, the color of a person determines what class he will belong to; in Puerto Rico, the class a person belongs to determines his color. This is a puzzling principle for Americans to understand, but it can be illustrated abundantly in Puerto Rico's social life.

As Puerto Ricans come to New York, or indeed with the rapid rise of the middle class in Puerto Rico itself, Puerto Ricans face the serious question of re-defining the meaning of color. Color can no longer be simply a sign of lower class status. In New York, or in the middle class of Puerto Rican cities, what is color going to mean now? Will people continue to be accepted widely in social gatherings, in occupation, in housing, in marriage, regardless of their color? This would be to continue the marvelous tradition of non-discrimination. Or will they adopt the American pattern of discriminating on the basis of color, regardless of the value and greatness of the human person, and thus embrace the injustice and distress that discrimination has involved in our American culture?

What is more, in New York, Puerto Ricans will be caught immediately in the strong pressure for upward mobility, for social and economic advancement, and they will realize the handicaps that one must face in this regard if he is identified as Colored on the mainland.

This has prompted a number of writers to conclude that the Puerto Ricans will split into two groups: those who will be identified as white; those who will become identified as Colored. In order to determine whether this was happening, I did a study last year of the behavior of Puerto Ricans in six Catholic parishes in New York. I chose parishes of a wide variety of characteristics from the parish most heavily populated with Puerto Ricans to others where they are scattered widely and sparsely among older residents. Observation and interviews provided abundant evidence that the practice of Puerto Ricans of accepting the social intermingling of people of all colors was continuing up till that time in New York. A study of the marriages of Puerto Ricans in these parishes over a four-month period indicated that twenty-five percent of the Puerto Rican marriages involved people of noticeably different shades of color. This prompted the conclusion that, up till the present time, the Puerto Ricans give strong evidence of continuing on the mainland the tradition of social relations between those of different color which is characteristic of the Island.

It seems clear, however, that if it is really going to continue, the Puerto Rican people themselves must make explicit the values on which their admirable social tradition is based. It is my sincere prayer and hope that they will continue their tradition; that they will make explicit the principles of human brotherhood, of universal respect for men and women that have been implicit in their culture. If they do, they will have brought a priceless contribution to the life of the mainland, and have succeeded in breaking as no other group has done, the resistance to integration in mainland cities.

Notes ►

1. There is an extensive literature on assimilation. One of the finest general discussions can be found in Oscar Handlin, *The Uprooted* (Boston: Little-Brown, 1951). An excellent treatment of first and second generations can be found in Hannibal G. Duncan, *Immigration and Assimilation* (Boston: D. C. Heath, 1933). It will also be discussed in any good text on minority groups such as Brewton Berry, *Race and Ethnic Relations* (Boston: Houghton Mifflin, 1958).

2. For some of the background, cf. Edith Abbott, *Historical Aspects of the Immigration Problem* (Chicago: Chic. Univ. Press, 1926), Sections IV & V. For the early New York experience cf. Robert Ernst, *Immigrant Life in New York City, 1825–63* (New York: Columbia Univ. Press, 1949).

3. Cf. Daniel Seligman, "The Enduring Slums," Chapter 4 in *The*

Exploding Metropolis, by the Editors of *Fortune* (New York: Double-day Anchor, 1958). Also Dan Wakefield, *Island in the City* (Boston: Houghton Mifflin, 1959), Chapter 8, "Orientation."

4. The best documentation on the exploitation of Puerto Rican workers is available in mimeographed form from the Association of Catholic Trade Unionists, 327 Lexington Ave., New York 16, N.Y. Some of this is reported in Lester Velie, *Labor, U.S.A.* (New York: Harper & Brothers, 1959), Chapter 13.

5. For a detailed treatment, cf. Joseph P. Fitzpatrick, "Integration of Puerto Ricans," *Thought,* Vol. XXX (Autumn, 1955).

6. For a detailed discussion of the following, an unpublished manu-script, "Attitudes of Puerto Ricans Toward Color," is available from the author, Joseph P. Fitzpatrick, S.J., at Fordham University, New York, 58, N.Y.

7. The existence of racial prejudice or discrimination is a seriously debated matter in the literature about Puerto Rico. José Celso Bar-bosa, an outstanding Puerto Rican, founder of the Republican Party on the Island, was a Negro. In his compilation of articles, *Problema de Razas* (San Juan: Imprenta Venezuela, 1937), he consistently con-trasts the situation of the Colored person in Puerto Rico with that of the United States. He insisted that racial discrimination did not exist on the Island. Tomas Blanco, *Prejuicio Racial en Puerto Rico* (San Juan: Biblioteca de Autores Puertoriqueños, 1942), takes a similar position. For the contrary position, cf. Maxine Gordon, "Race Pat-terns and Prejudice in Puerto Rico," *American Sociological Review,* XVI (April, 1949). A more detailed bibliography is given in the Fitzpatrick manuscript mentioned in note 6.

20▸ THE MUTUAL IMAGES
AND EXPECTATIONS
OF ANGLO-AMERICANS
AND MEXICAN-AMERICANS

OZZIE G. SIMMONS

Mexicans are one of the largest ethnic groups to have immigrated to the United States from other countries in the Western hemisphere. Of mixed Indian and white ancestry ("mestizos"), they are a frequent source of cheap labor and often remain a low-income group even in the second generation. Most Mexican-Americans live in the Southwest close to their country of origin, and they are constantly reenforced there by the arrival of new Mexican immigrants. Like other oppressed minorities, Mexicans are no strangers to occupational and wage discrimination, segregation in schools and housing, and even mob brutality. Their exploiters, the Anglo-Americans, brought to the relationship an ideology that originated in the former slave states—one that welcomed the Mexicans as cheap labor and social inferiors. Professor Simmons, in the article that follows, examines the reciprocal image-formation in the interaction of the dominant and minority groups.

▸ A NUMBER OF psychological and sociological studies have treated ethnic and racial stereotypes as they appear publicly in the mass media and also as held privately by individuals.[1] The present paper is based on data collected for a study of a number of aspects of the

Reprinted by permission from the author and *Daedalus*, published by the American Academy of Arts and Sciences, Brookline, Massachusetts (Spring, 1961), 286–99.

Based on an address at the annual meeting of the Mexican Christian Institute at San Antonio in 1958.

relations between Anglo-Americans and Mexican-Americans in a South Texas community, and is concerned with the principal assumptions and expectations that Anglo- and Mexican-Americans hold of one another; how they see each other; the extent to which these pictures are realistic; and the implications of their intergroup relations and cultural differences for the fulfillment of their mutual expectations.[2]

The Community

The community studied (here called "Border City") is in South Texas, about 250 miles south of San Antonio. Driving south from San Antonio, one passes over vast expanses of brushland and grazing country, then suddenly comes upon acres of citrus groves, farmlands rich with vegetables and cotton, and long rows of palm trees. This is the "Magic Valley," an oasis in the semidesert region of South Texas. The Missouri Pacific Railroad (paralleled by Highway 83, locally called "The longest street in the world") bisects twelve major towns and cities of the Lower Rio Grande Valley between Brownsville, near the Gulf of Mexico, and Rio Grande City, 103 miles to the west.

Border City is neither the largest nor the smallest of these cities, and is physically and culturally much like the rest. Its first building was constructed in 1905. By 1920 it had 5,331 inhabitants, and at the time of our study these had increased to an estimated 17,500. The completion of the St. Louis, Brownsville, and Mexico Railroad in 1904 considerably facilitated Anglo-American immigration to the Valley. Before this the Valley had been inhabited largely by Mexican ranchers, who maintained large haciendas in the traditional Mexican style based on peonage. Most of these haciendas are now divided into large or small tracts that are owned by Anglo-Americans, who obtained them through purchase or less legitimate means. The position of the old Mexican-American landowning families has steadily deteriorated, and today these families, with a few exceptions, are completely overshadowed by the Anglo-Americans, who have taken over their social and economic position in the community.

The Anglo-American immigration into the Valley was paralleled by that of the Mexicans from across the border, who were attracted by the seemingly greater opportunities for farm labor created by the introduction of irrigation and the subsequent agricultural expansion. Actually, there had been a small but steady flow of Mexican immigration into South Texas that long ante-dated the Anglo-American immigration.[3] At present, Mexican-Americans probably constitute about two-fifths of the total population of the Valley.

In Border City, Mexican-Americans comprise about 56 percent of the population. The southwestern part of the city, adjoining and sometimes infiltrating the business and industrial areas, is variously referred to as "Mexiquita," "Mexican-town," and "Little Mexico" by the city's Anglo-Americans, and as the *colonia* by the Mexican-Americans. With few exceptions, the *colonia* is inhabited only by Mexican-Americans, most of whom live in close proximity to one another in indifferently constructed houses on tiny lots. The north side of the city, which lies across the railroad tracks, is inhabited almost completely by Anglo-Americans. Its appearance is in sharp contrast to that of the *colonia* in that it is strictly residential and displays much better housing.

In the occupational hierarchy of Border City, the top level (the growers, packers, canners, businessmen, and professionals) is over-whelmingly Anglo-American. In the middle group (the white-collar occupations) Mexicans are prominent only where their bilingualism makes them useful, for example, as clerks and sales-men. The bottom level (farm laborers, shed and cannery workers, and domestic servants) is overwhelmingly Mexican-American.

These conditions result from a number of factors, some quite distinct from the reception accorded Mexican-Americans by Anglo-Americans. Many Mexican-Americans are still recent immigrants and are thus relatively unfamiliar with Anglo-American culture and urban living, or else persist in their tendency to live apart and maintain their own institutions whenever possible. Among their disadvantages, however, the negative attitudes and discriminatory practices of the Anglo-American group must be counted. It is only fair to say, with the late Ruth Tuck, that much of what Mexican-Americans have suffered at Anglo-American hands has not been perpetrated deliberately but through indiffer-ence, that it has been done not with the fist but with the elbow.[4] The average social and economic status of the Mexican-American group has been improving, and many are moving upward. This is partly owing to increasing acceptance by the Anglo-American group, but chiefly to the efforts of the Mexican-Americans them-selves.

Anglo-American Assumptions and Expectations

Robert Lynd writes of the dualism in the principal assumptions that guide Americans in conducting their everyday life and identifies the attempt to "live by contrasting rules of the game" as a characteristic aspect of our culture.[5] This pattern of moral compromise, symptomatic of what is likely to be only vaguely a conscious moral conflict, is evident in Anglo-American assumptions and expectations with regard to Mexican-Americans, which appear both in the moral principles that define what intergroup relations ought to be, and in the popular notions held by Anglo-Americans as to what Mexican-Americans are "really" like. In the first case there is a response to the "American creed," which embodies ideals of the essential dignity of the individual and of certain inalienable rights to freedom, justice, and equal opportunity. Accordingly, Anglo-Americans believe that Mexican-Americans must be accorded full acceptance and equal status in the larger society. When their orientation to these ideals is uppermost, Anglo-Americans believe that the assimilation of Mexican-Americans is only a matter of time, contingent solely on the full incorporation of Anglo-American values and ways of life.

These expectations regarding the assimilation of the Mexican are most clearly expressed in the notion of the "high type" of Mexican. It is based on three criteria: occupational achievement and wealth (the Anglo-American's own principal criteria of status) and command of Anglo-American ways. Mexican-Americans who can so qualify are acceptable for membership in the service clubs and a few other Anglo-American organizations and for limited social intercourse. They may even intermarry without being penalized or ostracized. Both in their achievements in business and agriculture and in wealth, they compare favorably with middle-class Anglo-Americans, and they manifest a high command of the latter's ways. This view of the "high type" of Mexican reflects the Anglo-American assumption that Mexicans are assimilable; it does not necessarily insure a full acceptance of even the "high type" of Mexican or that his acceptance will be consistent.

The assumption that Mexican-Americans will be ultimately assimilated was not uniformly shared by all the Anglo-Americans who were our informants in Border City. Regardless of whether they expressed adherence to this ideal, however, most Anglo-Americans expressed the contrasting assumption that Mexican-Americans are essentially inferior. Thus the same people may hold assumptions and expectations that are contradictory, although expressed at different times and in different situations. As in the case of their adherence to the ideal of assimilability, not all Anglo-Americans hold the same assumptions and expectations with respect to the inferiority of Mexican-Americans; and even those who agree vary in the intensity of their beliefs. Some do not believe in the Mexican's inferiority at all; some are relatively moderate or sceptical, while others express extreme views with considerable emotional intensity.

Despite this variation, the Anglo-Americans' principal assumptions and expectations emphasize the Mexicans' presumed inferiority. In its most characteristic pattern, such inferiority is held to be self-evident. As one Anglo-American woman put it, "Mexicans are inferior because they are so typically and naturally Mexican." Since they are so obviously inferior, their present subordinate status is appropriate and is really their own fault. There is a ready identification between Mexicans and menial labor, buttressed by an image of the Mexican worker as improvident, undependable, irresponsible, childlike, and indolent. If Mexicans are fit for only the humblest labor, there is nothing abnormal about the fact that most Mexican workers are at the bottom of the occupational pyramid, and the fact that most Mexicans are unskilled workers is sufficient proof that they belong in that category.

Associated with the assumption of Mexican inferiority is that of the homogeneity of this group—that is, all Mexicans are alike. Anglo-Americans may classify Mexicans as being of "high type" and "low type" and at the same time maintain that "a Mexican is a Mexican." Both notions serve a purpose, depending on the situation. The assumption that all Mexicans are alike buttresses the assumption of inferiority by making it convenient to ignore the fact of the existence of a substantial number of Mexican-Americans who represent all levels of business and professional achievement. Such people are considered exceptions to the rule.

Anglo-American Images of Mexican-Americans

To employ Gordon Allport's definition, a stereotype is an exaggerated belief associated with a category, and its function is to justify conduct in relation to that category.[6] Some of the Anglo-

American images of the Mexican have no ascertainable basis in fact, while others have at least a kernel of truth. Although some components of these images derive from behavior patterns that are characteristic of some Mexican-Americans in some situations, few if any of the popular generalizations about them are valid as stated, and none is demonstrably true of all. Some of the images of Mexican-Americans are specific to a particular area of intergroup relations, such as the image of the Mexican-American's attributes as a worker. Another is specific to politics and describes Mexicans as ready to give their votes to whoever will pay for them or provide free barbecues and beer.[7] Let us consider a few of the stereotypical beliefs that are widely used on general principles to justify Anglo-American practices of exclusion and subordination.

One such general belief accuses Mexican-Americans of being unclean. The examples given of this supposed characteristic most frequently refer to a lack of personal cleanliness and environmental hygiene and to a high incidence of skin ailments ascribed to a lack of hygienic practices. Indeed, there are few immigrant groups, regardless of their ethnic background, to whom this defect has not been attributed by the host society, as well as others prominent in stereotypes of the Mexican. It has often been observed that for middle-class Americans cleanliness is not simply a matter of keeping clean but is also an index to the morals and virtues of the individual. It is largely true that Mexicans tend to be much more casual in hygienic practices than Anglo-Americans. Moreover, their labor in the field, the packing sheds, and the towns is rarely clean work, and it is possible that many Anglo-Americans base their conclusions on what they observe in such situations. There is no evidence of a higher incidence of skin ailments among Mexicans than among Anglo-Americans. The belief that Mexicans are unclean is useful for rationalizing the Anglo-American practice of excluding Mexicans from any situation that involves close or allegedly close contact with Anglo-Americans, as in residence, and the common use of swimming pools and other recreational facilities.

Drunkenness and criminality are a pair of traits that have appeared regularly in the stereotypes applied to immigrant groups. They have a prominent place in Anglo-American images of Mexicans. If Mexicans are inveterate drunkards and have criminal tendencies, a justification is provided for excluding them from full participation in the life of the community. It is true that drinking is a popular activity among Mexican-Americans and that total abstinence is rare, except among some Protestant Mexican-Americans. Drinking varies, however, from the occasional consumption of a bottle of beer to the heavy drinking of more potent beverages, so that the frequency of drinking and drunkenness is far from being evenly distributed among Mexican-Americans. Actually, this pattern is equally applicable to the Anglo-American group. The ample patronage of bars in the Anglo-American part of Border City, and the drinking behavior exhibited by Anglo-Americans when they cross the river to Mexico indicate that Mexicans have no monopoly on drinking or drunkenness. It is true that the number of arrests for drunkenness in Border City is greater among Mexicans, but this is probably because Mexicans are more vulnerable to arrest. The court records in Border City show little difference in the contributions made to delinquency and crime by Anglo- and Mexican-Americans.

Another cluster of images in the Anglo-American stereotype portrays Mexican-Americans as deceitful and of a "low" morality, as mysterious, unpredictable, and hostile to Anglo-Americans. It is quite possible that Mexicans resort to a number of devices in their relations with Anglo-Americans, particularly in relations with employers, to compensate for their disadvantages, which may be construed by Anglo-Americans as evidence of deceitfulness. The whole nature of the dominant-subordinate relationship does not make for frankness on the part of Mexicans or encourage them to face up directly to Anglo-Americans in most intergroup contacts. As to the charge of immorality, one need only recognize the strong sense of loyalty and obligation that Mexicans feel in their familial and interpersonal relations to know that the charge is baseless. The claim that Mexicans are mysterious and deceitful may in part reflect Anglo-American reactions to actual differences in culture and personality, but like the other beliefs considered here, is highly exaggerated. The imputation of hostility to Mexicans, which is manifested in a reluctance to enter the *colonia*, particularly at night, may have its kernel of truth, but appears to be largely a projection of the Anglo-American's own feelings.

All three of these images can serve to justify exclusion and discrimination: if Mexicans are deceitful and immoral, they do not have to be accorded equal status and justice; if they are mysterious and unpredictable, there is no point in treating them as one would a fellow Anglo-American; and if they are hostile and dangerous, it is best that they live apart in colonies of their own.

Not all Anglo-American images of the Mexican are unfavorable. Among those usually meant to be complimentary are the beliefs that all Mexicans are musical and always ready for a fiesta, that they are very "romantic" rather than "realistic" (which may have unfavorable overtones as well), and that they love flowers and can grow them under the most adverse conditions. Although each of these beliefs may have a modicum of truth, it may be noted that they tend to reinforce Anglo-American images of Mexicans as childlike and irresponsible, and thus they support the notion that Mexicans are capable only of subordinate status.

Mexican-American Assumptions, Expectations, and Images

Mexican-Americans are as likely to hold contradictory assumptions and distorted images as are Anglo-Americans. Their principal assumptions, however, must reflect those of Anglo-Americans— that is, Mexicans must take into account the Anglo-Americans' conflict as to their potential equality and present inferiority, since they are the object of such imputations. Similarly, their images of Anglo-Americans are not derived wholly independently, but to some extent must reflect their own subordinate status. Consequently, their stereotypes of Anglo-Americans are much less elaborate, in part because Mexicans feel no need of justifying the present intergroup relation, in part because the very nature of their dependent position forces them to view the relation more realistically than Anglo-Americans do. For the same reasons, they need not hold to their beliefs about Anglo-Americans with the rigidity and intensity so often characteristic of the latter.

Any discussion of these assumptions and expectations requires some mention of the class distinctions within the Mexican-American group.[8] Its middle class, though small as compared with the lower class, is powerful within the group and performs the critical role of intermediary in negotiations with the Anglo-American group. Middle-class status is based on education and occupation, family background, readiness to serve the interests of the group, on wealth, and the degree of acculturation, or command of Anglo-American ways. Anglo-Americans recognize Mexican class distinctions (although not very accurately) in their notions of the "high type" and "low type" of Mexicans.

In general, lower-class Mexicans do not regard the disabilities of their status as being nearly as severe as do middle-class Mexican-

Americans. This is primarily a reflection of the insulation between the Anglo-American world and that of the Mexican lower class. Most Mexicans, regardless of class, are keenly aware of Anglo-American attitudes and practices with regard to their group, but lower-class Mexicans do not conceive of participation in the larger society as necessary nor do they regard Anglo-American practices of exclusion as affecting them directly. Their principal reaction has been to maintain their isolation, and thus they have not been particularly concerned with improving their status by acquiring Anglo-American ways, a course more characteristic of the middle-class Mexican.

Mexican-American assumptions and expectations regarding Anglo-Americans must be qualified, then, as being more characteristic of middle- than of lower-class Mexican-Americans. Mexicans, like Anglo-Americans, are subject to conflicts in their ideals, not only because of irrational thinking on their part but also because of Anglo-American inconsistencies between ideal and practice. As for ideals expressing democratic values, Mexican expectations are for obvious reasons the counterpart of the Anglo-Americans'—that Mexican-Americans should be accorded full acceptance and equal opportunity. They feel a considerable ambivalence, however, as to the Anglo-American expectation that the only way to achieve this goal is by a full incorporation of Anglo-American values and ways of life, for this implies the ultimate loss of their cultural identity as Mexicans. On the one hand, they favor the acquisition of Anglo-American culture and the eventual remaking of the Mexican in the Anglo-American image; but on the other hand, they are not so sure that Anglo-American acceptance is worth such a price. When they are concerned with this dilemma, Mexicans advocate a fusion with Anglo-American culture in which the "best" of the Mexican ways, as they view it, would be retained along with the incorporation of the "best" of the Anglo-American ways, rather than a one-sided exchange in which all that is distinctively Mexican would be lost.

A few examples will illustrate the point of view expressed in the phrase, "the best of both ways." A premium is placed on speaking good, unaccented English, but the retention of good Spanish is valued just as highly as "a mark of culture that should not be abandoned." Similarly, there is an emphasis on the incorporation of behavior patterns that are considered characteristically Anglo-American and that will promote "getting ahead," but not to the point at which the drive for power and wealth would become completely dominant, as is believed to be the case with Anglo-Americans.

Mexican ambivalence about becoming Anglo-American or achieving a fusion of the "best" of both cultures is compounded by their ambivalence about another issue, that of equality versus inferiority. That Anglo-Americans are dominant in the society and seem to monopolize its accomplishments and rewards leads Mexicans at times to draw the same conclusion that Anglo-Americans do, namely, that Mexicans are inferior. This questioning of their own sense of worth exists in all classes of the Mexican-American group, although with varying intensity, and plays a substantial part in every adjustment to intergroup relations. There is a pronounced tendency to concede the superiority of Anglo-American ways and consequently to define Mexican ways as undesirable, inferior, and disreputable. The tendency to believe in his own inferiority is counterbalanced, however, by the Mexican's fierce racial pride, which sets the tone of Mexican demands and strivings for equal status, even though these may slip into feelings of inferiority.

The images Mexicans have of Anglo-Americans may not be so elaborate or so emotionally charged as the images that Anglo-Americans have of Mexicans, but they are nevertheless stereotypes, overgeneralized, and exaggerated, although used primarily for defensive rather than justificatory purposes. Mexican images of Anglo-Americans are sometimes favorable, particularly when they identify such traits as initiative, ambition, and industriousness as being peculiarly Anglo-American. Unfavorable images are prominent, however, and, although they may be hostile, they never impute inferiority to Anglo-Americans. Most of the Mexican stereotypes evaluate Anglo-Americans on the basis of their attitudes toward Mexican-Americans. For example, one such classification provides a two-fold typology. The first type, the "majority," includes those who are cold, unkind, mercenary, and exploitative. The second type, the "minority," consists of those who are friendly, warm, just, and unprejudiced. For the most part, Mexican images of Anglo-Americans reflect the latter's patterns of exclusion and assumptions of superiority, as experienced by Mexican-Americans. Thus Anglo-Americans are pictured as stolid, phlegmatic, cold-hearted, and distant. They are also said to be braggarts, conceited, inconstant, and insincere.

Intergroup Relations, Mutual Expectations, and Cultural Differences

A number of students of intergroup relations assert that research in this area has yet to demonstrate any relation between stereotypical beliefs and intergroup behavior; indeed, some insist that under certain conditions ethnic attitudes and discrimination can vary independently.[9] Arnold M. Rose, for example, concludes that "from a heuristic standpoint it may be desirable to assume that patterns of intergroup relations, on the one hand, and attitudes of prejudice and stereotyping, on the other hand, are fairly unrelated phenomena although they have reciprocal influences on each other. . . ." [10] In the present study, no systematic attempt was made to investigate the relation between the stereotypical beliefs of particular individuals and their actual intergroup behavior; but the study did yield much evidence that both images which justify group separatism and separateness itself are characteristic aspects of intergroup relations in Border City. One of the principal findings is that in those situations in which contact between Anglo-Americans and Mexicans is voluntary (such as residence, education, recreation, religious worship, and social intercourse) the characteristic pattern is separateness rather than common participation. Whenever intergroup contact is necessary, as in occupational activities and the performance of commercial and professional services, it is held to the minimum sufficient to accomplish the purpose of the contact.[11] The extent of this separateness is not constant for all members of the two groups, since it tends to be less severe between Anglo-Americans and those Mexicans they define as of a "high type." Nevertheless, the evidence reveals a high degree of compatibility between beliefs and practices in Border City's intergroup relations, although the data have nothing to offer for the identification of direct relationships.

In any case, the separateness that characterizes intergroup relations cannot be attributed solely to the exclusion practices of the Anglo-American group. Mexicans have tended to remain separate by choice as well as by necessity. Like many other ethnic groups, they have often found this the easier course, since they need not strain to learn another language or to change their ways and manners. The isolation practices of the Mexican group are as relevant to an understanding of intergroup relations as are the exclusion practices of the Anglo-Americans.

This should not, however, obscure the fact that to a wide extent the majority of Mexican-Americans share the patterns of living of Anglo-American society; many of their ways are already identical. Regardless of the degree of their insulation from the larger society, the demands of life in the United States have required basic modifications of the Mexicans' cultural tradition. In material culture, Mexicans are hardly to be distinguished from Anglo-Americans, and there have been basic changes in medical beliefs and practices and in the customs regarding godparenthood. Mexicans have acquired English in varying degrees, and their Spanish has become noticeably Anglicized. Although the original organization of the family has persisted, major changes have occurred in patterns of traditional authority, as well as in child training and courtship practices. Still, it is the exceedingly rare Mexican-American, no matter how acculturated he may be to the dominant society, who does not in some degree retain the more subtle characteristics of his Mexican heritage, particularly in his conception of time and in other fundamental value orientations, as well as in his modes of participation in interpersonal relations.[12] Many of the most acculturated Mexican-Americans have attempted to exemplify what they regard as "the best of both ways." They have become largely Anglo-American in their way of living, but they still retain fluent Spanish and a knowledge of their traditional culture, and they maintain an identification with their own heritage while participating in Anglo-American culture. Nevertheless, this sort of achievement still seems a long way off for many Mexican-Americans who regard it as desirable.

A predominant Anglo-American expectation is that the Mexicans will be eventually assimilated into the larger society; but this is contingent upon Mexicans becoming just like Anglo-Americans. The Mexican counterpart to this expectation is only partially complementary. Mexicans want to be full members of the larger society, but they do not want to give up their cultural heritage. There is even less complementarity of expectation with regard to the present conduct of intergroup relations. Anglo-Americans believe they are justified in withholding equal access to the rewards of full acceptance as long as Mexicans remain "different," particularly since they interpret the differences (both those which have some basis in reality and those which have none) as evidence of inferiority. Mexicans, on the other hand, while not always certain that they are not inferior, clearly want equal opportunity and full acceptance now, not in some dim future, and they do not believe that their differences (either presumed or real) from Anglo-Americans offer any justification for the denial of opportunity and acceptance. Moreover, they do not find that acculturation is rewarded in any clear and regular way by progressive acceptance.

It is probable that both Anglo-Americans and Mexicans will have to modify their beliefs and practices if they are to realize more nearly their expectations of each other. Mutual stereotyping, as well as the exclusion practices of Anglo-Americans and the isolation practices of Mexicans, maintains the separateness of the two groups, and separateness is a massive barrier to the realization of their expectations. The process of acculturation is presently going on among Mexican-Americans and will continue, regardless of whether changes in Anglo-Mexican relations occur. Unless Mexican-Americans can validate their increasing command of Anglo-American ways by a free participation in the larger society, however, such acculturation is not likely to accelerate its present leisurely pace, nor will it lead to eventual assimilation. The *colonia* is a relatively safe place in which new cultural acquisitions may be tried out, and thus it has its positive functions; but by the same token it is only in intergroup contacts with Anglo-Americans that acculturation is validated, that the Mexican's level of acculturation is tested, and that the distance he must yet travel to assimilation is measured.[13]

Conclusions

There are major inconsistencies in the assumptions that Anglo-Americans and Mexican-Americans hold about one another. Anglo-Americans assume that Mexican-Americans are their potential, if not actual, peers, but at the same time assume they are their inferiors. The beliefs that presumably demonstrate the Mexican-Americans' inferiority tend to place them outside the accepted moral order and framework of Anglo-American society by attributing to them undesirable characteristics that make it "reasonable" to treat them differently from their fellow Anglo-Americans. Thus the negative images provide not only a rationalized definition of the intergroup relation that makes it palatable for Anglo-Americans, but also a substantial support for maintaining the relation as it is. The assumptions of Mexican-Americans about Anglo-Americans are similarly inconsistent, and their images of Anglo-Americans are predominantly negative, although these are primarily defensive rather than justificatory. The mutual expectations of the two groups contrast sharply with the ideal of a complementarity of expectations, in that Anglo-Americans expect Mexicans to become just like themselves, if they are to be accorded equal status in the larger society, whereas Mexican-Americans want full acceptance, regardless of the extent to which they give up their own ways and acquire those of the dominant group.

Anglo-Americans and Mexicans may decide to stay apart because they are different, but cultural differences provide no moral justification for one group to deny to the other equal opportunity and the rewards of the larger society. If the full acceptance of Mexicans by Anglo-Americans is contingent upon the disappearance of cultural differences, it will not be accorded in the foreseeable future. In our American society, we have often seriously underestimated the strength and tenacity of early cultural conditioning. We have expected newcomers to change their customs and values to conform to American ways as quickly as possible, without an adequate appreciation of the strains imposed by this process. An understanding of the nature of culture and of its interrelations with personality can make us more realistic about the rate at which cultural change can proceed and about the gains and costs for the individual who is subject to the experiences of acculturation. In viewing cultural differences primarily as disabilities, we neglect their positive aspects. Mexican-American culture represents the most constructive and effective means Mexican-Americans have yet been able to develop for coping with their changed natural and social environment. They will further exchange old ways for new only if these appear to be more meaningful and rewarding than the old, and then only if they are given full opportunity to acquire the new ways and to use them.

Notes ►

1. See John Harding, Bernard Kutner, Harold Proshansky, and Isidor Chein, "Prejudice and Ethnic Relations," in Gardner Lindzey (ed.), *Handbook of Social Psychology*, Cambridge, Addison-Wesley Publishing Company, 1954, vol. 2, pp. 1021–1061; and Otto Klineberg, *Tensions Affecting International Understanding*, New York, Social Science Research Council, 1950, Bulletin 62.

2. The term "Anglo-American," as is common in the Southwest, refers to all residents of Border City who do not identify themselves as Spanish-speaking and of Mexican descent. The Anglo-Americans of Border City have emigrated there from all parts of the United States and represent a wide variety of regional and ethnic backgrounds. The terms "Mexican-American" and "Mexican," as used here, refer to all residents of Border City who are Spanish-speaking and of Mexican descent. The term "Spanish-speaking" is perhaps less objectionable to many people, but for present purposes is even less specific than Mexican or Mexican-American, since it also refers to ethnic groups that would have no sense of identification with the group under consideration here.

3. For the historical background of the Valley, see Frank C. Pierce, *A Brief History of the Lower Rio Grande Valley*, Menasha, George Banta Publishing Company, 1917; Paul S. Taylor, *An American-Mexican Frontier*, Chapel Hill, University of North Carolina Press, 1934; and Florence J. Scott, *Historical Heritage of the Lower Rio Grande*, San Antonio, The Naylor Company, 1937.

4. Ruth D. Tuck, *Not with the Fist*, New York, Harcourt Brace and Company, 1946.

5. Robert S. Lynd, *Knowledge for What?* Princeton, Princeton University Press, 1948.

6. Gordon W. Allport, *The Nature of Prejudice*, Cambridge, Addison-Wesley Publishing Company, 1954.

7. For an analysis of Mexican-American value orientations and behavior in the occupational and political spheres, see Ozzie G. Simmons, Anglo-Americans and Mexican-Americans in South Texas: A Study in Dominant-Subordinate Group Relations (unpublished doctoral dissertation, Harvard University, 1952).

8. See *ibid.*, for a discussion of the Anglo-American and Mexican class structures.

9. Robert K. Merton, "Discrimination and the American Creed," in R. M. MacIver (ed.), *Discrimination and National Welfare*, New York, Harper and Brothers, 1949, pp. 99–128; John Harding, Bernard Kutner, Harold Proshansky, and Isidor Chein, *op. cit.*; Arnold M. Rose, "Intergroup Relations vs. Prejudice: Pertinent Theory for the Study of Social Change," *Social Problems*, 1956, 4: 173–176; Robin M. Williams, Jr., "Racial and Cultural Relations," in Joseph B. Gittler (ed.), *Review of Sociology: Analysis of a Decade*, New York, John Wiley and Sons, 1957, pp. 423–464.

10. Rose, *op. cit.*

11. Simmons, *op. cit.*

12. For cultural differences and similarities between Anglo-Ameri-

cans and Mexicans, see Simmons, *op. cit.*; Tuck, *op. cit.*; Lyle Saunders, *Cultural Difference and Medical Care*, New York, Russell Sage Foundation, 1954; Munro S. Edmonson, *Los Manitos: A Study of Institutional Values*, New Orleans, Middle American Research Institute, Tulane University, 1957, Publication 25, pp. 1–72; and Margaret Clark, *Health in the Mexican-American Culture*, Berkeley, University of California Press, 1959.

13. See Leonard Broom and John I. Kitsuse, "The Validation of Acculturation: A Condition to Ethnic Assimilation," *American Anthropologist*, 1955, 57: 44–48.

21 ► THE AMERICAN CATHOLIC IS CHANGING

JOHN LEO

Of all dominant and minority group relations in American society today, probably the most dynamic and improving is that between Roman Catholics and non-Catholics. Antipathy grounded in nativism flourished when the Irish Catholics arrived in large numbers in the nineteenth century. New immigration after 1890 brought millions of Roman Catholics and intensified the already hostile attitude of native-born Protestant Americans. In the 1940's and 1950's, church competition and the clash of religious and other cultural values replaced nativism as the chief basis of conflict. A series of charges by Paul Blanshard and others—that the growing power of the Roman Catholic Church threatened American freedom—rallied anti-Catholics all over the country.

But offsetting this were the inevitable Americanization of Roman Catholics—culminating in a Roman Catholic President of the United States—and Pope John and Pope Paul's encouragement of "updating" many of the procedures and policies of the Roman Catholic Church. The ecumenical movement has been almost revolutionary in bringing Catholics and non-Catholics together. The range of recent changes among American Catholics, as reviewed by Mr. John Leo, associate editor of a leading Catholic periodical, has implications for intergroup relations that would have been incredulous to Catholics and non-Catholics alike only a short time ago.

From *The New York Times Magazine*, November 14, 1965. © 1965 by The New York Times Company. Reprinted by permission of the author and publisher.

▶ Who is the American Catholic? One speaker used to begin his lectures this way: "The American Catholic is Bing Crosby, Bob Considine, George Meany, William Buckley, Clare Boothe Luce and Senator Joseph McCarthy. He is also Sargent Shriver, Dorothy Day, Dr. John Rock, Justice Brennan, Tom Dooley and Senator Eugene McCarthy. . . ."

All right. Catholics can be given credit for diversity—along with most other religious groups. But how different is the American Catholic from his neighbor?

The question gains immediacy both from the reverberations of Pope John's call for an *aggiornamento,* and from the rise of American influence within Catholicism. "America," says one European bishop, "is living in the 21st century, and the experience of Catholics there will have a lot to do with how the church adapts."

Well, then, how different *is* the American Catholic from his neighbor? The sociology is a bit thin, but the answer would have to be: not much. The social, cultural and economic state he finds himself in is a better index to his thinking and behavior than his religion. This is a fairly recent development, and visiting European Catholics usually miss no opportunity to remark (often with dismay) that the U.S. Catholic cannot be distinguished from any other American.

Nevertheless, there are differences. In general, the American Catholic is less likely than his non-Catholic neighbor to become a social activist, more likely to vote Democratic (until he moves to suburbia), less likely to excel in the academic world (particularly the sciences), more likely to have a large family, less likely to make "Who's Who."

If he reaches the top in American society, he is more likely to have made it through politics, the professions or show business. He is likely to stress order more than freedom, and more likely to favor strict laws enforcing sexual mores—though the pattern here seems to be breaking down.

Sociologists and historians think that the immigrant experience, not religious belief, is the key to these differences. In general, Catholics were latecomers to America, arriving in massive waves of migration between 1840 and 1920, mostly from Ireland, Central Europe and Italy.

According to the "immigrant theory," the course of American Catholicism has been determined by the cultural base of the immigrants, who were largely impoverished peasants and villagers, cut off from the intellectual traditions of their religion and their native lands. The ordinary prejudice against newcomers was heightened by the native American anti-Catholicism which Arthur Schlesinger Sr. called "the oldest and most ingrained of American prejudices." The result was that immigrant Catholicism turned in on itself, developing deep defensive traits, and devoting its energies to parochial affairs.

On its own terms, the young church was a sound success. Of all major branches of Catholicism, it became the only one to hold onto the working class and to avoid anti-clericalism. Its vitality—though directed inward—was high. Out of working-class salaries it built an enormous system of schools, hospitals and religious organizations. It also kept the loyalty of younger generations in an age when Catholicism could be a costly social handicap.

But for all that it paid a price. The cost of building the schools delayed the arrival of Catholics into the great American middle class—only with the prosperity following World War II did Catholics arrive in any numbers. Separate Catholic institutions, particularly the schools, enforced Catholic isolation. The values of intellect and imagination were hardly stressed and the church lost creative people of the first rank—Fitzgerald, O'Hara, Farrell and Eugene O'Neill. What intellectualism there was, was devoted to ingenious defenses of Catholic teaching. Disinterested scholarship was rare, and generally suspect.

Part of the legacy today is that American Catholics are dramatically underrepresented on the intellectual front. There are no great American Catholic scientists (though this seems to be true of Catholics everywhere). Neither are there Catholic philosophers, poets, theologians and writers in any proportion to the Catholic population.

A decade ago, Msgr. John Tracy Ellis, the historian, sent tremors through the American Catholic Church with an essay documenting the lack of Catholic intellectual activity, and implying that Catholics tended to rely rather complacently on the "immigrant theory" to explain it away. Since then, Catholics have conducted a profound—and often loud—investigation of the subject in an attempt to upgrade intellectual values. The job is far from done, although a recent study by Chicago sociologist Andrew Greeley shows that now, for the first time, Catholics are in graduate schools in proportion to their numbers.

The Ellis essay ended an era of puffy self-satisfaction, when

Catholics basked in the illusory glow of the so-called "religious revival" and counted success in terms of rising statistics on schools, communicants and converts. Monsignor Ellis touched off a decade of sweeping self-analysis (known in less sympathetic quarters as "the orgy of criticism"). Combined with the reforms of the Second Vatican Council, it has brought to the fore a generation of younger Catholics—vaguely referred to as "the new breed"—who are committed to secular values as well as the Catholic faith. Among other things, they have taken control of the major Catholic publishing outlets, thus assuring that rigorous self-criticism will continue. During 1965 alone, there have been no fewer than 12 bristling attacks on the Catholic press by individual bishops who consider it dangerously overcritical.

Education is one of the prime concerns. The Catholic Church in America has been committed to the ideal of "every Catholic child in a Catholic school." In the 19th century, the decision was received by the laity with some reluctance and grumbling, but in the 20th century, the pressure for more and more Catholic schools has come from laymen.

Today slightly more than half of the 11 million school-age Catholics are in Catholic elementary and secondary schools. But the proportion will not rise. In the past decade, Catholics have managed to add 1,550 schools to their system; in the same period, more than 14 million babies have been born to Catholic couples. The statistics suggest that perhaps only a third of the next generation of Catholics will attend Catholic schools.

Much of the push for Federal aid to parochial schools grows from the fear that a rush of government spending on public schools will price the Catholic schools out of the market and doom them to perpetual inferiority. As it is, the Catholic schools are economically viable today only because 100,000 nuns are willing to teach for token wages, sometimes as low as $20 a month.

Under these conditions, the Catholic schools have become the center of hot debate among Catholics. There are those who favor an all-out drive for Federal aid. Others think the church should resign itself to a nonexpanding school system, cut back on construction, and throw its weight behind the public schools. This is already the policy in the St. Louis Archdiocese—which, in 1962, placed a ban on school construction and expansion, and urged parents to vote for any bond issues necessary for the expansion of the public school system.

A small minority thinks the church should get out of the school business altogether and find less expensive but more dynamic ways of instructing its children. This strain of thought surfaced last year with publication of Mary Perkins Ryan's influential book "Are Parochial Schools the Answer?" It expressed the feeling that parochial schools drain away so much money and energy needed on other fronts that they have become white elephants. Meaningful parish activities often given way to naked fund-raising affairs designed merely to keep the schools afloat.

A popular belief, among many Catholics as well as non-Catholics, is that the parochial schools are inferior, but the evidence is not at all conclusive. Whether they are or not, many Catholic intellectuals argue that the differences in outlook between the Catholic who goes to public school and the Catholic educated at great sacrifice in a parochial school are too small to justify the expense of a separate school system. Others argue that the parochial schools are divisive, although a recent study at the University of Chicago does not bear this out.

Politically, the American Catholic has tended to be conservative, suspicious of central government. "Liberal" has been a dirty word, associated theologically with misguided attempts to make Catholicism palatable to non-Catholics by dropping a few essentials, and associated politically with free-wheeling relativism and secularism. As late as 1958, a popular Catholic magazine could run an anxious article on the vexing question: "Can a Catholic be a liberal?"

In part, the suspicion of liberalism goes back to the 19th century, when the European liberal movement was firmly anti-Catholic. When many of the immigrants came over, the liberal movement was involved in a direct physical attack on the papacy. Then, too, the Irish, who were to dominate American Catholicism, came from a static, conservative society, and one with a settled tradition of regarding the central government of the British as illegitimate. Parallel attitudes toward government existed among other immigrant groups. Most of the Italian immigrants, for example, came from the south, where government officials were unhelpful at best, and usually corrupt.

That Catholics came to be regular Democratic voters was not a choice for liberalism, but more or less a historical accident. It seemed that all their enemies were Republicans, and there was nowhere else to go. While the Jews, for instance, tended to see the

Democratic party as an instrument for social progress, no such vision descended upon the Irish. For them it was simply an instrument of self-interest and the leading channel of upward mobility.

In America, the inability to see government as a force for social progress is usually attributed to "rugged individualism." For American Catholics, it went hand in hand with spiritual individualism: the emphasis was on personal morality, personal devotion, personal salvation. In practice, American Catholicism did not seem to be a charter for communal concern, but a set of rules for a one-man obstacle race from earth to heaven. Episcopal thunderbolts tended to be hurled far more often at threats to personal morality, such as dirty movies, than at infractions of social morality, such as race prejudice or economic exploitation.

The tradition of individualism and social conservatism has put a strain on the traditional loyalty to the Democratic party. When Democratic Catholics from the city move to the suburbs, Republican values often seem suddenly much more congenial.

The emergence of the Communist issue hastened the process, presenting American Catholics with peculiar temptations toward superpatriotism. First of all, the Catholic Church identified the danger of Communism early. The sight of Franklin D. Roosevelt courting Stalin as late as 1945 sent resentments soaring; they were to boil over in the later investigations of "dupes" and "collaborators" who had been unsure about Communism while the church was so certain.

This spirit operated at full throttle during the McCarthy period. Precisely because they could not be found in the upper reaches of government, and had not taken part in the social causes of the thirties and forties, Catholics could note with some satisfaction that the Communist investigations would cast no reflections on *their* loyalty. In fact, the investigations were widely taken as long-awaited proof of Catholic reliability. As Daniel Patrick Moynihan wrote: "Harvard men were to be checked; Fordham men would do the checking."

It was no accident that McCarthy reserved special gusto for his attacks on the intellectuals of Harvard and "the striped-pants set" of the State Department, which many Catholics took as symbols of their cultural oppressors in America. In a way, many Catholics, particularly the Irish, were taking the occasion to settle some old scores.

But there are signs that the reflex action of anti-Communist proconservative bias is on the wane. In 1964, for example, 70 per cent of Catholics voted for Johnson rather than Goldwater. The Catholic vote, in fact, is losing its normal distinctiveness. Catholics voted more heavily for Johnson than for Kennedy. Eisenhower's vast strength among Catholics both in 1952 and 1956 shows how feeble the once-compelling ties to the Democratic party now are. (So do the indications that both Lindsay and Buckley did extremely well among Catholic voters in the recent New York mayoral election.) Since 1960, no clear pattern has developed in Catholic voting, and aside from faith-related issues such as a birth-control referendum, none is likely to reappear.

There is evidence, too, that Catholic "crusades" in the public order are on the wane. Nothing resembling Cardinal Spellman's all-out attack on "Baby Doll" has occurred in the sixties, though movies have become far more explicit on sexual matters. Censorship groups are now out on the fringe of Catholic life, and, significantly, they are now more likely to be interfaith efforts than purely Catholic forays.

The Supreme Court decision on school prayer drew loud complaints from many Catholics, but no crusade. By and large, Catholics seem to have opposed the Becker amendment to reinstall school prayer. "The Deputy," Rolf Hochhuth's play attacking Pope Pius XII, brought mob scenes and violence in much of Europe, but passed without incident in America. A good part of the Catholic press agreed with Hochhuth's thesis.

On birth control, which is still a potentially divisive problem in the public order, the attitudes of Catholics are in flux. The allocation of anti-poverty funds for birth control, and the further-reaching proposals now before Senator Gruening's committee, have produced isolated protests, some of them strong, but nothing like the furor touched off in 1959 over a single veiled suggestion, in a report to President Eisenhower, that foreign-aid funds might go to birth-control programs.

Catholics themselves are divided on the morality of birth control, as an average week's reading of the better Catholic journals will show. Immense pressure has been raised for a re-examination of the church's stand, and many pastors have reported birth control as the major reason for married couples' remaining away from the sacraments. What studies there are indicate that perhaps three out of 10 married Catholics practice birth control. One study in

North Carolina indicated that half of the Catholics there used contraceptives.

One recent poll shows that 61 per cent of American Catholics expect their church to modify its stand on the question. A 1964 survey indicated that just 49 per cent of Catholics considered contraception immoral, and just 23 per cent thought that the practice of birth control would prevent salvation.

Many Catholics, of course, still feel strongly about birth-control laws, but the sentiment is on the wane. The debate on contraception within Catholicism has taken much of the heart out of the fight. More important, the present generation of Catholics is much more conscious of the rights of others than the last.

Kenneth Underwood's book "Protestant and Catholic," which studied Catholic-Protestant relations in Holyoke, Mass., in the years 1947-48, indicated that Catholics, given the slightest opportunity, would not hesitate to ride roughshod over non-Catholics. Yet he noted the beginning of a pattern that has since emerged: Better-educated and higher-income Catholics tended to stand apart from pressure tactics and unenlightened clerical advice. They were loyal to the church, but not to religious efforts which seemed to restrict the rights of their neighbors.

Catholic-Protestant tensions have lessened dramatically in the last five years. The leading Catholic newspapers and magazines have Protestant columnists and regular contributors—sympathetic, but critical when necessary. Catholics are now inclined to think that Paul Blanshard, the author of "American Freedom and Catholic Power," whose attacks sent them into a defensive frenzy in the fifties, had some real points, though failing to understand the complexity of Catholicism and the self-corrective forces within it. Blanshard, for his part, is still critical, but hardly shrill; he has been seen dining with bishops in Rome.

The polls reflect the change. A 1964 study in the U.S. asked the question: "Do you agree that both Luther and the Catholic Church were both partly right and partly wrong in the dispute that led to their split?" Forty per cent of the Catholics who answered said yes, compared with 36 per cent of the Protestants. In the last two years, Catholic scholarship has produced a number of Reformation studies sympathetic to Luther.

According to one Catholic story, the bishops at the Vatican Council were all handed cards bearing a portrait of Luther; on the other side, the card read: "In your heart you know he's right."

Catholic lecturers, speaking to packed houses at $250 a throw, now open their talks with jokes that once were termed "anti-Catholic" and now are cheerfully received as "ecumenical."

The efforts of Popes John and Paul have helped spread this spirit, but it is likely that ecumenicism would have caught on in America even without them. Catholic-Protestant hostility is simply dated; on the Catholic side, the hostility and fear that go back to the immigrant period had to be brought in line with the normal pattern of amiable business and social relationships with Protestants. The immigrant emotions could not have held on much longer.

There is no doubt that the social and cultural freedom of American life is having a profound effect on the emerging generation of Catholics. So are the reforms set in motion by Pope John and the Second Vatican Council.

Over the last few years, the biggest question among American Catholics has been the role of the layman, both in and out of the church. Donald Thorman's "The Emerging Layman" and Daniel Callahan's "The Mind of the Catholic Layman" have been bestsellers among Catholics. The layman is clearly restless with his traditionally minor role in his church, and theological, liturgical and political developments have given him considerable leverage.

The "new-breed" American Catholic resists any idea that he is an agent of the church operating in society; he tends to be indifferent to institutional claims. Often he will bypass even the most progressive Catholic organizations in favor of work for secular service groups. The network of Catholic interracial councils, for instance, seems to hold less appeal for him than the established nonreligious civil-rights organizations. In short, he is anxious to enter the mainstream of American life, to end Catholic separatism and to identify Catholic efforts with the disenfranchised instead of the status quo.

No one knows how strong this movement is. Critics claim it represents only 1 per cent or 2 per cent of the Catholic population. But defenders maintain that evidence shows the new attitudes going deep into the population at large, not just the intellectual class.

At any rate, the American layman is more relaxed about his religion, particularly since Pope John and John F. Kennedy. He now thinks his Americanism is taken for granted, and his defensiveness is fading. As Catholics move in large numbers into the middle class, the temptation will be less toward putting religious strains on the public order than it will be to settle down complacently with a set of newly acquired bourgeois values. The reflex conservatism he felt, even as an outsider, might still make him an inordinately comfortable insider.

Internally, American Catholics have achieved vitality—without much expression of it in terms of social concern—and a high level of religious practice—without a very wide grasp of the implications of their faith. The Vatican Council has brought the best parts of their tradition to the fore; the American emphasis on freedom has girded them against the kind of authoritarianism that is continually a danger in a well-structured church. Their attitudes and values are very much in flux. Only time will tell which ones will prevail.

V THE AMERICAN NEGRO

AMERICAN NEGROES — comprising approximately one-tenth of the American population—surpass all other American minorities in strategic importance. The anomaly of their lower-caste status in a society that professes democracy has been central to their transformation into the most publicized ethnic group anywhere in the world. In their bitter struggle for equality, particularly their efforts to achieve desegregation since the Supreme Court Decision of 1954, American Negroes have offered the classical sociological illustration of the die-hard resistance of all caste-differentiated systems. But castes function most effectively in static, rural and agricultural settings; they become obsolete in dynamic, urban and industrial societies. The trend of social change would appear to favor the upgrading of American Negroes in the long run.

American Negroes defy a clear-cut racial definition in the physical anthropological sense, for they are enormously varied among themselves in appearance and genetic background. In fact, many are indistinguishable from so-called whites. Although they have indicated a preference for Protestantism, some are members of other major religious denominations and even many of the minor sects. Like American Indians, no label of nationality other than American accurately describes them. We might be justified in saying that Negroes are people who, because of the combination of such factors as appearance, descent and association think of themselves as Negroes and are so thought of by others.

The first Negro slaves were brought to this country in 1619 when a Dutch ship from Guiana reached Jamestown, Virginia, and sold twenty slaves to the plantations. By 1750 slavery was recognized by law in every American colony, but it became profitable only in the South. Negroes soon became so numerous in the South that in some areas they outnumbered the dominant whites. By the time of the first United States Census in 1790, there were almost one million Negro slaves in the United States, and nine-tenths of them were in the South.

In the opening piece of this section, Professor Harold Pfautz attempts to show that now, for the first time in our history, the Negro is free of the dominant white's definition of the intergroup situation.

22► THE NEW "NEW NEGRO": EMERGING AMERICAN

HAROLD W. PFAUTZ

► RECENT HISTORICAL research has demonstrated how, in the past, the place of Negroes in America has been largely determined and defined by the dominant whites.[1] During the course of the seventeenth and early eighteenth centuries, the indentured servant was relegated slowly but surely to the status of a slave. In the nineteenth century, the Abolitionist vision of Negroes as "free" was effectively doomed by the Compromise of 1877, a succession of conservative Supreme Court decisions, and the appearance of the Black Codes: American Negroes became "Jim Crow." Throughout the struggle for civil rights and equal opportunity which began to take form in the first quarter of the twentieth century as a reaction to the emasculation of Emancipation, however, there pulsed a fresh theme: the concept of the "New Negro." American Negroes began to carve out their own self-image.

Numerous versions were projected: Booker T. Washington's "industrious artisan," W. E. B. DuBois' "talented tenth" of the Negro "renaissance," and Marcus Garvey's back-to-Africa "Black Nationalist." Unfortunately, all were, precisely, projections; none provided effective and realistic rallying points for the total Negro community, and all were permeated essentially by the spirit of reform rather than revolution. Washington's concept was self-consciously accommodative; DuBois' message was oriented primarily to the Negro intelligentsia, and Garvey was heard only by the masses.

From *Phylon* (Winter, 1963), 360–68. Reprinted by permission of the author and publisher.

Throughout the 'twenties and 'thirties, where Negroes were not objects of a self-conscious paternalistic sympathy (as in the South), they were objects of formal political and economic charity (as in the North). Tolerance was the best of all possible worlds; things could improve; they could get better, but the basic formula of American Negro-white relations—"white over black"—could not be changed.

Indeed, as late as the 1940's, the essential mechanism governing the place of Negroes and their relationship to whites remained inviolate. The ubiquitous theme of Myrdal's classic analysis of the situation of American Negroes in 1944 was that white men act and Negroes react: "The Negro's entire life, and, consequently, also his opinions on the Negro problem, are, in the main, to be considered as secondary reactions to more primary pressures from the side of the dominant white majority." [2]

Today, however, white Americans find themselves facing a new "New Negro," incomprehensible to most of them and, therefore, frightening. In many ways the new "New Negro" is the first to bear legitimately the accolade, for in his essential character and conduct he is the first to belie genuinely the basic traditions of American race relations. Unlike his precursors he is, at long last and simply, an emerging American.

The new "New Negro" was born in the midst of World War II, was raised in its aftermath, and is coming to maturity in this, the second half of the twentieth century. In some respects the war served to accentuate primarily social forces and trends affecting the situation of Negroes which had been at work for some time; in other respects, it set into operation new forces. And the post-war years have witnessed not only the continuation of many of these trends, but their essential fruition.

In the first place, relative to the demands of military production, the war both speeded up and gave new direction to the emigration of Negroes from the South, a process which had been going on for almost half a century. More than a million Negroes left Southern states for Western as well as Northern states during the decade 1940–1950; and this trend has continued with approximately the same number emigrating during the period 1950–1960. As a result, while in 1940 more than three-fourths of all Negroes resided in Southern states, by 1960 this proportion stood at less than three-fifths and was still declining.[3]

As in the past, the destinations of most of the migrants were the big cities, New York, Chicago, Detroit, Los Angeles, and San Francisco. The geographic redistribution was, therefore, accompanied by an equally dramatic shift in residential status: in 1940, more than one-half of all Negroes lived in rural areas; by 1960, almost three-fourths were urban residents.[4]

Inextricably bound up with these geographical and residential changes was a fundamental shift in occupational status: in 1940, more than two-fifths of all employed Negro males were engaged in agricultural pursuits, which figure had been reduced to 15 percent by 1960.[5]

In other words, in less than a generation the American Negro population had been transformed from regional, rural, and agricultural to essentially national, urban, and industrial. Geographically, residentially, and occupationally, Negroes are rapidly becoming "American," for these are the demographic modes of the dominant white majority.

Not unrelated to these revolutionary changes has been a less pervasive but equally salient socio-economic transformation, carrying with it an even greater potential for the validation of the self-concept of the new "New Negro" as "American"—the appearance in significant numbers of a middle class in terms of education and income. To be sure, large over-all income and educational differences between Negroes and whites still exist and will continue to exist for some time to come. The absolute numbers, however, clearly attest to the existence of a Negro middle class, another American mode. By 1960, more than 200,000 non-white youths were enrolled in colleges and professional schools, and more than 400,000 non-white families had annual incomes of $8,000 or more.[6]

Two other wartime occurrences which set the stage for even more dramatic post-war changes were the military service of large numbers of Negroes and formal anti-discriminatory and desegregation policies and practices initiated by the federal government and by military authorities. More than a million Negroes were inducted into the various branches of the armed forces between 1940 and 1946, over one-half of whom saw service overseas.[7] The experience, whether domestic or foreign, provided the core of a social generation of American Negroes with a new perspective on the provincial nature of their segregated world at home as well as an enlarged vision of what might be possible in the future. Significantly, a study of post-war migration plans of soldiers indicated that whereas 82 percent of the white soldiers expressed an intention to return to their former homes, this was true of only 66 percent of the Negroes.[8]

In the second place, while ideological elements in World War II might have been irrelevant for motivation for combat, they did function to dramatize publicly as never before the "American Dilemma," and to raise in pointed fashion the question of the meaning of democracy for race relations. To this new perspective of Negro soldiers was added the concept of the "double-V"—victory for democracy at home as well as overseas—for Negroes who did not see military service.

In the face of the political threat of A. Philip Randolph's "March on Washington" movement, the federal government, through President Roosevelt's Executive Order 8802, gave an official accolade to, and established a mechanism for, promoting non-discrimination in defense industries and government employment by creating the Commission on Fair Employment Practices. In addition, for reasons of strictly military efficiency and expediency, the army introduced a limited integration process among combat units serving in the European theatre of operations during the final phase of the battle for Germany.

Each of these wartime experiments in the use of governmental authority to lessen discrimination led to more intensive and extensive efforts in the post-war period. The Korean conflict proved an even greater stimulus to the enlightened race policies of the military, so much so that by 1953, *Time* magazine could describe the armed forces as having struck "the biggest single blow against segregation in the U.S." In 1945, Governor Dewey affixed his signature to the Ives-Quinn bill, making New York the first state to adopt a peacetime fair employment practices act. Moreover, although federal F.E.P.C. legislation has yet to be achieved, by 1962 more than half the states had enacted statutes prohibiting discrimination in many different areas: employment, housing, education, recreation, as well as various places of public accommodation. In addition, numerous municipalities passed anti-discrimination ordinances and created "race relations" or "human relations" commissions of various types. More recently, the Civil Rights Acts of 1957 and 1960, numerous court decisions on all judicial levels, and President Kennedy's housing order have given further official support to the aspirations of American Negroes as well as provided broader avenues for their entrance into traditionally closed and typically prestigeful white-collar and professional occupations and the American way of life in general.

Needless to say, the final and most significant fruition of all these trends and events was the Supreme Court decision of 1954, outlawing segregation in the public schools. Regardless of the extent to which its immediate impact may have been emasculated by the 1955 decision to rely on local authorities to comply "with all deliberate speed" and by the resistance offered by Southern state legislatures and citizens' pro-segregation movements, the 1954 decision armed Negroes with a manifesto for revolution. In effect, it introduced a new mirror for self-conception and provided a mechanism for collective action. The argument over the "sociological" versus the "legal" basis of the decision may have academic interest for lawyers as well as propaganda value for Citizens' Councils, but the edict has been clearly sociological in its impact. It redefined publicly the basic postulate of American race relations —separate, henceforth, was to be inherently unequal! The majesty and power of the federal courts have literally sparked a revolt that has grown to explosive proportions in a context of resonant social changes and cultural drifts.

To all of this must be added certain other post-war developments which have functioned further to shake up the Negro community, to exacerbate the fault in the social relationship between Negro and white, and to provide further support for the projection of a new self-concept as a basis for independent individual and collective action on the part of Negroes throughout the country. Among these have been what Otis and Beverly Duncan have referred to as the "piling up" of Negroes in the big cities (together with a correlative flight of middle-class whites to the suburbs),[9] a high level of urban renewal activity which has resulted in massive and obvious disproportionate dislocations of urban Negroes (together with the vertical extension of the Black Belt in the drift of Negroes into public housing projects),[10] and, finally, the emergence of the independent African nations.

The "piling up" of urban Negroes and the suburban flight of middle-class whites have brought into focus the North's race problem, making more patent and problematic *de facto* school segregation, as well as increasing the political potential of urban Negroes on all levels of government—federal, state, and city. The difficulties of relocating Negroes displaced by urban renewal projects in increasingly obvious discriminatory and prejudicial community climates of opinion have not only reached the point of threatening the entire renewal program of the dominant whites but also have provided a rallying point for all classes in the Negro community. And although probably less salient to many individual Negroes than the above developments, the rise of the new African nations surely functions to underwrite the ego strength of the new "New Negro." Here, at least, the analogy between the experiences of foreign-born whites and Negroes in America might have some validity: Marcus Hansen's principle of the third generation interest ("what the son wishes to forget, the grandson wishes to remember") has the potential for operating with a vengeance in the case of the Negro "eighth generation"! [11]

Parenthetically, another significant development in regard to race relations in world perspective is the fact that the theoretical cat is finally out of the bag: just as the theological rationale for racial discrimination fell before the onslaught of the crude Darwinistic biology, the naïve physical anthropology, and the ethnocentric psychology of the nineteenth century, so these pseudo-scientific rationalizations have fallen victim to the more objective and relativistic behavioral sciences and the more sophisticated genetics of the twentieth century. To all concerned, and especially to non-whites, the ultimate basis of racial minority status has been revealed to lie primarily and simply in the fact of unequal power. As an American, therefore, the new "New Negro" increasingly turns his attention to the ballot as his Maxim gun.

Finally, if the World War II generation of American Negroes was shaken out of its traditional lethargy and provincial blindness by its wartime experiences, the post-war generation of Negro youth has been educated in a manner and in numbers which represent a motivation and capacity for bringing about fundamental changes in the pattern of American race relations as has never before existed. Not only the skills but the values and goals which are necessary for full participation in the American way of life—liberal and professional education, white-collar occupations, and, above all, "respectability"—have been assimilated by a large cadre of Negro adolescents and young adults. Having been assimilated and given the factors and forces operating in the contemporary situation, these abilities and values will emerge. Negro youth is the bellwether and epitome of the new "New York"; it has played (and will continue to play) a prominent role in the growing ability of the Negro community, nationally and locally, to initiate independent action and successfully to make collective demands on the dominant whites for equal treatment and opportunity.

The social psychological consequences of the more or less silently working demographic forces and economic processes as well as of the historical run of events during the war and post-war decades are, precisely, the development of a new concept of self on the part of American Negroes. And new self-concepts have always been the first basis and final result of social revolutions.

The signs are everywhere, and the contrast with the past is dramatically instructive. Even the terms currently used to discuss the situation of Negroes in the United States—"revolution," "revolt," "rebellion"—attest to the emergence of the new "New Negro" as an American.[12] It is not just a half-century but a sociological light year from the leaderless and completely passive Negro community at the mercy of riotous white violence in Atlanta in 1906 to the sophisticated leadership of Martin Luther King and the collective solidarity behind the Montgomery bus boycott in 1956.

"Sit-ins," "wade-ins," "kneel-ins," picket lines, economic boycotts, selective buying campaigns, civic associations, and legal suits make clear the increasing ability of the Negro community to mobilize itself for independent collective action. A new leadership has appeared which is no longer accommodating and beholden for its status to the dominant white majority and no longer ill-trained and confined to a traditional "protest within the status quo." [13] Willing and able to go beyond the established legal and conventional community norms and institutional channels to achieve immediate ends which often have legal as well as moral sanction, its ultimate goal is nothing less than full and equal status and opportunity as Americans.

Parenthetically, the past experiences of the dominant white leadership with both the Urban League and the National Association for the Advancement of Colored People constitute questionable bases for predicting the acts of or imputing motives to this new "New Negro." The social work background of the Urban League together with its assimilation into the community organization complex in local communities have made its accommodative success as dangerous and debilitating as that of a religious sect whose success in "the world" is the key to its fundamental failure. On the other hand, the commitment of the N.A.A.C.P. to the legal form of the struggle between the races necessarily involves a time-scale which, given the pace of change in contemporary race relations, brings about increasing dissatisfaction and defection on the part of many of its constituents, Negroes as well as whites.

In 1946, Branch Rickey felt compelled to advise Jackie Robinson that if he wished to break the color barrier in organized baseball, he would have to learn "to take it without dishing it out." [14] But ten years later, when Robinson left the Big Leagues, he was "dishing it out." This, in microcosm, encapsulates what is "new" in the new "New Negro." Reduced to individual terms, this essentially is what being an American means: the assumption of self-worth and personal autonomy as a starting point. In collective terms, to paraphrase a recent remark by Robert B. Johnson, Negroes are "men in motion," a minority on the move.[15] This, too, has ever been a cardinal element in the social character of the American.

All significant social changes basically involve changes in the minds and often in the hearts of men. Paradoxically, while getting men to change their minds about that which they hold most dear is usually the most difficult thing to accomplish, it is also the most inevitable. Ortega reminds us, however, "Man does not have a nature, he has a history." Race relations are fundamentally a matter of history, and history is inherently change. When a Dick Gregory can make a public joke out of tribal etiquette and an Ossie Davis can make a farce out of the myth of the Old South, race relations mores are surely in the way of being reduced to the status of quaint folkways.

If, in the past, the informing tradition of American Negro-white relations has been that white men act and Negroes react, the present attests to the essential reversal of this formula. The increasing autonomy of Negroes in thought and action provides a growing empirical basis for the maturation of the new "New Negro's" self-concept as an American. For this is not only what the new "New Negro" wants to be; in the final analysis, it is the only thing he can be.

If, in the past, there has been a guilty dissociation between democratic theory and democratic practice, does the future promise a convergence?

To be sure, there are resistances to this wave of the future in American race relations both within and without the Negro community. Within, there are the ubiquitous and seldom discussed vested interest in segregation and the often wasteful competition among Negro leaders and groups for power and status, aggravated by the social and psychological distance between the "black bourgeoisie" and the Negro lower class. There is also the inevitable burden of the past that necessarily slows the pace of present and future movement.

In regard to the first, it is obvious that many segments of the old Negro middle class have much to lose by desegregation. The ghetto has always been a small world; businessman or professional, the captive market necessarily provides a sheltered arena for competition, and the struggle for success necessarily takes on a note of unreality. Moreover, the ghetto is also an incomplete world, often failing to provide the full range of perspectives that must be brought to bear on decisions concerning strategy and tactics for success in the battle for full equality and opportunity.

In regard to the second, in the internecine struggle among the leaders and between the classes, "the race" provides a final leaven if a working consensus cannot be achieved on more rational grounds. Even the grass roots is on the move, however much respectable Negro elements may decry the verbal and ceremonial extremism of the Black Muslims.

As for the burden of the past—the fact, for example, that "the disparity between white and non-white levels of educational attainment in the general adult population can hardly disappear in less than three quarters of a century" [16]—this can, in the final analysis, only slow, not stop, the inevitable emergence of the new "New Negro."

Outside the Negro community there is, ubiquitously, "the man," bewildered by the pace of social change, filled with status anxiety, and inheritor of the traditions of racial prejudice and discrimination that have permeated American society from its very beginnings. But no significant social change has ever taken place without opposition and, often, without violence. And, unfortunately, there is no reason to believe that the revolution in American race relations will not continue to involve opposition as well as incidents of violence. On the other hand, in the face of the social trends and cultural drifts as well as the historical events that have spawned and succored the new "New Negro," "tokenism," "massive resistance," White Citizens' Councils, political gerrymandering, and even the lurking threat of physical violence become more patently quixotic and anachronistic, more surely dangerous, and more certainly ineffective. For the self-concept of the new "New Negro" is not (as in the past) the function of either the myths or the anxieties of the dominant whites. Its viability as well as its content have been carved out of and are anchored in empirical processes and unalterable events.

In the final analysis, conflict opens the way to assimilation: the new "New Negro" was not only born in conflict, but he will continue to mature only in the crucible of conflict. Sociologically speaking (as Simmel pointed out long ago), conflict is inherently a socializing process.[17] It is segregation and such forms of accommodation as the traditional caste-like structuring of race relations that have minimized the possibilities of communication and consensus and contributed to the invisibility of Negroes both as individuals and as a problem in America.

Notes ▶

1. Cf., *e.g.*, C. Vann Woodward, *The Strange Career of Jim Crow* (New York, 1957), Oscar Handlin, *Race and Nationality in American Life* (New York, 1957), and Stanley Elkins, *Slavery* (Chicago, 1959).

2. Gunnar Myrdal *et al.*, *An American Dilemma* (New York, 1944), p. li.

3. United States Bureau of the Census, *1940 Census of Population, Vol. II, Characteristics of the Population, United States Summary* (Washington, D.C., 1943), Table 23, p. 53, and United States Bureau of the Census, *1960 Census of Population, United States Summary, General Population Characteristics* (Washington, D.C., 1961), Table 55, p. 163.

4. *Ibid.*, *1940 Census of Population, op. cit.*, Table 21, p. 51 and *1960 Census of Population, op. cit.*, Table 44, p. 145.

5. United States Department of Labor, "The Economic Situation of Negroes in the United States," Bulletin S-3 (Washington, D.C., October, 1960), Table 12, p. 13.

6. *Ibid.*, Table 23, p. 41.

7. Selective Service Systems, *Special Groups, Special Monograph No. 10* (Washington, D.C., 1953), Table 53, p. 111.

8. *Ibid.*, I, p. 170.

9. Otis Dudley Duncan and Beverly Duncan, *The Negro Population of Chicago* (Chicago, 1957), p. 143, *passim*.

10. Cf., Harold Kaplan, "Urban Renewal in Newark, N.J., The Power Structure of a 'Successful Program' " (Mimeographed; no date).

11. Marcus L. Hansen, *The Problem of the Third Generation Immigrant* (Rock Island, Illinois, 1938), pp. 9–10.

12. Cf., *e.g.*, Dan Wakefield, *Revolt in the South* (New York, 1960) and Louis E. Lomax, *The Negro Revolt* (New York, 1962).

13. Cf., *e.g.*, Harold W. Pfautz, "The Power Structure of the Negro Sub-Community: A Case Study and a Comparative View," *Phylon*, XXIII (Second Quarter, 1962), 156–66; Lewis M. Killian and Charles U. Smith, "Negro Protest Leaders in a Southern Community," *Social Forces*, XXXVIII (March, 1960), 253–57; in James B. McKee, "Community Power and Strategies in Race Relations: Some Critical Observations," *Social Problems*, VI (Winter, 1958–59), 195–203.

14. John Roosevelt Robinson, *Jackie Robinson, My Own Story*, as told to Wendell Smith (New York, 1948).

15. Cf. Robert B. Johnson, "Changing Status of the Negro in American Life," *Journal of Intergroup Relations*, I (Spring, 1960), 56–71.

16. Otis Dudley Duncan, "Population Trends, Mobility and Social Change" (Mimeographed. Prepared for the American Association of Colleges for Teacher Education, Committee on Studies, Seminar on Dimensions of American Society, October 4–18, 1961), p. 53.

17. Georg Simmel, *Conflict and the Web of Group Affiliations*, trans. Kurt H. Wolff and Reinhard Bendix (Glencoe, Illinois, 1955), p. 14.

23 ► SINCE THE SUPREME COURT SPOKE

ANTHONY LEWIS

The ten years that followed the landmark Supreme Court decision of 1954 calling for the racial desegregation of the public schools may in the long run become the most important decade in all three and a half centuries of American race relations. According to Mr. Anthony Lewis—a distinguished journalist who has kept close watch on the "racial decade"—we now have an irreversible revolution in the patterning of Negro-white relations.

► SHORTLY AFTER noon on May 17, 1954, reporters waiting in the Supreme Court press room for what they thought would be routine opinions were suddenly told to go to the courtroom. There Chief Justice Earl Warren was reading his opinion for the Court in Case No. 1 on the docket that term, *Brown et al. v. Board of Education of Topeka et al.* For minutes the audience listened without a sure clue to the outcome. Then the Chief Justice read:

"We come then to the question presented. Does segregation of children in public schools solely on the basis of race, even though the physical facilities and other 'tangible' factors may be equal, deprive the children of the minority group of equal educational opportunities? We believe that it does."

Ten years after that moment in history we can see it as the spark of a revolution in American attitudes toward the race problem. During the turbulent decade the stereotype of the apathetic, satisfied Negro has forever been destroyed; the Federal Government has abandoned a hands-off attitude of 80 years' standing and come to the point of total commitment against racial segregation; the hypocrisy of the South and the complacency of the North have been undermined by the new Negro militancy. Perhaps most important, the indifference of white America toward the race problem has been shattered; everyone knows that it is the great domestic issue facing this country and will be in the years ahead.

Now we stand at a new turning point, the start of an even more intense and dangerous phase in the racial struggle. In the great cities of the North new civil rights groups are using more aggressive tactics and demanding special steps to undo the wrongs of the past—tactics and demands that are producing a backlash of white antagonism. In the South the last rural strongholds of total resistance to change are being challenged. In Washington, Congress is at the point of making its first broad commitment to the task of reform begun 10 years ago by the Supreme Court.

Change of the dimensions experienced in the racial field over the last decade does not just begin at a point in time; it builds on history. There were pressures working for change in American race relations before 1954: the industrialization and urbanization of the South, bringing with them social anonymity; the weakening of regional differences in this country by the impact of mass communications; universal training in armed forces that were being desegregated; a slow growth in the Negro's legal and political power.

But revolutions require a spark. For the revolution in this country's racial situation, it was surely the school decision.

Men live by symbols, and school segregation was a special symbol to the white Southerner. Nor was it illogical that racial separation should carry more emotional weight in schools than elsewhere. Attendance in schools was compulsory and there children of an impressionable age were exposed to a culture. Intermingling of the races could not help but affect their outlook. Any breakdown in school segregation necessarily endangered perpetuation of the Southern myth that all Negroes are by nature distinct and inferior.

For the Negro, too, the all-white school was a symbolic citadel. The pitifully unequal, not to mention separate, education afforded most Negroes in the South was clearly—so overwhelmingly clearly—an obstacle to Negro progress.

What, then, have been the results and the lessons of that Supreme Court decision of 10 years ago?

It may, more than anything else, have given the Negro hope. The Supreme Court of the United States, pinnacle of the white Establishment, had understood at last that segregated institutions were not and could not be equal. The law was on the Negro's side now—often a faraway law, it is true, offering little immediate protection against the local pressures of white supremacy, but still giving hope of ultimate justice.

It gave the Negro a courage and a will that few, or even he himself, had known he had. Who will forget the picture of a few little colored children walking into a school past jeering, hating white faces? After that, the children had to endure in many cases a life without friends in school, often a life of secret abuse and terror. Their parents faced economic reprisal as well as fear for the children. And still they persisted.

The struggle to carry out the school decision encouraged Negroes to speak out for other rights. It surely helped to inspire such events of this remarkable decade as the Montgomery bus boycott, the Freedom Rides, the sit-ins. Even in the voting field, the school struggle was relevant. Many outsiders believed it would be more logical for Negroes in the South to concentrate first on obtaining the right to vote. But that right, basic as it was, may have been too impersonal to arouse the Southern Negro from apathy and fear. It took the drama of school desegregation and then of the protest movements to bring the possibility of freedom alive; then the Negroes began standing in those long, patient lines outside registrars' offices.

Violent Southern resistance to the school decision awakened Northern white opinion to the meaning of racism. Most Northerners had gone through life without thinking about how it would feel to have a black skin. Then came those scenes outside the schools in Little Rock and New Orleans—the women screaming "Nigger," the mob clawing at a Catholic priest. Those in the North who saw those events on television, or read about them, were not likely to miss the unreasoning hatred and inhumanity. The North is not pure of heart, but its official institutions work to eradicate inequality, not to maintain it.

The Federal Government was at last moved to action in race matters. President Eisenhower, who had done nothing to encourage acceptance of the Supreme Court decision, and was planning to do nothing, intervened when Gov. Orval Faubus and his mob at Little Rock forced the Federal hand.

Southern excesses in other areas similarly aroused Northern opinion and the Federal Government. Brutal assaults on the Freedom Riders in Alabama in 1961 led Attorney General Robert F. Kennedy to dispatch a force of marshals and then to ask the Interstate Commerce Commission for an order that has virtually wiped out segregation in bus and rail terminals. The pictures of dogs assaulting Negro demonstrators in Birmingham in 1963 were instrumental in President Kennedy's decision to propose the broadest civil rights legislation ever seriously urged on Congress.

These years have demonstrated the extraordinary role of law as a shaper of opinion in this country. Events proved the foolishness of President Eisenhower's view that the law could not affect racial prejudice. "I don't believe you can change the hearts of men with laws or decisions" was what he often said.

That was just what the Supreme Court had written in 1896, in the decision upholding the constitutionality of separate facilities for Negroes. "Legislation is powerless," the opinion said, "to eradicate racial instincts or to abolish distinctions based upon physical differences."

The point is not that laws and decisions can end all racial feelings; of course not. But they can either encourage or inhibit prejudice. As a wiser Supreme Court said in 1950, when it held that a Negro university student could not be made to sit at a segregated desk:

"The removal of the state restrictions will not necessarily abate the individual and group predilections, prejudices and choices. But at the very least the state will not be depriving appellant of the opportunity to secure acceptance by his fellow students on his own merits."

Moreover, law does affect patterns of external conduct, slowly forcing people to conform at least superficially to new standards. Over time, habits may affect feelings. One of the most touching little episodes of the racial struggle in the last 10 years was the statement of two segregationist white girls in Central High School, Little Rock, that after meeting Negro children their ideas had changed: "My parents and a lot of the other students and their parents think that the Negroes aren't equal to us. But—I don't know. It seems like they are, to me."

One of the terrible tragedies was the solemn advice of Southern leaders, perhaps most significantly Senator Harry F. Byrd of Virginia, that the law could be resisted with impunity. It has taken much time and even the spilling of blood to demonstrate the difference between criticizing a court decision and organizing physical resistance to it. The cost has been the degrading of the entire political process in one section of the country.

Now, at last this country's deep underlying reverence for law seems to be prevailing in most of the South. The South has begun to learn that the Supreme Court's interpretation of the Constitution, when it has the support of the rest of the country, cannot be resisted indefinitely. It has begun to learn that change is inevitable in race relations, that the movement for equal rights has powerful momentum behind it. It has begun to learn that the South cannot stand alone, that it is part of a larger country and that the United States is part of a world in which men with white skins are outnumbered by the black and brown and yellow.

But a companion lesson is that law is not enough. This is a moralistic as well as a legalistic country, and the pace of change in race relations was as revolutionary as it was because the American conscience was touched.

Dr. Martin Luther King Jr. and his doctrine of nonviolent resistance, one of the remarkable developments of the period, combined the American religious tradition with the spirit of Gandhian protest. The young followers of Dr. King, sitting quietly at lunch counters as they were verbally and physically abused, brought a needed spiritual content to the movement for racial justice.

Those brave students ended, moreover, the possibility of anyone taking seriously the South's traditional claim that *its* Negroes were contented—outside agitators were causing all the trouble. The peaceful protesters caught the imagination and sympathy of the North.

Now, as we stand at the start of a new phase in race relations, the Negro sees much that is undone. He knows that he is twice as likely to be unemployed as a white man, that his median family income is only half the white family's. In the rural counties of the South recognition of Negro rights is still miniscule, and there is intransigence in Southern cities from Birmingham to Jackson. United States Senators still stand up and admit men are kept from voting because of their color. In Mississippi it is still worth a Negro's job—and perhaps his life—to try to vote.

In practical terms not much of a dent has been made on school segregation; throughout the South only 1 per cent of Negro children are actually in classes with whites. In the great cities—North and South—it is Negroes who more and more fill up the slums and attend the worst schools. In innumerable ways a colored skin remains an enormous handicap in the United States.

The white man sees the problem from the opposite end of the telescope. He sees what has happened in 10 years and thinks it is astonishingly much. Segregation has ended at hundreds of lunch counters and hotels and theaters in the South and has all but disappeared in transportation. Every Southern state but Mississippi has made at least a token start on school desegregation. Negro political power has risen, South and North. The Supreme Court has removed the legal basis for virtually every official discrimination on account of race.

For the first time a President—Kennedy, then Johnson—has condemned segregation as morally unjust. Congress, after 80 years of silence, has passed two civil-rights acts and is considering a third that would bring Federal power to bear in many new ways.

As we look ahead, it is possible to foresee a gradual end to the remaining official discrimination in the South. The force of the effort to open the polling places and the schools and the parks will mount. One can even hope, within the next 10 years, to see some Senators from the Deep South liberated from the awful weight of racist politics.

Not that the South can be forgotten now. It will take the most grueling effort by the Justice Department—and perhaps more legislation—to end the blatant discrimination that remains there.

But it is as a national problem that race relations will primarily be seen in the next decade. The challenge is to overcome the legacy of inequality everywhere—to open unions and companies to Negro workers, to provide education and training that Negroes have not had, to let Negroes escape from the slums, to break the cycle of poverty and ignorance. After the cruel refusal of white plumbers to work by the side of a few Negroes and Puerto Ricans in New York City we know that not only the South has a race problem.

For the immediate future, the most obvious danger is that increasing Negro militancy will lose white support. We know that extremist tactics may be used by Negroes in the North as well as whites in the South.

It is ironic that Negro advances have helped to pave the way for the present turmoil. The cowed Negro of a generation ago, deprived of even the most basic rights of citizenship, would not have had the courage—or the folly—to attempt to disrupt a President's speech at a World's Fair. The gains made so far have enabled the Negro to see his inequality more clearly and have given him the means to demand faster progress. But it must be so. Change in so deep-rooted a social problem as racial discrimination can hardly take place without turmoil.

Stall-ins, dumping of garbage on the Triborough Bridge, school boycotts—tactics such as these have alienated the most sympathetic whites. It is impossible to explain away the primary votes for Gov. George Wallace of Alabama, a wild man embarrassing even to most Southern politicians. The racial issue has begun to frighten the Northern white.

The great question for the next decade, therefore, is whether the revolution in race relations can be contained within the framework acceptable to enlightened white opinion.

The Negro faces a choice as the new period opens. He can go on following the course that has brought him so far in what seems to others so short a time—the course of reason and restraint. Or he can give way to frustration at what seems to him centipedal progress and listen to the counsels of disorder, of anarchy. For those who now threaten to take over the Negro movement from the responsible leaders are essentially anarchists; they have given up on our system and would as soon destroy it.

For the white majority there is a choice, too. It can react to increasingly militant Negro tactics with hatred and fear. Or it can react, in President Johnson's phrase, with compassion. It can meet the legitimate grievances.

Hardly any revolution in history, however noble its origins, has occurred without a spilling-over of hatred and irrationality. The race relations revolution so far has been a unique effort to join a society rather than to overthrow it. What we are about to find out is whether Americans, white and Negro, will permit the revolution to continue on that course.

In a sense it should not be disturbing that all the country is now engaged in the race problem. The pretense that the problem existed only in the South was just that, a pretense, and it is better to have the truth out, however painful it is.

Indeed, one of the greatest changes in the last 10 years has been simply an awareness of the racial issue. It is hard to recall the pervasive indifference to racial discrimination in this country 10 years ago, or even more recently. We have come a long way when thousands of Northern college students sign on to spend their summers helping Negroes to register in the South or to get a better education in the North.

In his "An American Dilemma," published in 1944, Gunnar Myrdal wrote:

"The Negro problem is not only America's greatest failure but also America's great opportunity for the future. If America should follow its own deepest convictions, its well-being at home would be increased directly. At the same time America's prestige and power abroad would rise. . . . America can demonstrate that justice, equality and cooperation are possible between white and colored people. . . . *America is free to choose whether the Negro shall remain her liability or become her opportunity.*"

The choice is even more urgently before us now.

24 ► THE NEGRO'S MIDDLE-CLASS DREAM

C. ERIC LINCOLN

What is the clearest aspiration of American Negroes aside from equality or first-class citizenship? Some argue that the evidence favors the goal of middle-class status. In the article that follows, Professor Lincoln traces the historical beginning of middle-class life for American Negroes all the way back to slave days, and shows the evolution of a Negro bourgeoisie as the inevitable consequence of the Negro's sharing in the dominant values of the white man's social-class structure.

► A FAMOUS PROFESSOR at a large university used to begin one of his lectures in social psychology with a description of the characteristics of a typical American family. After he had described the family's income, address, religion, the kind of car they drove, organizations to which they belonged and the occupation of the father, he would then demand to know what social class the family belonged to. But before the students could answer, the professor would add as an apparent afterthought: "Oh, yes, I forgot to mention that this is a *Negro* family!" Inevitably, the students were stymied. What had begun as a simple problem became insolubly complex by the addition of the word "Negro."

Where do Negroes fit into the prevailing American class structure? Most sociologists say they don't. Negroes have a *parallel* social structure, somewhat—but not entirely—analogous to that of whites. This social parallelism, or two-caste society, is created by

From *The New York Times Magazine*, October 25, 1964. © 1964 by The New York Times Company. Reprinted by permission of the author and publisher.

the color barrier which, with the rarest exceptions, prevents lateral movement from class to class between Negroes and whites. As a prominent Negro matron said in Detroit, "We Negroes and whites visit each other at times, and frequently we belong to the same civic organizations and attend the same functions, but the lines are there, and no one has to say where they are."

The Negro class structure had its roots in the institution of American slavery, which, in ignoring the African's cultural presumptions, leveled all classes, and force-fused highly disparate individuals and groups into one conglomerate mass—"the Negro slave," or simply, "the Negro," a word which, in America, became synonymous with "slave" or the "descendant of slaves." Prince and servant, Eboe and Mandingo, Moslem and spirit-worshipper were all the same to the slave master, who saw them only as commodities to be bought and sold, or as a labor supply for his vast plantations.

Whatever the basis of past distinctions, the Negro social structure in America had to evolve out of conditions connected with plantation life, and within a context which recognized the absolute superiority of the white slave owner (although not necessarily that of the small, nonslave-holding white farmers, who supplied the "overseer" class, and who were looked upon by house servants and slave owners alike as "poor white trash").

The Negro's "society," then, had four more or less distinct social classes. In ascending order, they were: (1) field hands (who had least contact with the socializing influences of the white environment); (2) mechanics and artisans (bricklayers, carpenters, iron workers, bakers, etc., who were frequently hired by the month or the year to merchants or builders in the cities); (3) valets, butlers, maids, cooks and other household servants (whose frequent personal contact with whites made them the most "acculturated" class); and (4) free Negroes (who had bought their freedom or had become free by manumission—often because of faithfulness or some heroic exploit).

As slaves, the house-servant class had by far the highest proportion of mulattoes. While this did not by any means exempt them from the normal rigors incident to being slaves, including sale, the light-skinned mistresses of the slave masters were often granted petty privileges and their children were more frequently given their freedom than those of any other class.

At the end of the slave period, the mulattoes sought to establish themselves as a distinct occupational and social class within the Negro subculture. For the most part, they continued as servants and retainers to their erstwhile masters—as dressmakers, barbers, coachmen and the like. For more than a generation they clung tenuously to a certain degree of status derived from catering exclusively to the "quality" folk (as they had done in slavery) under the then current slogan of (serving) "mighty few white folks and no niggers a'tall!"

By the turn of the century, however, as the economy of the South began to revive, the mulatto "retainers" were progressively displaced by European immigrants and poor whites who were suddenly willing to do "Negro work." From that date neither occupation nor color has been a reliable index of social standing among Negroes.

Today, a light skin is not an automatic key to social status. In this day of the Negro's increasing race pride and his subtle impulse to nationalism, a light skin *can* be a handicap, especially if it is associated with "recent" miscegenation. Mass education and the indiscriminate rise to power and money of significant numbers of Negroes irrespective of their grandparents' station in the slave society have all but destroyed the effectiveness of the Negro's private color bar. Leadership in civil rights as well as in the professions has long since passed from the mulatto class. As a matter of fact, the number of mulattoes in the general Negro population seems to be declining steadily, and there is no evidence that legal integration will soon replace clandestine miscegenation in restoring the ratio of light color.

There is no unanimity of opinion as to what proportion of today's Negroes fall into the traditional "lower," "middle" and "upper" classes of the Negro social structure. Prof. Tillman Cothran, head of the graduate department of sociology at Atlanta University, estimates that "not more than 25 per cent of the Negro population can be called middle class by any reasonable standards. And not more than 5 per cent can be called upper class."

Other sociologists have argued that if one applies the full spectrum of criteria by which the white social structure is measured—ranging from income to education, affiliation, residence, etc.—the Negro middle class is reduced to 4 per cent or 5 per cent of the Negro population, and the Negro upper class vanishes altogether.

Such an estimate is, I think, too drastic. If the theory of parallel social structure is valid (and there seems to be no other way to measure "class" in an essentially segregated society), certainly it can be shown that Negroes and whites of similar education and income exhibit many of the same desires, restraints, conformities and general patterns of behavior.

America's self-image is that of an essentially equalitarian society best represented by the middle class. Most Americans concede that there are a few snobs and millionaires at the top, and a few poor people in Appalachia, or somewhere, at the bottom, but America is middle class, and most Americans identify themselves as belonging to the middle class.

Implicit in this identification is a belief in "democracy" and "fair play," and also the expectation of "the good life"—a home, a car, a regular vacation, an education for the children, regular promotions, and maybe even extras like a boat or a summer place. Despite the pessimism of the sociologists, more and more Negroes share this dream, and to an increasing degree they are making it come true for themselves and their children.

The Negro middle class is made up primarily of Negro professionals, with school teachers probably constituting the largest single bloc. Teachers, along with doctors, lawyers, college professors, small businessmen, ministers, and postal workers have traditionally made up the bulk of the Negro middle class.

However, the recent availability of new kinds of jobs not previously held by Negroes has begun to modify the character of this group. Technicians, politicians, clerical and sales personnel, social workers, labor-union officials, minor government bureaucrats, and an increasing managerial class in such agencies as Federal housing and local units of national corporations have helped broaden the occupational range of the Negro middle class.

Under the Kennedy-Johnson Administration a few Negroes have been appointed to the upper echelons of Government officialdom, and within the past two or three years a few Negroes have reached executive status in white corporations. A recent dinner in New York honored seven Negroes who were vice presidents or held managerial positions in major firms. In Washington, Dr. James Nabrit, president of Howard University, and Dr. Frank Jones have been elected to the board of directors of a major bank. And in that city, several Negroes have been elected to the Board of Trade.

It is difficult to set a salary range for a given social class because social status does not depend upon money alone. Some upper-class whites are impoverished, but their families have once held fortunes and they have traditions of culture and attainment. Since the American Negro's family traditions seldom antedate the Civil War, Negro society puts an undue emphasis on money and material acquisitions. It is often said by Negro critics themselves that "anybody with a dollar, no matter where he stole it, can belong to Negro society."

Most Negroes, like most other Americans, earn their living legitimately, of course, but because of job discrimination and lack of skills, the total income of the typical middle-class Negro family will be substantially lower than that of a typical white family of the middle class. An arbitrary figure of $7,500 a year as the average income of a middle-class family would severely limit the number of Negroes who could be called middle-class.

Some Negro families do exceed a $7,500 income, but the vast majority of those who do are families in which both husband and wife work full time. Very frequently among home-buying Negroes, the head of the family works at two jobs, and occasionally at three. Such supplementary work or "moonlighting"—often driving a taxi, waiting on tables, tending bar or bellhopping—is known as "a hustle," a term quite familiar to the Negro middle class.

In many of the large cities of the North such as New York or Boston where undeveloped land is nonexistent, the middle-class Negro, who has the means and the desire to live elsewhere, is locked in the black ghetto. Only with difficulty can he find a house or apartment outside the ghetto in a white community. As a consequence, many Negroes despair of ever leaving the slums, no matter what their education or income.

Money that would normally go for a new house is spent in the hopeless task of refurbishing antiquated apartments, or in conspicuous consumption which somehow helps them to forget the horror of living in the nation's Harlems. (In the South, the housing problem is not nearly so acute. Space for building can be had in most Southern cities, although it is likely to be in a segregated community.)

The style of living of the Negro middle class does not differ radically from that of its white counterpart. Bridge is a favorite pastime among both men and women. Those who have the leisure belong to innumerable social clubs. An increasing number of Negro men play golf and participate in water sports where facilities are available. In the South, fishing and hunting are favorite pastimes, but only if one has the full regalia of dress, and all the latest equipment shown in the sports magazines.

To a far greater degree than whites, Negroes maintain affiliation in the graduate chapters of their college fraternities and sororities, and these organizations are important indexes of social stratification. Women of a given sorority tend to marry men of its fraternal opposite number. Together, the eight major Negro sororities and fraternities constitute the nucleus of any imaginary "blue book" of Negro society.

The children of the Negro middle class are taught to aspire to middle-class standards. They take lessons in piano and creative dancing on Saturday mornings and attend carefully planned parties on Saturday night. A few are sent East to private schools.

Sometimes the interpretation of middle-class values takes an unusual twist. A Negro matron in a Memphis department store, for example, refused to corral her two children who were busily chasing through the store and littering the aisles with merchandise. She explained: "The white kids do it and the salesclerks think it's cute. I don't want my children inhibited by feeling that they can't do anything any other kids can do."

In Washington, among those aspiring to the middle class, or those who are recently "in," status is measured by the quantity and the cost of whisky served one's guests. The most conspicuous feature in such a home will be the bar appointments, and it is considered equally insulting for a guest to refuse a drink as it is for the host to offer his guests "cheap whisky." One Washingtonian gained prominence in his set by consistently being first to serve rare and expensive imports before they were well known in the Negro community. He learned what was "in" by frequenting an exclusive liquor store patronized by high Government officials.

It used to be said that the difference between a Negro making $50 a week and driving a Cadillac and a white man making $100 a week and driving a Chevrolet was that the Negro, having nowhere to live, needed the bigger car to sleep in! On Atlanta's West Side, where the Cadillac (or Lincoln) frequently comes with a split-level ranch house, it is popular to have the main (or "status") car match the house in color and appointments.

A second car for the Negro professional family is not unusual. Unlike most white middle-class families having two cars, the Negro's second car is likely to be as big and expensive as his first. An expensive automobile to drive to work is often as much a matter of personal prestige for the working Negro woman as for her husband. Hence, it is common to see large numbers of Pontiacs, Oldsmobiles and Mercurys parked near the schools where Negro women are employed as teachers.

A cottage at Oak Bluffs, on Martha's Vineyard, or in Maine or Upper Michigan can be claimed by a few. A very small number of Negroes go to Europe and to the Caribbean or Mexico on vacation. A sort of pilgrimage to Africa has high status value for those seeking to "understand their pre-Western heritage."

Some Negroes are in the middle class because there is nowhere else for them to go. These few might be considered "upper class" but there is a certain incongruity in talking about a Negro "upper class" so long as the color barrier operates to bar Negroes who are otherwise qualified from full participation in American social life. "There may not be an upper class," says Clarence Coleman, southeastern director of the National Urban League, "but there is a 'power élite' which abstracts itself from the rank and file of the middle class and participates to an important extent in the decision-making of the white power structure where Negroes are concerned."

Certainly this power élite does exist. But where it was not created by the white establishment, its power derives from white recognition and respect. Militant civil-rights leaders have discovered this again and again when the white establishment has refused to negotiate with the Negro community except through "recognized channels."

The Negro middle class, like any middle class, is preoccupied with making secure its hard-won social position. This is a characteristic of middle-class aspirations.

Because of this preoccupation the Negro middle class has been criticized frequently for not being more deeply and realistically involved in the struggle for civil rights. The criticism is well placed, for given more manpower, more money and more dedication, it is obvious that more walls could be breached. But this is not the whole story, and the lack of total involvement may not be an accurate index of middle-class feelings and intentions.

Much of the criticism has come from within the ranks of the middle class itself. The Urban League's Clarence Coleman sees the middle class as the buffer between the militants, whose aspirations are frequently unrealistic in terms of present possibilities, and the power élite which seems concerned to protect itself and its privileged positions from too rapid social change.

James A. Tillman Jr., executive director of the Greater Minneapolis Fair Housing Program and a frequent writer on problems of social change, describes the Negro middle class as "that class of Negroes who have bought the inane, invalid and self-defeating notion that the black man can be integrated into a hostile white society without conflict."

Tillman denounces the power élite as "the fixers and go-betweens who cover up rather than expose the violent nature of racism. They are," he declares, "the most dangerous clique in America."

Tillman's sentiments are echoed by Cecil Moore, militant civil-rights attorney and head of the Philadelphia N.A.A.C.P. Moore, who himself came from an accomplished West Virginia family, insists that "the Negro middle class, and all those who consider themselves above the middle class, 'subsist on the blood of the brother down under,' the brother they are supposed to be leading. Who do these Negroes think they're kidding?" he asks, and then answers his own question. "They're kidding nobody but the white folks who are willing to pay 'philanthropy' to keep from having to come to grips with the central problem, which is 'full and complete citizenship for all Americans, *right now!*'"

Despite all such criticism, however, the Negro middle class has borne the brunt of the civil-rights protest. Critics of the so-called "Black Bourgeoisie" have not always given them credit for the maturity and social responsibility upon which the Negro's fight for first-class citizenship has finally depended. The civil-rights fight, at least insofar as it visualizes an integrated society, is a middle-class fight. The N.A.A.C.P., CORE, the Urban League and the followers of Dr. Martin Luther King are all middle-class. (Indeed, the lower-class Negro has yet to be stirred by the promise of integration. He is more concerned with such immediate needs as jobs and housing than with abstract values like integration. He looks neither to Martin Luther King nor to Roy Wilkins; in fact, the leader of the black masses has yet to appear.)

In Atlanta and other Southern cities during the massive sit-ins of 1962–63, housewives baked pies, made sandwiches and provided transportation for the students. Negro businessmen donated food, gasoline and other supplies. Then doctors, nurses, professors and businessmen walked the picket lines. Similar middle-class support has assisted the activities of CORE in New York, Cleveland and other cities in the North. Voter registration is essentially a middle-class project.

Middle-class leadership and support of the civil-rights movement has not been without ambivalence. Desegregated schools frequently mean that Negro teachers will lose their jobs. Negro businessmen often lose their most competent clerical help to recently desegregated industries. Negro restaurants, drug stores, real-estate firms and the like may be adversely affected by desegregation. Some Negro churches have lost members to white churches. In a fully integrated society, the Negro middle class would lose its identity. Indeed, it would cease to exist.

Some Negroes recognize all this, of course, and fight against it. Nor can it be said that the majority of the middle class is active in the rights struggle. What can be said is that the struggle is for the most part led, financed and supported by the Negro middle class and, of course, its white allies.

Certainly, Negro leadership has become a "profession," and in some cases a lucrative one. Yet most Negroes trying to help improve things are in search of neither fame nor fortune and may be themselves disadvantaged by the race issue. A. Maceo Walker and Jesse Turner of Memphis, for example, both executive officers of a sensitive banking business that has important white as well as Negro depositors, come to mind. These men and others like them have little to gain for themselves personally, yet they have given leadership to the civil-rights movement in their city for years. Other cases could be cited across the country.

In Washington, I talked with the distinguished Negro attorney, Belford Lawson, and his wife, Marjorie McKenzie, who, as associate judge of the Juvenile Court there, is no less distinguished. The Lawsons were undisturbed about the "black backlash" against the Negro middle class, although they felt that the middle class was just beginning to realize its responsibilities to the Negro masses. Nor did they recognize a middle-class backlash against the lower class (which has been roundly criticized by some Negroes for rioting in the streets and undoing the patient and painful accomplishments of middle-class leaders).

"We must press on to the next phase," Lawson said. "And it would be foolish to wait until all of us have reached the place a few of us have reached today. Negroes, like other people, move at different rates of speed. Our circumstances vary. Now we have a handful of civil rights and no money. Our next front is economic. We want to buy stocks in banks and corporations and sit on their boards. Every time a Negro reaches an executive position in a major corporation, he is in a better position to help that Negro in the streets without a job."

Mr. Lawson believes that it is time to stop complaining and to move on into the American mainstream. "Breaking into the white man's economy" he believes to be essential to any further progress on the part of Negroes. "In Washington," he says, "where many social and cultural affairs are integrated, many doors would open if the Negro would only push on them."

Negroes are pushing—for status and respectability and economic security. They are less concerned with integration for integration's sake than they are with being comfortable—middle-class —and unhindered in enjoying all that America has to offer. The riots in the city streets are not the work of sinister Communist agents, except where such agents move in to exploit an already festering social situation. Nor are they the work of hopheads and hoodlums bent on the destruction of the fruits of years of patient interracial effort.

They are the social expressions of pent-up anxiety and frustration which derive from the hopelessness of the conditions under which those people live. *They* cannot hope for "the good life." *They* cannot appropriate the "middle-class image," the American norm for democratic living.

I sat recently in a comfortable middle-class home in northwest Washington talking with Jerry Coward and his wife, both school teachers in the District of Columbia school system. "You know, when we moved into this neighborhood five years ago," Jerry said, "the whites all threatened to move out. A few stayed. And since that time, two brand-new white families have moved in, right down the block. Professional people, too. When white people start moving into, instead of away from, a Negro neighborhood, I guess we've got it made."

I guess they have.

25 ► THE NEGRO'S PROBLEM IS THE WHITE'S

ELI GINZBERG

The thesis that the American Negro's problem is also the white's problem was formulated most explicitly and systematically in Gunnar Myrdal's An American Dilemma, *published in 1944. It means not only that the white power structure traditionally defined the pattern of American race relations, but also that the Negro's efforts to improve his social, economic and political statuses have serious consequences for the ninety percent of Americans who are not Negro. Professor Eli Ginzberg, an economist who has become a specialist in manpower problems, maintains that Negroes have made gains when whites have pragmatically recognized the advantages they themselves could derive from such gains.*

► The "NEGRO PROBLEM" does not involve the Negro alone; it is a problem facing the whole country. For 350 years, white America has stood the Negro off. Why it did so, and with what consequences, are lessons we should study carefully.

During World War II, I found that many senior members of the military—intelligent men with whom I had daily dealings—seemed to have different views of the Negro from mine. In searching for an explanation, I realized many of these officers were from the South. They had grown up during the early years of the century, and their image of the Negro was still a reflection of the one they acquired in youth. I, on the other hand, came from a

From *The New York Times Magazine*, February 9, 1964. © 1964 by The New York Times Company. Reprinted by permission of the author and publisher.

Northern state. All of us, therefore, Northerners as well as Southerners, are prisoners of time and perspective. Even the effective leaders of today's Negro protest movement sometimes act as if history began yesterday. The real challenge is to broaden and deepen our perspective beyond the limits of our own individual experience.

The first conclusion to be derived from history is that our democracy, by conception and commitment, was a white democracy only. The Negro was excluded from the Declaration of Independence and from the Constitution. The Great Abolitionist, William Lloyd Garrison, was right when he said that, from this point of view, the Constitution was "a pact with the devil." The Negro was counted out. Much of the intractable difficulty American democracy has experienced with respect to the Negro citizen, therefore, comes from having to restructure its basic institutions to make room for him. Gunnar Myrdal, the distinguished Swedish economist and author of the first comprehensive study of the Negro, "An American Dilemma," was wrong, in my opinion, when he said that there has been a conflict between our convictions and our actions. He complimented us, because he misunderstood the problem. We never had a commitment, as a nation, to the Negro.

The Constitution—the basic law of the land—dealt with the Negro in three ways: first, it stipulated that Congress could put an end to the slave trade but not before 1808; second, it authorized the Federal Government to return runaway slaves to their owners; and, third, it provided that a slave would be counted as three-fifths of a man in determining the basis of representation in the House of Representatives—hardly the type of legislation to justify Myrdal's belief that we had a democratic commitment to the Negro. A further piece of evidence is that no President of the United States from George Washington to William Howard Taft had any answer to the problem presented by Negroes in white America except to suggest, in one way or another, that they leave the country.

The second historical fact is that although the Negro has mostly lived in the South, the North and the West have also been, and remain, generally hostile to him. Even today, the Administration is finding it difficult to persuade Republicans from states where there are few Negroes to agree to the passage of a broad civil-rights bill.

The South has never had the determining voice. The destiny of the Negro in America has always been shaped primarily by the attitudes and actions of white citizens in the North and West, who were not interested in the Negro and made no commitments to him. As early as the drafting of the Constitution, and many times thereafter, the North said to the South: "We will not interfere in your relationships with the Negro if you will not interfere with some of our basic economic policies."

The third conclusion from history is that such gains as Negroes have been able to make usually came when whites did not have to pay for them—or when they wanted something from the Negro or from each other. Negro slaves had a chance to win their freedom during the Revolutionary War when the British offered to free all those who would fight for them. George Washington, who had at first refused to take Negroes into the army, then permitted them to enlist. Later, when North and South engaged in fratricidal war, Lincoln himself said that he would settle the war gladly even if he could not free a single Negro. He believed his primary responsibility as Chief Executive was to settle the war; emancipation was merely a military expedient.

It is only since 1940, when the North needed and wanted Negro labor in pursuit of the defense effort and of economic growth, that the Negro has begun to make significant gains. When the country finally needed Negro manpower, Negroes were able to advance as citizens.

The New Deal was established because President Roosevelt was concerned about the problems of the handicapped third of the population—the people who were badly fed, badly housed and had no work. Under his leadership, we were able to establish Federal programs that incidentally embraced the Negro. Not all of them provided him with significant benefits, however.

Those measures that required the cooperation of the states and local areas—such as the agricultural programs—were of limited advantage to the Negro. But where Federal power was exercised in programs like Social Security, unemployment insurance and public works, the Negro enjoyed the benefits equally.

History thus points to two conclusions: that animosity, indifference and neglect have characterized the attitude of the white population toward the Negro in both the North and the South; and that most of the Negro's progress to date has been made through the economic self-interest of the white community rather than through its active encouragement.

How, then, do we stand now—and what are the prospects? Despite the fact that Negroes are more urbanized today than the white population (roughly 75 per cent live in urban communities), the rural South remains the center of poverty, unemployment, underemployment, undereducation and racialism in its most aggravated forms.

One and a half million Negroes left the South in the nineteen-fifties but despite that tremendous migration, there will have to be another one soon. There is no future for *all* the whites and Negroes who still remain on Southern farms. Dr. C. E. Bishop of North Carolina State College of Agriculture and Engineering has estimated that of the million and a half young people between the ages of 10 and 20 still employed on the land in the South, only 150,000 will be needed by the end of the decade. President Kennedy made much the same calculation in his manpower report. He stated that only about one in 10 of the young people now growing up in the farm areas of the United States—and an even smaller percentage in the South—had a chance of making a living in agriculture.

These poorly educated, poorly trained whites and Negroes naturally gravitate toward the large cities. But urban areas that used to be so hospitable to new arrivals and offered a place for anyone with a strong back, are no longer conglomerations of first-generation immigrants—they have become third- and fourth-generation middle-class communities. The yawning gap between these farm migrants and the cities' residents makes for an entirely new source of social tension.

Even those Negroes who have started up the income and occupational scale—who escaped to the cities in the nineteen-forties and did well in the wartime and postwar booms—are in trouble. They are heavily concentrated in those sectors of the economy that are most affected by automation and technological change—on Detroit assembly lines, in Chicago meat-packing plants and the steel mills of Pittsburgh. These are the industries where semi-skilled laborers are being squeezed out—and Negroes loom very large in their ranks.

At the height of the Korean War, unemployment among Negroes was approximately 4 per cent—considerably below the level in the work force as a whole in recent years. Today, the level of Negro unemployment is 11 to 12 per cent or even higher.

Another element in the problem is that the Negro birth rate is now considerably above the white birth rate—for many reasons, including improvements in health and consequent reductions in sterility. This comes at a time when the number of young people available for work is already increasing phenomenally and both white and Negro youngsters are having more and more difficulty finding jobs.

Despite this gloomy picture, however, there is one encouraging piece of evidence. In both North and South, a growing minority of Negroes have managed to climb up the economic and occupational ladder. In Chicago, for instance, 30 per cent of the Negro families have a higher income than 50 per cent of the white families. In the West, the nonwhite income distribution is almost the exact counterpart of income distribution among the white population of the South.

This suggests that our complicated, diffuse and widely differentiated society offers many options, many ways to go around obstacles, that permit members of disadvantaged minorities to escape from the slough.

Nevertheless, the general drift of the economy and the rapid increase in the labor force do present a formidable problem for an underprivileged group. One crucial index makes this clear: In the last 10 years approximately 800,000 new jobs have been created annually; but even without reducing the present level of unemployment—which is much too high—we need half as many again each year just to absorb the tremendous increase in the number of youngsters coming of working age.

And, despite a growing national income, there is nothing on the horizon at the moment to inspire much confidence in our ability to achieve this aim. President Johnson recently emphasized the rapid gains that the economy had made during the past two and a half years: $100 billion more in gross national product, and 2.5 million more jobs. But put these figures together and they show that it took $40 billion of additional G.N.P. to create one million additional jobs!

What bearing do these economic and manpower trends have on the strategy and tactics of the civil-rights movement? So far, the great contribution of the protest movement has been to underscore, first for the Negro and then for the white community, that the Negro must become a full partner in an America that historically had no place for him and no commitment to receive him. The protest movement has said plainly that all Negroes must have all of the rights—civil and political—that were conferred by three Constitutional Amendments after the Civil War but which were never adequately enforced.

But no minority can bring about this desired end by itself. Power in a democracy rests with the majority. Against a backdrop of white animosity or lack of interest, the only answer is to find potential allies for the Negroes among the poor, the ill-educated, the unemployed and the menially employed (together, a considerable part of the white community), as well as the Spanish-speaking community and some other minority groups.

Allies, however, come at a price. In the perspective of our democratic tradition, it appears that if a minority's program is to gain the support of others, it must somehow serve their needs as well as its own.

It becomes important, therefore, to determine what white America is willing to do for white Americans—and thus incidentally for the Negro.

Approached in this light, the history of the new federalism from Roosevelt to Johnson seems to indicate that if acceptable programs can be found for improvements in education, health and welfare, and for urban renewal, all those in need of special Government help in these areas will have a chance to get it.

Education alone is too slow an answer to the Negroes' problem. It is necessary to move along on the educational front, but the real emergency is in the employment situation. We have—on the books—a Congressional commitment to full employment passed in 1946 with the strong support of both parties, but it has never been fully implemented.

To revive the Employment Act of 1946 would be a major attack on racialism, and there is a good possibility of its political success because there are even more white youngsters who need a chance to work than Negro youngsters. If this were done, we would then have short-run job and long-run educational programs supporting each other. A balance must be found among multiple programs— those which Negroes should attempt to accomplish largely on their own (such as protest and civil rights); objectives, like improved welfare and rehabilitation programs, which they must work toward in alliance with others, and full employment, which is a challenge to all groups in our society.

In the absence of such a program, however, it would be understandable if large parts of the Negro community chose to give up the struggle, as the Black Muslims have suggested, and withdraw, either physically or spiritually, from America. It would be understandable if their despair reached the point of total alienation.

But I believe that the trials, suffering and victories of Negro men, women and children over the last 350 years have not been in vain. It has taken the nation much too long to admit the Negro to full citizenship, but we are at last on the threshold of establishing a biracial society based on freedom and equality for all. It is late but it is also early, for no other nation has ever attempted this.

26 ► DESEGREGATION IN AMERICAN SOCIETY: THE RECORD OF A GENERATION OF CHANGE

J. MILTON YINGER

A comparative, cross-cultural perspective reveals that although some forms of segregation (in the broad sense of the term) are accepted everywhere, others are opposed because they conflict with basic cultural values and are socially disruptive. In the United States, pressures toward desegregation have developed in almost all aspects of social life. Professor Yinger now describes the extent of the change and comments on the probable future course of events.

► WE HAVE HEARD such terms as revolution and explosion so often in recent years that they have lost all shock value. This should not cause us to forget that this *is* a period of dramatic change—not least of all in the nature of intergroup contact. There are patterns of racial and cultural relations in the United States that were difficult to imagine twenty-five years ago. Although not without exceptions, the strongest trends have been in the direction of greater integration. An attempt will be made here to document that fact carefully and explore some of its significance for American society.

The term integration is used in various ways. In referring to an integrated society, this commonly implies one in which the mem-

From *Sociology and Social Research*, 47, 4 (July, 1963), 428–45. Reprinted by permission of the author and publisher.

This article first appeared in a modified form in *A Minority Group in American Society* (New York: McGraw-Hill, 1965).

bers, regardless of race, religion, or national origin, move freely among one another, sharing the same opportunities and the same public facilities and privileges on an equal basis. Does the term imply also the absence of any barriers to purely private associations? Yes, if one is thinking of full integration; for we are dealing with a variable that can have many different scale values, from little to much.

Whereas integration is a state of affairs, desegregation is a process—a process of change within a society during which the degree of segregation is reduced. This too is a variable; desegregation can range from a small increase in the amount of interaction across group lines (three or four Negro children admitted to a formerly all-white school) to a major reduction in the number and height of the barriers to association. In this sense, it is not entirely meaningful to say that a factory or school or church has "been desegregated"—as if one were speaking of an either-or situation. But we shall occasionally use that phrase to mean that a formerly fully segregated situation has taken one or more steps toward integration. In most instances the first step is the most difficult and critical, thus partly justifying reference to it as desegregation.

It is important to ask how the process of desegregation is set in motion, sometimes breaking up stable patterns of segregation that have existed for many generations. There are varieties of segregation in all societies. To some degree it is the natural expression of group identity and function. Some forms of segregation are repugnant to a society, however, because they violate its basic values or because they create enormous problems.

Conflict over segregation may occur because the lines of separation that are taken for granted or approved in a society do not remain static. As a result of social change which creates new issues for the nation to handle, forms of segregation become unacceptable that formerly were allowed. But since the change hits individuals and regions in different ways and at different rates, there is often a period of sharp controversy during which some persons say, "the old way represents a desirable pluralism and a legitimate separation," while others say, "the old way represents a threat to the health of the society."

The United States is now in the midst of such a process of redefinition with respect to racial and religious segregation. It is no longer simply taken for granted; the older patterns of intergroup relations are rapidly being modified. Urbanization and industrialization, America's world position, and the growth in economic and political power among minority-group members strongly support the integration process. It is well also to note that desegregation has become a national, not simply a southern question. The economy is increasingly national in scope, as Arkansas businessmen painfully learned after 1957. And the migration of minority-group members has brought the question of segregation directly to the attention of almost every region of the country. Virtually all of the persons of Puerto Rican descent, many of the Mexican-Americans, and over forty per cent of the Negroes in the United States now live in the North and West.

The Record of Change

For two generations after the Civil War segregation was taken for granted by almost everyone. There were changes during this period, but the pace was so slow that even the cumulative effect over several decades was slight. Then, beginning perhaps in the early 1930's, there was a quickening in the rate of change, particularly in the South. Although it started from a lower base, the South has been industrializing and urbanizing more rapidly than the rest of the nation for the last twenty-five years. Among other things, this has meant a tremendous migration of Negroes away from the rural areas, most of them to northern cities. In the 1940's, 1,245,000 non-whites (almost all of them Negroes) migrated to the North and West. In the 1950's migration was even heavier: 1,457,000 non-whites, one out of seven of those living in the South in 1950, moved out of the region. At the same time, the colored population of southern cities increased at a rapid rate, a fact of great significance in understanding the process of desegregation; for interaction in the city, as sociologists have long observed, is significantly different from life on the plantation.[1]

It would be a mistake, in this account of desegregation, to forget the vigor and local effectiveness of the opposition. Since the purpose of this paper is to measure the steps being taken toward integration, however, I shall not record the evidence of this opposition—the schools that have been closed, the violence, the devices used to try to prevent colored citizens from registering to vote, and other signs that segregation is approved by some people. In some places, schools and parks have been closed rather than accept an order to integrate them. A tiny amount of integration is being used in other localities in the hope that a token change will satisfy Federal courts and other agencies that are pressing for desegregation. Such facts are important for the student of American society. More important, however, are the evidences of change. It is not surprising that strong forces seek to preserve an established institutional pattern. It is more noteworthy that extensive change is underway in almost every aspect of national life.

Judicial and Legal Changes

Among the most influential developments have been the Supreme Court decisions and the local, state, and federal laws which together have severely narrowed the legal basis for segregation. Without attempting any complete catalogue, one can indicate the scope of the legal change by listing several of the Court decisions and laws. In 1915 the Supreme Court declared that "grandfather clauses" in state constitutions or statutes, patently designed to prevent Negroes from voting, were unconstitutional. In 1917, laws that required housing segregation were barred; and in 1948 the Court ruled that private "restrictive covenants" designed to preserve segregated areas could not be upheld in the courts. One of the major decisions was handed down in 1944, when the "white primary"—the basic device for the disfranchisement of Negroes— was barred by the Supreme Court. Beginning in 1938 and reaching a climax in 1954, with its decision outlawing segregation in all public education, the Supreme Court set in motion the process of school desegregation. In 1946, segregation in interstate travel was banned; and in 1955 the Court ruled against segregation in public recreational facilities.

Such decisions as these did not, of course, immediately transform the practices against which they were directed. What the Supreme Court decisions do represent is a major transformation of the Plessy v. Ferguson doctrine (1896) which established the principle of "separate but equal" as legally acceptable. That Court decision can be thought of as the judicial equivalent of the political "compromise of 1876." It represented a period of indifference on the part of the Supreme Court to laws and practices of segregation and discrimination, because in practice, during the next forty years, segregation meant "separate and unequal." Reversal of the Plessy v. Ferguson decision came in two stages. At first the Court became more and more insistent that if facilities were separate they must at least be equal. But in the school decision of 1954 a significant second stage was reached: segregated facilities were declared to be inherently unequal.

Of the scores of local, state and federal laws supporting the process of desegregation, the following are perhaps the most important: Twenty states, beginning with New York in 1945, and over forty cities, have passed enforceable Fair Employment Practices laws. They vary widely in scope and in the powers granted to enforcement commissions; but their total effect has been to increase significantly the employment opportunities of minority-group workers. Sixty per cent of the population of the country, including nearly one half of the minority-group population, resides in states and cities covered by these laws. Since 1950, seventeen states and many cities have passed Fair Housing Practices laws. Most of the statutes refer only to "publicly assisted" housing (which, however, now includes a high proportion of the houses being built); but a growing number bar discrimination in much of the privately financed housing as well. On the federal level, the Civil Rights bills of 1957 and 1960, concerned primarily with voting rights, were the first civil rights bills passed by Congress since 1875.

Politics

These judicial and legal developments can partly be understood as a result of changes in the United States affecting the political power of minority groups, especially of Negroes, who constitute over ten per cent of the population. Three factors are of greatest importance in these changes: The elimination of the "white primary" in 1944 has been followed by a steady increase of Negro registration and voting in the South. In 1944 there were approximately 250,000 registered Negro voters in the South; in 1962 there were nearly one and a half million. (It should be noted that this represents only about twenty per cent of the potential Negro electorate, compared with a registration of sixty per cent among whites.) Inevitably the increased voting power of Negroes has resulted in competition for their support in some districts. In most areas where Negro voters are important they have won better police protection, more attention to their school needs, and an abatement in racist campaigns.

The second cause of the change has been the growth in size and importance of the white, urban middle class in the South. Their political interests do not all coincide with those of the landed gentry. Intra- and inter-party competition is developing. And where parties and politicians compete, they seek votes from formerly neglected groups. Urban voters are grossly under-represented in American politics, particularly on the state level, and particularly in the South. This important fact is beginning to change as a result of the Supreme Court decision barring practices that support gross inequality of representation among voters.

The third force affecting the political role of minorities in the United States has been the vast migratory movement of Negroes to northern cities. In at least eight industrial states, colored voters now hold strategic "balance of power" positions. To neglect their interests is to court defeat.

The effect of these three developments, supported by the increase in educational level and economic power of minorities, has been to give strong political impetus to the desegregation process. The 1960 election illustrates decisively the strategic importance of colored voters. The average shift from the Republican to the Democratic ticket between 1956 and 1960 was eight per cent, just barely enough to elect President Kennedy. Among Negro voters, however, there was a shift of sixteen per cent. Had the Democrats increased their vote among Negroes by only the eight per cent that was the national average, Mr. Nixon would now be president. President Kennedy's margin of victory in Texas, South Carolina, Illinois, New Jersey, Michigan and several other states was far smaller than the number of votes he received from Negroes. These simple facts have not been overlooked by either party and will surely affect future campaigns.

The Armed Forces

Closely related to the legal and political changes that we have discussed has been the desegregation of the armed forces of the United States since 1950. With only minor exceptions, all branches of the service segregated colored from white troops before and during the Second World War. This policy was abruptly changed when President Truman, after receiving the report of his Committee on Equality of Treatment and Opportunity in the Armed Services in 1950, ordered an immediate and rapid integration of all branches of the service. By 1954 the *New York Times* could write, perhaps only slightly prematurely, that racial integration in the armed forces is "one of the biggest stories of the twentieth century." In a period of three or four years, most of the barriers to the participation of colored Americans were removed. They are still vastly under-represented in the National Guard and in the officer corps, particularly of the Navy and the Marines. This latter fact is partly indicative of the lack of seniority and the lack of training. Only to a residual degree does it represent the lack of equal treatment. Integration of the armed forces has been accompanied by integration of government owned shore installations and other facilities for civilian employees and of schools for the children of service men. It has also meant that more Negroes are getting skilled training, some are receiving increased income, and throughout the services there has been an increase of equal-status contact across race lines.

Employment and Income

In this brief listing I can only illustrate the changes affecting minority-group families that are taking place in the American economic system. Particularly since 1940 colored workers have made substantial gains in the income and skill levels of their jobs. Not all of the gains have been accompanied by desegregation; but the tendency is for the walls of separation to be lowered along with the lowering of income and skill differentials.

The average income of nonwhite families in 1930 was approximately thirty per cent of the income of white families; by 1960 it had increased to sixty per cent. Viewing these facts, one can remark the continuing large contrast or emphasize the extent of the reduction in the differential—and be correct either way. If the trend is of greatest interest, however, we should stress the closing of the income gap, roughly at the rate of one per cent per year. If this trend were to continue, by the end of the century the average income of white and colored families would be equal.

Perhaps the most important aspect of the economic situation is the changing job pattern. Although still seriously disprivileged, the colored population has made important gains in the stable core of urban jobs for men—doubtless the best index of its place in the American economy. On the white collar level (professional, managerial, clerical, and sales jobs), the percentage of white males increased, between 1940 and 1962, from 30.3 to 41.2, while the percentage of nonwhite males in these jobs increased from 5.6 to 16.0. Although the latter change is slightly smaller in absolute amount (10.4 per cent to 10.9 per cent), it is a much larger relative gain for the nonwhites. On the semi-skilled and skilled job levels, colored men made steady gains during the same period. The increase among white workers was from 34.3 per cent to 38.6 per cent; among nonwhites it was 16.6 per cent to 32.7 per cent. Most of these workers were recruited from the ranks of the unskilled and from among farm laborers, hence the new jobs represented significant improvement in their economic status.[2]

On the other hand, colored workers have persistently been hit much more severely by unemployment. Because their jobs are more often on the lower levels of skill, they are more seriously affected by automation. Participation in apprenticeship programs and skilled crafts has increased only slightly since World War II.

On balance, the forces have supported a slow trend toward job improvement for nonwhite Americans. Urban migration, improved education, industrial unions, state and local Fair Employment Practices laws, federal civil service and contract policy, and perhaps most importantly the high level of economic prosperity in the nation sustain the gains among minority-group workers. Some of these forces have had ambivalent results, to be sure, but their net effect has been to support the desegregation of the economy of the United States.

Housing

The extensive migratory movement of colored families into the cities of the nation and the improvement of their incomes, among other factors, have focused increasing attention on residential segregation. In many ways this is more a northern than a southern question, for the most numerous blocks of segregated houses are in the large northern cities. Many Yankees who criticize the South for its segregated schools defend housing arrangements that have many of the same consequences for race relations and for personality development that school segregation has.

Housing desegregation has proceeded more slowly than almost any other phase of the process of change of the last generation. Most contractors and developers build for white families only; a few build for colored families; and a tiny fraction—a few score throughout the nation—build integrated projects. There are many integrated public housing units; yet there is a tendency among some of these to drift toward segregation. Even the process of urban redevelopment sometimes increases segregation: the deteriorated housing, often occupied by minority-group families, may be replaced by units too expensive for them. They are forced into the already overcrowded segregated areas, contributing to their further deterioration.

Some persons who accept integration in public facilities or in jobs resist the idea of desegregating housing because it represents a change near the "social" end of the scale of contact. This feeling is complicated by the fact that a house is a major lifetime expenditure. Housing costs are high; and for many years housing has been in short supply in most parts of the United States. The increase of the nonwhite population of the cities has been far more rapid than the increase in housing available to them—with resulting pressure and tension. In such a setting, powerful interests are able to profit by the sale of exclusiveness on one hand and by overcrowding on the other.

The Commission on Race and Housing has estimated that one-sixth of the American people are to some degree restricted in their choice of residence. Many of them, as a result, are forced into slums. These accommodations for minority-groups in the United States are probably an improvement over those previously available. But our national income and our national standards for minimum housing have also gone up, increasing the gap between what we have and what we accept as a national goal and policy.[3]

The consequences of residential segregation are severe, both for those who experience it and for the total community. Housing segregation usually leads to other forms of segregation—in schools, parks, churches, hospitals, and public accommodations. It is often associated with discrimination in such forms as poorer police and fire protection, lower standards of sanitation, and lax enforcement of housing codes. Their lack of choice in housing makes colored Americans vulnerable to rental and purchase prices up to forty per cent higher than white Americans pay for equivalent accommodations—a heavy overcharge for those least able to pay. Many slum residents are recent migrants to the city. They have a great deal to learn about how to live in a city, but their isolation blocks them from the pressures to learn. The group is turned in on itself, developing its own code of behavior in a context of frustration and hopelessness. The motivation and self-conceptions of segregated children are negatively influenced in a setting of separating subcultures and contracultures.

It is not only the minority-group member who suffers from this situation. The total community loses potential skills. Residential segregation creates conditions within which hostility and anti-social behavior can develop. It promotes the growth of slums, with a variety of negative effects on a community; and when the slums are cleared, the displaced population, often unable to afford the new housing, "piles up" into other areas, making new slums. Segregation creates problems in the foreign relations of the United States. And by increasing distant and stereotype-laden contact, it promotes prejudices that tear the fabric of community life.[4]

Although segregation in housing is the overwhelmingly common fact, a close look will reveal even in this aspect of national life important tendencies toward desegregation. A new trend began— insofar as one can give a date to such a social process—about 1950, and in the last five years it has shown a significant increase in strength. The Federal Housing Authority and other governmental agencies concerned with housing at first considered segregated housing both natural and desirable. In the last decade, however, they have increasingly allowed and encouraged the development of integrated projects. In 1963 President Kennedy issued a long-awaited administrative order that all new governmentally assisted housing must be rented or sold without regard to race, religion, or national origin.

State and local laws, as well as federal actions, are beginning to restrict housing segregation. These laws are based not only on the constitutional grounds of due process (the illegality of being taxed without sharing equally in the benefits), but also on the police power of the community (the right to protect itself against blight and the unhappy consequences of residential deterioration). Several other forces are beginning to support the desegregation of housing. Some labor unions, with interracial membership, are entering the mortgage market. There is evidence for a general reduction in prejudice and a slight shift in attitudes toward integrated residential areas, perhaps based on the growing acquaintance with the favorable responses of those who live in such areas. A few score private builders are now explicitly developing interracial districts.[5] And a large number of churches have circulated open-occupancy covenants. These are the reverse of the restrictive covenants that extra-legally (but not yet illegally) segregate so many American neighborhoods along racial and religious lines. Thousands of church members have signed pledges similar to this: "I will welcome into my neighborhood as a resident any person of good character, regardless of race, religion, or national origin." Thus they seek to weaken the assertion that segregation persists only because residents will not accept integrated neighborhoods.

The total effect of such recent developments in the field of housing is difficult to assess. Supported as they are, however, by other pressures toward desegregation, it seems likely that they will grow in strength and that housing desegregation will proceed at a cumulatively more rapid pace.

Education

No aspect of the process of desegregation has received more attention than the changes in American schools. I need scarcely mention the strategic importance of education, both to individuals and to the whole group, in a society based on democratic political forms and diverse occupational skills. Those blocked from educational advance are kept in low status even if other influences favor their development. A group that is given educational opportunities has a powerful instrument with which to improve its status, even if for the moment other influences are unfavorable. Certainly the extent, if not always the quality, of our educational opportunities is an exciting and important part of the American resolve to maintain an open society.

The long run trend has been to make the educational ladder available to more and more groups in the United States. Desegregation is only the most recent manifestation of this trend. I shall not review here the series of Court decisions and the voluntary changes that have, since the late nineteen-thirties, slowly expanded the educational opportunities of colored Americans and reduced the barriers of segregation. An important turning point was reached in 1954 when the Supreme Court ruled that any segregation in public schools was unconstitutional. This was followed in 1955 by an order that all school districts must proceed "with all deliberate speed" (for the Court recognized that there would be difficult problems to solve) to integrate their schools.

At the time of the 1954 decision, all of the schools in the southern region (17 states plus the District of Columbia) were segregated. By the beginning of 1963 over thirty per cent of the biracial school districts (972 of 3058) had been desegregated to some degree; but the range was wide. The states can be classified into four groups. First are those which have had extensive integration (nearly half of the Negro children go to school with white children; and ninety per cent of the biracial school districts have been desegregated): Washington, D.C., West Virginia, Delaware, Missouri, Kentucky, Maryland, and Oklahoma are in this group. One state, Texas, has had slight desegregation (174 out of 919 biracial school districts, involving two per cent of the Negro pupils). There has been token integration in nine states, ranging from one student on the college level in Mississippi and South Carolina to several hundred in Tennessee. The six additional states in this group are Virginia, Arkansas, North Carolina, Florida, Louisiana, and Georgia. And in Alabama segregation is still nearly complete. In total, 7.8 per cent of the Negro children in the southern region now go to school with white children.[6]

Desegregation of graduate schools and colleges began before the 1954 Supreme Court decision and has been carried farther than on the primary and secondary levels. Over half of the public colleges and universities of the South now admit colored students. Although the proportion is not large—is minute in fact in the Deep South—there are now perhaps seven thousand Negro students enrolled in institutions of higher education that were entirely segregated a few years ago. And there are white students in fifteen of the fifty formerly all-Negro colleges.

In terms of the number of persons involved, there has not yet been a major desegregation of schools in the South. The steps taken so far have been accompanied by extensive litigation, some merely token compliance with court orders, and, in a few instances, violence. In my judgment, however, the more important fact is that an essentially irreversible process has begun.

Although school desegregation is primarily a southern question, there are many quasi-segregated schools in northern and western cities produced by the concentration of nonwhite families in a few residential areas. A survey made by the American Jewish Committee in 1957 found that 20 per cent of the public schools in Chicago, 43 per cent in Cincinnati, 22 per cent in Cleveland, 21 per cent in Detroit, 15 per cent in Los Angeles, 20 per cent in New York, 27 per cent in Philadelphia, and 7 per cent in San Francisco had nonwhite majorities. This situation is not identical with one produced by total and officially enforced segregation; there is a substantial minority of white pupils in many of the schools mentioned above. Yet it cannot be denied that a significant proportion of the colored children, and the Mexican and Puerto Rican children as well, in the large cities of the North and West attend schools in which intergroup contact is at a minimum. And the proportion attending such schools is likely to go up, as white families move from the cities to suburbs where few or no colored families reside.

Several procedures have been developed by school boards and administrative staffs to try to reduce the number of quasi-segregated schools. Skillful districting (gerrymandering in reverse) can sometimes be used to assign minority-group children to several schools. (The same procedure has been used, of course, and continues to be in some instances, to concentrate colored children in a few schools.) New York City transports several thousand pupils out of their districts in an effort to disperse heavy concentrations of Negro and Puerto Rican children in some schools. A few communities have shifted from the neighborhood concept for elementary schools to a plan calling for the assignment of all first and second grade children to one school, third and fourth graders to another, fifth and sixth graders to another. Although this increases problems of transportation, it can, at least in small and medium sized cities, reduce the tendency toward segregation in schools. It may, in addition, have significant educational advantages.

Such procedures as these, however, can only slightly reduce school segregation that rests upon the fact that many American cities contain large subcommunities of nonwhites. Significant changes in the school pattern are dependent upon future developments in urban renewal programs, housing practices, and the economic position of minority groups.

Churches

It has often been said that "eleven o'clock Sunday morning is the most segregated hour of the week." Although this has been substantially true, changes since World War II require modification of the statement. There are so many churches in the United

States, with such widely divergent practices, that any brief summary is liable to error. It is hopeful that the net result of citing the following items will be to convey an accurate impression.

In the South, local congregations, almost without exception, are segregated. Resistance to integration gets strong support from some churches and ministers, particularly of the sectarian, fundamentalist variety. Most of the clergy in the middle and upper class churches either avoid any reference to the question of segregation or call for Christian understanding without specifying what steps are required at the given moment. Faced with the problem of holding a divided or segregationist-minded congregation together, they turn to less controversial issues.

On the other hand, there is evidence that many ministers approved of the Supreme Court decision outlawing school segregation (80 per cent of the Protestant ministers from the South who responded to an inquiry from *Pulpit Digest* supported the Court). Ministerial associations in Richmond, Nashville, Atlanta, and other cities have appealed for peaceful desegregation of schools (if not of their own churches). Ministers have been prominent among the few white southerners who have taken active, and often courageous, parts in the integration process. And every major denomination in the South—still excluding the fundamentalist sects—has gone on record favoring the Supreme Court decision.

In the North, most local congregations are still segregated. As in the South, the churches of the lower classes, of the recent migrants from rural areas, the small "storefront" and other fundamentalists groups oppose integration. A large majority of the local congregations belonging to the established denominations are also segregated. It should be noted, however, that this is not always a sign of unwillingness to accept colored members. There may be no Negroes or other nonwhites living in the area or they may feel no desire to become associated with a "white church." Moreover, a significant minority, perhaps ten per cent, of the established northern churches, Protestant and Catholic, now have some interracial character. This is a very recent development, most of the desegregation having occurred in the last decade. Usually it means, not that there has been extensive integration, but that a small number of families of Oriental descent or Negro families have joined a formerly all-white church. They are typically professional and business people whose education and income are similar to those of the other members. In a few instances, usually in areas of a city where there has been a large increase in the nonwhite population, more extensive integration of congregations, and occasionally of ministerial staffs, has occurred.

Altogether, one can find in these various trends among churches a sensitive index to the currents of desegregation.

Public Accommodations

Generalization in this area is even more difficult and hazardous than in the others we have discussed. There are tens of thousands of publicly and privately owned facilities to serve the "general public," and their policies range from full integration to total segregation. Despite this diversity, however, I think it is correct to state that there has been extensive desegregation in the use of public accommodations since World War II. What is some of the evidence for this statement?

Before the War, segregation in hotels and restaurants was the rule, even in major northern cities. Conventions with multiracial membership were able to secure accommodations, but individual colored persons were often denied service. Almost all of the states of the North already had civil rights statutes requiring that all businesses catering to the general public must grant service without regard to race, religion, or national origin. (Twenty-eight states now have such laws.) But the laws were repeatedly violated without penalty. After the War this situation began to change for a number of reasons: The growing economic power of colored Americans made it more costly to neglect them as customers; their increased political participation made it more costly to neglect the enforcement of civil rights statutes; new state and local anti-discrimination commissions have been assigned some responsibility in civil rights matters; and public attitudes are significantly more favorable to integrated facilities. Virtually all of the larger hotels, restaurants, and theatres are now desegregated in the major northern and western cities. This is less true of some of the smaller businesses and in the smaller cities.

There has also been desegregation in "border" cities, most particularly in Washington, D.C. Despite the difficulties caused by segregation in the nation's capital, most of its public facilities were segregated until 1950. Without specifying the details of the shift, let me simply state that as a result of such forces as administrative action, Court decisions, international incidents, and a general change in the climate of opinion, the major hotels and restaurants, the theatres, swimming pools, and (in a somewhat different connection) the schools have been desegregated. To those acquainted with Washington in the early nineteen-fifties and before, the speed and extent of the change are truly dramatic. There have been similar if not always such extensive changes in St. Louis, Cincinnati, Louisville, Baltimore, and other border cities.

The least extensive but perhaps the most significant changes have occurred in the South. In a region where there are no state civil rights statutes and where opposition to desegregation is strongest, there have nevertheless been steps taken toward integration of public facilities that were difficult to imagine even five years ago. In 1946 the Supreme Court ruled against segregation in interstate travel and the terminals connected with it. The purchase of interstate tickets on a non-segregated basis became standard practice on buses, trains, and airplanes within a few years; changes in the terminals have been slower. Between 1955 and 1957, several decisions by the Supreme Court and other federal courts invalidated state and local laws requiring segregated seating on public conveyances and required the integration of public recreational facilities. Although these decisions have not been widely enforced, as we are well aware because of the spotlight focused on the Freedom Riders, we need also to note that dozens of southern cities have desegregated their buses, almost all have eliminated segregated terminals, and a few have opened their public recreational facilities to all races.

Perhaps more significant than these developments, which were aided by court decisions, has been the desegregation of lunch counters in drug and department stores in many parts of the South. The "sit-in" movement has generated some opposition and violence, but far more often has opened lunch counters to persons of all races by peaceful demonstration and negotiation. Negro college students, white businessmen, and several private "human relations" organizations have largely been responsible for this change which, since 1960, has desegregated hundreds of lunch counters and some restaurants in at least nine southern states.

Desegregation has not proceeded far in the South; it is virtually nonexistent in the rural areas; but a significant start has been made in the cities.

Sports

Few types of human endeavor have more objective criteria of excellence than sports. If exclusion on the presumed grounds of lack of preparation or talent is disguised prejudice, it is easily exposed by the facts. In many parts of the country, high school and college athletic teams have been integrated for decades, a fact well underscored by a look at the record books or at an American Olympic team. Since professional football, when it appeared, drew most of its players from college teams, it rather quickly hired players regardless of race, although resistance to this policy continued as late as 1961. Such individual sports as boxing have long been used by boys from low status groups to improve their income and status.

Perhaps the most dramatic step toward integration of sports was Branch Rickey's decision, in 1946, to add a Negro player to the Brooklyn Dodgers. In Jackie Robinson he found an almost ideal person to take the lead. His athletic talent was unquestionable; he was able to take the verbal and physical abuse without retaliation and without letting it disturb his playing; and yet he also conveyed the impression to those who abused him that he was not accepting their definition of his role nor shrinking from them. When we now see the list of Negro, Puerto Rican, and Mexican stars in the major leagues of the United States, it is difficult to remember how thoroughly segregation prevailed on the teams only fifteen years ago. The consequences reach far beyond the sports arena. There are dozens of stars with whom Negro boys can identify; there is a quickening of pride; there is an increase in equalitarian contact.

In the last few years, the first steps toward desegregation of golf and tennis have been taken, most notably shown by the success of Althea Gibson on the courts of Wimbledon and Forest Hills. Public golf courses and tennis courts are open to all in most northern communities and in a few cities of the South. Private clubs, however, continue to be segregated in most cases throughout the country.

Conclusion

This brief catalogue of changes in American race relations during the last generation can only give a hint of the desegregation process. It is primarily a record of public acts and institutional changes, with little reference to the "tone" with which individuals have received and participated in those changes. Individual responses are important of course. The course of events when changes are accepted reluctantly, under fear of penalty, is different from the consequence of a new pattern that is accepted enthusiastically. Yet this contrast can easily be exaggerated, particularly if one is interested in long-run developments. Contemporary sociology emphasizes the extent to which the public definition of events, the institutional structure within which group interaction takes place, affects the individual's response. Within the last twenty-five years that public definition, as it applies to race relations, has been drastically changed in the United States. The extent of the change so far accomplished is reshaping individual attitudes in such a way that further change becomes more likely.

The fact that the present balance of forces is producing desegregation does not mean that the process is inevitable. We can say with some confidence that if present trends continue further desegregation seems likely. But present trends may not continue. Economic prosperity and growth have certainly supported the growth of integration. The rapid development of urban areas and the related heavy migration of minority-group persons, although their effects have been somewhat ambivalent, have lent support to desegregation. Without trying to list all the variables that affect the speed and direction of change, I would mention at least the following additional ones: The international situation, the presence of organized groups, the appearance of leaders with strategic skills, and the strength of the movement to extend and improve education. Most of these influences support desegregation now and seem likely to in the future.

There are some forces that may work in the opposite direction if they continue to operate. Although the concentration of Negroes in the rural counties of the South is much reduced, there is a strong tendency for them to be reconcentrated in the center of the large industrial cities. During the first 150 years of the nation's history, there was a steady decline in the proportion of the population that was non-white. Since 1940, this trend has been reversed and we can expect a small increase in the proportion of the population that is non-white (from 11.3 per cent in 1960 to perhaps 14 per cent in 2000). This does not seem to me to be a very important variable among those affecting desegregation, but if other factors were blocking further integration, the demographic situation might support them. And finally, the strength of "isolationist" and hostile movements among minorities—the Black Muslims are the most important current example—must be taken into account. Virtually all minority-group organizations now support desegregation, but this would not necessarily continue to be the case if the process of integration were to stop or significantly slow down.

What then can one say in summary regarding the prospects for continuing desegregation? It seems highly probable that further extensive desegregation will take place. The three hundred year era during which race symbols have been important in determining a person's life chances and in group relations in most of the western world is coming to an end. Its fundamental roots in slavery, in conquest, in colonialism and imperialism, in the sharp cultural differences often found, in plantation economies, and in the Civil War are all broken. (It is by no means impossible, however, that a reciprocal racism, already apparent in some measure, will develop, as more "non-white" peoples rise to military, economic, and political power. This would be one of history's bitter ironies were it to occur even as the European and European-derived peoples eliminated race from their perspectives. Lessons learned too late are not uncommon in human experience.)

Within the United States race lines are fading. That does not mean that a Negro will be elected mayor of New York, or of Birmingham, tomorrow (although the former may not be many decades away). Racial disprivilege will outlive the twentieth century, but in less and less extensive ways. If the United States takes as many steps toward full integration in the next twenty-five years as she has in the preceding twenty-five—and this seems fully likely —the country will have accomplished a major social transformation, deeply affecting the whole course of its development, within a half century. Seldom are such vital reorganizations accomplished so swiftly.

Notes ▶

1. See J. Milton Yinger and George E. Simpson, "Can Segregation Survive in an Industrial Society?" *Antioch Review*, 8 (Spring, 1958), 15–24.

2. United States Department of Labor, "The Economic Situation of Negroes in the United States," Bulletin S-3, Revised, 1962.

3. Commission on Race and Housing, *Where Shall We Live* (Berkeley: University of California Press, 1958).

4. See *ibid.* and Davis McEntire, *Residence and Race* (Berkeley: University of California Press, 1960).

5. Eunice Grier and George Grier, *Privately Developed Interracial Housing: An Analysis of Experience* (Berkeley: University of California Press, 1960).

6. *Southern School News*, 9 (December, 1962), 1.

27 ► THE CHANGING CHARACTER OF NEGRO PROTEST

JAMES H. LAUE

A major change has taken place in the desegregation process during the last ten years. It is characterized by growing militancy on the part of thousands of Negro and white Americans, and the growth in influence of six major civil rights organizations. The initiative for change has shifted from the hands of a relatively few professional desegregationists to large numbers of average citizens who are now willing to confront the segregated system through direct action. The growth and immediate success of the sit-in movement in 1960 added a third method of effective protest— activism—to the legal and educational means which had been employed before. It is found that significant desegregation in America has taken place only after the development of crisis situations which demanded rapid resolution by community deci- sion-makers. The movement is turning to an essentially political phase, requiring the major civil rights groups to utilize all three methods more fully in co-ordinated programs. An indication of the success of such co-operative programs is the Voter Education Project, which registered more than 550,000 new Negro voters in the South from 1962 to 1964.

James H. Laue is Assistant Professor of Sociology and Anthro- pology at Emory University. He serves as a consultant on problems of youth and human relations with the Community Relations Service of the U.S. Department of Commerce. His research and articles have been in the areas of intergroup relations and religion.

From *The Annals of the American Academy of Political and Social Science*, Vol. 357 (January, 1965), 119–26. Reprinted by permission of the author and publisher.

▶ IN 1955, MOST Americans had not even heard of most of the organizations whose reports are included in this section. Yet today, just ten years later, the desegregation movement in America has reached its highest peak of energy and effectiveness, largely through the efforts of thousands of Negro and white Americans working through these six groups—the National Association for the Advancement of Colored People (NAACP), the National Urban League, the Southern Regional Council (SRC), the Congress of Racial Equality (CORE), the Southern Christian Leadership Conference (SCLC), and the Student Nonviolent Co-ordinating Committee (SNCC).

Many Americans ten years ago probably could have named the NAACP as one organization working for desegregation, mainly because of its long history of legal action culminating in the 1954 United States Supreme Court decision banning segregation in the public schools. The other five groups, however, were either little known or nonexistent ten years ago. Today, most of them are familiar to anyone who reads a newspaper—a good indication of how rapidly the character of Negro protest is changing.

From Professionalism to Personal Militancy

These changes may be summarized by comparing the basic means of protest today to those of even a few years ago. For most of the twentieth century, most American civil rights supporters were willing to contribute financially only to organizations like the NAACP, whose staff professionals carried through the front lines activity. The crucial difference today is the active personal participation of thousands of persons who are willing to risk their jobs, social status—and, in some cases, their lives—to protest segregation. In short: "Year by year and month by month, Negroes have been growing more militant, more immediatist, more fed up with limited successes and tokenism." [1]

This change from an attitude of professionalism to one demanding personal commitment—"putting your body on the line," as student sit-inners put it—has had three important correlates:

(1) *The transfer of initiative for change from the hands of a relatively few civil rights professionals, religious leaders, and "white liberals" to the broad backs of militant individuals of every color and calling.* Prior to 1954, the approach of desegregation

strategists was basically legal and educational. Low educational levels, lack of economic and political power, and the resulting scarcity of articulate Negro leadership necessarily had kept the drive for equal rights in the hands of a few skilled professionals. Discrimination was rigidly institutionalized, and change was generally slow and piecemeal.[2]

But almost overnight after the Montgomery bus boycott of 1955–1956, the initiative for change shifted to average citizens whose segregation-bred frustration had been spilling over into action at an ever-increasing rate. Organizations and their leaders were still important, to be sure, but their role was becoming one of channeling and structuring the energy for change which was releasing itself among growing numbers of citizens. "Hurry up so we can catch up with our followers!" has become a common feeling among civil rights leaders.[3]

(2) *The development in the last ten years of a full-scale social movement for desegregation.* Sporadic protests against racism in America have been going on since the first Africans jumped overboard rather than be sold into slavery some 400 years ago. But not until the Montgomery bus boycott and its catapulting of Dr. Martin Luther King, Jr., into nationwide prominence was the final groundwork laid for development of a widespread desegregation movement. Montgomery dramatically showed Negroes a new technique—nonviolent direct action—which had won immediate gains in a hard-core segregationist area of the Deep South. More importantly, Dr. King was a *person* (not an organization or a court decision), a living symbol of achievement with whom Negroes could identify in their strivings for self-fulfillment. So it was that nonviolence was added to legalistic and educational approaches to desegregation.

The sense of movement crystallized in 1960 when the lunch counter sit-ins among Southern Negro college students attracted immediate response from students and organizations throughout the nation. Dr. Leslie Dunbar, Executive Director of the Southern Regional Council, has observed that, almost from the beginning, the sit-ins were referred to by both participants and observers as a "movement," but that no one ever spoke of the "school desegregation movement." From 1960 on, this new-found sense of movement and direction has, among other things, increased the tempo of desegregation, led to the birth of new civil rights organizations and the revitalization of existing ones, and hastened the national political confrontation with the problem which culminated in the comprehensive civil rights law of July 1964.

(3) *The growing importance of organizational structures in channeling and co-ordinating the energy generated by the emergence of the desegregation movement.* Movements cannot live by charisma alone—and the current desegregation drive is no exception. Ours is an organizational society, so while laymen and their mass militant activism have become a major source of initiative for change, this energy can be effective in the long run only if it is appropriately organized and directed. Efficient organization has become increasingly important as segregationist community leaders learn to deal with direct action demonstrations, and organizations like the White Citizens Council retaliate with stronger economic and political sanctions. All in all, these conditions have helped to hasten the growth of militancy in the desegregation movement among religious and labor leaders as well as the formal civil rights leadership.

Three Types of Protest

It is in this context of changing participation and leadership, I believe, that the strategies of the six major organizations should be viewed. There have been three basic methods employed in the desegregation effort, which we shall label legal, educational, and activist. The civil rights groups may be distinguished on the basis of which one of these strategies makes up the major part of their approach to the problem: (1) *legal*—appeal to law through filing suits, court litigation, encouraging favorable legislation, and the like (NAACP); (2) *educational*—appeal to reason through researching, informing, consulting, persuading and negotiating with political and economic leaders (Urban League, Southern Regional Council); (3) *activist*—appeal to morality through direct personal confrontation of the enforcers and tacit bystanders of the segregated system, usually through nonviolent direct action in the area of public accommodations (CORE, SCLC, SNCC).

While the major approach of each organization can be characterized by one of the three terms in this typology, it should be noted that (1) most of the groups today employ the other two strategies to some extent and (2) the relative emphasis on the three techniques varies within each organization over time, often depending on the external situation. Using the same framework, the history of protest in the twentieth century may be viewed as an accumulation of effective strategies, beginning with the basically educational approach which the NAACP and the Urban League followed upon their founding in 1909 and 1910, respectively, adding the turn to effective legal means of the NAACP in the 1930's and the Southern Regional Council's area educational function in the 1940's, and including, finally, the growing importance of direct action with CORE (1942), SCLC (1957), and SNCC (1960).

Two essentially educationist strategies have been used in varying degrees by all of the organizations: publications and the sponsoring of workshops and conferences. All the groups publish regular newsletters in addition to issuing special releases and pamphlets. Publications as a means of fund-raising are becoming increasingly important for all the groups, with the exception of the Southern Regional Council and the Urban League, for whom more stable foundation support is a major source of income. Another important form of communication—the workshop or conference—has been a major activity of the educationists and an important part of the programs of all the organizations. Such meetings generally have been of two types: (1) to bring Negroes and whites together for intergroup experiences not provided in a segregated society,[4] and (2) to train leaders and supporters in the philosophy and techniques of the organization.

The role of each of the groups now may be assessed in terms of the general typology of protest techniques, and changes in four important dimensions of group life—goals, strategies, leadership and membership/support.

The Legalists

NATIONAL ASSOCIATION FOR THE ADVANCEMENT OF COLORED PEOPLE (1909)

Goals: To end racial discrimination and segregation in all public aspects of American life.[5]

Strategies: Educational activities important—especially in voting—but legal and legislative techniques have been major approach since the 1930's, when courts began consistently upholding unconstitutionality of public segregation. Approach has expanded considerably since 1960, when rapid success of sit-ins spurred more direct action.[6]

Leadership: Board determines policy, but effective leadership at executive level from Roy Wilkins, Executive Secretary since 1955 —and with the organization for thirty years. Grass-roots leadership shared by local executive secretary and president of chapter in larger communities.

Membership and Support: Dues-paying membership of more than 400,000 in 1,600 chapters throughout the United States. Effectively utilizes structure of Negro church, with many clergymen as branch presidents, especially in South.

The Educationists

NATIONAL URBAN LEAGUE (1910)

Goals: "Opportunity, keynote of American freedom, has been the theme of the National Urban League since its founding."[7]

Strategies: Social work and community organization emphasis. Educational, consulting, and persuasive activities designed to convince employers and government officials that equal opportunity is economically as well as morally right. Important programs include youth talent search and training, promoting compliance with federal equal opportunity regulations, research on Negro-white demographic differences, and wide distribution of findings in such pamphlets as "Economic and Social Status of the Negro in the United States."[8]

Leadership: Highly trained national staff, full-time professional local directors. Increasing militancy since Whitney M. Young, Jr., became Executive Director in 1961—reflected in Young's proposal for a "Marshall Plan for Negro Americans" and his full participation in the March on Washington.

Membership and Support: Nonmembership organization, supported largely by foundation grants. Some 8,000 volunteers and staff members throughout the nation.[9]

SOUTHERN REGIONAL COUNCIL (1944) [10]

Goals: "To attain, through research and action, the ideals and practices of equal opportunity for all peoples in the South."[11]

Strategies: Maintenance of a reputation for careful and objective research makes SRC a respected spokesman on Southern economic, political, and social problems. It has done much through this role to legitimate the ideal of desegregation in the South. Not an activist organization; therefore has unique access to the media, business leaders, educators, religious leaders, and government officials, and is able to serve as mediator between activist groups.[12] Organization and service of state and local human relations councils. Wide circulation of journal, New South, and numerous releases, reports and pamphlets. Representative examples: "What the Supreme Court Said" (1955); "The Economic Effect of School Closing" (1959); "Integration and Industry: What Price Tag for 'Massive Resistance'?" (1960); "The Federal Executive and Civil Rights: A Report to the President" (1961); and "The Price We Pay [for Discrimination]" (1964).

Leadership: Professional staff trained in political science, law, economics, sociology, journalism, governed by Board of Directors. Rapid staff growth with new programs since 1960. Executive Director is Dr. Leslie W. Dunbar, widely respected as knowledgeable on race relations and the South.

Membership and Support: Nonmembership organization, supported largely by foundation grants. Volunteers and some staff in state and local human relations councils. Several thousand academicians, agency personnel, religious, educational, and economic and political leaders subscribe to publications.

The Activists [13]

CONGRESS OF RACIAL EQUALITY (1942)

Goals: To abolish racial discrimination through application of the Gandhian philosophy and techniques of nonviolent direct action.[14]

Strategies: Pioneered nonviolent direct action demonstrations with sit-ins, stand-ins, wade-ins, in the North in 1940's and 1950's; Journey of Reconciliation to test interstate bus facilities in Middle South in 1947; supplied intensive leadership training for sit-inners in 1960's; led Freedom Rides in 1961. Like other activists, approach is basically moral, confronting society's sense of right and wrong directly instead of working through law or reason. Recent leader in organizing voter registration and community centers in Deep South.

Leadership: Small, action-trained national staff including field workers; volunteer leadership on National Council and in local chapters. National Director since 1961: James Farmer, a founder in 1942, has gained position of major leadership in civil rights movement in short time.

Membership and Support: Small active membership organized in approximately 50 local chapters; required commitment to continuous direct action on local level keeps active membership small. Rapid growth in local chapters and all phases of program since sit-ins began in 1960. About 10,000 financial supporters in 1960, now well over 60,000.

SOUTHERN CHRISTIAN LEADERSHIP CONFERENCE (1957)

Goals: "To achieve full citizenship rights, and total integration of the Negro in American life . . . to disseminate the creative philosophy and technique of nonviolence . . . to secure the right and unhampered use of the ballot for every citizen . . . to reduce the cultural lag." [15]

Strategies: Founded to spread techniques of Gandhian nonviolence which brought desegregation on Montgomery's buses, [16] SCLC remains basically direct actionist in approach. Educational and legal work often implemented through direct action. Most important contribution to strategies of movement: highly professional citizenship education and voter-registration schools, training indigenous leaders from throughout the South.

Leadership: SCLC was formed as an organizational embodiment of *the* major symbol of direct action in America—Dr. Martin Luther King, Jr., who is President. Day-to-day policy and implementation under leadership of Executive Director Reverend Andrew J. Young, who succeeded Reverend Wyatt Walker in 1964. Rapid expansion of office and field staff since 1961, including Directors of Citizenship Education and Voter Education; nonprofessional local leadership—mostly clergymen.

Membership and Support: Approximately one hundred affiliates —church groups, civic organizations, and the like—in some thirty states, mainly engaged in fund-raising. Budget increased ten times from 1960 to 1964 with expanding program in direct action and voting. Major fund-raising source: Freedom Rallies with Dr. King speaking in all parts of the country, sponsored by affiliates.

STUDENT NONVIOLENT CO-ORDINATING
COMMITTEE (1960)

Goals: In 1960, to build "a social order of justice permeated by love." In 1963, to build "an interracial democracy [that] can be made to work in this country." [17]

Strategies: Formed to facilitate communication among sit-inners in 1960, SNCC worked primarily in mass nonviolent direct action for first year. Significant change in 1961: decision to take the movement into rural Black Belt through voter-education work. SNCC field secretaries, living on close to subsistence salaries, are more consistently on the rural front lines than any other group. Organized first large voter projects in rural Georgia and Alabama, and laid groundwork for the now extensive voter work in Mississippi. Major strategic contribution: building indigenous leadership through field secretary-led projects in Deep South.

Leadership: Co-ordinating Committee of representative sit-in groups in 1960 became full-time staff of fifteen leave-of-absence students in 1961; grew to more than 200 field secretaries in 1964. Policy-makers James Forman and Robert Moses envision program designed to revolutionize Deep South political and economic caste system.

Membership and Support: "Not a membership organization, but rather an agency attempting to stimulate and foster the growth of local protest movements." [18] Financial support from voluntary contributions, aided by foundations in voter work, Northern Student Movement, and various Northern Friends of SNCC groups.

A Generalization: Crisis Brings Change

The major generalization deriving from these data is that in virtually every case of desegregation in the United States, change has come only after the development of a crisis situation which demanded rapid resolution by a community's leadership structure. It may have been a legal mandate which had to be met, or the loss of business due to demonstrations, or the fear of school closings—any situation defined by the decision-makers as a severe enough crisis to demand solution.

This Crisis-Change model provides the framework for understanding how the three strategies have worked together in the desegregation process. A crisis arises whenever a significant number of elements in the social structure deviate from expected patterns enough to threaten the system's equilibrium. In terms of our typology, such threats to the status quo may come from court cases and equal-opportunity legislation (legalist), or through some form of mass protest (activist). In either case, crisis within a community must be resolved ultimately through face-to-face negotiation (educationist). Or: Activists may test the constitutionality of a law, be bailed out and defended by the legalists, while the educationists help the community adjust if the case produces a new legal definition of the situation.

The Politicizing of the Protest Movement

Though strategies differ, the emerging goal of all the civil rights organizations seems to be social and economic self-help within a framework of equal opportunity.[19] All the groups reflect this orientation in their growing concern for development of indigenous leadership.

But social and economic self-help and equal opportunity are only possible within representative political institutions. Thus, it is not surprising that the Negro protest is already well into an essentially political phase. There are numerous indications already: citizenship education, voter registration, the Mississippi Summer Project, and the Mississippi Freedom Party's challenge at the 1964 Democratic National Convention. The real measure of things to come, however, was begun early in 1962: the massive— an initial three-year grant of more than $500,000—Voter Education Project sponsored by several foundations, blessed by the federal government, co-ordinated by the Southern Regional Council, and carried out by the other five organizations plus many more. In its first two years, the Project had, among other things, registered more than 550,000 new Negro voters in the South.[20]

The increasing reliance on political means will call for still greater commitment and organizational skills. It must, in fact, combine the best of the three strategies discussed here in order to succeed. Assuming this trend, we may conclude with several predictions about the course of the protest in the next few years:

(1) The need for greater technical sophistication—in interpreting and defending provisions of the civil rights law, or in behind-

the-scenes consulting with community leaders through crisis periods, for instance—may produce a trend to a new kind of professionalism, but at a much broader and more militant level than the pre-1954 variety.

(2) In the North, civil rights advocates and community leaders will work more closely together for equal opportunity in housing and jobs in an effort to avoid more ghetto riots like those of last summer.

(3) In the South, the activists will necessarily gain increasing support from legalists and educationists as they continue to challenge local custom and thereby demand enforcement of federal law—and protection of their very lives.

(4) Finally, we can expect to see more of the trend to cooperation manifested in the Council of Federated Organizations,[21] the National Conference on Religion and Race,[22] the March on Washington, and the formation of the United Council on Civil Rights Leadership. In short, the civil rights groups will be putting aside past differences over strategy as the growing sophistication of segregationist resistance—North and South—makes continued reintegration of the movement itself a practical and moral necessity.

Notes ▶

1. August Meier, "The Civil Rights Movement: The Growth of Negro Influence," *Current*, No. 42 (October 1963), p. 40.

2. The plea for "time to voluntarily desegregate" proved to be no answer to the problem then, just as it is not now. Change has only come about as a result of people and groups acting *through* time, and integration leaders in America learned this through many years of generally unsuccessful attempts at friendly persuasion.

3. President Benjamin Mays of Morehouse College made this comment when the March on Washington started spontaneously on its route without waiting for the official signal, and other leaders present agreed that this was an accurate symbol of the whole Negro protest—from research notes, August 28, 1964.

4. This type of workshop is, of course, more frequent with the educationist organizations. A number of other groups have sponsored such meetings since the 1940's, the most important of which are the American Missionary Association—annual Race Relations Institute at Fisk University in Nashville; the Fellowship of Reconciliation; the War Resisters League; the Southern Conference Educational Fund;

the National Student Association; the Anti-Defamation League; and the National Conference of Christians and Jews.

5. "This is the NAACP" (New York, April 1960). The basic goal has been the same since the group was founded.

6. Recently the NAACP Youth Council marched on the National Board to demand the right to engage in more direct action programs (Art Sears and Larry Still, "Demand for More Action, Funds, Pushes Groups Closer Together," *Jet*, Vol. 24, July 18, 1963, p. 20).

7. "A Fair Chance in the Race of Life" (New York: National Urban League, 1962).

8. Published in 1962, utilizing 1960 census data.

9. *PAR: Newsletter of the National Urban League* (Winter 1962), p. 1.

10. An outgrowth of the Commission on Interracial Co-operation, which had been in existence for some twenty-five years.

11. Statement from Council letterhead.

12. See the conclusion of this paper for a discussion of the Council's role in the Voter Education Project.

13. Basic information on the activists—CORE, SCLC and SNCC —from observations, documents and interview data in the files of James H. Laue.

14. Condensed from the masthead of CORE's newsletter, *The CORElator*, and "This is CORE"—publicity pamphlet.

15. Condensed from masthead of the *SCLC Newsletter*.

16. SCLC's distribution of Dr. King's books and other writings is a major method of diffusing nonviolent philosophy and strategies.

17. Conference, April 1960, and statement from a descriptive pamphlet on SNCC, August 1963. The difference in the two phases represents a "secularization" which is a common tendency in social movements as they mature.

18. *Ibid.*, August 1963.

19. Note that the stated goals of the legalists and educationists are phrased strictly in secular terms, while all of the activist groups have said that they are striving toward goals with definite philosophical (that is, Gandhian) or theological (Judaeo-Christian) bases.

20. Southern Regional Council release, August 2, 1964.

21. "COFO," a united project of the NAACP, CORE, SCLC, SNCC and other groups.

22. Attended by 600 representatives of all major faiths in America in Chicago, January 1963.

VI ETHNIC ASSIMILATION AND INTERMARRIAGE

ASSIMILATION is a crucial and inevitable process in the incorporation of American minorities into the fabric of the host society. Yet there is no consensus about its exact meaning and how it takes place.

For some Americans assimilation means the gradual absorption of a minority by a dominant group. The end product is alleged to be the loss of the minority's identity and the emergence of an enlarged and homogenous society. This dubious over-simplification of what actually occurs in dominant-minority relations is based on an analogy, for assimilation was originally a conceptualization of a physiological process wherein foreign substances are ingested by a living organism and transformed into harmonious body cells.

In the sociological sense, however, assimilation does not necessarily mean the total and inevitable homogenization of the social units involved in any sustained interaction, nor does it refer to an exclusively one-way process in which the minority passively accepts what is offered it by the dominant group and loses its own character. If it is not these things, then what is it? According to Professor Milton Gordon, a recognized authority on the sociology of assimilation, it is a process that divides into seven basic subprocesses, sequentially related to each other. Cultural or behavioral assimilation (i.e., acculturation) comes first, followed by structural, marital, identificational, attitude receptional (absence of prejudice), behavior receptional (absence of discrimination), and finally civic assimilation (absence of value and power conflict).

The keystone of the arch of assimilation, Professor Gordon contends, is not acculturation but rather structural assimilation—the large-scale entrance by ethnic minorities into the cliques, clubs and primary-group institutions of the "core" subsociety, comprised of white, Anglo-Saxon Protestants. So far, American society has undergone widespread ethnic acculturation, but with regard to the other six subprocesses, assimilation has advanced considerably less.

28 ► ASSIMILATION IN AMERICA: THEORY AND REALITY

MILTON M. GORDON

► THREE IDEOLOGIES or conceptual models have competed for attention on the American scene as explanations of the way in which a nation, in the beginning largely white, Anglo-Saxon, and Protestant, has absorbed over 41 million immigrants and their descendants from variegated sources and welded them into the contemporary American people. These ideologies are Anglo-conformity, the melting pot, and cultural pluralism. They have served at various times, and often simultaneously, as explanations of what has happened—descriptive models—and of what should happen—goal models. Not infrequently they have been used in such a fashion that it is difficult to tell which of these two usages the writer has had in mind. In fact, one of the more remarkable omissions in the history of American intellectual thought is the relative lack of close analytical attention given to the theory of immigrant adjustment in the United States by its social scientists.

The result has been that this field of discussion—an overridingly important one since it has significant implications for the more familiar problems of prejudice, discrimination, and majority-minority group relations generally—has been largely preempted by laymen, representatives of belles lettres, philosophers, and apologists of various persuasions. Even from these sources the amount of attention devoted to ideologies of assimilation is hardly exten-

Reprinted by permission from the author and *Daedalus*, published by the American Academy of Arts and Sciences, Brookline, Massachusetts (Spring, 1961), 263–85.

sive. Consequently, the work of improving intergroup relations in America is carried out by dedicated professional agencies and individuals who deal as best they can with day-to-day problems of discriminatory behavior, but who for the most part are unable to relate their efforts to an adequate conceptual apparatus. Such an apparatus would, at one and the same time, accurately describe the present structure of American society with respect to its ethnic groups (I shall use the term "ethnic group" to refer to any racial, religious, or national-origins collectivity), and allow for a considered formulation of its assimilation or integration goals for the foreseeable future. One is reminded of Alice's distraught question in her travels in Wonderland: "Would you tell me, please, which way I ought to go from here?" "That depends a good deal," replied the Cat with irrefutable logic, "on where you want to get to."

The story of America's immigration can be quickly told for our present purposes. The white American population at the time of the Revolution was largely English and Protestant in origin, but had already absorbed substantial groups of Germans and Scotch-Irish and smaller contingents of Frenchmen, Dutchmen, Swedes, Swiss, South Irish, Poles, and a handful of migrants from other European nations. Catholics were represented in modest numbers, particularly in the middle colonies, and a small number of Jews were residents of the incipient nation. With the exception of the Quakers and a few missionaries, the colonists had generally treated the Indians and their cultures with contempt and hostility, driving them from the coastal plains and making the western frontier a bloody battleground where eternal vigilance was the price of survival.

Although the Negro at that time made up nearly one-fifth of the total population, his predominantly slave status, together with racial and cultural prejudice, barred him from serious consideration as an assimilable element of the society. And while many groups of European origin started out as determined ethnic enclaves, eventually, most historians believe, considerable ethnic intermixture within the white population took place. "People of different blood" [sic]—write two American historians about the colonial period, "English, Irish, German, Huguenot, Dutch, Swedish—mingled and intermarried with little thought of any difference." [1] In such a society, its people predominantly English, its white immigrants of other ethnic origins either English-speaking or derived largely from countries of northern and western Europe whose cultural divergences from the English were not great, and its dominant white population excluding by fiat the claims and considerations of welfare of the non-Caucasian minorities, the problem of assimilation understandably did not loom unduly large or complex.

The unfolding events of the next century and a half with increasing momentum dispelled the complacency which rested upon the relative simplicity of colonial and immediate post-Revolutionary conditions. The large-scale immigration to America of the famine-fleeing Irish, the Germans, and later the Scandinavians (along with additional Englishmen and other peoples of northern and western Europe) in the middle of the nineteenth century (the so-called "old immigration"), the emancipation of the Negro slaves and the problems created by post-Civil War reconstruction, the placing of the conquered Indian with his broken culture on government reservations, the arrival of the Oriental, first attracted by the discovery of gold and other opportunities in the West, and finally, beginning in the last quarter of the nineteenth century and continuing to the early 1920's, the swelling to proportions hitherto unimagined of the tide of immigration from the peasantries and "pales" of southern and eastern Europe—the Italians, Jews, and Slavs of the so-called "new immigration," fleeing the persecutions and industrial dislocations of the day—all these events constitute the background against which we may consider the rise of the theories of assimilation mentioned above. After a necessarily fore-shortened description of each of these theories and their historical emergence, we shall suggest analytical distinctions designed to aid in clarifying the nature of the assimilation process, and then conclude by focusing on the American scene.

Anglo-Conformity

"Anglo-conformity" [2] is a broad term used to cover a variety of viewpoints about assimilation and immigration; they all assume the desirability of maintaining English institutions (as modified by the American Revolution), the English language, and English-oriented cultural patterns as dominant and standard in American life. However, bound up with this assumption are related attitudes. These may range from discredited notions about race and "Nordic" and "Aryan" racial superiority, together with the nativist political programs and exclusionist immigration policies which such notions entail, through an intermediate position of favoring immigration from northern and western Europe on amorphous, unreflective grounds ("They are more like us"), to a lack of opposition to any source of immigration, as long as these immigrants and their descendants duly adopt the standard Anglo-Saxon cultural patterns. There is by no means any necessary equation between Anglo-conformity and racist attitudes.

It is quite likely that "Anglo-conformity" in its more moderate aspects, however explicit its formulation, has been the most prevalent ideology of assimilation goals in America throughout the nation's history. As far back as colonial times, Benjamin Franklin recorded concern about the clannishness of the Germans in Pennsylvania, their slowness in learning English, and the establishment of their own native-language press.[3] Others of the founding fathers had similar reservations about large-scale immigration from Europe. In the context of their times they were unable to foresee the role such immigration was to play in creating the later greatness of the nation. They were not at all men of unthinking prejudices. The disestablishment of religion and the separation of church and state (so that no religious group—whether New England Congregationalists, Virginian Anglicans, or even all Protestants combined —could call upon the federal government for special favors or support, and so that man's religious conscience should be free) were cardinal points of the new national policy they fostered. "The Government of the United States," George Washington had written to the Jewish congregation of Newport during his first term as president, "gives to bigotry no sanction, to persecution no assistance."

Political differences with ancestral England had just been written in blood; but there is no reason to suppose that these men looked upon their fledgling country as an impartial melting pot for the merging of the various cultures of Europe, or as a new "nation of nations," or as anything but a society in which, with important political modifications, Anglo-Saxon speech and institutional forms would be standard. Indeed, their newly won victory for democracy and republicanism made them especially anxious that these still precarious fruits of revolution should not be threatened by a large influx of European peoples whose life experiences had accustomed them to the bonds of despotic monarchy. Thus, although they explicitly conceived of the new United States of

America as a haven for those unfortunates of Europe who were persecuted and oppressed, they had characteristic reservations about the effects of too free a policy. "My opinion, with respect to immigration," Washington wrote to John Adams in 1794, "is that except of useful mechanics and some particular descriptions of men or professions, there is no need of encouragement, while the policy or advantage of its taking place in a body (I mean the settling of them in a body) may be much questioned; for, by so doing, they retain the language, habits and principles (good or bad) which they bring with them." [4] Thomas Jefferson, whose views on race and attitudes towards slavery were notably liberal and advanced for his time, had similar doubts concerning the effects of mass immigration on American institutions, while conceding that immigrants, "if they come of themselves . . . are entitled to all the rights of citizenship." [5]

The attitudes of Americans toward foreign immigration in the first three-quarters of the nineteenth century may correctly be described as ambiguous. On the one hand, immigrants were much desired, so as to swell the population and importance of states and territories, to man the farms of expanding prairie settlement, to work the mines, build the railroads and canals, and take their place in expanding industry. This was a period in which no federal legislation of any consequence prevented the entry of aliens, and such state legislation as existed attempted to bar on an individual basis only those who were likely to become a burden on the community, such as convicts and paupers. On the other hand, the arrival in an overwhelmingly Protestant society of large numbers of poverty-stricken Irish Catholics, who settled in groups in the slums of Eastern cities, roused dormant fears of "Popery" and Rome. Another source of anxiety was the substantial influx of Germans, who made their way to the cities and farms of the mid-West and whose different language, separate communal life, and freer ideas on temperance and sabbath observance brought them into conflict with the Anglo-Saxon bearers of the Puritan and Evangelical traditions. Fear of foreign "radicals" and suspicion of the economic demands of the occasionally aroused workingmen added fuel to the nativist fires. In their extreme form these fears resulted in the Native-American movement of the 1830's and 1840's and the "American" or "Know-Nothing" party of the 1850's, with their anti-Catholic campaigns and their demands for restrictive laws on naturalization procedures and for keeping the foreign-born out of political office. While these movements scored local political successes and their turbulences so rent the national social fabric that the patches are not yet entirely invisible, they failed to influence national legislative policy on immigration and immigrants; and their fulminations inevitably provoked the expected reactions from thoughtful observers.

The flood of newcomers to the westward expanding nation grew larger, reaching over one and two-thirds million between 1841 and 1850 and over two and one-half million in the decade before the Civil War. Throughout the entire period, quite apart from the excesses of the Know-Nothings, the predominant (though not exclusive) conception of what the ideal immigrant adjustment should be was probably summed up in a letter written in 1818 by John Quincy Adams, then Secretary of State, in answer to the inquiries of the Baron von Fürstenwaerther. If not the earliest, it is certainly the most elegant version of the sentiment, "If they don't like it here, they can go back where they came from." Adams declared: [6]

They [immigrants to America] come to a life of independence, but to a life of labor—and, if they cannot accommodate themselves to the character, moral, political and physical, of this country with all its compensating balances of good and evil, the Atlantic is always open to them to return to the land of their nativity and their fathers. To one thing they must make up their minds, or they will be disappointed in every expectation of happiness as Americans. They must cast off the European skin, never to resume it. They must look forward to their posterity rather than backward to their ancestors; they must be sure that whatever their own feelings may be, those of their children will cling to the prejudices of this country.

The events that followed the Civil War created their own ambiguities in attitude toward the immigrant. A nation undergoing wholesale industrial expansion and not yet finished with the march of westward settlement could make good use of the never faltering waves of newcomers. But sporadic bursts of labor unrest, attributed to foreign radicals, the growth of Catholic institutions and the rise of Catholics to municipal political power, and the continuing association of immigrant settlement with urban slums revived familiar fears. The first federal selective law restricting immigration was passed in 1882, and Chinese immigration was cut off in the same year. The most significant development of all, barely recognized at first, was the change in the source of Euro-

pean migrants. Beginning in the 1880's, the countries of southern
and eastern Europe began to be represented in substantial numbers for the first time, and in the next decade immigrants from
these sources became numerically dominant. Now the notes of a
new, or at least hitherto unemphasized, chord from the nativist
lyre began to sound—the ugly chord, or discord, of racism. Previously vague and romantic notions of Anglo-Saxon peoplehood,
combined with general ethnocentrism, rudimentary wisps of genetics, selected tidbits of evolutionary theory, and naive assumptions
from an early and crude imported anthropology produced the
doctrine that the English, Germans, and others of the "old immigration" constituted a superior race of tall, blonde, blue-eyed
"Nordics" or "Aryans," whereas the peoples of eastern and southern Europe made up the darker Alpines or Mediterraneans—both
"inferior" breeds whose presence in America threatened, either by
intermixture or supplementation, the traditional American stock
and culture. The obvious corollary to this doctrine was to exclude
the allegedly inferior breeds; but if the new type of immigrant
could not be excluded, then everything must be done to instill
Anglo-Saxon virtues in these benighted creatures. Thus, one educator writing in 1909 could state: [7]

These southern and eastern Europeans are of a very different type
from the north Europeans who preceded them. Illiterate, docile,
lacking in self-reliance and initiative, and not possessing the Anglo-
Teutonic conceptions of law, order, and government, their coming has
served to dilute tremendously our national stock, and to corrupt our
civic life. . . . Everywhere these people tend to settle in groups or
settlements, and to set up here their national manners, customs, and
observances. Our task is to break up these groups or settlements, to
assimilate and amalgamate these people as a part of our American race,
and to implant in their children, so far as can be done, the Anglo-
Saxon conception of righteousness, law and order, and popular government, and to awaken in them a reverence for our democratic institutions and for those things in our national life which we as a people
hold to be of abiding worth.

Anglo-conformity received its fullest expression in the so-called
Americanization movement which gripped the nation during
World War I. While "Americanization" in its various stages had
more than one emphasis, it was essentially a consciously articulated movement to strip the immigrant of his native culture and
attachments and make him over into an American along Anglo-

Saxon lines—all this to be accomplished with great rapidity. To use an image of a later day, it was an attempt at "pressure-cooking assimilation." It had prewar antecedents, but it was during the height of the world conflict that federal agencies, state governments, municipalities, and a host of private organizations joined in the effort to persuade the immigrant to learn English, take out naturalization papers, buy war bonds, forget his former origins and culture, and give himself over to patriotic hysteria.

After the war and the "Red scare" which followed, the excesses of the Americanization movement subsided. In its place, however, came the restriction of immigration through federal law. Foiled at first by presidential vetoes, and later by the failure of the 1917 literacy test to halt the immigrant tide, the proponents of restriction finally put through in the early 1920's a series of acts culminating in the well-known national-origins formula for immigrant quotas which went into effect in 1929. Whatever the merits of a quantitative limit on the number of immigrants to be admitted to the United States, the provisions of the formula, which discriminated sharply against the countries of southern and eastern Europe, in effect institutionalized the assumptions of the rightful dominance of Anglo-Saxon patterns in the land. Reaffirmed with only slight modifications in the McCarran-Walter Act of 1952, these laws, then, stand as a legal monument to the creed of Anglo-conformity and a telling reminder that this ideological system still has numerous and powerful adherents on the American scene.

The Melting Pot

While Anglo-conformity in various guises has probably been the most prevalent ideology of assimilation in the American historical experience, a competing viewpoint with more generous and idealistic overtones has had its adherents and exponents from the eighteenth century onward. Conditions in the virgin continent, it was clear, were modifying the institutions which the English colonists brought with them from the mother country. Arrivals from non-English homelands such as Germany, Sweden, and France were similarly exposed to this fresh environment. Was it not possible, then, to think of the evolving American society not as a slightly modified England but rather as a totally new blend, culturally and biologically, in which the stocks and folkways of Europe, figuratively speaking, were indiscriminately mixed in the political pot of the emerging nation and fused by the fires of American influence and interaction into a distinctly new type?

Such, at any rate, was the conception of the new society which motivated that eighteenth-century French-born writer and agriculturalist, J. Hector St. John Crèvecoeur, who, after many years of American residence, published his reflections and observations in *Letters from an American Farmer.*[8] Who, he asks, is the American?

He is either an European, or the descendant of an European, hence that strange mixture of blood, which you will find in no other country. I could point out to you a family whose grandfather was an Englishman, whose wife was Dutch, whose son married a French woman, and whose present four sons have now four wives of different nations. *He* is an American, who leaving behind him all his ancient prejudices and manners, receives new ones from the new mode of life he has embraced, the new government he obeys, and the new rank he holds. He becomes an American by being received in the broad lap of our great *Alma Mater.* Here individuals of all nations are melted into a new race of men, whose labours and posterity will one day cause great changes in the world.

Some observers have interpreted the open-door policy on immigration of the first three-quarters of the nineteenth century as reflecting an underlying faith in the effectiveness of the American melting pot, in the belief "that all could be absorbed and that all could contribute to an emerging national character."[9] No doubt many who observed with dismay the nativist agitation of the times felt as did Ralph Waldo Emerson that such conformity-demanding and immigrant-hating forces represented a perversion of the best American ideals. In 1845, Emerson wrote in his Journal:[10]

I hate the narrowness of the Native American Party. It is the dog in the manger. It is precisely opposite to all the dictates of love and magnanimity; and therefore, of course, opposite to true wisdom. . . . Man is the most composite of all creatures. . . .Well, as in the old burning of the Temple at Corinth, by the melting and intermixture of silver and gold and other metals a new compound more precious than any, called Corinthian brass, was formed; so in this continent,—asylum of all nations,—the energy of Irish, Germans, Swedes, Poles, and Cossacks, and all the European tribes,—of the Africans, and of the Polynesians,—will construct a new race, a new religion, a new state, a new literature, which will be as vigorous as the new Europe which came out of the smelting-pot of the Dark Ages, or that which earlier emerged from the Pelasgic and Etruscan barbarism. *La Nature aime les croisements.*

Eventually, the melting-pot hypothesis found its way into historical scholarship and interpretation. While many American historians of the late nineteenth century, some fresh from graduate study at German universities, tended to adopt the view that American institutions derived in essence from Anglo-Saxon (and ultimately Teutonic) sources, others were not so sure.[11] One of these was Frederick Jackson Turner, a young historian from Wisconsin, not long emerged from his graduate training at Johns Hopkins. Turner presented a paper to the American Historical Association, meeting in Chicago in 1893. Called "The Significance of the Frontier in American History," this paper proved to be one of the most influential essays in the history of American scholarship, and its point of view, supported by Turner's subsequent writings and his teaching, pervaded the field of American historical interpretation for at least a generation. Turner's thesis was that the dominant influence in the shaping of American institutions and American democracy was not this nation's European heritage in any of its forms, nor the forces emanating from the eastern seaboard cities, but rather the experiences created by a moving and variegated western frontier. Among the many effects attributed to the frontier environment and the challenges it presented was that it acted as a solvent for the national heritages and the separatist tendencies of the many nationality groups which had joined the trek westward, including the Germans and Scotch-Irish of the eighteenth century and the Scandinavians and Germans of the nineteenth. "The frontier," asserted Turner, "promoted the formation of a composite nationality for the American people. . . . In the crucible of the frontier the immigrants were Americanized, liberated, and fused into a mixed race, English in neither nationality nor characteristics. The process has gone on from the early days to our own." And later, in an essay on the role of the Mississippi Valley, he refers to "the tide of foreign immigration which has risen so steadily that it has made a composite American people whose amalgamation is destined to produce a new national stock." [12]

Thus far, the proponents of the melting pot idea had dealt largely with the diversity produced by the sizeable immigration from the countries of northern and western Europe alone—the "old immigration," consisting of peoples with cultures and physical appearance not greatly different from those of the Anglo-Saxon stock. Emerson, it is true, had impartially included Africans, Polynesians, and Cossacks in his conception of the mixture; but it was only in the last two decades of the nineteenth century that a large-scale influx of peoples from the countries of southern and eastern Europe imperatively posed the question of whether these uprooted newcomers who were crowding into the large cities of the nation and the industrial sector of the economy could also be successfully "melted." Would the "urban melting pot" work as well as the "frontier melting pot" of an essentially rural society was alleged to have done?

It remained for an English-Jewish writer with strong social convictions, moved by his observation of the role of the United States as a haven for the poor and oppressed of Europe, to give utterance to the broader view of the American melting pot in a way which attracted public attention. In 1908, Israel Zangwill's drama, *The Melting Pot*, was produced in this country and became a popular success. It is a play dominated by the dream of its protagonist, a young Russian-Jewish immigrant to America, a composer, whose goal is the completion of a vast "American" symphony which will express his deeply felt conception of his adopted country as a divinely appointed crucible in which all the ethnic divisions of mankind will divest themselves of their ancient animosities and differences and become fused into one group, signifying the brotherhood of man. In the process he falls in love with a beautiful and cultured Gentile girl. The play ends with the performance of the symphony and, after numerous vicissitudes and traditional family opposition from both sides, with the approaching marriage of David Quixano and his beloved. During the course of these developments, David, in the rhetoric of the time, delivers himself of such sentiments as these: [13]

America is God's crucible, the great Melting Pot where all the races of Europe are melting and re-forming! Here you stand, good folk, think I, when I see them at Ellis Island, here you stand in your fifty groups, with your fifty languages and histories, and your fifty blood hatreds and rivalries. But you won't be long like that, brothers, for these are the fires of God you've come to—these are the fires of God. A fig for your feuds and vendettas! Germans and Frenchmen, Irishmen and Englishmen, Jews and Russians—into the Crucible with you all! God is making the American.

Here we have a conception of a melting pot which admits of no exceptions or qualifications with regard to the ethnic stocks which will fuse in the great crucible. Englishmen, Germans, Frenchmen, Slavs, Greeks, Syrians, Jews, Gentiles, even the black and yellow races, were specifically mentioned in Zangwill's rhapsodic enumeration. And this pot patently was to boil in the great cities of America.

Thus around the turn of the century the melting-pot idea became embedded in the ideals of the age as one response to the immigrant receiving experience of the nation. Soon to be challenged by a new philosophy of group adjustment (to be discussed below) and always competing with the more pervasive adherence to Anglo-conformity, the melting-pot image, however, continued to draw a portion of the attention consciously directed toward this aspect of the American scene in the first half of the twentieth century. In the mid-1940's a sociologist who had carried out an investigation of intermarriage trends in New Haven, Connecticut, described a revised conception of the melting process in that city and suggested a basic modification of the theory of that process. In New Haven, Ruby Jo Reeves Kennedy [14] reported from a study of intermarriages from 1870 to 1940 that there was a distinct tendency for the British-Americans, Germans, and Scandinavians to marry among themselves—that is, within a Protestant "pool"; for the Irish, Italians, and Poles to marry among themselves—a Catholic "pool"; and for the Jews to marry other Jews. In other words, intermarriage was taking place across lines of nationality background, but there was a strong tendency for it to stay confined within one or the other of the three major religious groups, Protestants, Catholics, and Jews. Thus, declared Mrs. Kennedy, the picture in New Haven resembled a "triple melting pot" based on religious divisions, rather than a "single melting pot." Her study indicated, she stated, that "while strict endogamy is loosening, religious endogamy is persisting and the future cleavages will be along religious lines rather than along nationality lines as in the past. If this is the case, then the traditional 'single-melting-pot' idea must be abandoned, and a new conception, which we term the 'triple-melting-pot' theory of American assimilation, will take its place as the true expression of what is happening to the various nationality groups in the United States." [15] The triple melting-pot thesis was later taken up by the theologian, Will Herberg, and formed an important sociological frame of reference for his analysis of religious trends in American society, *Protestant-Catholic-Jew*.[16] But the triple melting-pot hypothesis patently takes us into the realm of a society pluralistically conceived. We turn now to the rise of an ideology which attempts to justify such a conception.

Cultural Pluralism

Probably all the non-English immigrants who came to American shores in any significant numbers from colonial times onward—settling either in the forbidding wilderness, the lonely prairie, or in some accessible urban slum—created ethnic enclaves and looked forward to the preservation of at least some of their native cultural patterns. Such a development, natural as breathing, was supported by the later accretion of friends, relatives, and countrymen seeking out oases of familiarity in a strange land, by the desire of the settlers to rebuild (necessarily in miniature) a society in which they could communicate in the familiar tongue and maintain familiar institutions, and, finally, by the necessity to band together for mutual aid and mutual protection against the uncertainties of a strange and frequently hostile environment. This was as true of the "old" immigrants as of the "new." In fact, some of the liberal intellectuals who fled to America from an inhospitable political climate in Germany in the 1830's, 1840's, and 1850's looked forward to the creation of an all-German state within the union, or, even more hopefully, to the eventual formation of a separate German nation, as soon as the expected dissolution of the union under the impact of the slavery controversy should have taken place.[17] Oscar Handlin, writing of the sons of Erin in mid-nineteenth-century Boston, recent refugees from famine and economic degradation in their homeland, points out: "Unable to participate in the normal associational affairs of the community, the Irish felt obliged to erect a society within a society, to act together in their own way. In every contact therefore the group, acting apart from other sections of the community, became intensely aware of its peculiar and exclusive identity."[18] Thus cultural pluralism was a fact in American society before it became a theory—a theory with explicit relevance for the nation as a whole, and articulated and discussed in the English-speaking circles of American intellectual life.

Eventually, the cultural enclaves of the Germans (and the later arriving Scandinavians) were to decline in scope and significance as succeeding generations of their native-born attended public schools, left the farms and villages to strike out as individuals for the Americanizing city, and generally became subject to the influences of a standardizing industrial civilization. The German-American community, too, was struck a powerful blow by the accumulated passions generated by World War I—a blow from which it never fully recovered. The Irish were to be the dominant and pervasive element in the gradual emergence of a pan-Catholic group in America, but these developments would reveal themselves only in the twentieth century. In the meantime, in the last two decades of the nineteenth, the influx of immigrants from southern and eastern Europe had begun. These groups were all the more sociologically visible because the closing of the frontier, the occupational demands of an expanding industrial economy, and their own poverty made it inevitable that they would remain in the urban areas of the nation. In the swirling fires of controversy and the steadier flame of experience created by these new events, the ideology of cultural pluralism as a philosophy for the nation was forged.

The first manifestations of an ideological counterattack against draconic Americanization came not from the beleaguered newcomers (who were, after all, more concerned with survival than with theories of adjustment), but from those idealistic members of the middle class who, in the decade or so before the turn of the century, had followed the example of their English predecessors and "settled" in the slums to "learn to sup sorrow with the poor." [19] Immediately, these workers in the "settlement houses" were forced to come to grips with the realities of immigrant life and adjustment. Not all reacted in the same way, but on the whole the settlements developed an approach to the immigrant which was sympathetic to his native cultural heritage and to his newly created ethnic institutions.[20] For one thing, their workers, necessarily in intimate contact with the lives of these often pathetic and bewildered newcomers and their daily problems, could see how unfortunate were the effects of those forces which impelled rapid Americanization in their impact on the immigrants' children, who not infrequently became alienated from their parents and the restraining influence of family authority. Were not their parents ignorant and uneducated "Hunkies," "Sheenies," or "Dagoes," as that limited portion of the American environment in which they moved defined the matter? Ethnic "self-hatred" with its debilitating psychological consequences, family disorganization and juvenile delinquency, were not unusual results of this state of affairs. Furthermore, the immigrants themselves were adversely affected by the incessant attacks on their culture, their language, their institutions, their very conception of themselves. How were they to maintain their self-respect when all that they knew, felt, and dreamed, beyond their sheer capacity for manual labor—in other words, all that they *were*—was despised or scoffed at in America? And—unkindest cut of all—their own children had begun to adopt the contemptuous attitude of the "Americans." Jane Addams relates in a moving chapter of her *Twenty Years at Hull House* how, after coming to have some conception of the extent and depth of these problems, she created at the settlement a "Labor Museum," in which the immigrant women of the various nationalities crowded together in the slums of Chicago could illustrate their native methods of spinning and weaving, and in which the relation of these earlier techniques to contemporary factory methods could be graphically shown. For the first time these peasant women were made to feel by some part of their American environment that they possessed valuable and interesting skills—that they too had something to offer—and for the first time, the daughters of these women who, after a long day's work at their dank "needletrade" sweatshops, came to Hull House to observe, began to appreciate the fact that their mothers, too, had a "culture," that this culture possessed its own merit, and that it was related to their own contemporary lives. How aptly Jane Addams concludes her chapter with the hope that "our American citizenship might be built without disturbing these foundations which were laid of old time." [21]

This appreciative view of the immigrant's cultural heritage and of its distinctive usefulness both to himself and his adopted country received additional sustenance from another source: those intellectual currents of the day which, however overborne by their currently more powerful opposites, emphasized liberalism, internationalism, and tolerance. From time to time, an occasional educator or publicist protested the demands of the "Americanizers," arguing that the immigrant, too, had an ancient and honorable culture, and that this culture had much to offer an America whose character and destiny were still in the process of formation, an America which must serve as an example of the harmonious

cooperation of various heritages to a world inflamed by nationalism and war. In 1916 John Dewey, Norman Hapgood, and the
young literary critic, Randolph Bourne, published articles or ad-
dresses elaborating various aspects of this theme.

The classic statement of the cultural pluralist position, however,
had been made over a year before. Early in 1915 there appeared in
the pages of *The Nation* two articles under the title "Democracy
versus the Melting-Pot." Their author was Horace Kallen, a Har-
vard-educated philosopher with a concern for the application of
philosophy to societal affairs, and, as an American Jew, himself
derivative of an ethnic background which was subject to the
contemporary pressures for dissolution implicit in the "Americanization," or Anglo-conformity, and the melting-pot theories. In
these articles Kallen vigorously rejected the usefulness of these
theories as models of what was actually transpiring in American
life or as ideals for the future. Rather he was impressed by the way
in which the various ethnic groups in America were coincident
with particular areas and regions, and with the tendency for each
group to preserve its own language, religion, communal institutions, and ancestral culture. All the while, he pointed out, the
immigrant has been learning to speak English as the language of
general communication, and has participated in the over-all economic and political life of the nation. These developments in
which "the United States are in the process of becoming a federal
state not merely as a union of geographical and administrative
unities, but also as a cooperation of cultural diversities, as a
federation or commonwealth of national cultures," [22] the author
argued, far from constituting a violation of historic American
political principles, as the "Americanizers" claimed, actually represented the inevitable consequences of democratic ideals, since
individuals are implicated in groups, and since democracy for the
individual must by extension also mean democracy for his group.

The processes just described, however, as Kallen develops his
argument, are far from having been thoroughly realized. They are
menaced by "Americanization" programs, assumptions of Anglo-
Saxon superiority, and misguided attempts to promote "racial"
amalgamation. Thus America stands at a kind of cultural crossroads. It can attempt to impose by force an artificial, Anglo-Saxon
oriented uniformity on its peoples, or it can consciously allow and
encourage its ethnic groups to develop democratically, each em-

phasizing its particular cultural heritage. If the latter course is followed, as Kallen puts it at the close of his essay, then,[23]

The outlines of a possible great and truly democratic commonwealth become discernible. Its form would be that of the federal republic; its substance a democracy of nationalities, cooperating voluntarily and autonomously through common institutions in the enterprise of self-realization through the perfection of men according to their kind. The common language of the commonwealth, the language of its great tradition, would be English, but each nationality would have for its emotional and involuntary life its own peculiar dialect or speech, its own individual and inevitable esthetic and intellectual forms. The political and economic life of the commonwealth is a single unit and serves as the foundation and background for the realization of the distinctive individuality of each *natio* that composes it and of the pooling of these in a harmony above them all. Thus "American civilization" may come to mean the perfection of the cooperative harmonies of "European civilization"—the waste, the squalor and the distress of Europe being eliminated—a multiplicity in a unity, an orchestration of mankind.

Within the next decade Kallen published more essays dealing with the theme of American multiple-group life, later collected in a volume.[24] In the introductory note to this book he used for the first time the term "cultural pluralism" to refer to his position. These essays reflect both his increasingly sharp rejection of the onslaughts on the immigrant and his culture which the coming of World War I and its attendant fears, the "Red scare," the projection of themes of racial superiority, the continued exploitation of the newcomers, and the rise of the Ku Klux Klan all served to increase in intensity, and also his emphasis on cultural pluralism as the democratic antidote to these ills. He has since published other essays elaborating or annotating the theme of cultural pluralism. Thus, for at least forty-five years, most of them spent teaching at the New School for Social Research, Kallen has been acknowledged as the originator and leading philosophical exponent of the idea of cultural pluralism.

In the late 1930's and early 1940's the late Louis Adamic, the Yugoslav immigrant who had become an American writer, took up the theme of America's multicultural heritage and the role of these groups in forging the country's national character. Borrowing Walt Whitman's phrase, he described America as "a nation of nations," and while his ultimate goal was closer to the melting-pot idea than to cultural pluralism, he saw the immediate task as that of making America conscious of what it owed to all its ethnic groups, not just to the Anglo-Saxons. The children and grandchildren of immigrants of non-English origins, he was convinced, must be taught to be proud of the cultural heritage of their ancestral ethnic group and of its role in building the American nation; otherwise, they would not lose their sense of ethnic inferiority and the feeling of rootlessness he claimed to find in them.

Thus in the twentieth century, particularly since World War II, "cultural pluralism" has become a concept which has worked its way into the vocabulary and imagery of specialists in intergroup relations and leaders of ethnic communal groups. In view of this new pluralistic emphasis, some writers now prefer to speak of the "integration" of immigrants rather than of their "assimilation." [25] However, with a few exceptions,[26] no close analytical attention has been given either by social scientists or practitioners of intergroup relations to the meaning of cultural pluralism, its nature and relevance for a modern industrialized society, and its implications for problems of prejudice and discrimination—a point to which we referred at the outset of this discussion.

Conclusions

In the remaining pages I can make only a few analytical comments which I shall apply in context to the American scene, historical and current. My view of the American situation will not be documented here, but may be considered as a series of hypotheses in which I shall attempt to outline the American assimilation process.

First of all, it must be realized that "assimilation" is a blanket term which in reality covers a multitude of subprocesses. The most crucial distinction is one often ignored—the distinction between what I have elsewhere called "behavioral assimilation" and "structural assimilation." [27] The first refers to the absorption of the cultural behavior patterns of the "host" society. (At the same time, there is frequently some modification of the cultural patterns of the immigrant-receiving country, as well.) There is a special term for this process of cultural modification or "behavioral assimilation"—namely, "acculturation." "Structural assimilation," on the other hand, refers to the entrance of the immigrants and their descendants into the social cliques, organizations, institutional activities, and general civic life of the receiving society. If this process takes place on a large enough scale, then a high frequency of intermarriage must result. A further distinction must be made between, on the one hand, those activities of the general civic life which involve earning a living, carrying out political responsibilities, and engaging in the instrumental affairs of the larger community, and, on the other hand, activities which create personal friendship patterns, frequent home intervisiting, communal worship, and communal recreation. The first type usually develops so-called "secondary relationships," which tend to be relatively impersonal and segmental; the latter type leads to "primary relationships," which are warm, intimate, and personal. With these various distinctions in mind, we may then proceed.

Built on the base of the original immigrant "colony" but frequently extending into the life of successive generations, the characteristic ethnic group experience is this: within the ethnic group there develops a network of organizations and informal social relationships which permits and encourages the members of the ethnic group to remain within the confines of the group for all of their primary relationships and some of their secondary relationships throughout all the stages of the life cycle. From the cradle in the sectarian hospital to the child's play group, the social clique in high school, the fraternity and religious center in college, the dating group within which he searches for a spouse, the marriage partner, the neighborhood of his residence, the church affiliation and the church clubs, the men's and the women's social and service organizations, the adult clique of "marrieds," the vacation resort, and then, as the age cycle nears completion, the rest home for the elderly and, finally, the sectarian cemetery—in all these activities and relationships which are close to the core of personality and selfhood—the member of the ethnic group may if he wishes follow a path which never takes him across the boundaries of his ethnic structural network.

The picture is made more complex by the existence of social class divisions which cut across ethnic group lines just as they do those of the white Protestant population in America. As each ethnic group which has been here for the requisite time has developed second, third, or in some cases, succeeding generations, it has produced a college-educated group which composes an upper middle class (and sometimes upper class, as well) segment of the larger groups. Such class divisions tend to restrict primary group relations even further, for although the ethnic-group member feels a general sense of identification with all the bearers of his ethnic heritage, he feels comfortable in intimate social relations only with those who also share his own class background or attainment.

In short, my point is that, while *behavioral assimilation* or acculturation has taken place in America to a considerable degree, *structural assimilation*, with some important exceptions has not been extensive.[28] The exceptions are of two types. The first brings us back to the "triple melting pot" thesis of Ruby Jo Reeves Kennedy and Will Herberg. The "nationality" ethnic groups have tended to merge within each of the three major religious groups. This has been particularly true of the Protestant and Jewish communities. Those descendants of the "old" immigration of the nineteenth century, who were Protestant (many of the Germans and all the Scandinavians), have in considerable part gradually merged into the white Protestant "subsociety." Jews of Sephardic, German, and Eastern-European origins have similarly tended to come together in their communal life. The process of absorbing the various Catholic nationalities, such as the Italians, Poles, and French Canadians, into an American Catholic community hitherto dominated by the Irish has begun, although I do not believe that it is by any means close to completion. Racial and quasi-racial groups such as the Negroes, Indians, Mexican-Americans, and Puerto Ricans still retain their separate sociological structures. The outcome of all this in contemporary American life is thus pluralism—but it is more than "triple" and it is more accurately described as *structural pluralism* than as cultural pluralism, although some of the latter also remains.

My second exception refers to the social structures which implicate intellectuals. There is no space to develop the issue here, but I would argue that there is a social world or subsociety of the intellectuals in America in which true structural intermixture among persons of various ethnic backgrounds, including the religious, has markedly taken place.

My final point deals with the reasons for these developments. If structural assimilation has been retarded in America by religious and racial lines, we must ask why. The answer lies in the attitudes of both the majority and the minority groups and in the way these attitudes have interacted. A saying of the current day is, "It takes two to tango." To apply the analogy, there is no good reason to believe that white Protestant America has ever extended a firm and cordial invitation to its minorities to dance. Furthermore, the attitudes of the minority-group members themselves on the matter have been divided and ambiguous. Particularly for the minority religious groups, there is a certain logic in ethnic communality, since there is a commitment to the perpetuation of the religious ideology and since structural intermixture leads to intermarriage and the possible loss to the group of the intermarried family. Let us, then, examine the situation serially for various types of minorities.

With regard to the immigrant, in his characteristic numbers and socioeconomic background, structural assimilation was out of the question. He did not want it, and he had a positive need for the comfort of his own communal institutions. The native American, moreover, whatever the implications of his public pronouncements, had no intention of opening up his primary group life to entrance by these hordes of alien newcomers. The situation was a functionally complementary standoff.

The second generation found a much more complex situation. Many believed they heard the siren call of welcome to the social cliques, clubs, and institutions of white Protestant America. After all, it was simply a matter of learning American ways, was it not? Had they not grown up as Americans, and were they not culturally different from their parents, the "greenhorns?" Or perhaps an especially eager one reasoned (like the Jewish protagonist of Myron Kaufmann's novel, *Remember Me To God*, aspiring to membership in the prestigious club system of Harvard undergraduate social life) "If only I can go the last few steps in Ivy League manners and behavior, they will surely recognize that I am one of them and take me in." But, alas, Brooks Brothers suit notwithstanding, the doors of the fraternity house, the city men's club, and the country club were slammed in the face of the immigrant's offspring. That invitation was not really there in the first place; or, to the extent it was, in Joshua Fishman's phrase, it was a " 'look me over but don't touch me' invitation to the American minority group child." [29] And so the rebuffed one returned to the homelier but dependable comfort of the communal institutions of his ancestral group. There he found his fellows of the same generation who had never stirred from the home fires. Some of these had been too timid to stray; others were ethnic ideologists committed to the group's survival; still others had never really believed in the authenticity of the siren call or were simply too passive to do more than go along the familiar way. All could now join in the task that was well within the realm of the sociologically possible—the build-up of social institutions and organizations within the ethnic enclave, manned increasingly by members of the second generation and suitably separated by social class.

Those who had for a time ventured out gingerly or confidently, as the case might be, had been lured by the vision of an "American" social structure that was somehow larger than all subgroups and was ethnically neutral. Were they, too, not Americans? But they found to their dismay that at the primary group level a neutral American social structure was a mirage. What at a distance seemed to be a quasi-public edifice flying only the all-inclusive flag of American nationality turned out on closer inspection to be the clubhouse of a particular ethnic group—the white Anglo-Saxon Protestants, its operation shot through with the premises and expectations of its parental ethnicity. In these terms, the desirability of whatever invitation was grudgingly extended to those of other ethnic backgrounds could only become a considerably attenuated one.

With the racial minorities, there was not even the pretense of an invitation. Negroes, to take the most salient example, have for the most part been determinedly barred from the cliques, social clubs, and churches of white America. Consequently, with due allowance for internal class differences, they have constructed their own network of organizations and institutions, their own "social world." There are now many vested interests served by the preservation of this separate communal life, and doubtless many Negroes are psychologically comfortable in it, even though at the same time they keenly desire that discrimination in such areas as employment, education, housing, and public accommodations be eliminated. However, the ideological attachment of Negroes to their communal separation is not conspicuous. Their sense of identification with ancestral African national cultures is virtually nonexistent, although Pan-Africanism engages the interest of some intellectuals and although "black nationalist" and "black racist" fringe groups have recently made an appearance at the other end of the communal spectrum. As for their religion, they are either Protestant or Catholic (overwhelmingly the former). Thus, there are no "logical" ideological reasons for their separate communality; dual social structures are created solely by the dynamics of prejudice and discrimination, rather than being reinforced by the ideological commitments of the minority itself.

Structural assimilation, then, has turned out to be the rock on which the ships of Anglo-conformity and the melting pot have foundered. To understand that behavioral assimilation (or acculturation) without massive structural intermingling in primary relationships has been the dominant motif in the American experience of creating and developing a nation out of diverse peoples is to comprehend the most essential sociological fact of that experience. It is against the background of "structural pluralism" that strategies of strengthening intergroup harmony, reducing ethnic discrimination and prejudice, and maintaining the rights of both those who stay within and those who venture beyond their ethnic boundaries must be thoughtfully devised.

Notes ►

1. Allan Nevins and Henry Steele Commager, *America: The Story of a Free People* (Boston, Little, Brown, 1942), p. 58.

2. The phrase is the Coles's. See Stewart G. Cole and Mildred Wiese Cole, *Minorities and the American Promise* (New York, Harper & Brothers, 1954), ch. 6.

3. Maurice R. Davie, *World Immigration* (New York, Macmillan, 1936), p. 36, and (cited therein) "Letter of Benjamin Franklin to Peter Collinson, 9th May, 1753, on the condition and character of the Germans in Pennsylvania," in *The Works of Benjamin Franklin, with notes and a life of the author,* by Jared Sparks (Boston, 1828), vol. 7, pp. 71–73.

4. *The Writings of George Washington,* collected and edited by W. C. Ford (New York, G. P. Putnam's Sons, 1889), vol. 12, p. 489.

5. Thomas Jefferson, "Notes on Virginia, Query 8," in *The Writings of Thomas Jefferson,* ed. A. E. Bergh (Washington, The Thomas Jefferson Memorial Association, 1907), vol. 2, p. 121.

6. *Niles' Weekly Register,* vol. 18, 29 April 1820, pp. 157–158; also, Marcus L. Hansen, *The Atlantic Migration, 1607–1860,* pp. 96–97.

7. Ellwood P. Cubberly, *Changing Conceptions of Education* (Boston, Houghton Mifflin, 1909), pp. 15–16.

8. J. Hector St. John Crèvecoeur, *Letters from an American*

Farmer (New York, Albert and Charles Boni, 1925; reprinted from the 1st ed., London, 1782), pp. 54–55.

9. Oscar Handlin, ed., *Immigration as a Factor in American History* (Englewood, Prentice-Hall, 1959), p. 146.

10. Quoted by Stuart P. Sherman in his Introduction to *Essays and Poems of Emerson* (New York, Harcourt Brace, 1921), p. xxxiv.

11. See Edward N. Saveth, *American Historians and European Immigrants, 1875–1925* (New York, Columbia University Press, 1948).

12. Frederick Jackson Turner, *The Frontier in American History* (New York, Henry Holt, 1920), pp. 22–23, 190.

13. Israel Zangwill, *The Melting Pot* (New York, Macmillan, 1909), p. 37.

14. Ruby Jo Reeves Kennedy, "Single or Triple Melting-Pot? Intermarriage Trends in New Haven, 1870–1940," *American Journal of Sociology*, 1944, 49: 331–339. See also her "Single or Triple Melting-Pot? Intermarriage in New Haven, 1870–1950," *ibid.*, 1952, 58: 56–59.

15. ———— "Single or Triple Melting-Pot? . . . 1870–1940," p. 332 (author's italics omitted).

16. Will Herberg, *Protestant-Catholic-Jew* (Garden City, Doubleday, 1955).

17. Nathan Glazer, "Ethnic Groups in America: From National Culture to Ideology," in Morroe Berger, Theodore Abel, and Charles H. Page, eds., *Freedom and Control in Modern Society* (New York, D. Van Nostrand, 1954), p. 161; Marcus Lee Hansen, *The Immigrant in American History* (Cambridge, Harvard University Press, 1940), pp. 129–140; John A. Hawgood, *The Tragedy of German-America* (New York, Putnam's, 1940), *passim*.

18. Oscar Handlin, *Boston's Immigrants* (Cambridge, Harvard University Press, 1959, rev. ed.), p. 176.

19. From a letter (1883) by Samuel A. Barnett; quoted in Arthur C. Holden, *The Settlement Idea* (New York, Macmillan, 1922), p. 12.

20. Jane Addams, *Twenty Years at Hull House* (New York, Macmillan, 1914), pp. 231–258; Arthur C. Holden, *op. cit.*, pp. 109–131, 182–189; John Higham, *Strangers in the Land* (New Brunswick, Rutgers University Press, 1955), p. 236.

21. Jane Addams, *op. cit.*, p. 258.

22. Horace M. Kallen, "Democracy *versus* the Melting-Pot," *The Nation*, 18 and 25 February 1915; reprinted in his *Culture and Democracy in the United States* (New York, Boni and Liveright, 1924); the quotation is on p. 116.

23. Kallen, *Culture and Democracy. . . .*, p. 124.

24. *Op. cit.*

25. See W. D. Borrie *et al.*, *The Cultural Integration of Immigrants* (a survey based on the papers and proceedings of the UNESCO Conference in Havana, April 1956), Paris, UNESCO, 1959; and William S. Bernard, "The Integration of Immigrants in the United States" (mimeographed), one of the papers for this conference.

26. See particularly Milton M. Gordon, "Social Structure and Goals in Group Relations"; and Nathan Glazer, "Ethnic Groups in America; From National Culture to Ideology," both articles in Berger, Abel, and Page, *op. cit.*; S. N. Eisenstadt, *The Absorption of Immigrants* (London, Routledge and Kegan Paul, 1954); and W. D. Borrie *et al.*, *op. cit.*

27. Milton M. Gordon, "Social Structure and Goals in Group Relations," p. 151.

28. See Erich Rosenthal, "Acculturation without Assimilation?" *American Journal of Sociology*, 1960, 66: 275–288.

29. Joshua A. Fishman, "Childhood Indoctrination for Minority-Group Membership and the Quest for Minority-Group Biculturism in America," in Oscar Handlin, ed., *Group Life in America* (Cambridge, Harvard University Press, forthcoming).

29 ► INTERMARRIAGE AND THE JEWISH FUTURE

MARSHALL SKLARE

Intermarriage obviously is inextricably and functionally related to assimilation, both in terms of promoting it and at the same time being a result of it. Among dominant ethnic groups, such as the Southern white Anglo-Saxon Protestants, there is fear of racial intermarriage; whereas among ethnic minorities, no group demonstrates so much anxiety about the threat of intermarriage to its values of homogeneity, identity and survival as do the Jews. In the following article, Dr. Marshall Sklare, research director of the American Jewish Committee, discusses the implications of recent studies of intermarriage for the survival of the Jews as a group.

► AMERICAN JEWS have always had a reputation for resisting intermarriage, and they still serve as a model in this respect for other ethnic and religious groups who worry about their future in a pluralist society. Just as the Jewish alcoholic or juvenile delinquent is thought to be a rare exception, so the Jewish son who brings home a Gentile bride is generally considered a sport. Within the Jewish community itself, the danger of intermarriage is always felt to be there, of course, but the prevailing attitude—even among those who are knowledgeable about Jewish matters or professionally concerned with Jewish welfare—is that the threat of the problem has been surprisingly well contained in America.

One result of this complacency is that the Jewish agencies have

Reprinted from *Commentary*, 37, 4 (April, 1964), 46–52, by permission of the author and publisher. Copyright © 1964 by the American Jewish Committee.

sponsored or conducted practically no research in the area of intermarriage. Social planning agencies have extensively investigated other community problems as a matter of course—the needs of the aged, the convalescent, the refugee, the maladjusted family, etc.—and the defense agencies have examined anti-Semitism from diverse angles, ranging from studies of the personality of the active bigot to investigations of attitudes toward Jews in rural counties where there are no Jews, merely "images" of them. By contrast, what little hard data we have on the subject of intermarriage comes mainly from the work of independent scholars (often as a by-product of broader projects), and not from the research facilities of the official community.

This surprising lack of interest in a matter more crucial to Jewish survival than any other is not, of course, wholly the product of faith in intuition or of wishful thinking. Actually, the small measure of relevant research that was done in the past has tended to reinforce complacency. The earliest study of intermarriage was Julius Drachsler's *Democracy and Assimilation,* which received a good deal of attention at the time of its publication in 1920. On the basis of an examination of about 100,000 marriage licenses issued in New York City between 1908 and 1912, Drachsler found that of all white groups in the city, the Jews were least prone to marry outsiders. The Jewish intermarriage rate of 1.17 per cent was scarcely higher than that of interracial marriages among Negroes, and Drachsler bracketed the two together as a "low-ratio group," as opposed to the "middle-ratio" groups (Italians and Irish) and the "high-ratio" groups (English, Germans, Swedes, and others).

A second investigation that was influential in confirming the Jewish reputation for endogamy was conducted in New Haven by Ruby Jo Reeves Kennedy. Published in the *American Journal of Sociology* in 1944 (a follow-up article appeared in 1952), the Kennedy study was to reach a wide audience through Will Herberg's extensive use of it in *Protestant-Catholic-Jew.* Kennedy's conclusions were in close keeping with those of Drachsler. She found that for all the years investigated—1870, 1900, 1930, and 1940—Jews had the lowest intermarriage rate in the city. The Italians were the only ethnic group which approached them in endogamy, and even their rate of intermarriage was several times higher.

All this must have seemed impressive evidence to the leaders of the Jewish community, just as it did—and does—to the scholars themselves. For example, the most recent sociological investigation of American-Jewish life, C. B. Sherman's *The Jew within American Society*, continues to take a highly optimistic view of the intermarriage problem. Comparing newer statistics with those collected by Drachsler, Sherman remarks that "considering the degree of acculturation to which the Jewish community has attained during the period, the surprise is not that the increase has been so big, but that it has been so small." Much the same point is made by Nathan Glazer and Daniel P. Moynihan in *Beyond the Melting Pot*. Commenting on the Kennedy study, the authors note that the persisting pattern of endogamy sharply distinguishes the Jews of the United States from those of other countries in which Jews have achieved wealth and social position, such as Holland, Germany, Austria, and Hungary in the twenties. There the intermarriage rates were phenomenally high." [1]

But even more influential, perhaps, than the Drachsler and Kennedy studies in establishing the Jewish reputation for continued endogamy was a report by the Bureau of the Census based on its Current Population Survey of March 1957 (the only such survey to include a question on religion). In its sample of 35,000 households, the Bureau found that only 7.2 per cent of the husbands or wives of Jews were of a different faith. The comparable figure for Protestants was 8.6 per cent, and for Catholics it was 21.6 per cent.

These statistics gave many people within the Jewish community reason to believe that the Jews were still doing quite well: after all, the Catholics, who had made a much more conscious effort than Jews to foster separatism, were faced with an intermarriage rate that was almost three times as high. Moreover, the Jewish rate was all the more heartening in view of the absolute size of the group and the insignificant percentage it comprised of the population as a whole. In his annual review of demographic data in the 1959 *American Jewish Year Book*, Alvin Chenkin, statistician for the Council of Jewish Federations and Welfare Funds, described 7.2 as a "nominal" percentage; if marital selection had taken place entirely at random, Chenkin pointed out, the Jewish intermarriage rate would have approached 98 per cent.

Since the 7.2 figure has become the most widely quoted statistic in recent discussions of intermarriage and currently provides the main source of reassurance in the Jewish community, it is worth taking a closer look at what it actually means. Quite apart from whether comparisons in this area between majority and minority groups are valid at all (a case could be made that they are not), there remains the fact that almost everyone who has cited the figure has failed to heed the Bureau's *caveat* that its statistics on intermarriage were probably subject to a larger margin of error than would result from normal sampling variation. (In an unusual aside, the Bureau noted that while it had told its personnel not to assume the same religion for all members of a given family and directed them to ask about each adult member of a household separately, some interviewers might have overlooked this instruction.)

Other implications of the 7.2 per cent figure have also been ignored. No one has bothered to relate it, for instance, to the well-known fact that considerably more Jewish men intermarry than do Jewish women (at least seven out of every ten Jews who intermarry are men), so that as a consequence some Jewish women must either marry Gentiles or remain single. Spinsterhood does not, to be sure, affect the intermarriage rate, but it does influence another crucial demographic factor: the birth-rate. Nor is this the only indirect consequence of intermarriage. For example, all other things being equal, the smaller the size of any group, the higher will be its rate of intermarriage; or to put it the other way around, the higher the proportion of the minority to the total population, the smaller will be the impact of "randomization" upon it. Thus, since the general population in the United States is growing, the Jewish population must also grow in order to escape further attrition by randomization. Should the size of the Jewish population only remain constant, the group's intermarriage rate would inevitably rise.

However, the most crucial point which has been generally overlooked in evaluating the 7.2 figure is that it represented the *ratio* of intermarried to inmarried couples and not the *current* rate of intermarriage among Jews. The statistic, in other words, was cumulative—included were people who had taken their vows in Czarist Russia where intermarriage was forbidden, as well as people who had married in the United States; people belonging to the virtually closed community of the immigrant generation, as well as people living in the wide world of the fourth generation. The *current* rate, then, may well be at least double that of the Bureau's cumulative ratio. And even the cumulative ratio is bound to soar in the decades ahead with the thinning-out of the ranks of those who are presently keeping it down—first- and second-generation Jews.

In short, the grounds for the American Jewish community's optimism are by no means as firm as they have been assumed to be by laymen and sociologists alike. Interestingly enough, the present state of Jewish endogamy seems to have been grasped more firmly by the novelists than by the sociologists. Even a hasty run-down of the work of such writers as Bernard Malamud, Saul Bellow, Philip Roth, Leslie Fiedler, Bruce Jay Friedman, Herbert Gold, Jack Ludwig, Myron Kaufmann, Neal Oxenhandler, etc., reveals how much recent American fiction has dealt with marriage or the strong possibility of it between a Jew and a Gentile. That the stance taken toward the question, moreover, is usually not in the least militant or didactic is significant evidence that among those who might be expected to be in closest touch with the climate of the times, the high incidence of intermarriage is no longer a matter of controversy.

Within the organized Jewish community itself, the publication last year in the *American Jewish Year Book* of Erich Rosenthal's article "Studies of Jewish Intermarriage in the United States," is one of the first signs that this community may at last be preparing to recognize that a problem does exist.[2] (In the sixty-three previous volumes of the *Year Book*, the subject was dealt with only once—in a brief two pages.)

In his pioneering study, Rosenthal provides a sophisticated analysis of statistical data concerning intermarriage in the state of Iowa and in the city of Washington, D.C. According to Rosenthal's findings, during the years 1953–59, only 57.8 per cent of the marriage licenses applied for by Jews in Iowa *listed both applicants* as Jewish. (Iowa and Indiana are the two jurisdictions in the United States where the marriage-license form includes a query on religion.) Religion, then, still plays a role in the marital choices of Iowa Jews—42.2 per cent, after all, represents a far smaller intermarriage rate than would be produced by randomization. Nevertheless, as Rosenthal suggests, unless the figure drops sharply in the future, the final chapter in the history of Iowa's Jewish community will have been reached by the end of this century.

Of course, the current situation in Des Moines, Davenport, and other Iowa communities is not an accurate reflection of what is happening in the major cities and their suburbs, where the great majority of American Jews still live. But at the very least this section of Rosenthal's study does point up the fact that the problem is most critical where the Jewish population is small both in absolute and relative terms. Moreover, in the other section of his study, Rosenthal reminds us that even in a middle-sized Jewish community like that of Washington, D.C. (with 81,000 members it ranks as the seventh largest Jewish community in the nation), the cumulative ratio is now almost twice the Census Bureau's figure. And since a significant segment of the Jewish population resides in communities of this size, the problem of Jewish survival there cannot be shrugged off as one might be tempted to do with the problem in Iowa.

Rosenthal utilizes a 1956 survey of Washington's Jewish population which was unusually resourceful in locating the unaffiliated Jew. Although the issue of intermarriage was of secondary interest in the design of the study, it was found that in 13.1 per cent of the households including a married Jew, either the husband or wife was Gentile. This percentage is probably somewhat higher than the average for middle-sized Jewish communities—Washington's Jews not being known for the intensity of their Jewish commitment. But that does not really modify the import of the figure, particularly since there is reason to believe that the current rate of intermarriage in Washington substantially exceeds 13.1 per cent. Rosenthal himself does not offer a current rate, but he does provide tabulations on the rate for successive generations: 1.4 per cent for the first generation; 10.2 per cent for the second; and 17.9 per cent for the third. Since it can be assumed that the great majority of Washington's Jews who are marrying in 1964 belong to the third generation, the 17.9 figure is probably very close to the current rate.

Besides offering a sharp corrective to Jewish complacency about the rate of intermarriage today, these statistics provide an occasion for calling into question a good many dated notions about the psychological and social conditions under which intermarriage now takes place. One traditional view, for example, holds that the Jew who marries a Gentile often does so to escape the social disabilities of being Jewish (the prototype here is someone like August Belmont). Though this motive was no doubt decisive in the marital choices of a fair number of mobile, *nouveaux-riches*, or socially ambitious Jews of an earlier period, it seems to have much less force in the present age when many traditional status distinctions are being swept away and the old-time social arbiters are becoming increasingly ineffective. And as the hospital boards, country clubs, suburbs, and corporations that were once the exclusive preserve of the Protestant upper class become more democratic in their admission policies, we can expect that this reason for intermarriage will become even less significant. One can already observe from Rosenthal's data on Iowa that social-climbing is probably not an important element in intermarriage in that state. Lutherans, Methodists, and Presbyterians comprise the three largest Protestant denominations in Iowa, in that order, and in the marriages contracted between Jewish men and Protestant women these three denominations rank in the same order; furthermore, Iowa Jews marry into the plainspun society of the Baptists about as frequently as they do into the prestigious milieu of the Episcopalians. Such inferences are, of course, less than precise, but it seems clear that if social climbing were a leading cause of intermarriage, Jewish men in Iowa would ignore many of the girls they choose to marry.

Along with the habit of interpreting intermarriage as a form of status-seeking, there is still a tendency to view it as a form of escape from the burdens of Jewishness and the harassments of anti-Semitism—as, in short, the most effective method of assimilation. This explanation, too, undoubtedly had some relevance at an earlier period in American Jewish history (though never nearly as much as it did among European Jewry), but it is increasingly beside the point at a time when the penalties and risks of being Jewish are obviously on the wane. Indeed, if intermarriage were a response to the threat of anti-Semitism, particularly in a state as remote from the scenes and memories of Jewish persecution as Iowa is, there should currently be less, rather than more, of it.

Other standard explanations of intermarriage take psychological rather than social factors as the governing ones, finding the source of the impulse to intermarriage not in the confrontation of the Jew with Gentile society, but in the early relationship between parent and child. Serious conflicts at this stage—so the notion goes —will be expressed later on in the attempt by the child to avoid a marital pattern similar to that of his parents. In its more simplistic form, this theory holds that marriage to an outsider is a gesture of hostility toward the parents, the point being to rob them of the pleasure they would obtain from a "suitable" match, shame them before relatives and friends, and deprive them finally of the consolation of Jewish grandchildren. The more complex form of the same theory regards intermarriage as part of a syndrome of general revolt from the mores and aspirations of the parents, often manifesting itself in bohemianism, political radicalism, or other types of identification with socially alienated and/or dissident groups.

But were this theory particularly pertinent, one would expect Jewish-Gentile marriages to be most prevalent in the second generation, where the trauma of acculturation was most decisively experienced and the generational conflict was at its most intense. However, intermarriage rates, as we have already noted, are clearly higher in the third generation; and in addition, as we shall soon see, Jewish-Gentile marriages are particularly prevalent among certain Jewish groups who are very much at home in the culture.

At best, the existence of a correlation between childhood conflicts and marital choices is easier to assume than it is to demonstrate. In analyzing the data on intermarriage contained in the recent "Midtown Manhattan Study" [3] the sociologist Jerold Heiss began with the standard idea that those whose early family life showed marked signs of disruption or had otherwise been unsatisfactory would be more likely to intermarry than those with relatively stable childhoods. But he discovered that this idea could not be sustained. The family backgrounds of the exogamous Jews in the study were not exceptional in terms of conflict, and actually showed fewer cases of parental divorce, separation, and desertion than did the backgrounds of the endogamous Jews surveyed.

In attempting to revise traditional perspectives on the causes of intermarriage, one is even more hampered by the scarcity of research that has been done into the sociological and psychological aspects of the problem than in trying to determine the current rate of intermarriage. The few studies and essays allowing one to draw certain limited inferences about the personal motives and social context that foster exogamy happen to involve professional groups —mainly in the academy—which are marginal to the community life of American Jewry. Therefore, one cannot regard these findings as telling us anything definitive about the "typical" behavior of American Jews who choose to marry outside the faith. On the other hand, there is good reason not to discount them altogether, since most of the people concerned are Jews who grew up in metropolitan Jewish communities, who lead fairly conventional lives, and who practice highly respected professions. It should also be borne in mind that as writers, teachers, scientists, psychoanalysts, and so forth, they serve as models to their younger contemporaries who in increasing numbers are forsaking the Jewish business and community ties of their parents' generation and seeking careers in the professions. Thus, the influence of, say, the exogamous college teacher in legitimizing intermarriage can far outweigh the fact that his importance is statistically very small in relation to the total Jewish population.

According to a recent study conducted by Rabbi Henry Cohen, approximately 20 per cent of the Jewish faculty members at the University of Illinois—well over twice the national average—are married to Gentile women. This is a significant figure because Illinois has a reputation for academic and social conservatism, being neither particularly adventurous in its curriculum nor particularly "highbrow" in its faculty. We can therefore assume that the pattern here is more typical than it would be at experimental colleges like Antioch or Reed, or fashionable universities like Yale or Chicago. There is also a comparatively large Jewish student body on the Illinois campus; in contrast to a college such as Swarthmore, for example—which has been described as an "intermarriage mill"—the University of Illinois is a favorite choice of Midwestern parents eager to avoid this peril. (In fact, it was on the Illinois campus that America's first Hillel Foundation was established some forty years ago.)

The Jewish population of Champaign-Urbana numbers about 250 families, which are almost equally divided between town and gown. One of Rabbi Cohen's most suggestive findings on intermarriage was the unexpected disparity between the 20 per cent ratio for the faculty members and a 6.5 per cent ratio for the Jewish townspeople. The contrast between town and gown is even more striking in view of the respective family backgrounds of both groups, which, if anything, would have led one to expect their respective intermarriage rates to be reversed. Most of the Jewish faculty members (chiefly mathematicians, physicists, psychologists, and sociologists) arrived in Champaign-Urbana during the last few years; they are mainly sons of East European immigrants and grew up in predominantly Jewish neighborhoods; almost all described their parents as affiliated with either Orthodox or Conservative synagogues. The townspeople, on the other hand—chiefly manufacturers, wholesalers, retailers, and professionals—include a group descended from "old" German-Jewish families who are firmly rooted in the community and whose predominant background is Reform.

What lies behind the disparity in the intermarriage rates of these two groups? Rabbi Cohen points out that many of the Jewish teachers and researchers at the University of Illinois (and presumably the overwhelming majority of the intermarried couples) hold to a point of view—"Academic Commitment" he calls it—which fulfills a function analogous to that of religious faith:

How many aspects of religious faith and fellowship we find in the Academic Commitment! There is the dominant philosophy of naturalism. Its method is scientific; its faith, that all being can be explained in terms of a single order of efficient causation in which a supernatural Deity has no place; its morality, the ideals of humanism rooted in finite human experience; its messianic hope, that man—through understanding the consequences of his actions—can build a better world.

As against the case of the Gentile society of Champaign-Urbana, there are a number of Gentile academicians on the Illinois campus who do not consider affiliation with a religious institution to be a necessary sign of respectability. Furthermore, Jewish life in Champaign-Urbana—ethnic, religious, or cultural—depends largely on the town community, most of whose members are attached in one way or another to Jewish organizations. The academicians, on the other hand, range, according to Rabbi Cohen, from "the strongly identified who are trying to preserve Jewish culture in a Midwestern cornfield [to] the cosmopolite who feels that there are enough barriers between people . . . without the clannishness of the Jews." Once the memories of Jewish culture become vague, he writes, the town Jew can still find reasons to remain within the fold: he retains a latent supernatural faith, and the larger community expects him to be Jewish. By contrast, once the faculty Jew ceases to find meaning in the ethnic fellowship or the folkways, he has neither traditional belief nor strong social pressure to help him maintain his commitment.

If intermarriage among academicians on a campus as conservative as the University of Illinois is so high, it should not surprise us that there are cities with larger and more active Jewish communities where intermarriage rates among special segments of the Jewish population are even higher. New Haven is a good example. Champaign-Urbana has many Jewish physicians, but New Haven also has a fairly substantial group of psychoanalysts. In a study which appeared several years ago under the title *Social Class and Mental Illness: A Community Study*, A. B. Hollingshead and

Frederick C. Redlich studied the therapists as well as the patients. They found that 83 per cent of New Haven analysts "came from Jewish homes," and of these some 64 per cent were intermarried. This startling figure exceeds even the current level of the geographically isolated Jewish community of Iowa, and is, of course, many times higher than the general rate in New Haven itself. What accounts for such a high rate of intermarriage among individuals who, like their counterparts in Illinois, were born and raised in communities thickly settled by Jews, whose families were active in Jewish affairs, and who practice a profession second only to the rabbinate in its proportion to Jews? One answer is suggested by Redlich and Hollingshead who point out that the great majority of the New Haven analysts "consider themselves representatives of classical psychoanalysis; when the discussion turns in that direction they look down their classical analytical noses at their colleagues who have a Jungian, Horneyan or Sullivanian orientation." Thus the psychoanalysts of New Haven have an even more sharply defined "commitment" than the academicians of Champaign-Urbana (so much so that they maintain virtually no contact with their psychiatrist colleagues in New Haven who are directive or organic in orientation), and this professional commitment probably is as binding as that of the Illinois professors.

In our context, perhaps the most interesting fact to emerge from the New Haven study is that apart from marital choice and the lack of religious affiliation, the analysts do not appear to be alienated in any profound sense from the culture in which they live. Far from exhibiting any left-wing political beliefs and sympathies, they tend toward the attitudes of the old-fashioned American who started from humble beginnings and achieved success as a result of hard work. Living in the best residential areas of New Haven, enjoying high incomes which they have earned (unlike many Protestants in the same area) "largely through their own efforts and abilities," their individual social mobility has been such that 73 per cent of them have won a higher station in life than their fathers, 79 per cent have surpassed their brothers-in-law, and 83 per cent have outdistanced their brothers.

Their essential conformity to middle-class ideals is nowhere better shown than in their attitude to their children's education. While denying any desire to impose their own values upon their offspring, their typical response to the question "How much education do you want for your children?" was: "As much as they want; college is the minimum." On the whole, they have no contact with Jewish life, yet as Hollingshead and Redlich put it: "Doubt and confusion is apparent in their response on how they would like to have their children trained religiously." Presumably the rate of intermarriage among the children of these analysts will be very high, although the children's motives will obviously be different from those which led their fathers to intermarry. But even where both parents are Jewish, there will no doubt be a high rate of intermarriage among the children in this group.

Thus far we have concentrated on the behavior of the Jew in relation to intermarriage, but perhaps the newest factor in the situation is the change in the position of the Gentile. Once we shift our focus to the Gentile, it becomes evident that intermarriage is increasing not only because the Jew is moving out into the general society, but also because the tastes, ideas, cultural preferences, and life-styles preferred by many Jews are more and more coming to be shared by non-Jews. In the Herzl Institute volume referred to above, this process is commented upon by Richard Rubenstein, a well-known Hillel rabbi currently at the University of Pittsburgh. As Rubenstein sees it, in the course of "emancipating" themselves, many of the bright middle-class Gentile girls who attend the better colleges are attracted by the political liberalism characteristic of Jewish students or by their equally characteristic avant-gardism in intellectual and aesthetic matters. To the allure of the "Jewish" cultural style is added the fact that Jews are in, but still not completely of, the society. In other words, where Jewish alienation used to inhibit contacts with Gentiles (several decades ago, the heavily Jewish radical movements on the college campuses experienced considerable difficulty in appealing to the rest of the student body), it now operates in a subtle way to foster them. For, as Rabbi Rubenstein says, it is precisely this delicate balance between acceptance and marginality which is sought after by girls who do not want Bohemian husbands but rather respectable ones who are somewhat "different." In addition, the marked rise in egalitarianism on the college campuses following World War II has done much to promote a climate in which dating, and in some cases marrying, outside one's social group is no longer regarded as deviant behavior, and on the more "advanced" campuses even confers some degree of status. And finally, these changes in the social atmosphere of the college community run parallel to developments in the occupational world, for to a greater extent than ever before, Jews are now working with Gentiles as colleagues instead of serving them as merchants or free professionals.

What all this suggests is that the old notions about the causes of intermarriage are beginning to look as outmoded as the causes themselves. Both on the folk level and in more sophisticated terms, these notions invariably involved the imputation of some defect in the contracting parties. If a Gentile girl agreed to marry a Jew, it must be because no Christian would have her, or because she had made herself sexually available as no Jewish girl would deign to do. Similarly, if a Jewish man married a Gentile girl, it must be because no Jewish girl would have him, or because he was a self-hater or a social climber. Whatever their applicability to individual cases, it takes no great insight to realize that approaches like these—which stress the deviancy and inferiority of the person who intermarries—serve the dual function of reinforcing the practice of endogamy and allaying fears about the threat of intermarriage. By impugning the motives of exogamous Jews, or by attributing them to dark forces outside the Jewish community, the challenge that intermarriage poses to the prevailing values of the group is vanquished—at least for the moment. The difficulty, however, is that these assumptions of pathology—social or personal—no longer explain either the rate or the reasons for exogamy among Jews. This is not to say that intermarriage can already be considered a routine phenomenon and that the motives which impel Jews to choose Gentile mates are basically no different from those which lead them to marry Jews. Nevertheless, from the evidence that has begun to accumulate, it is becoming impossible to view intermarriage as an indication either of personal aberration or of social persecution. In a recent study of middle-class intermarried couples residing in the Boston area, Maria and Daniel Levinson conclude that:

intermarriage is not . . . a unitary phenomenon. It occurs under a variety of psychological and social conditions and has varying consequences. Psychologically it is not purely a neurotic manifestation, although neurotic motives may enter to varying degrees. Nor is it to be seen solely as an "escape" from the Jewish group or as a means of securing social or financial gain, although motives of this kind play a part in some cases.

Heiss's analysis of the Midtown Study supports this conclusion. Surveying the mental-health rating assigned each respondent by a board of psychiatrists, he found that there was no significant difference between the mean rating achieved by those who had intermarried and those who had not.

It is precisely the "healthy" modern intermarriages which raise the most troubling questions of all to the Jewish community in general, and Jewish parents in particular. When his child inter-marries, the Jewish parent guiltily feels that in some way he must be responsible. Yet how is he to oppose the match? Chances are that he believes that love is the basis of marriage, that marriage is the uniting of two individuals rather than two families, and that the final determination of a mate is his child's prerogative. This complex of ideas (which constitutes a radical departure from the norm, if not always the practice, of traditional Jewish society) came to be embraced by some of the more advanced members of the first generation in America, by a majority of the second genera-tion, and by an overwhelming proportion of the third. How then can the parent ask his child to renounce what he himself believes in? Moreover, the liberalism of the Jewish parent—his commit-ment to the idea of equality and his belief in the transitory character of the differences which distinguish people from one another—serves to subvert his sense of moral rectitude in opposing intermarriage. For if he is at all in the habit of personal candor, he must ask himself if the Gentile is any less worthy of the Jew than the Jew is of the Gentile.

The second-generation parent or adviser usually manages to escape this dilemma by falling back on the argument of happiness. Experience, he will say, is the best teacher, and what it teaches is that intermarriage seldom works out well. And he will cite figures to show that exogamous couples have higher divorce rates than those who marry within the fold. Thus the need to confront the painful contradictions in his own position is evaded, and he can oppose his child's intermarriage with a good conscience.

In the writings of such founding fathers of the contemporary American Jewish community as Isaac Mayer Wise or Solomon Schechter, the assumption is that Jewish survival is entirely pos-sible in a free society. But having finally established themselves in such a society, Jews are now coming to realize that their survival is still threatened—not by Gentile hostility but by Jewish indiffer-ence. This is what finally makes intermarriage so bitter a dilemma to confront. On the one hand, it signifies the fulfillment of the

Jews' demand for acceptance as an individual—a demand he has been making since the Emancipation; on the other hand, it signifies a weakening of Jewish commitment. In short, it casts into doubt American Jewry's dual ideal of full participation in the society and the preservation of Jewish identity. And once the rate of intermarriage is seen to be growing, the contradiction in the basic strategy of American-Jewish adjustment is nakedly exposed.

As the horns of this dilemma sharpen and press closer, the very least one can hope from the Jewish community is that it will eventually surrender the cherished diagnoses and nostrums that have come to obfuscate the true nature of the problem. A more realistic confrontation is necessary, and that requires a much larger body of research than we now possess on the current rate of intermarriage in the country as a whole. It also requires much more information about the Jews who intermarry and about the causes and consequences of their doing so. So, too, there is a need for studies to evaluate the various methods in use to combat intermarriage, particularly those involving Jewish education. And demographic research will have to be done at regular intervals so that a reliable trend line can be established.

A candid and pertinent discussion of intermarriage will also require a more critical examination of Jewish attitudes than we have had in the past. One immediately thinks of the issue of conversion, which many Jews seem to regard as a token, last-gap measure in a developing process of assimilation; but is it? There is also the obvious, but usually ignored, problem of birth-rate. One reason why a rising rate of intermarriage is of such pressing significance is that the birth-rate of native-born Jews has been so low. (This, in part, is why comparisons between Jewish and Catholic intermarriage rates have helped to confound rather than clarify the issue.) If a greater proportion of second-generation Jewish parents had permitted themselves to have even three children rather than one or two, the present situation would be far more hopeful so far as Jewish survival is concerned. But the fact is that the fertility rate of the second generation dropped catastrophically, and with hardly a word of discussion about it among Jewish leaders. Reform and Conservative rabbis decided, for all practical purposes, to exempt the question of contraception from the area of the sacred, implying that a decision about family size was of strictly private concern. Orthodox spokesmen were not prepared to go this far in the direction of secularization, but they preferred to concentrate on other issues such as maintaining the practice of *kashruth*.

The threat posed by intermarriage may change all this, and there is a possibility that it will also change the way most Jews think about their Jewish responsibilities. Typically, the American-Jewish notion has been that to be a good Jew means doing something for some other Jew; it means, in short, philanthropy. As the problem of intermarriage grows in urgency, however, the Jewish community in America will for the first time have to face an issue which is highly personal—almost anti-philanthropic—in character. And if the emphasis on philanthropic activism has allowed American Jews to avoid confronting the stark question: "What do you stand for when you wish to remain separate?"—the defense against intermarriage will necessarily involve a coming to terms, sooner or later, with what one is defending.

As the evidence accumulates that Jewish survival in America literally depends upon each individual Jew—and in an entirely different way than it did in the past—the answer to the question, "What do you stand for when you remain separate?" may well demand the development of a new consciousness in the community. This will not be the first time in history that social conditions have impelled a people to philosophical discussion and involvement. If the problem of intermarriage should engender such a consciousness—the kind which has been foreign to the activism of American Jewry—it will have had a positive effect on the quality of Jewish life. If it does not, the negative consequences are indeed ominous to contemplate.

Notes ▶

1. According to the statistics of Arthur Ruppin, these rates were as high as 20 and 30 per cent.

2. Another work was also published last year—*Intermarriage and Jewish Life*, edited by Werner J. Cahnman (The Herzl Press and the Jewish Reconstructionist Press, 212 pp., $5.00)—which consists of papers read at a conference organized by the Herzl Institute. This is the first book on the subject sponsored by any American Jewish organization.

3. It is worth noting that this study found 18.4 per cent of all marriages involving Jews to be exogamous.

VII NEW PROGRAMS AND TECHNIQUES IN CHANGING AMERICAN RACE RELATIONS

VII

Finding the solutions to problems in dominant-minority relations is no longer regarded as the responsibility of the minority groups themselves. Along with the conviction that hostility is costly to all has come the realization that policy, program and technique are the business of all.

There is no agreement on the goals of action programs in bringing about change in ethnic relations, for there are at least five different targets: homogeneity, tolerance, cultural pluralism, peace and equality. Similarly, there are differences of opinion concerning the techniques and programs that would be most effective in reaching these goals. Until evaluation and action research give us better answers, we shall probably continue to employ a variety of measures in trial and error. Our most earnest search and experimentation for new and more effective programs and techniques has been in the case of Negro-white relations. In fact, as Professor Dan Dodson suggests in the first article of this last section, it is conceivable that we need to reexamine our uncritical opposition to all quota systems, for it is quite possible that benign quotas, such as are found in interracial housing, are desirable and practical first steps toward eventual equality.

30 ► CAN INTERGROUP QUOTAS BE BENIGN?

DAN W. DODSON

► For those concerned with intergroup relations, one of the most baffling issues is that of engineering desegregation programs so that ratios of peoples are maintained toward each other in such proportions that the weight of numbers of one group does not constitute a threat to the other. Most would concede that there is a relation between proportion of those to be integrated and the successful attempt to maintain stabilized relations in the desegregated groups. We are not too sure what other factors are involved, however. In the high school situation in New York City the experience seems to be that as the Negro proportion in the student population becomes a percentage of around 30 the white group starts to withdraw *en masse*. When they start withdrawing, the better students of the Negro group also leave, so that the school becomes a greatly reduced student body, frequently composed of adjustment students. Wadleigh had to be closed as a high school because of this type of failure. Benjamin Franklin High School and Boys High in Brooklyn are rapidly facing similar predicaments. There may be others which are unknown to this writer.

At the neighborhood level, the elementary schools make out better. Here proportions of Negroes to whites seem to make little difference up to and well beyond the 50 per cent point. Stable and sustained mixed elementary school populations are achieved in most neighborhoods with little difficulty.

Seeley reported in *Crestwood Heights* that when the Jewish

From the *Journal of Intergroup Relations* (Autumn, 1960), 125–33. Reprinted by permission of the author and publisher.

population started migrating into the community they were widely and warmly accepted. When they became an identifiable and self-conscious group the relations became more formal between them and the other population. As their numbers passed the one-fourth proportion, hostility and conflict ensued, and around the 35 per cent point the large-scale withdrawal of the Christian group started.

A theory of benign quotas is being tested in residential housing by the Milgrim Associates in their projects. The assumption is that whites do not mind living with Negro neighbors provided they can be assured that the values of the dominant group will not be "drowned" by the numbers of Negroes. Hence there is a consciously established quota system in which some houses are held off the white market to assure that some Negroes are accommodated. The controversy over this bold venture has not subsided. Deerfield Park in Illinois has been torn by strife over it. Intergroup relations leaders in public agencies who have to enforce fair housing laws and public policies have privately expressed concern over what they would do should a complaint be filed against such a developer who discriminated in his attempt to achieve some semblance of balance in the racial backgrounds of residents in such projects.

In New York City, as in many other communities, there is asked increasingly the question as to what can be done with the public housing to keep it integrated. Many whites are reluctant to live in projects with Negroes—especially if they are the minority. Likewise, many Negroes do not want to live in projects where they are a small minority—especially if they have to live long distances from the Negro communities to do so. Also in many of the City projects, sometimes referred to as low middle income, fewer Negroes are financially able to afford the rentals. With a backlog of applications amounting to some 67,000 composed mainly of Negro and Puerto Rican populations, what should be the responsibility of public authority to *seek* eligible continental whites to move into the projects to help maintain interracial balances? A few years back, one leader openly advocated formal quotas in one project in the Bronx as a means of maintaining a stable racial balance.

In the private volunteer organizations a like problem exists. The new group in a changing neighborhood tends to be Negro or Puerto Rican. If the agency serves needs it concentrates heavily on the minority groups. If it values integration of all peoples, it invariably reaches the place where it must pass over some of the minority constituency in order to hold the majority group. This is discrimination.

These are illustrative of the issues before us today as we wrestle with the problems of desegregation. The problem is not new, either in philosophy or practice. What is new is the changing relationship of groups to each other. The basic philosophy of intergroup relations in crashing through institutionalized segregation and *apartheid* policies was most clearly stated by Justice Harlan in the famous *Plessy v. Ferguson* decision. In his dissent he stated that any arm of government in dealing with people should be "color blind." "Without regard to race, creed or color" has been the phraseology of all anti-bias laws so far enacted. Obviously such legislation was targeted to the abolition of institutionalized "Jim Crow." Its objective was to destroy formal policies of discrimination. In this context we were not satisfied with "tokenism" as a philosophy. The fight on college quotas in this and many other states suggests that token integration as an institutionalized policy is unsatisfactory. The complaint of the South today is over "token" integration. We all deplore the policy of the agency which employs one Negro and places him in a prominent spot as evidence of integration. We refer to such a person as "Exhibit A."

In this first phase of desegregation, Harlan's statement and the phraseology of the law have been of tremendous importance. In New York City the first housing authority administrator was able to get integrated housing because he said "This is public housing. Being public it is available to all the public who qualify, without regard to race, creed or color." In a like measure the laws against discrimination have said "You do not have to employ a man on any other basis than before, except that race, creed or color shall not be a factor in his qualification."

Today, however, when it comes to integration as contrasted to desegregation, the shoe is on the other foot. The Supreme Court decision in May 1954 can be, and is, widely interpreted to mean that children reared in segregation are traumatized in their perception of self. This has injected a new value into the picture. This value indicates that when segregation, either enforced or *de facto*, occurs it is the responsibility of government to use positive means to break it up. This cannot be done by being color blind. It was evident to me that the New Rochelle School system had become increasingly segregated, *de facto*, by a policy of not considering who was Negro and who was white, i.e., by being color blind. On the other hand, to take into account race in employment, housing (in New York), public accommodations, or education would be a violation of the law. Thus the means used to achieve the objective of stable, integrated racial balances appear to be at variance with the present anti-discrimination laws, especially if public agencies are involved.

Another limitation to the honest evaluation of the situation is our paucity of knowledge about such group problems. All, I am sure, would concede that there is nothing magic about a percentage of 30 or 40 or any other. The use of such a number becomes dangerous because it reinforces stereotypes about what such proportions should be and limits experimentation on how to deal with the many other variables. As I suggested in the New Rochelle Report, undoubtedly another variable is that of the climate in which the group interacts. There are some instances in which whites have come into Negro-majority situations and remained. It should be pointed out that the whites began as an infinitesimally small minority and ultimately took over the Georgetown section in Washington, D.C. A racially balanced neighborhood was achieved in the Bolton Hill section of Baltimore in a comparable way. Another factor is that of the nature of the group. A task oriented group undoubtedly would respond differently to one that was a socially oriented one.

Another factor related to achieving stabilized intergroup balances is the weight of a historical past. For instance an agency which refuses to integrate as a neighborhood changes, frequently finds itself *surrounded* by minority group persons. Integration becomes a *cause célèbre* in some such instances. Hence, when the color line is ultimately broken, it is like the weakening of a dam which has held back pent-up waters. In such instances too often nothing can be done to keep racial balance. The Bedford branch of the Y.M.C.A. in Brooklyn is a good example.

The next question to be raised is "How effective are quotas, anyway?" If the agency is facing rapid neighborhood change, usually they have little effect. Some there are who would say that when imaginative volunteer leadership cannot succeed in holding integrated groups there is no hope for quotas unless there is resort to coercion.

Before serious consideration is given to formal quotas, all other means of achieving balance should be exhausted. What are these? One is selection through program emphasis. Sometimes it is possible to maintain racial balance through programming. The Bronx High School of Science fulfills this purpose. The reason the high school division has moved from comprehensive schools to such special schools is due, in no small part, to this problem of racial and ethnic mixing. In a like manner I recommended to the Educational Alliance that a program which was Jewish in content would of itself restrict non-Jewish participation and perhaps attract sufficient persons of the faith background to preserve the integrity of the institution as a Jewish agency.

A second type of alternative is selective recruitment. This is particularly useful for some types of agencies. The housing authority personnel can seek assistance from local organizations to get qualified persons of select backgrounds to apply. A dean of a popular college told me once that he could fill his entire freshman class from Brooklyn without lowering his admission standards and 95 per cent of them would be Jewish. This led to selective recruitment and regional quotas rather than racial quotas. Some of the private schools which are heavily homogeneous in enrollment are extremely generous with scholarships for those of other backgrounds in order to keep some integration and the practice is defended for precisely the same reason as the court ruled, i.e., segregated education is *ipso facto* inferior.

Another device is school districting or other policy programs. In public education zoning for racial balance holds many possibilities. For example, Princeton, New Jersey, integrated the schools by sending the first three grades to one building and the other grades to the second school plant. This mixed the children and provided wholesome integration. The proposed New Rochelle plan for a K-3 (Kindergarten through third grade) school in the Negro community and the distribution of the older children in schools outside the Negro district is suggestive.

In New Rochelle we declined to recommend sending children by bus to schools outside their community purely for desegregation purposes. However, where this as a value can be achieved along with other educational values such as relieving overcrowding it becomes a useful device.

After all the possibilities are exhausted, however, there is still the issue to which this paper is addressed. "Can racial quotas be justified?" "If so, under what circumstances?" I am sure few of us are doctrinaire on this issue. For myself, for official, i.e., public agencies, I would say no! I well realize there are great traumas to personality of both Negroes and whites stemming from what has been a historical past. These biases make it difficult to achieve an integrated community. I have a lot of sympathy for public officials who are experimenting with programs designed to achieve mixed groups in public agencies. Their objectives are good. I have not been able to bring myself to an endorsement of such a program, however.

With 67,000 applicants for public housing, for instance, and many of these consisting of families of several members living in one room, it is hard to endorse holding an apartment vacant hoping some one with a white skin will apply and pass by those in such need.

If such programs of benign quotas are launched it appears that the following points should be clear: (1) What are the criteria by which one establishes what the quota should be? 20 per cent, 30 per cent, 90, etc.? (2) Can such a quota be defended as an interim or "phase" operation? There is the assumption here that all desire a society where, ultimately, there is free association of peoples, yet, when quotas are established they tend to become "frozen," institutionalized and difficult to change. (3) How are the "weightings" established by which "desegregation" as a value transcends "non-discrimination" as a value? It should be noted that unless there is "discrimination" there is little problem. (4) How can the "phase operation" be terminated when it has outlived its usefulness? Once social structure is created it tends to resist change. (5) Are we sure we are not injecting our own values to deprive even minority people of their right to self-segregation? Does this threaten the entire pattern of grouping around social and religious interests? For example in one neighborhood in New Rochelle over 90 per cent of the children in the school are Jewish in background. These are homes of the $40,000 class. Most such upper income people could have chosen—with some search—more integrated neighborhoods in which to live. Does such a policy of quota programming deny this privilege?

Private agencies are in a less vulnerable position, although they too face the dilemma that—pushed too far—quotas mean discrimination. Where such measures are employed it should be clear, even here, that there is an element of experiment in it; that there are clearly delineated procedures for sharing the fruits of the experiment with others.

In summation my position is as follows: (1) As we move beyond *desegregation* toward integration, we move away from Justice Harlan's position on the role of government as regards race, creed and color. (2) Public and private agencies both must take into account race or creed if creative roles are to be developed and maintained.

This "due regard for race or creed" cannot, however, be used as an excuse to resort to preferential treatment of people because of race, creed or color. In such areas as housing and education where weighting of variables includes the need for mixed association as a social value, it should be very clear how and in what way this value takes precedence over the need for service as a value. Perhaps the establishment of these weights is the next task ahead.

31 ► SHOULD THERE BE "COMPENSATION" FOR NEGROES?

WHITNEY M. YOUNG, JR. AND KYLE HASELDEN

Another new challenge to our earlier concepts of action programs in race relations is the question concerning the desirability of giving the minority more-than-equal or preferred treatment in jobs, housing and other economic and social facilities in order to make up for the long years of deprivation and to break the chain of intergenerational stagnation of status. Debating the validity and wisdom of this doctrine of compensation that grew out of the civil rights movement are Mr. Whitney Young of the National Urban League and Mr. Kyle Haselden of The Christian Century.

"Domestic Marshall Plan"–(*Whitney M. Young, Jr.*)

In 1948, by instituting the Marshall Plan to aid the war-torn countries of Europe, the United States took a step unparalleled in history. Recognizing the special need of the nations shattered by World War II, the people of this country committed some $17 billion in money, machines and technical aid to help our neighbors overseas to take their place again in the community of free nations.

This rightful action was in keeping with the long tradition of America's moral, political and economic credo. We have long given special, emergency aid to the oppressed, the sick, the handi-

From *The New York Times Magazine*, October 6, 1963. © 1963 by The New York Times Company. Reprinted by permission of the authors and publisher.

capped and deprived. In recent years, we have seen this concept put into action through our aid—in employment, education and welfare—to Hungarian and Cuban refugees. We see it annually carried out in the form of emergency help to "depressed" and "disaster" areas, suffering from joblessness or devastation by hurricanes, drought and other misfortunes. The "G.I. Bill of Rights" after World War II was, in a sense, a recognition of the special need of our discharged veterans for education, housing, employment and other benefits.

Recently, the National Urban League has attracted nationwide attention with its proposal for a temporary "more-than-equal" program of aid for Negro citizens. In the current drive for civil rights, with its demonstrations, marches and sit-ins, this proposal has confused many white Americans. They ask: Is the Negro not to be satisfied by equality alone? Or, is he seeking, not equality, but preference? In the face of these questions, our history should teach us that what the Urban League proposes is not only directly in the American tradition, but has the arguments of racial justice, economic practicality and morality—secular as well as religious—behind it.

On an economic level, the hard but simple fact—borne out by comparative statistics on unemployment, income, mortality rates, substandard housing and education—is that the past of the Negro exists in the present. Citizens everywhere must realize that the effects of over 300 years of oppression cannot be obliterated by doing business as usual. They must know, too, that in today's complex, technological society, a strong back and a will to succeed are no longer sufficient to break the bonds of deprivation, as was the case with minority groups in the past. For, in addition to the ordinary forces affecting one's way of life, the Negro's struggle into America's mainstream has been thwarted by the barriers of discrimination and denial based on the color of his skin.

The facts speak for themselves. Today, the average Negro family earns $3,233, as compared with $5,835 for the white family—a difference of 45 per cent. This gap has widened by two percentage points in the last decade alone. It has widened because the Negro started receiving too little, too late. More than 75 per cent of Negro workers are found in the three lowest occupational categories—service workers, semi-skilled workers, and unskilled and farm labor—the categories most affected by the geometric growth of automation. These same categories include less than 39 per cent of white workers.

By the same token, one out of every six Negro dwellings are substandard, as compared with one in 32 white dwellings. One in every four Negro women with pre-school children is working away from home. Of the school dropouts, 21 per cent are Negro; only 7 per cent of high school graduates are Negroes. Unemployment rates for Negroes are from two and one-half to three times higher than those for white workers.

To overcome these conditions the National Urban League declares that the nation must undertake an immediate, dramatic and tangible "crash program"—a domestic Marshall Plan—to close this intolerable economic, social and educational gap, which separates the vast majority of Negro citizens from other Americans. Unless this is done, the results of the current heroic efforts in the civil-rights movement will be truly an illusion, and the struggle will continue, with perhaps tragic consequences.

In its plea for such a domestic Marshall Plan, the Urban League is asking for a special effort, not for special privileges. This effort has been described as "preferential treatment," "indemnification," "special consideration," "compensatory activity." These are "scare" phrases that obscure the meaning of the proposal and go against the grain of our native sense of fair play.

We prefer that our recommendations be seen as necessary and just corrective measures that must be taken if equal opportunity is to have meaning. They are necessary, because only by such means can the majority of Negro citizens be prepared to assume the increased responsibilities that they will face in a more integrated society. They are just, because such an effort alone can repair the devastation wrought by generations of injustice, neglect, discrimination and indifference, based on race.

To put it another way, the scales of equal opportunity are now heavily weighted against the Negro and cannot be corrected in today's technological society simply by applying equal weights. For more than 300 years the white American has received special consideration, or "preferential treatment," if you will, over the Negro. What we ask now is that for a brief period there be a deliberate and massive effort to include the Negro citizen in the mainstream of American life. Furthermore, we are not asking for equal time; a major effort, honestly applied, need last only some 10 years. This crash program must be a cooperative effort by all agencies, institutions and individuals, public and private.

The elements of the crash program, or domestic Marshall Plan, would include:

Education: For the deprived child—Negro as well as white— provision for first-class schools, with the most modern facilities and the best and most experienced teachers. These are necessary to help him realize his potential and prepare him to take advantage of greater educational opportunity. Necessary also is intensified remedial instruction in the lower grades for culturally deprived and retarded pupils. Schools and colleges must find new ways to seek out Negro youths with undeveloped talents. Similarly adult education programs must be expanded and geared to the needs of citizens lacking the basic literary and technical skills.

Employment: A planned effort to place *qualified* Negroes in all categories of employment, at all levels of responsibility. This would mean that employers would consciously seek to hire qualified Negro citizens and would intensify apprenticeship and training programs to prepare new Negro employees and upgrade those already employed. Labor unions, too, must make a conscientious effort to include Negroes in their membership and training programs.

Further, where Negroes have not been employed in the past at all levels, it is essential that there be conscious preferment to help them catch up. This does not mean the establishment of a quota system—an idea shunned by responsible Negro organizations and leaders. But, because we are faced with the hypocrisy of "tokenism," where the presence of two or three Negro employes is passed off as integration, we are forced, during the transitional stages, to discuss numbers and categories. We demand, in all fairness, that the Negro not be expected to bear the brunt of unemployment.

Housing: Racial ghettos eliminated by providing genuine housing opportunities on the basis of need and financial ability. Programs of redevelopment and relocation, planned to provide both low-income housing and a racial diversity, are needed throughout our communities. This will require the active participation of real estate brokers as well as homeowners.

Health and Welfare: Public and private agencies seeking to provide the best personnel and facilities in low-income neighborhoods, and increased counseling services to troubled families. Here, particularly, the churches and schools must combine efforts to help Negro families develop a deeper sense of parental and community responsibility.

Finally, qualified Negro citizens should be sought and named to public and private boards and commissions, particularly those which shape employment, housing, education, and health and welfare policies. In achieving this objective, we would develop strong, responsible leadership within the Negro community. Also, we would prompt private foundations, business and government to reassess the extent and aims of their financial contributions to established Negro leadership and organizations.

The program outlined here has a simple, practical aim: to provide the Negro citizen with the leadership, education, jobs and motivation that will permit him to help himself. It is not a plea to exempt him from the independence and initiative demanded by our free, competitive society. It makes practical economic sense as a measure to reduce unemployment and welfare costs and to increase our productivity and national income by including Negro citizens in the benefits of our rich society. President Kennedy's economic advisers estimated that our gross national product could be raised 2.5 per cent, were the Negro worker's earnings commensurate with the nation's average.

This program makes historical sense as a rehabilitation of the damage inflicted upon the Negro by generations of injustice and neglect. He, too, has given his blood, sweat and tears to the building of our country; yet, where the labor and initiative of other minority groups have been rewarded by assimilation within the society, the black American has been isolated and rejected.

The domestic Marshall Plan has profound moral and religious justification. Our country is in dire jeopardy as long as it has within its body politic a socially and economically deprived group of citizens, whether they be actually enslaved or denied the full benefits of equality and freedom by an insidious economic and psychological slavery. In this sense, the crash programs that we propose are not an effort to impose the guilt and sins of a past generation on our present white community. This is an appeal for all Americans, working together, to rid present-day America of its sickening disease and its moral shame.

The Negro is in revolt today, not to change the fabric of our society or to seek a special place in it, but to enter into partnership in that society. It is a revolt with which every American should sympathize. Already a few educational and business institutions are working with intensified effort, special consideration, if you will, in solving this problem. We have the material and spiritual resources as a country to meet the challenge and accomplish the urgent task ahead. All we need is the will to act and the spirit of decency and sacrifice which abounds in our land.

"Parity, Not Preference"–(*Kyle Haselden*)

An increasing number of Negro and white Americans agree that securing complete freedom and total equality for the Negro is this nation's No. 1 domestic issue and that justice for the deprived one-tenth of the nation's population is the end toward which the whole society should move speedily. Unanimous in this agreement, they nevertheless disagree as to the permissible and effective means to that end.

Varied in their temperaments, their religious convictions, their sense of what is prudent and practical, these Americans prefer one or another of the various strategies which seek racial justice. The options range from the doctrine of violent rebellion against white domination at one extreme to a patient yet active appeal to the nation's creeds, congresses and courts at the other. Between these extremes fall various nonviolent strategies and schemes, each with its own supporters.

Unfortunately there are, in the ranks of men and women genuinely committed to racial justice, some who insist that unanimity of purpose requires uniformity of plan. They insist that whites and Negroes who share their objective also adopt their methods—however unruly, eccentric and impractical those methods—or accept vilification for Uncle Tomism. This absolutist, autocratic spirit believes that justice for the Negro is the ultimate criterion of all human action and that this end validates any means, whatever practicality or religious principle may dictate to the contrary.

This is a dangerous mood. It divides those who seek justice for Negroes; it alienates influential moderates unnecessarily; and, most serious, this authoritarian spirit lures the Negro into activities which corrupt his purpose and defeat his ultimate hope.

In the struggle for racial justice a technique is not valid simply because it annoys the white man or because it promises some temporary advantage to the Negro. It is valid only if it honors the moral ground on which the Negro makes his claim for justice, respects the right of all men to the same justice, preserves in the human relationship values which are equivalents of justice, and promotes rather than prevents the Negro's progress.

The idea of compensation, which has been suggested as a device to equalize competition between whites and Negroes, fails these crucial tests. By compensation—in the passive rather than the active sense—is meant compensation *for* the Negro rather than *by* the Negro. It has been proposed that the Negro cannot succeed in his search for freedom and equality unless there is an arbitrary—in fact, artificial—removal of the academic, cultural and professional lag forced upon him by over two centuries of slavery and by another of exploitation. It is argued further that the Negro's years of involuntary, payless servitude established a collectible claim against the descendants of those who enslaved and exploited him.

How can this debt be paid? The proposal is that the Negro be given preference in employment wherever a vacancy occurs, a premium in salary, and a quota system guaranteeing that one-tenth of all people hired by firms, professional enterprises and industries be Negroes. Even though this proposal is obviously unfeasible, what shall we say of it as a theory?

Compensation must be rejected as an equalizer of competition between Negroes and whites for several reasons, all of which rest on the grounds to which the Negro appeals in his demand for freedom and equality.

First, compensation for Negroes is a subtle but pernicious form of racism. It requires that men be dealt with by society on the basis of race and color rather than on the basis of their humanity. It would therefore as a public policy legalize, deepen and perpetuate the abominable racial cleavage which has ostracized and crippled the American Negro. Racism, whoever may be its temporary beneficiary, should be eliminated from the social order, not confirmed by it.

Second, preferential economic status for Negroes would penalize the living in a futile attempt to collect a debt owed by the dead. The 20th-century white man is no more to blame for the fact that his ancestors bought and held slaves than are 20th-century Negroes for the fact that some of their ancestors captured and sold slaves. This is the ironic tragedy of exploitation. It leaves with the descendants of the exploiters a guilt they cannot cancel and with the descendants of the exploited a debt they cannot collect.

Third, a scheme which gives Negroes preference in employment and a premium in salary would bestow on Negroes the debilitating social status which has for centuries cursed the initiative and enterprise of the white man in the South. Preferred status for the Negro, however much society may owe him a debt, will inevitably destroy in him the initiative and enterprise required of a minority people in a highly competitive society. Slavery corrupts ambition and self-reliance; so, too, does patronizing social status.

Fourth, compensation for Negroes would be unfair to other minorities handicapped by their history or by rapid social and industrial change: Puerto Ricans, Mexican-Americans, migrants of all races, Indians, coal miners and others. Negroes are entirely right in demanding that they be hired, paid and promoted on their merit and in boycotting those enterprises which discriminate on a racial basis. But they are not right in demanding an artificial scheme which is unworkable, racist, destructive of initiative and unfair to other struggling Americans.

Our goal should be parity, not preferment, and there are three things we must do, none of them pleasant, none easy, if we are to attain it.

First, there must be a total, across-the-board desegregation of American society. Wherever the white man will not voluntarily surrender the psychic and material advantages of racial discrimination, the Negro must use the law, his power as a consumer, his increasing political leverage, and coercive nonviolent protests to assail and destroy the color structures of our society.

Equality of opportunity is an elemental civil right specifically declared in the sacred documents of the United States. Withholding that right from any people because of their race profanes every tenet in the political and religious creeds of the American people. Denying that right encumbers and humiliates 20,000,000 American citizens. The first business of the nation is the total elimination of racial discrimination and its component, racial segregation.

Such liberation, however, would leave the Negro still handicapped by centuries of poor schooling and by his long exclusion from most trades and professions. A desegregated society would open to the Negro opportunities which are rightfully his and should be granted to him but for which centuries of neglect and abuse leave many of his race inadequately prepared. Even though all racial bars were removed, most Negroes could not, in a free and impartial society, compete on equal terms with most white people for jobs and preferments.

But this, as we have noted, is a handicap which Negroes share with another one-tenth of the population, whose competitive strength has also been sapped by an unfortunate history or by the entrapping eddies of industrial development.

Our second task, therefore, is to undertake a nationwide crash program for the education, training and employment of the under-privileged, underdeveloped one-fifth of the nation, a domestic Point Four which would give to the employable a fair chance and to the unemployable qualifying education and training. Such a program would be based not on race but on need. Negroes would of course be the chief beneficiaries of an educational and economic crash program, because of the predominant number of deprived Negroes. But a domestic Point Four program aimed at the needs of *all* the nation's backward peoples would close rather than widen the nation's racial cleavage.

Finally, irritating as it may be, the fact might as well be faced that no immigrant or minority group has ever made its way into the mainstream of American life without studying and working harder and longer than the general population. This is the third task as it now confronts the Negro.

During their long pilgrimage through slavery and semi-slavery, most Negroes did not have an incentive for the kind of active self-compensation by which other minorities have climbed out of humiliating servitude into respected equality with other ethnic groups. Slavery and peonage do not generally encourage ambition. Even now the Negro must divert himself—his native abilities and his acquired skills, his initiative and enterprise, his devotion and endurance, his ablest leadership—from the pursuits followed by free men to the claiming of those dignities and opportunities which are the birthright of every American citizen. Yet the hard historical fact is that self-compensation is essential if he is to escape that social substratum into which a cruel history and an arrogant, avaricious white man have coerced him.

Along with several million Caucasian Americans, most Negroes need a lift from their Government if they are to overcome the handicaps of a tragic history. More than that, however, Negroes need to throw off the white man's domination if they are to discover at last what they can do for themselves unencumbered in an open society.

32 ▸ THE LIMITS OF EFFECTIVE LEGAL ACTION

ALEXANDER M. BICKEL

Social scientists and lawyers find it necessary from time to time to remind Americans that the enactment of law and the pronouncement of court decisions do not, in themselves, effect social change in general or change race relations in particular. Professor Bickel now warns us against this unwarranted faith in law with special reference to the Civil Rights Act of 1964.

▸ INITIAL COMPLIANCE with Title II, the public accommodations title of the Civil Rights Act of 1964, which was the only provision imposing an immediate duty on the general public, has been rather better than expected. A survey of 53 cities of over 50,000 population in the 19 states that have no public accommodations laws, which was conducted by the Community Relations Service within weeks after enactment of the statute, showed that as early as then, over two thirds of the relevant facilities, including hotels, motels, restaurants, theaters, sports facilities, parks, and libraries, had been desegregated. There was some variation, to be sure. The two-thirds figure applied to motels in only 46 cities, for example, and to sports facilities in only 48. And some of the desegregation represented by these figures had taken place before the statute was enacted. Nevertheless, what one Justice Department official called major compliance—conspicuous places in substantial cities—was a fact shortly after Title II became law.

These heartening statistics must not delude us into thinking that the public accommodations title (let alone the rest of the act) is now effective and that the problem is solved. It is an all too common delusion with us that the way to dispose of a social problem finally is to pass a law and then forget it, and we are naturally prone to seize on facts that seem to confirm what we wish to believe. But the evidence so far is not conclusive. There is some basis for feeling sanguine, no doubt. And yet a good initial response is not infrequently achieved by laws whose implementation later gives rise to many difficulties. It seemed for a while, after enactment of the Eighteenth Amendment, that prohibition would prove effective. So the Wickersham Commission reported ruefully a decade later. And for the first two years or so there was a good deal of voluntary compliance with the Supreme Court's school desegregation decision of 1954. In both instances, of course, there was plenty of trouble later.

Voluntary compliance may loom large at first because there are always people who have been waiting—out of timidity or inertia—for the law to nudge them into doing what they have really considered the right and profitable thing to do all along. The forces of resistance, on the other hand, need time to cohere and to encourage themselves. It is noteworthy in this connection that some good missionary work by the Department of Justice and others in 1963–1964 succeeded in obtaining considerable desegregation even before there was a law to comply with. Mostly it was chain organizations and establishments in metropolitan areas that agreed to desegregate. This has, by and large, continued to be the pattern. Compliance is far from universal in hard-core areas. And we cannot be sure that all the desegregation in the cities was genuine, rather than a token show to be followed by subterfuges of various kinds. Again, conspicuous initial compliance does not mean much if the Negro community does not fairly continuously use the facilities involved, either because of inertia or because of economic and other pressures skillfully and quietly exerted to discourage genuine integration. Finally, there is the problem of the large number of "private clubs" that are newly rising all over the South.

These caveats are not meant to suggest that the public accommodations title and other portions of the Civil Rights Act are likely to fail, or that they can work, as Mr. Goldwater said in the Senate, only if we institute a police state. The point is that the act is likely—it is virtually bound to—fail if we take the fatuous assumption that it is bound to succeed. Laws are not always effective simply because they are there and because violators are subject to suit. To think so is to forget what the late Roscoe Pound almost fifty years ago called "the limits of effective legal action," to forget that only in a certain kind of social and political situation is law self-executing through its own institutions, and that there are times when extralegal resources must be brought to the aid of the law in order to make it attain its end. Enactment and enforcement of law are sometimes only episodes, even if the single most important and influential ones, in a long and varied process by which society, working through a number of institutions, manages to realize a given purpose.

The limits of law are the limits of enforcement, and the limits of enforcement are the conditions of a free society; perhaps, indeed, the limits of government altogether. If substantial portions of the statute book had to be enforced by direct action—whether through civil or criminal litigation—against large numbers of people, we would have a very different and infinitely more disagreeable society than we do. To be sure, there is always a residuum of the antisocial, whose numbers the enforcement process, most often the criminal process, strives to reduce, although never with absolute success. And there may be laws, such as narcotics statutes, which some people may be simply incapable of obeying. Still, laws about killing and stealing, about the payment of taxes, about contracts, about torts, about labor relations, and even about traffic are effectively, if never absolutely, in force. And yet we have a free society, not a police state. We invest relatively limited resources in the effort to enforce law, and we sacrifice relatively little of other values in the process. The well-known secret of this operation is that most people, most of the time, need only to be made aware of the law in order to obey it. Much of litigation is the consequence of differences of opinion about what the law is or ought to be, not of failure to obey what is clearly the law.

In a simple system, when, as Pound pointed out,

men demand little of law and enforcement of law is but enforcement of the ethical minimum necessary for the orderly conduct of society, enforcement of law involves few difficulties. All but the inevitable anti-social residuum can understand the simple program and obvious purposes of such a legal system. . . . On the other hand, when men demand much of law, when they seek to devolve upon it the whole burden of social control, when they seek to make it do the work of the home and of the church, enforcement of law comes to involve many difficulties. . . . The purposes of the legal order are [then] not all upon the surface and it may be that many whose nature is by no means anti-social are out of accord with some or even with many of these purposes.

It is then, Pound added, that "we begin to hear complaint that laws are not enforced and the forgotten problem of the limitations upon effective legal action once more becomes acute." [1]

When people in the millions or even hundreds of thousands are opposed, intensely, consistently, and on principle, to a law bearing directly on their conduct of ordinary affairs, effective enforcement is possible, if at all, only through military occupation. Effective enforcement in the face of determined and widespread opposition is possible, this is to say, only if the private conduct that is to be regulated is subject to more or less continuous official scrutiny and to more or less continuous coercion. It makes no difference, with regard to the enforcement problem, that the opposition is nationally in a minority. As Walter Lippmann remarked in 1926, writing about prohibition, "when the object is to regulate personal habit and social custom, the majority which matters is the majority of the community concerned." [2]

People in the sort of numbers we are talking about will, of course, control some state governments and many other local authorities, and these in turn may decline to cooperate in the enforcement of locally unpopular federal law. But the chief source of the difficulty is not that the federal government lacks the basic police power and is helpless without the cooperation of the states. The heart of the matter is that no normal police and prosecuting activity can be effective in such circumstances. Nothing short of the pervasive presence of armed men will do.

As a temporary measure, in case of a breakdown of elementary public order, this has proved necessary in the past, may again be necessary on future occasions, and is well within the authority and capability of the federal government. But as a regular and more or less permanent device, it is something from which we recoil, deeming it destructive of the values of a free society, and in the end, quite possibly, counterproductive even in terms of its immediate aim. The true alternatives, therefore, are reducing the opposition by a process of inducement and persuasion, or abandoning the law. Abandonment of the law is not incompatible with occasional enforcement in pitched circumstances. And abandonment does not have to be formal, at least not immediately; the law may stay on the books for a while, it may even be observed in some parts of the country, but if it is substantially abandoned in practice, that in the end is what really matters. Noncompliance is contagious, and the statute book will conform to the practice.

Most laws, very nearly all laws, it need hardly be repeated, are readily accorded general acquiescence, and are easily effective. But that the alternatives otherwise are as I have stated them, that there are times when law does not gain general consent merely by virtue of having been authoritatively pronounced, and that lacking such consent it cannot be effective—this is demonstrated by anti-gambling statutes, which coexist with widespread gambling, and by laws regulating common sexual practices, which lie largely in disuse. Further, dramatic proof of the proposition may be drawn from two notorious experiences in American history.

The Fugitive Slave Act of 1850 was enacted as part of that year's broad compromise on the slavery problem, engineered by Henry Clay and seconded by Webster in the famous 7th of March speech. The act had firm support in the Constitution. But it was repugnant to much of the North. Emerson, no wild abolitionist, called it "this filthy enactment," and wrote in his journal: "I will not obey it, by God!" Others, like Theodore Parker of Boston, agitated against it publicly and fiercely. William R. Day, then a boy in Ravenna, Ohio, later a justice of the Supreme Court of the United States, remembered to the end of his days the heated meetings and resolutions against the act, and retained a sense of the limits of federal law. Many Northern states passed "personal liberty laws," as they were called, which were inconsistent with the act and were really thinly veiled attempts to nullify it. Efforts to enforce the Fugitive Slave Act were often resisted by mobs, were in any event not significant, and soon pretty well ceased. The end result was a hardening and broadening of Northern antislavery sentiment.

Nearly three quarters of a century later prohibition was imposed on the country by constitutional amendment. The amendment was proposed by the necessary two-thirds vote of the Congress, and ratified by the legislatures of ten more states than necessary, forty-six in all. There was some thought that the amendment might, paradoxically, itself be unconstitutional, and the matter was carried to the Supreme Court by distinguished counsel, but the Court held otherwise.[3] In some states prohibition was effective, and almost everywhere it abolished the old-fashioned saloon. But in many areas, and signally throughout the urban United States, enforcement soon became a shambles. Large numbers of people discovered, if they had ever thought about it before, that they did not really want prohibition. The Volstead Act was, of course, openly disdained. Perfectly respectable and substantial people advised violation of it, and public officials condoned violation, to say the least. By the middle of the decade, when repeal did not yet seem a realistic possibility, leaders of opinion talked of nullification in one form or another. "Conscience and public opinion," wrote Arthur T. Hadley, president emeritus of Yale, in 1925, "enforce the laws; the police suppress the exceptions." In this instance, conscience and public opinion opposed the law, and the exceptions were the rule. Hence no enforcement was possible; the law was no law.[4] And it wasn't. When, under President Hoover, an effort was made to achieve more widespread and efficient enforcement, the only result was that sufficient steam was finally generated for actual repeal.

What do these ominous lessons from history teach about prospects for realization of the aims of the Civil Rights Act of 1964? It is first to be remarked that the Fugitive Slave Act *was* an immoral law, and that the Eighteenth Amendment attempted to regulate conduct that is morally neutral, and as to which one's neighbor or a majority of one's countrymen ought, of right, have no power to impose their views. The Civil Rights Act of 1964 is a very different affair.

Now, such judgments are not to be escaped. They are decisive, and if by any chance the Civil Rights Act cannot validly be distinguished in this fashion from the Fugitive Slave Law and the Prohibition Amendment, then it may meet their fate. That is the blunt truth, and we may as well be aware of it. If, on the other hand, as so many believe, the Civil Rights Act is a just law, embodying minimal moral requirements that a national majority may properly attempt to impose on everyone, then what the earlier experiences teach is that the country now faces a task of persuasion and inducement, a task of political and social leadership and education.

Pronouncement of the law is the first step, and in itself an important persuasive and educational action. It must be followed not merely by a concerted campaign to convince everyone of the morality and justice of the law but also by an effort to bring home to the minority the intensity with which by far the greater number of their fellow citizens hold to the law. This will appeal to the minority's interest, which goes beyond the immediate issue, in conforming to the wishes of a national majority, with which, we may assume, they desire to continue in mutual profit to form part of a single body politic. The crucial point is that there is in prospect a contest of wills. We must not think that it was resolved in Congress and is now behind us. The preponderant majority and the resistant minority remain, in the phrase that was so popular in the Kennedy administration at the time of the Cuban missile crisis, eyeball to eyeball, and if the majority relaxes, in a failure of patience or in discontinuity of purpose, as it did after Reconstruction, or if it thinks it can devolve its responsibility on some enforcement officials in Washington and forget about it, as it largely did during Reconstruction, the law is from that moment moribund.

A normal rate of enforcement is part of the process of persuasion and inducement. Litigation, even if its other consequences are not overly onerous, is at the least expensive, and the possibility of it will deter in some measure, for although not nearly everyone can be sued, no one knows who may be. But other means of pressure and inducement must also be employed, by the government and by private groups and interests favoring the law. The inducement of compliance with this law must be a consideration at every one of the countless points at which the activities of the federal government—both the civil and military establishments—touch on the private sector and constitute an actual or potential source of benefits. Private entities—not only the Negro organizations but all who would like to see this statute rendered fully effective—have an obligation to exert economic, social, and moral pressure and to set an unwavering example. If it is understood that the triumphant passage of this civil rights statute launched a great reforming enterprise, to be carried on by the society as a whole and not merely by the enforcing arm of the federal government, then there is every probability of success.

Notes ▶

1. Address Before the Pennsylvania Bar Association, June 27, 1916, 22 *Pa. B.A. Rep.* 221 (1916).

2. W. Lippmann, "Our Predicament under the Eighteenth Amendment," *Harper's*, vol. 154, p. 51.

3. National Prohibition Cases, 253 U.S. 350 (1920).

4. A. T. Hadley, "Law Making and Law Enforcement," *Harper's*, vol. 151, p. 641.

33 ► WHAT NEXT? FIVE NEGRO LEADERS REPLY

KENNETH B. CLARK

JAMES FARMER

MARTIN LUTHER KING, JR.

A. PHILIP RANDOLPH

ROY WILKINS

As the last item of reading in both the section and the book, we turn to an unusual collective attempt to foresee what action will be needed in the future of American race relations. Five of the leading personalities in the American Negro's fight for civil rights try to identify the next goals and tactical steps in the American people's efforts to achieve racial equality.

"More Effective Techniques"–(*Kenneth B. Clark*)

The Aug. 28 march demonstrated the discipline, the seriousness, the persistence and the insistence of the bulk of American Negroes and some whites that racial injustices must now be eliminated from American life. Yet it is possible that the "success" of the march could confuse the issue and delay the attainment of the goal of racial equality. Some Negroes could interpret the demonstration as evidence of direct political power and believe the fact that it occurred will magically produce the desired results. And some whites could congratulate themselves on the fact that Negroes were permitted to let off steam harmlessly.

From *The New York Times Magazine*, September 29, 1963. © 1963 by The New York Times Company. Reprinted by permission.

Such ideas, although comforting, would be serious misinterpretations of the meaning of the current civil-rights movement. Any political or other actions based upon them would be in error and probably tragic in their consequences.

In a most disturbing sense, a society which permitted the perpetrators of 28 bombings in Birmingham to remain free and unpunished, a society which permits the convicted killer of a Negro woman to complete his harvest before enjoying the luxury of six months in a white prison, a society in which the highest elected official of a state incites the primitive passions of his people for personal political gain, a society which can continue to accept flagrant and subtle forms of racism in the same generation in which the horrors of death camps were exposed to the world is a society in serious trouble.

Negro organizations and their white allies must now develop precise and more effective techniques to deal directly with the areas of resistance to racial injustice in America. They must consolidate and conserve past gains and use them as the basis for removing the existing inequities. Specifically:

Ways must be found to make the Congress of the United States and the various state legislative bodies more sensitive and responsive to the present mood of urgency.

Serious negotiations with the leaders of American labor and of individual unions should be initiated and sustained.

If these discussions do not result in the elimination of patterns of racial exclusion from the American labor movement then more direct action techniques must be developed and used until these goals are obtained.

More systematic organized and sustained forms of selective patronage should be used by Negroes to eliminate the remaining forms of racial discrimination in employment and in places of public accommodation.

The problem of residential segregation has to be attacked by direct action and effective protests against the discriminatory practices of banks, real-estate groups and offending landlords.

Police brutality must be curbed and law-enforcement agencies and officials made to understand that it is their duty and responsibility to protect all citizens impartially. If this cannot be done by reason it must be done by disciplined civil disobedience.

Desegregation of schools, from the elementary through graduate and professional levels, must be accelerated. The present snail's pace of grudging tokenism should give way to a pace more consistent with the letter and the spirit of the May 17, 1954, Supreme Court decision and the trained manpower needs of the nation. Here, too, it may be necessary, unfortunately, for Negroes to develop and use appropriate, nonviolent direct-action approaches.

Massive pressure for voter registration among Negroes in the South must be developed and sustained without regard to the risk. The executive and judicial branches of the Federal Government must protect the constitutional rights of Negroes to vote and participate in their government. These rights either must be enforced by representation sanctions against the states or Negroes must find some way of withholding the taxes paid in these states in direct proportion to their representation. Taxation without representation is still tyranny.

As for the next steps, apathy, indifference, battle weariness, return to inertia and wishful thinking are some of the major dangers to be counteracted. The momentum of the Negro surge for equality during the past few years and particularly during recent months has been admirable—but also exhausting. The challenge now is to sustain the dynamism of recent demonstrations until the legitimate goals are achieved.

"We Cannot Afford to Fail"—(*James Farmer*)

Governor Wallace of Alabama is probably most to blame for the outrage of Birmingham. However, Wallace is not alone. All of us share the blame because we have not done enough to end racial injustice. I have not been able to sleep since Birmingham because I have not done enough. Those who are not on the picket lines share the blame. Those who remain silent share the blame. Those who are neutral share the blame.

Birmingham will not stop the movement. It will not slow it down, rather it will help speed up the process of mass involvement of the Negro community.

No longer are we just a few scattered militants and intellectuals. Now the revolt has cut across the formerly divisive lines of class, cultural achievement and education to a greater extent than ever before; even the timorous, the former "Uncle Toms," have been swept along in the tide of Negro self-consciousness and revolt against discrimination. They have become involved not so much by choice as by necessity. The realization has come to most Negroes that there is no escape for them as individuals. We are in what might be called the "everyman" stage of development in the struggle.

The problems are obviously enormous. To mention just two: (1) Sloganeering is frequently mistaken for a program. (2) A dangerous racial polarization in the national community seems possible.

To combat the first problem, more sweep needs to be given to the present revolutionary struggle by analysis and criticism and creative thought as well as by more detailed planning.

Real differences in point of view should be expressed and encouraged. Unity of goal should not be mistaken for uniformity of action and approach.

In combating the second danger, the march on Washington was a good first step. Its interracial character was impressive. Now we need steps to make constructive use of the millions of potential white allies according to the stage of their present commitment in the struggle. Ways must be found to let each add his thrust to the movement as far as he is at present willing to go, without hampering or holding back those who are willing to go further. Churches and unions must be encouraged to go beyond lip service and to take specific action for equality.

Direct-action demonstrations will be continued, but objectives should be more clearly pointed out in each campaign—both for better understanding among the demonstrators and for greater appreciation and support among the general public. In addition, means of maintaining the discipline of nonviolence need to be tightened. We require schools and workshops in every area of the country to train demonstrators and potential demonstrators in the discipline of nonviolence. We need, also, to train special cadres to monitor each mass demonstration, to stop trouble before it occurs, to isolate difficulties and move the demonstration on.

Our ultimate objective is equality—economic, political, educational, cultural, social. These things will not be achieved merely by breaking down the barriers of segregation and discrimination. The wounds inflicted by 350 years of deprivation will not be erased automatically. Nothing short of a massive program of remedial education and training for skills can even begin to solve the problem. The nation cannot afford to fail to take the necessary compensatory steps to advance those whom it has deprived over the years. Such a program requires billions of dollars—perhaps as much as $3,000,000,000 a year for a period of five or 10 years—in order to be effective. Money in that amount can come only from the Government. It may be the President's prime opportunity to achieve lasting greatness.

"In a Word—Now"–(*Martin Luther King, Jr.*)

Victor Hugo once said that progress is the mode of man; that when it is blocked, just as an obstacle in a river makes the water foam, so an obstacle to progress makes humanity seethe.

Any plan for the future, therefore, which seeks to calm troubled waters will have to sweep barriers away, rather than pour oil over turbulent tides.

The hundreds of thousands who marched in Washington marched to level barriers. They summed up everything in a word —NOW. What is the content of NOW?

Everything, not some things, in the President's civil-rights bill is part of NOW.

Immediate and effective Federal action to curb the shocking police brutality in the South is an urgent part of NOW. Just lately, the Department of Justice has indicted leaders of the civil-rights movement in Albany, Ga., and Birmingham, Ala., alleging that false statements were made under oath. This zealousness to punish Negroes for statements is in sharp contrast to the inaction of the same department in hundreds of cases of extreme police brutality.

The right to vote is part of NOW. To walk unafraid to the ballot box and cast a free vote remains still a myth in most of the South.

Unemployment is a form of brutality, especially violent for those who live on the edge of poverty. Negroes have twice as much of it as others. NOW means jobs, F.E.P.C., training, leveling obstacles of discrimination and the creation of new jobs by public works.

These are some of the imperatives of NOW. If they are met, the passionate determination Negroes have recently made so manifest can be mellowed without being compromised. Then slower, long-range planning can begin.

The far-reaching solutions for lifting the "weight of centuries" will necessarily involve systematic liquidation of ghetto life, loans and grants to provide equal opportunities for the unequally equipped, adult education, remedial clinics for damaged families and individuals and integrated housing construction on a scale commensurate with the extent of slums, rather than with the extent of budgets.

The present spontaneous, largely disorganized and spasmodic methods of piecemeal approaches, differing from city to city, and with a variety of tempos, will have to give way to broad national planning. A nation which could put more than 11,000,000 men in arms in a few short years, which poured torrents of sophisticated munitions from hundreds of thousands of coordinated facilities and deployed them in war, has the capacity to master a problem of much less complexity. It needs only the same will it possessed when it felt its existence threatened.

The long-deferred issue of second-class citizenship has become our nation's first-class crisis. We can deal with it now, or we can drive a seething humanity to a desperation it tried, asked and hoped to avoid.

"Filibuster of the People"–(A. *Philip Randolph*)

The objective of Aug. 28 was more than civil-rights legislation. The full march was a challenge to the conscience of the country; it was a creative dialogue between Negroes and their white allies, on the one hand, and the President, the Congress and our American democratic society, on the other. Its aim was to achieve a national consensus not only for civil-rights legislation—but for its implementation.

Historically, the social forces of revolutions have been expressed through human beings. Hence, the leadership of the civil-rights revolution cannot escape the moral responsibility for the maintenance of the highest order of unselfish, courageous and uncompromising fidelity to the ideals, values, hopes and faith of this sacred crusade for the recognition of, and respect for, the God-given human rights of Americans of color.

What then, is to be done?

First, Negro civil-rights leadership must maintain unity without uniformity.

Second, the coalition of the Negro community with the labor and church communities that supported the march must be preserved, broadened and deepened. If freedom is indivisible then the fight for freedom by those forces devoted to freedom should be indivisible. Negroes—like other minority groups—cannot win their rights alone. The coalition of moral forces represented by civil-rights, labor and church groups is unquestionably one of the most powerful instrumentalities yet devised to help create that ethical basis for interracial brotherhood which is imperative to give meaningfulness to civil-rights laws.

Third, demonstrations in the streets—a recognized American tradition—by Negroes and their white allies must continue without relaxation until basic, tangible progress in the acquisition of jobs and apprenticeship training for jobs in industry, unions and government, and the abolition of race bias in public accommodations, schools and housing is made.

Had it not been for demonstrations in the streets of Birmingham, Ala., and other cities in the North and South, it is quite unlikely that President Kennedy would have submitted his package of proposals for civil-rights legislation to the Congress. If street demonstrations were necessary to secure this action by the President, it is reasonable to assume that further street demonstrations will be indispensable to bring about the enactment of the proposals into laws, without emasculation.

Fourth, major emphasis should be placed upon building the unity of Negro leadership together with a coalition of the Negro, labor and church communities. This, of course, is the job of existing civil-rights organizations. No new movement is necessary.

The Birmingham tragedy—the wanton bombing of a church and the murder of four little girls—marked not only a breakdown of law and order but also has shaken and weakened the faith and confidence of Negroes and, no doubt, of numerous liberal-minded white people in constitutional government and our free, democratic, Christian society. It damages the image of the United States in Africa in particular, and the world of color in general.

It is a matter of record that no white person or mob in the South responsible for the murder of a Negro has ever been brought to justice. However, Negroes, despite this unspeakable crime, must not forsake or abandon the nonviolent philosophy as a framework within which they should carry on their relentless struggle for the abolition of race bias.

We have no choice but to fight ceaselessly for civil-rights legislation. If it should be killed, joblessness will continue to worsen, and humiliation in places of accommodation will go on unabated.

Then frustration—even desperation—may burst into fires of violent interracial conflict. Indeed, if the civil-rights revolution is aborted by a counterrevolution, symbolized by the filibuster, it may not only turn against white America but move to devour its own children.

"Negroes Want In"–(Roy Wilkins)

Negroes demand an end to the bestiality of Birmingham with its bombings and slaughter of innocent children. The spectacle of the Federal Government helpless in the face of such terror is incomprehensible to a people who have fought and died in its defense and who properly look to it for protection of their rights and lives. Failure to provide such protection increases frustration and seriously imperils continuance of the nonviolent character of the Negro protest. Prompt, effective action to end this terror is imperative.

The painfully slow pace of past desegregation can no longer be tolerated. To insist upon acceleration is neither radical nor extremist. It is rational and necessary.

Negroes want *in* in American society, and they want the ways opened *now*. They reject separation, whether advocated by the Black Muslims, the White Citizens Councils or the Communist party. They are committed to a pluralistic society with equal rights, opportunities and freedom for all.

Equally clear are the indicated next steps. There is no likelihood of an abatement of the present upsurge of militancy among Negroes. What is required now more than ever is responsible militancy. Not demonstrations for demonstrations' sake. But demonstrations for specific purposes, pressed uncompromisingly, but conducted in an orderly fashion.

The presence of thousands of white persons in the Washington march revealed to Negroes and to the nation that colored citizens are not alone in this struggle for equal rights. A vast reservoir of goodwill exists in the white populace. This goodwill must be cultivated and mobilized for effective action in the struggle. The religious groups—Protestant, Catholic and Jewish—demonstrated by their participation in the march that they are prepared now to go beyond resolutions and to take an active role. Liberal elements in the labor movement reiterated the demand for an end to the color bar in employment.

The church groups exert influence in areas where Negroes and other traditional civil-rights advocates are politically weak. With organized religion in support of the President's civil-rights bill, the chances for its enactment will be greatly enhanced. Senators from states where the issue of civil rights has not been regarded heretofore as urgent may be persuaded to vote for cloture to shut off a Senate filibuster.

The church groups can be an important factor in gaining support of both Republican and Democratic members of Congress in the nonindustrial states of the Midwest and Rocky Mountain regions. How they vote may well determine the outcome of the legislation.

Meanwhile, the civil-rights groups must redouble their efforts to increase the Negro vote in all regions, pursue a course of responsible militancy, conduct a vast program of public information, and enlist the active support of all possible elements within the American society.

Further Reading

A LITERATURE as prolific as that which describes and analyzes problems in ethnic relations in the modern world can only be sampled superficially in a book of this size. However, the student who wishes to pursue the subject in greater breadth and depth may find the following bibliography a useful guide. To conform with this volume's emphasis on contemporary readings, the bibliography includes only pertinent monographs and journal articles that have been published since 1960. For earlier publications, the reader should consult bibliographies available in most standard sourcebooks and monographs on ethnic relations—such as *Sociological Abstracts* and the *Inventory of Research in Racial and Cultural Relations*; and periodicals such as *Commentary, Crisis, Interracial News Service, Journal of Intergroup Relations, Journal of Negro History, Phylon, Race, Rights,* and *Southern School News.*

General Aspects of Minorities

Antonovsky, Aaron. "The Social Meaning of Discrimination," *Phylon* (Spring, 1960), 81–95.

Berkowitz, Leonard, and James A. Green. "The Stimulus Qualities of the Scapegoat," *Journal of Abnormal and Social Psychology* (April, 1962), 293–301.

Bettelheim, Bruno, and Morris Janowitz. *Social Change and Prejudice,* New York: The Free Press, 1964.

Blalock, H. M., Jr. "A Power Analysis of Racial Discrimination," *Social Forces* (October, 1960), 53–59.

Catton, William R., Jr. "The Functions and Dysfunctions of Ethnocentrism: A Theory," *Social Problems* (Winter, 1960–61), 201–11.

———, and Chick Hong Sung. "The Relation of Apparent Minority Ethnocentrism to Majority Antipathy," *American Sociological Review* (April, 1962), 178–91.

Clark, Kenneth B. *Prejudice and Your Child,* Boston: Beacon Press, 1963.

Coon, Carleton S. *The Origin of Races*, New York: Alfred A. Knopf, 1962.

Diab, Lutfy. "Factors Affecting Studies of National Stereotypes," *Journal of Social Psychology* (February, 1963), 29–40.

Ehrlich, Howard. "Stereotyping and Negro-Jewish Stereotypes," *Social Forces* (December, 1962), 171–76.

Grimshaw, Allen D. "Relationships Among Prejudice, Discrimination, Social Tension, and Social Violence," *Journal of Intergroup Relations* (Autumn, 1961), 302–10.

Hamblin, Robert L. "The Dynamics of Racial Discrimination," *Social Problems* (Fall, 1962), 103–21.

Hughes, Everett C. "Race Relations and the Sociological Imagination," *American Sociological Review* (December, 1963), 879–90.

Killian, Lewis M., and Charles M. Grigg. "Urbanism, Race, and Anomia," *American Journal of Sociology* (May, 1962), 661–65.

Klineberg, Otto. "Life Is Fun in a Smiling, Fair-Skinned World," *Saturday Review* (February 16, 1963), 75–76.

Kren, George M. "Race and Ideology," *Phylon* (Summer, 1962), 166–77.

Lenski, Gerhard E. *The Religious Factor*, New York: Doubleday, 1963.

Lieberson, Stanley. "A Societal Theory of Race and Ethnic Relations," *American Sociological Review* (December, 1961), 902–10.

Mack, Raymond. *The Sociology of Minorities*, New York: Anti-Defamation League of B'nai B'rith, 1963.

McCord, William, *et al.* "Early Familial Experiences and Bigotry," *American Sociological Review* (October, 1960), 717–22.

Medalia, Nahum Z. "Assumptions on Race Relations: A Conceptual Commentary," *Social Forces* (March, 1962), 223–27.

Montagu, Ashley. "The Concept of Race," *American Anthropologist* (October, 1962), 919–28.

Raab, Earl, and Seymour Lipset. *Prejudice and Society*, New York: Anti-Defamation League of B'nai B'rith, 1963.

Rokeach, Milton. *The Open and Closed Mind*, New York: Basic Books, 1960.

Yinger, J. Milton. "Social Forces Involved in Group Identification and Withdrawal," *Daedalus* (Spring, 1961), 247–62.

Minority Problems Outside American Society

Berreman, Gerald D. "Caste in India and in the United States," *American Journal of Sociology* (September, 1960), 120–27.

Cairns, H. A. C. *The Clash of Cultures: Early Race Relations in Central Africa*, New York: Frederick A. Praeger, 1965.

Glass, Dorothy. *London's Newcomers: the West Indian Migrants*, Cambridge: Harvard University Press, 1961.

Griffith, J. A. G., *et al. Coloured Immigrants in Britain*, London: Oxford University Press, 1960.

Katz, Jacob. *Exclusiveness and Tolerance: Studies in Jewish-Gentile Relations in Medieval and Modern Times*, New York: Oxford University Press, 1961.

Phillips, Norman. *The Tragedy of Apartheid*, New York: David McKay, 1961.

Shuval, Judith T. *Immigrants on the Threshold*, New York: Atherton Press, 1963.

Spooner, F. P. *South African Predicament: The Economics of Apartheid*, New York: Frederick A. Praeger, 1961.

Minority Problems in American Society

Glazer, Nathan, and Davis McEntire (eds.). *Studies in Housing and Minority Groups*, Berkeley: University of California Press, 1960.

——, and Daniel P. Moynihan. *Beyond the Melting Pot: The Negroes, Puerto Ricans, Jews, Italians and Irish of New York City*, Cambridge: The M.I.T. Press and Harvard University Press, 1963.

Glenn, Norval D. "Some Changes in the Relative Status of American Minorities," *Phylon* (Summer, 1963).

Grier, Eunice, and George Grier. *Discrimination in Housing*, New York: Anti-Defamation League of B'nai B'rith, 1960.

Handlin, Oscar. "Historical Perspectives on the American Ethnic Group," *Daedalus* (Spring, 1961), 220–32.

Heer, David M. "The Marital Status of Second-Generation Americans," *American Sociological Review* (April, 1961), 233–39.

Kramer, Judith R., and Seymour Leventman. *Children of the Gilded Ghetto*, New Haven: Yale University Press, 1961.

Laurenti, L. *Property Values and Race*, Berkeley: University of California Press, 1960.

Lieberson, Stanley. "Suburbs and Ethnic Residential Patterns," *American Journal of Sociology* (May, 1962), 673–81.

——. *Ethnic Patterns in American Cities*, New York: The Free Press, 1963.

Marrow, Alfred J. *Changing Patterns of Prejudice*, New York: Chilton, 1962.

Mendelson, Wallace. *Discrimination*, Englewood Cliffs: Prentice-Hall, 1962.

Palmore, Erdman, and John Howe. *Residential Integration and Property Values*, New York: Anti-Defamation League of B'nai B'rith, 1962.

Rose, Peter I. *They and We: Racial and Ethnic Relations in the United States*, New York: Random House, 1964.

Raab, Earl (ed.). *American Race Relations Today*, New York: Doubleday, 1962.

Tumin, Melvin M. *An Inventory and Appraisal of Research on American Anti-Semitism,* New York: Anti-Defamation League of B'nai B'rith, 1961.

Williams, Robin M., Jr. *Strangers Next Door: Ethnic Relations in American Communities,* Englewood Cliffs: Prentice-Hall, 1964.

Yinger, J. Milton. *Anti-Semitism: A Case Study in Prejudice and Discrimination,* New York: Anti-Defamation League of B'nai B'rith, 1964.

American Immigrant Minorities

Gans, Herbert. *The Urban Villagers: Group and Class in the Life of Italian-Americans,* Glencoe: The Free Press, 1962.

Greeley, Andrew M., and Peter G. Rossi. *The Education of Catholic Americans,* Chicago: Aldine, 1966.

Heller, Celia S. *Mexican American Youth,* New York: Random House, 1966.

Kung, Shien Woo. *Chinese in American Life,* Seattle: University of Washington Press, 1962.

Lee, Calvin. *Chinatown, U.S.A.,* New York: Doubleday, 1965.

Lee, Rose Hum. *The Chinese in the United States of America,* Hong Kong: Hong Kong University Press, 1960.

Rogow, Arnold (ed.). *The Jew in a Gentile World: An Anthology of Writings about Jews by non-Jews,* New York: Macmillan, 1961.

Senior, Clarence. *Strangers—Then Neighbors: From Pilgrims to Puerto Ricans,* New York: Anti-Defamation League of B'nai B'rith, 1961.

Sexton, Patricia C. *Spanish Harlem,* New York: Harper and Row, 1965.

Sherman, C. Bezalel. *The Jew Within American Society,* Detroit: Wayne State University Press, 1961.

The American Negro

Baldwin, James. *The Fire Next Time,* New York: Dial Press, 1962.

Berry, Brewton. *Almost White,* New York: Macmillan, 1963.

Broom, Leonard, and Norval D. Glenn. *Transformation of the Negro American,* New York: Harper and Row, 1965.

Burns, W. Haywood. *The Voices of Negro Protest in America,* New York: Oxford University Press, 1963.

Clark, Kenneth B. *Dark Ghetto,* New York: Harper and Row, 1965.

Dreger, R. M., and K. S. Miller. "Comparative Psychological Studies of Negroes and Whites in the United States," *Psychological Bulletin* (September, 1960), 361–402.

Erskine, Hazel Gaudet. "The Polls: Race Relations," *Public Opinion Quarterly* (Spring, 1962), 137–48.

Essien-Udom, E. U. *Black Nationalism: A Search for Identity in America*, Chicago: The University of Chicago Press, 1962.

Franklin, John Hope (ed.). *Three Negro Classics*, New York: Avon, 1965.

Ginsberg, Eli. *The Negro Potential*, New York: Columbia University Press, 1963.

Harlem Youth Opportunities Unlimited. *Youth in the Ghetto*, New York, 1964.

Hill, Herbert (ed.). *Soon, One Morning*, New York: Alfred A. Knopf, 1963.

Jackson, Esther Merle. "The American Negro and the Image of the Absurd," *Phylon* (Winter, 1962), 359–71.

Jones, LeRoi. *Blues People*, New York: Morrow, 1963.

Killian, Lewis M., and Charles M. Grigg. *Racial Crisis in America: Leadership in Conflict*, Englewood Cliffs: Prentice-Hall, 1964.

King, Martin Luther, Jr. *Why We Can't Wait*, New York: Harper and Row, 1963.

Lincoln, C. Eric. *The Black Muslims in America*, Boston: Beacon Press, 1961.

Lomax, Louis E. *The Negro Revolt*, New York: Harper and Row, 1962.

Miller, Elizabeth W. *The Negro in America: A Bibliography*, Cambridge: Harvard University Press, 1966.

Murphy, Raymond J., and Howard Elinson (eds.). *Problems and Prospects of the Negro Movement*, Belmont: Wadsworth, 1966.

Osofsky, Gilbert. *Harlem: The Making of a Ghetto*, New York: Harper and Row, 1966.

Pettigrew, Thomas F. *A Profile of the Negro American*, New York: D. Van Nostrand, 1964.

Pfautz, Harold W. "The Power Structure of the Negro Sub-Community," *Phylon* (Summer, 1962), 156–66.

Record, Jane Cassels, and Wilson Record. "Ideological Forces and the Negro Protest," *The Annals* (January, 1965), 89–96.

Reimers, David M. *White Protestantism and the Negro*, New York: Oxford University Press, 1965.

Silberman, Charles E. *Crisis in Black and White*, New York: Random House, 1964.

Sterling, Dorothy, and Benjamin Quarles. *Lift Every Voice: The Lives of W. E. B. DuBois, Mary Church Terrell, Booker T. Washington and James Weldon Johnson*, New York: Doubleday, 1965.

Taeuber, Karl E., and Alma F. Taeuber, *Negroes in Cities*, Chicago: Aldine, 1965.

Thompson, Daniel C. *The Negro Leadership Class*, Englewood Cliffs: Prentice-Hall, 1963.

Vander Zanden, James W. *Race Relations in Transition: The Segregation Crisis in the South*, New York: Random House, 1965.

Welsch, Erwin K. *The Negro in the United States: A Research Guide*, Bloomington: Indiana University Press, 1965.

Assimilation and Intermarriage

Bugelski, B. R. "Assimilation through Intermarriage," *Social Forces* (December, 1961), 148–53.

Cahnman, Werner J. (ed.). *Intermarriage and Jewish Life*, New York: Herzl Press and Jewish Reconstructionist Press, 1963.

Gordon, Milton M. *Assimilation in American Life*, New York: Oxford University Press, 1964.

Heiss, Jerold S. "Premarital Characteristics of the Religiously Intermarried in an Urban Area," *American Sociological Review* (February, 1960), 47–55.

Mayer, John E. *Jewish-Gentile Courtships*, Glencoe: The Free Press, 1961.

Rosenthal, Erich. "Acculturation Without Assimilation? The Jewish Community of Chicago," *American Journal of Sociology* (November, 1960), 275–88.

————. "Studies of Jewish Intermarriage in the United States," *American Jewish Year Book*, 1963.

Programs and Techniques of Intergroup Change

Ball, Harry V., *et al.* "Law and Social Change: Sumner Reconsidered," *American Journal of Sociology* (March, 1962), 532–40.

Breed, Warren. "Group Structure and Resistance to Desegregation in the Deep South," *Social Problems* (Summer, 1962), 84–94.

Campbell, Ernest Q. "Moral Discomfort and Racial Desegregation —An Examination of the Myrdal Hypothesis," *Social Forces* (March, 1961), 228–34.

Cohen, Oscar. "The Case for Benign Quotas in Housing," *Phylon* (Spring, 1960), 20–29.

Grigg, Charles M., and Lewis M. Killian. "The Bi-Racial Committee as a Response to Racial Tensions in Southern Cities," *Phylon* (Winter, 1962), 379–82.

Hughes, Langston. *Fight for Freedom: The Story of the NAACP*, New York: Norton, 1962.

Humphrey, Hubert H. (ed.). *School Desegregation: Documents and Commentaries*, New York: Crowell, 1964.

Konvitz, Milton B., and Theodore Leskes. *A Century of Civil Rights*, New York: Columbia University Press, 1961.

Morland, Kenneth. *Southern Schools: Token Desegregation and Beyond*, New York: Anti-Defamation League of B'nai B'rith, 1963.

Robison, Joseph B. "Legislation Against Bias—Possibilities and Limitations," *The Journal of Intergroup Relations* (Winter, 1959–60).

Stember, Charles H. *Education and Attitude Change: The Effect of Schooling on Prejudice Against Minority Groups*, New York: Institute of Human Relations Press, 1961.

Thompson, Daniel C. "The Rise of the Negro Protest," *The Annals* (January, 1965), 18–29.

Tumin, Melvin M. *Segregation and Desegregation: A Digest of Recent Research*, New York: Anti-Defamation League of B'nai B'rith, 1963.

Vander Zanden, James W. "The Non-Violent Resistance Movement Against Segregation," *American Journal of Sociology* (March, 1963), 544–50.

Waskow, Arthur I. *From Race Riot to Sit-In, 1919 and the 1960's*, New York: Doubleday, 1966.

Index

ABOUT THE EDITOR

MILTON L. BARRON, *professor and former chairman of the Department of Sociology and Anthropology, The City College of New York, and executive officer of the Ph.D. program in Sociology, The City University of New York, was educated at Yale University. In 1943 he served with the Department of Justice and has been a member of the faculties of St. Lawrence University, Syracuse University, and Cornell University, and visiting professor at Wells College, Columbia University, New York University, and Yeshiva University. In the academic year 1962–63 Dr. Barron was a Fulbright Lecturer at Bar-Ilan University (Israel). Among his many books are* The Juvenile in Delinquent Society, 1954; American Minorities, 1957; The Aging American, 1961; *and* Contemporary Sociology, 1964. *Dr. Barron lives with his family in Dobbs Ferry, New York.*

A NOTE ON THE TYPE

The text of this book is set in Electra, a typeface designed by W(illiam) A(ddison) Dwiggins for the Mergenthaler Linotype Company and first made available in 1935. Electra cannot be classified as either "modern" or "old style." It is not based on any historical model, and hence does not echo any particular period or style of type design. It avoids the extreme contrast between "thick" and "thin" elements that marks most modern faces, and is without eccentricities which catch the eye and interfere with reading. In general, Electra is a simple, readable typeface which attempts to give a feeling of fluidity, power, and speed.

W. A. DWIGGINS (1880–1956) was born in Martinsville, Ohio, and studied art in Chicago. In 1904 he moved to Hingham, Massachusetts, where he built a solid reputation as a designer of advertisements and as a calligrapher. He began an association with the Mergenthaler Linotype Company in 1929, and over the next twenty-seven years designed a number of book types, of which Metro, Electra, and Caledonia have been used very widely. In 1930 Dwiggins became interested in marionettes, and through the years made many important contributions to the art of puppetry and the design of marionettes.

*Composed, printed, and bound by
Kingsport Press, Inc., Kingsport, Tenn.
Typography by Leon Bolognese*